HITLER'S
AMBIVALENT ATTACHÉ

Also by Alfred M. Beck

The Corps of Engineers:
The War against Germany (coauthor)

With Courage: The U.S. Army Air Forces
in World War II (general editor)

HITLER'S AMBIVALENT ATTACHÉ

Lt. Gen. Friedrich von Boetticher in America, 1933–1941

ALFRED M. BECK

POTOMAC BOOKS, INC.
WASHINGTON, D.C.

First Paperback Edition 2006
Copyright © 2005 by Potomac Books, Inc.

Library of Congress Cataloging-in-Publication Data

Beck, Alfred M., 1939–
    Hitler's ambivalent attaché : Lt. Gen. Friedrich von Boetticher in America, 1933–1941 / Alfred M. Beck.
        p. cm.
    Includes bibliographical references and index.
    Hardcover ISBN 1-57488-877-3 (alk. paper)
    1. Boetticher, Friedrich von, 1881–1967. 2. Diplomats—Germany—Biography. 3. Germany—Foreign relations—1933–1945. 4. United States—Foreign relations—Germany. I. Title.
    DD247.B623B43 2005
    940.54—dc22

                                                              2004013425

        Paperback ISBN-10: 1-57488-878-1
        Paperback ISBN-13: 978-1-57488-878-2

Printed in the United States of America on acid-free paper that meets the American National Standards Institute Z39-48 Standard.

Potomac Books, Inc.
22841 Quicksilver Drive
Dulles, Virginia 20166

First Edition

10 9 8 7 6 5 4 3 2 1

For
Nelle, Ellen, Audrey, and Caroline,
Just because . . .

Contents

PREFACE

Lt. Gen. Friedrich von Boetticher was Germany's only military attaché in the United States between the two world wars. He was his country's sanctioned military observer in the capital of the nation whose contributions of fresh troops had swung the balance against Germany in the last year of World War I. The United States was a strategic cipher whose potential as an ally of those powers arrayed against Germany in the late 1930s might have given the National Socialist government some pause in any predatory plans for its neighbors. What Adolf Hitler may have learned of American national preparedness in diplomatic pouch and cable traffic from Washington at the time is of compelling interest. How much the German dictator read or heeded the news is a question of equal significance. This book attempts to answer those questions.

In its earliest form, this study had the narrower purpose of evaluating the content and accuracy of assessments of the American Army that von Boetticher wrote during his eight years in Washington. That research produced some new observations on the man and his tenure in Washington and rehearsed the anti-Semitic references that peppered the diplomatic and attaché dispatches of the time. The attaché's reports and cables that contained this sort of phraseology and any assessment dismissive of American industrial potential particularly attracted the attention of editors of published documentary records collections of German diplomatic dealings in the 1930s. Such indispensable standard sources as the *Documents on German Foreign Policy,* published in two long-running series under U.S. State Department auspices between 1949 and 1983 [eventually with German language versions], are often skewed in their emphasis because of the necessity of selecting representative documents rather than printing the entire overwhelming run of material. Published research mentioning von Boetticher tended to focus on this aspect of his written record as well and often assessed his judgments as one-sided and predictable.

This much-revised rendition of his story has become more of a biography of the attaché. It seeks neither to improve on his reputation nor to enlarge upon a man who remains a secondary figure, but to explore the personal, bureaucratic, and political contexts in which the attaché operated so as to offer wider understanding of his role in the events of the time. Newly unearthed materials offer dimension to his service offsetting the sometimes simpler notions about him that appear in much of the literature on German-American prewar diplomatic relations.[1]

Information on von Boetticher's career and service is surprisingly voluminous. The primary raw material for the original study is drawn from the microfilmed Captured German Records Collection at the National Archives and Records Administration in Washington, D.C. These files contain the hundreds of reports that von Boetticher wrote on American affairs. Though as much as two-thirds of the original material survived the war and is now in the public record, many of the attaché reports for the period April 1936 through September 1939 were destroyed in fires in 1942 at the German military archives at Potsdam and in the air raids of February 1945 that further ravaged the German military record. The reports from 1933 to 1936 even show the effects of this in the film record; many of the microfilm frames contain only the image of a charred oval of paper in the middle of which the substance of the message is still readable. The German archivists in Freiburg im Breisgau provided me with microfilmed copy of some missing material to fill gaps in the period 1936 to 1939, but this amounted to only about 250 pages for the entire three-year period. The photographs reproduced are variously from von Boetticher's organized collection of papers now in official custody in Germany; the estate files of his assistant attaché, Peter Riedel; and U.S. Army sources; or the result of my own camera work. Some of the imagery is from the old ACME news archives, today owned by the Corbis Corporation, and used with its permission.

The latter stages of this research project also had the happy effect of further gathering up von Boetticher papers not yet contained in German or American archives. Under a newly sovereign Federal Republic of Germany in the 1950s, the German Military Archives was reconstituted in Freiburg im Breisgau as part of a larger Bundesarchiv headquartered in Coblenz. This institution established a collection of von Boetticher's papers catalogued under his name and the general provenance file heading N323. Von Boetticher contributed papers to this collection during his lifetime. The extent of these files appeared fixed at the general's death in September 1967, but there was more to come. In dissolving her father's estate in Germany, Hildegard Marsden, General von Boetticher's younger daughter, emptied his household in Bielefeld [North Rhine-Westphalia] and dispatched all of his remaining effects to her own home in Ontario. When she died there in April 1988, after a distinguished career at the University of Waterloo, her son invited me to assess several large cartons of documents that proved to be of inestimable value in reflecting upon the general's entire career, from his earliest schooling through the last days of his life. A few moments of poring through this trove convinced me that this was something of a "lost codex" that belonged in official German archives. The German Embassy in Washington, through the offices of Brig. Gen. (Generalmajor) Baron Hasso von Uslar, German defense attaché in the United States from 1986 to 1990, arranged to transfer this collection via a Luftwaffe diplomatic channel flight to Freiburg in January 1989. At the same time, what had been for me a project finished and done with for over a decade suddenly took on new life. In June 1989, Dr. Manfred Kehrig, director of the German military archives and a retired colonel of infantry in the Bundeswehr Reserve, allowed me full access to the forwarded material. His support and his helpful commentary on the later life of General von Boetticher added many details to the story. A military historian in his own right, Dr. Kehrig became especially close to the subject of this book while completing his own research on the reestablishment of a clandestine German attaché system in the early 1920s. How von Boetticher contributed to this effort as a young staff officer is also recounted here.

Though a trained field artilleryman, von Boetticher spent a career in the traditional form of intelligence called HUMINT, for human intelligence, even before his dispatch to the United States. The role of a sanctioned observer of a host country's military establishment was already in decline by the time of von Boetticher's service in Washington. Less emphasized after 1945, the posting of officers to assess foreign armies and navies firsthand competed with much more elaborate technical means of gathering information in the Cold War atmosphere following the demise of the Axis. The exchange of attachés was still conditioned in 1940, however, by formal diplomatic protocol and courtesy, and the record left for the historian has much the same feel as that prized by students of traditional diplomatic history. The social setting in Washington, in fact, ruled much of the effectiveness of members of the foreign attaché corps there. The common bond among professional military officers, especially those who have faced each other across hostile lines, is also a feature of the story. Von Boetticher brought to this as well a considered reputation as a military historian. His interests and accomplishments in this field alone added to his continued effectiveness with American officers and even scholars amid rising political tensions.

Biography remains among the more demanding pursuits of historical investigation. Entering the mind of a subject like this one, examining motive, and reconstructing the life of relatively obscure figures is daunting enough even in the presence of abundant documentation. In this study, the personality and formation of a German officer of the Wilhelmine era emerges more clearly than it has before. A literate man of more than average education, Friedrich von Boetticher wrote almost compulsively, keeping daily journals from at least 1904 until the end of his life. This made more feasible the penetration of sometimes self-generated myth surrounding the man. It soon became clear that von Boetticher characterized his mission in the United States in highly ideal terms.

Widespread contemporary interest in Holocaust history has also promoted reinterpretation of the *dramatis personae* of the Third Reich, including its Washington attaché. The taint associated with anyone who wore the uniform of the Nazi regime is an acknowledged factor in more recent literature; some have sorted the actors in this violent episode simply as victims, perpetrators, or bystanders. Though certainly not a victim in the sense of this historiography, von Boetticher hardly measures up as a perpetrator of

1

THE KAISER'S
SOLDIER ENDURES

IN the early summer of 1941, the American capital was tense with the expectation of worsening war news. Though England had held out against a German aerial onslaught through the turn of the year, the Wehrmacht had now turned on the Soviet Union. Breathtaking victories threatened to bring the Nazi regime to complete control of the Continent while American opinion was still heavily in favor of keeping the conflict at more than arm's length. David Brinkley, then a young news reporter and later one of America's premier television journalists, recounted a curious apparition in Washington at the time. In a memoir appearing nearly fifty years later, he recalled a short, thick-featured man with a bull neck bulging over the collar of a German military uniform fairly ablaze in ribbons and medals. This figure in jackboots haunted newsstands, peering through a monocle at the daily foreign and domestic press. Feverishly he bought up copies of newsprint for dispatch to Berlin. The comic-opera character, reddish hair in a Prussian brush cut, was Lt. Gen. Friedrich von Boetticher, the German military attaché. The only sensible report this officer ever sent home, Brinkley maintained, was about some rocket experiments in 1936 by a then-obscure American scientist named Robert Goddard.[1]

For more than eight years, between April 1933 and December 1941, this officer served two ranking ambassadors and a chargé d'affaires acting for Nazi Germany in Washington. Hardly the stereotypical Prussian of Brinkley's recollection, von Boetticher was indeed short of stature and a bit jug eared but never wore cropped hair, even as a junior officer, and never in his life affected a monocle.[2]

As military attaché, he assiduously represented his nation and its military establishment in times of increasingly intractable political relations before the American entry into World War II. Surviving German diplomatic and military records of the time preserve many of his reports. Seized and published after the war, these reproduced a selection of his wide-ranging summaries that betrayed an overriding faith in the political influence of American General Staff officers and the strength of American isolationist sentiment against "Jewish" politicians. There was too an apparently disdainful underestimation of the American military-industrial capability before the war. A peripheral figure, von Boetticher was accused of misjudging the productive potential of the United States and misleading Hitler with overly optimistic reports. What he actually told German authorities in Berlin is strikingly different from what his detractors later claimed.

Judging from his early career, von Boetticher was a man of ability. He was the cultured product of a classical, humanistic tutelage and the technically brilliant German military educational system. The son of a bourgeois father, he entered the exalted caste of German General Staff officers before his thirtieth birthday. His livelihood as a professional soldier survived the German defeat in World War I, and he earned a reputation in the truncated Weimar military establishment as an advisor in several international conferences after the guns went silent.

The future attaché had a cosmopolitan background. His family's history in the nineteenth century ranged over two continents and three nationalities. The Boetticher name was known by that time in two widely separate areas in Europe, the German Rhineland and the Baltic area known as the Kurland, a peninsula forming the eastern shore of the Gulf of Riga. Friedrich's father descended from the Kurland branch. The maternal lineage originated in Hull, the English Yorkshire seaport on the Humber River, and the Boyes trading family centered in that city.[3] This side of the family genealogy produced one unusual aspect of von Boetticher's background that contributed to his value in diplomatic missions.

Thomas Phillips Boyes, shown in one family history as a wholesaler, was the commercial representative of the Hull firm in Hamburg. Used to keeping close records of events and accounts, he noted in his Bible the whirlwind courtship and marriage of his eighteen-year-old daughter, Anne Caroline, to Hermann Anton

Wippermann, whose father owned one of the larger German trading houses in the city. Betrothed on October 8, 1848, the couple married only twenty days later. By 1857, Wippermann, then the thirty-one-year-old father of a son and a daughter, decided on a new venture in the United States, where the Boyes family had holdings in the American West. He settled in what is today Davenport, Iowa, and on October 4, 1859, Anne Caroline bore a second daughter, Agathe Isabella Victoria, an American citizen by the accident of her birth in what was still an American frontier territory.

Hermann Wippermann's troubles mounted, though, and he failed in Iowa. Shortly after the arrival of his last child, his wife returned to Hamburg while he struggled with his fate. In February 1860, he wrote a tearful letter home relating how he had pawned the watch his father had given him; this resulted in the dispatch of an undisclosed sum, enough to repay his debts and even rent a small farm that he worked with a single helper. By December of that year, he was miserable with the absence of his family. He poured out his woe in another letter saying, "I hate this country from the depths of my soul, it is a country where Mammon rules, a land of swindles . . . where flowers do not smell and women do not love."[4] Family sources offer no hint of Wippermann's involvement with another woman, but in 1863, he managed to get home, broken in spirit and in health, and died of tuberculosis that December. His wife outlived him by not quite two years. She died in August 1865 at a family home in Hamm in the Ruhr, leaving three children in the care of her father, whose Bible kept the record of it all. In his advancing years, Thomas Boyes transplanted these youngsters to Dresden, where he had bought a new estate just before his daughter's death. There he found a private school headed by a Fräulein Leonhardi for six-year-old Isabella, as she was known.

On October 4, 1880, her twenty-first birthday, Isabella Wippermann married Walther Boetticher, a physician. Aside from his medical practice, he pursued the classics and local historical research. In 1902, he produced a five-part study of his local area, which earned him an honorary doctorate from the University of Breslau and a patent of nobility that added the *von* before the family name. Dr. von Boetticher imparted this pursuit of historical study to the first of his children, Friedrich, born October 14, 1881, while the medical practice centered in the village of Berthelsdorf bei Herrenhut, near Dresden. By the turn of the century, the doctor had three more children, and fortune clearly favored him. The second son went into the German Colonial Office, the third into law. The remaining child, Hildegard, was Friedrich's particular favorite. Successful and respected, typically representative of the German *Mittelstand*, their father eventually acquired an estate, *die Lössnitz*, overlooking the Elbe River at Oberlössnitz, just outside the city.[5]

Friedrich's education was classical. From his American-born and British-bred mother he acquired an ability in English that left him equally fluent in two languages; he later took up French and spoke that with near-native fluency as well.[6] He finished formal schooling at the gymnasium in nearby Bautzen, where he showed the beginnings of a fine literary style. He wrote unceasingly, and from the earliest years of his military life, he kept extensive journals and notebooks. Longhand copies of German classical poetry and even such English-language classics as T. S. Eliot's "The Waste Land" and "Definition of Culture" survive as evidence of his linguistic pursuits and his eclectic tastes.[7] On April 1, 1900, at the age of nineteen, after briefly considering a call to the ministry, he left the family estate to join the 28th Saxon Field Artillery Regiment at Pirna, the start of a military career spanning forty-five years.[8]

Von Boetticher began auspiciously. The artillery specialty was an evolving but primary combat arm when he joined the Saxon Army as a *Fahnenjunker*[9] in 1900. Ballistics was an esoteric science before the introduction of aircraft and motorization to military formations. At the time, Prussian military opinion was also divided into rival factions, the cavalry still arguing the merits of thundering charges by densely packed horse. Artillery, on the rise in importance and numbers, was split between field gun battalions and heavier fortress batteries; field (and horse) artillery debated whether the field guns should accompany the infantry or remain in semiconcealed positions in order to be effective against an enemy. In many quarters of the infantry, the aristocratic leadership disdained the support of the other arms, preferring to slug it out on "honorable" terms in frontal assaults.[10] Promoted to lieutenant in August 1901, von Boetticher transferred to the 64th Saxon Field Artillery Regiment on October 1, remaining there until his posting to the Prussian Kriegsakademie (War Academy) nine years later. In the interim, he continued service with the regiment, earning credit for his successful relations with a group of Chemnitz reservists known for their "red" politics. In one of his last accomplishments with the unit, he managed a two-week training stint in command of these men without incident.[11] Von Boetticher's recollection of this episode in reminiscences more than fifty years later does not fully convey the attitudes of the German Army of the time toward social democracy. The fears that the army's isolated and aloof position would be undermined by the necessity to recruit manpower presumed tainted with the bacillus of working-class revolutionary ardor were always at the fore. The Wilhelmine Army instinctively combated reforming urges, Reichstag parliamentarianism, and any challenge to its cherished position as a major—and untouchable—pillar of the state. Not only did the army actively oppose outside political proposals for change, but its recruit training programs also prohibited suspect literature, songs, and speech.[12] Regimental routine was employed to convey accepted attitudes and inspire loyalty to the semifeudal military system and the kaiser at its head. That the army was an educator of youth and a means of transmitting civic value and national esprit was part of its antisocialist mission; convictions about the notion of military elites serving as formative influences within national life manifested themselves again in von Boetticher's later service in Washington.

As a twenty-six-year-old senior lieutenant, von Boetticher had become regimental adjutant when his commanding officer advised him in the fall of 1907 to take the examination for the Kriegsakademie, a preserve once dominated by Prussian aristocrats. Von Boetticher disappointed his colonel by revealing that he had something else in mind before considering the next step in a career.[13]

On November 14, 1907, von Boetticher married Olga von Wirsing in a definite coup, for his bride was above his social station. Her father was a retired officer of the 106th Infantry Regiment. The von Wirsing name was also of the established German nobility with a family seat in Stuttgart (Württemburg), while von Boetticher's ennobled status was only five years old at this time. On her mother's side, Olga von Wirsing descended from the von Valois, a Huguenot family.[14] Their wedding took place in the *Thomaskirche* in Leipzig; the couple spent three days in the Austrian capital.[15] Despite Friedrich's idyllic description of the beginnings of his marriage, this was a life of duty and unquestioning service for the wife of a German officer.[16] Von Boetticher always wrote and spoke of her with an exaggerated courtesy that seemed almost required and rote for men of his calling and caste. Of his three children, two daughters and a son, he was the proud father, though life for his son would bring its eventual adversity.

Shortly after his promotion to senior lieutenant on May 22, 1909, von Boetticher stood the examination for the Kriegsakademie. Between the turn of the century and 1914, an average of 800 men attempted the test each year; only 20 percent, about 160 candidates, were accepted.[17] When he began the three-year curriculum in October 1910, the prestigious institution was still heavily influenced by the spirit of the narrow if technocratically gifted Alfred von Schlieffen. As Prussian chief of staff for nearly a decade, this rigid soldier redirected the strategic attention of German war planning from east to west and had produced a grand scheme for annihilating the French Army in a modern-day Cannae, a decisive battle of encirclement.[18] Forcibly retired in January 1906 for his role in the first Moroccan crisis of the previous year, von Schlieffen was still the grand old man to the young generation of general staffers, and von Boetticher revered him. The school's curriculum enforced rigorous, independent study guided by a picked faculty of the best military minds, meant in these circumstances to be role models to their students. The school was regarded, even among the other great powers in the world at the time, as the best training facility of its kind, and academy graduates assumed the aspect of demigods in a German society that deferred almost instinctively to military rank and uniforms.[19]

Von Boetticher's performance at the War Academy foretold his next step. Graduates ordinarily went off to field units and military assignments deliberately chosen to get them away from their original specialties and broaden their points of view. Promoted to captain on October 1, 1913, von Boetticher received what can only be seen as a prize billet. His posting to the Great General Staff itself was fateful on several levels. On February 1, 1914, he joined the Railway Directorate of the Staff, at the center of war contingency planning and administration for the railroad net so vital to von Schlieffen's plan. As a relatively junior officer, von Boetticher was caught up in the refinements of a machine without which there could have been no such grand scheme. He plunged into the intricacies of bulk railroad logistics and timetables.

More immediate for his future was his close association at this point with the chief of the Railway Directorate since 1912, then–Lt. Col. Wilhelm Groener. Groener was a man on the rise, though the son of a mere noncommissioned officer from Württemburg. Von Boetticher shared his status of protégé to this man with several others, who later achieved prominence for good or ill, among them Kurt von Schleicher and Kurt von Hammerstein-Equord.[20] He had resolved one problem of advancement for junior officers in many military establishments. In coming to the notice of Groener at a crucial point in his career, von Boetticher also acquired for himself a mentor. Colloquially known in the American army as a godfather, this is a senior officer who takes an interest in the careers of talented juniors whom he identifies and sponsors.[21] In the elite German General Staff (as in armies elsewhere), senior officers encouraged potential in the same way. Younger men caught the reflected aura of higher-ranking men, and the senior officers found their own reputations enhanced by the achievements of their picked successors. Though the mentoring system has obvious uses, overplaying it can also lead to the rise of warring factions within any entrenched bureaucracy. Groener's favor would influence von Boetticher's career.

Barely six months after von Boetticher joined the Railroad Directorate, war struck. Following the assassination of the Austrian archduke and his wife in the Bosnian capital of Sarajevo, Germany gave assurances to Austria in the latter's ultimatum to Serbia. As the two hostile alliances dominating European politics squared off against each other, von Boetticher spent days and nights in the War Ministry. If the mobilization plans left the great iron safe that stood within view of his desk, war was imminent.

Events took heed only of emotion then. On Friday evening, July 31, 1914, tight-lipped officers left the building, each carrying a briefcase stuffed with the detailed orders of march for each of the German field armies.[22] Groener appeared suddenly at the Railroad Directorate that night, collected the supply of his favorite cigars from his own office, and quietly presented them to von Boetticher. He would not enjoy another one, he said, until Germany was victorious.[23] Outside the War Ministry, roistering crowds sang in patriotic euphoria as the nation rushed to war.[24]

With somber efficiency, the Imperial German Army mobilized. The declaration of war gave Groener the new sobriquet of Chief of Field Railways within the General Headquarters that now took the field. The subtle change in name signified that he ceased being a planning functionary and had taken over an operating command to execute the rail movement plans for the expected war on two fronts. The entire top echelon of the Railway Directorate, including Captain von Boetticher, now transferred to the new field command according to plan. Groener's writ extended literally to individual train stations in the smallest German towns. He controlled a network that appropriated German locomotives and cars from their peacetime schedules and sent them with the entrained active army to assigned debarkation points at the eastern and western frontiers. The marvelous, clockwork precision concealed for the moment the plan's basic flaws: diplomacy surrendered to the demands of railroad timetables, and the tempo of the great plan left no possibility for a peace initiative even at this late hour. The entire scheme further depended for success on a deliberate violation of a neutral neighbor, since von Schlieffen and his successors perceived that the broad plain in the middle of Belgium made it the only feasible avenue for the immense flanking maneuver against the French Army. Even as the advance elements arrived at their destinations, the plans integrated the transport of all the mobilized reserve units from their depots in the German interior to the fronts.[25]

Groener entrusted his protegé with a series of detached assignments in the mobilization and through the first year of the war, leaving him to exercise independent judgment and responsibility. On August 12, 1914, the thirty-two-year-old von Boetticher commanded the military train carrying the High Command of Field Marshal Helmuth von Moltke to the western German border to direct the encirclement of the French capital. A few days before Christmas, Groener dispatched him east to the German headquarters in Posen on the Russian front as a rail liaison officer under Field Marshal Paul von Hindenburg. Given the complexities of supplying German armies during the battles around the Masurian Lakes in January 1915, Groener's choice reflected his confidence in von Boetticher, who proved equal to these assignments.[26] On May 18, 1915, he arrived at the headquarters of General Kommando XXVII as the *Bahnbeauftragter*, or railroad deputy, a general staff officer's billet. By midyear, he was back at Dadizeele, the Belgian location of Groener's command in the west.

In the late summer of 1915, a year of stalemate from the English Channel to the Swiss border in the west had already reduced the war to fruitless bloodletting. Frontal infantry assaults followed artillery preparations in attempts to carry fixed positions. The rapid victory that was the object of Great Staff planning had eluded the

German leadership. On the Russian front, some maneuver was still possible in the grand spaces that characterized that war theater. Maneuver alone could not substitute for decision over Russia, however tactically successful, and Germany sought new initiatives for decision in the east, one that would remove Russia from the war. While all this transpired, new developments in the Balkans absorbed von Boetticher and added to his accomplishments for much of the rest of the conflict.

Inept Austrian attempts at the war's outset to humble Serbia produced only routs for the Habsburg armies. German forces now joined their ally for the next try. By late September 1915, combined Austrian and German forces massed on the Sava and Danube Rivers for another determined thrust south. A nervous Greek government begged the western Allies for some show of support in the region, and Allied landings began at the Hellenic port of Salonika at the head of the Aegean Sea. Sensing a windfall in an impending German victory, the less-than-gifted Czar Ferdinand of Bulgaria, a blood relative of the German kaiser, bargained for tracts of Serbian territory as the price for his own entry into the war on Germany's side. On October 12, 1915, he sent two field armies—more than 300,000 men—into the Serbian rear as the Germans crossed the Sava; the combined forces routed the Serbs, who withdrew what they could through Albanian ports.[27]

The quick victory did little to relieve the impasse on the German western front, but with Bulgaria now allied to the Central Powers, a new, unencumbered route opened to another, more distant German ally. The Danube, navigable along 1,200 miles from the German city of Ulm to the Black Sea port of Varna, became a cheap and unobstructed logistical highway for military supply destined for Turkish forces directed by a German military legend, Gen. Liman von Sanders. Groener established in the Bulgarian capital a command known as the Plenipotentiary General Staff Officer in Sofia (*Bevollmächtigte Generalstabsoffizier in Sofia*), reporting directly to himself as chief of field railways. In late October 1915, von Boetticher joined Maj. Karl von Stockhausen, another veteran of the Field Railways Directorate, in Sofia as second in command.[28] This organization regulated the entire bulk logistics flow by water on the Danube and all the associated rail traffic feeding the river ports. The Sofia central office controlled all the freight cars in seven subordinate harbors along the river and in two Black Sea ports; it saw to the regular delivery of matériel to Turkish transfer commissions that were moving the goods to their army. In addition, the command supplied Bulgarian military formations and was responsible for all strictly military rail transport inside Bulgaria. With an area of operations extending from depots in Germany to the harbor of Constantinople itself, the widespread network never operated with more than seventy German officers.[29] On March 5, 1917, with von Stockhausen's transfer to the Russian front, von Boetticher assumed command and ran the net for more than a year.

What von Boetticher managed in Sofia cannot be underestimated, but by 1918 the area had become a backwater. The last major operation von Stockhausen and von Boetticher supplied in the region was the stroke by Field Marshal August von Mackensen against Rumania in the late summer of 1916 following that country's opportunistic declaration of war against Austria-Hungary. With the front stabilized again to the advantage of the Central Powers by the autumn of the year, the Russian cause began its fitful dissolution. But for a young captain in 1918, a military career could only suffer if he did not see some real action. That entailed somehow getting to the Western Front.

In the Wilhelmine Reich, the Great Prussian Staff controlled all German military operations in wartime, but the forces employed in the field still comprised units raised and equipped by the four larger individual German states: Prussia, Württemburg, Bavaria, and Saxony. Each at this time still retained its own officers' rolls and promotion lists and conferred its own distinctive military decorations. With the dawn of 1918, von Boetticher began appeals to the personnel office of his native Saxon Army for a transfer to a combat division. By early February, he had obtained a promise that his wishes would be represented at the Saxon War Ministry.[30] Even as von Boetticher successfully conspired at his own participation in larger events, the German High Command initiated the last battle for a decision in the stalemated west on March 21, 1918.

Von Boetticher reported to his first combat command in the west during the mass transfers of German soldiery from the east through the spring and summer of 1918. With a unit from his home principality for the first time in eight years, he became the "first General Staff officer," or I-a (*eins-ah*, the combined chief of staff and operations officer for the unit) in German military jargon, of the 241st Saxon Infantry Division on June 23.[31] This Saxon division apparently escaped the declining troop morale common to German front-line units in the west at this time, because it was a veteran of fighting in the east.[32] Once in the west, the division rapidly lost combat effectiveness in the last grinding act of the war in France.[33] With the failure of Ludendorff's great spring offensive, German initiative was gone forever. In the desperate defensive battles that followed for German arms through the summer, American troops poured into Europe at a rate of 250,000 a month, making the Allied armies irresistible. The first General Staff officer of the 241st could only plan withdrawals, especially in the slow and bloody pullout around Soissons in July. Here the division had two of its three regiments badly cut up. It was thereafter relegated to the army reserve and saw action against American forces in the sector east of the Meuse River between November 5 and the Armistice six days later.[34] His performance during the summer battles nevertheless won von Boetticher the *St. Heinrichs Orden*, the oldest Saxon decoration for valor.[35]

Germany could not stem the Allied tide in the west, and other fronts began rapidly caving in. On September 15, the Austrian government sued for peace, the Turkish Army on the Palestine front broke on the eighteenth, and the Bulgarians collapsed on the twenty-fifth. On Sunday, September 29, 1918, the German High Command, deeply struck at the deterioration of its field armies, met at the Hotel Britannique in Spa, the Belgian town that served as the German headquarters in the west. First Quartermaster General Ludendorff in particular, despite his later denials, had already decided that an immediate armistice was imperative to avoid complete military collapse. Germany was alone and incapable of fighting on, loath as its leadership was to admit it.[36] The generals consulting at Spa had soon to contend as well with the influence of the American president, whose Fourteen Point program loomed large in the German mind as the basis for peace offers and subsequent talks. Woodrow Wilson's diplomatic shadow continued to lengthen as the American contribution to the Allies grew. He insisted repeatedly through the end of October on dealing with a new German leadership not connected with the direction of the war or in any way representative of traditional German militarism. Not only Ludendorff's continued service but also the kaiser's presence itself jeopardized German chances for a cease-fire. The war was lost and conditions attaching to a prospective armistice now required a fundamental change in the German system of government, too.[37]

In the wings at this moment was Wilhelm Groener. Groener's achievement as military railroad czar earlier in the war had led to another assignment running successive aspects of the so-called Hindenburg Program. In May 1915, he had organized continuing imports of bulk food from Rumania to supplement dwindling German stocks, all diminished by the Allied naval blockade of the country.[38] In October 1916, after the German failure to reduce the French fortress of Verdun, the new German Supreme Command under Ludendorff and Hindenburg nominated Groener head of the War Office, a newly established central function that was to manage not just food deliveries, but the whole disparate German war effort at home.[39] Groener had bested a series of dirty jobs, a fact that alienated many of his officer-colleagues the more. His, too, was Germany's highest military decoration, the *Pour le Merite*, not for combat leadership, but for his masterly management of the field railways supporting German arms on all fronts.

Groener's pragmatic management of often impossible choices brought him into close contact with the Social Democratic leadership of the time; his acquiescence to workers' needs for living wages and adequate working conditions had him balancing the conflicting tensions of the German war economy, the front, and the agendas of the radical independent socialists and communists in the factories. Groener had kept the lid on this corrosive mix by threatening dire consequences for any strike in the factories, but also by meting out fair treatment for German workers. Within a year, the Supreme Command proved itself incapable of leaving Groener to his own proven devices, with his colleague Ludendorff now decidedly cool toward him and openly distrusting the leftward drift of the war-industrial programs in the Reich. One of Ludendorff's minions engineered a bureaucratic spat that resulted in Groener's relief and his dispatch first to a divisional command in the west and then to a position as chief of staff at Kharkov for the German Army occupying the Ukraine.[40]

With the failures of the spring offensive and the operations into late summer to retrieve the situation in the west, combined in the fall with the High Command's meddling in responses to the Allies over peace terms, Hindenburg and Ludendorff both handed the kaiser resignations in a stormy scene on October 26. The increasingly besieged emperor accepted only Ludendorff's, whose replacement as first quartermaster general was eventually Groener.

Returning now from Kiev to the west through Berlin, the former field railway chief grasped fully the hopelessness of the German cause at the front and the discontents of the working classes at home. With his detailed proficiency in the logistics of wholesale rail transport, Groener would now, among other things, have to engineer mass German troop withdrawals to positions behind the Rhine.[41] His varied wartime experience prepared him little for the self-delusion and indecision among cabinet officials and the remaining High Command, continuously backpedaling in their earlier resolve for an armistice once they learned of Allied conditions. The kaiser, at the Spa headquarters since October 30, added to the uncertain atmosphere in the pressure mounting for his own abdication as the emperor of Germany; the Allies would not deal with his person or tolerate his presence in armistice and peace negotiations at hand.

Groener became central to the ensuing German drama of defeat and survival. On November 4, while he was in Berlin consulting with Prince Max of Baden, revolution broke across Germany. Naval units at Kiel mutinied at the order for a suicidal foray against the blockading British fleet. Three days later, radicals in Munich proclaimed a Bavarian Soviet modeled on the workers' and peasants' local organizations in Russia. With these events crowding the German leadership, Groener addressed a meeting of thirty-nine senior German generals called to Spa on the eighth. None of these field army commanders could guarantee the reliability of his own unit if called upon to quash the revolution; in the communications unit serving the Supreme Headquarters itself, the enlisted signal troops had established a revolutionary council.[42] Groener, finally, in Hindenburg's withdrawn presence, added his voice to those advocating abdication, revealing to the vacillating kaiser that there was no hope of his leading the German Army in France back over the Rhine to crush the revolution at home. Wilhelm now agreed only to desert the emperor's throne, but to remain as King of Prussia. On the ninth, events in Berlin overtook the absent Wilhelm when his complete abdication from all offices was prematurely announced to a milling crowd in front of the Reichstag building.[43] The exhausted chancellor, Prince Max, had resigned. A tailor's son, Friedrich Ebert, became the first Social Democratic chancellor of Germany and the head of a republic that replaced the Hohenzollern monarchy as the ruling system in the nation.

In the midst of this, Groener seized an opportunity. Late that same evening, he telephoned Ebert in Berlin. The two agreed to a measured quid pro quo. Groener offered the new republican government the army's backing in return for the government's support of the army during the forthcoming withdrawals in the west. Ebert guaranteed continued bulk supply deliveries from Germany for the troops still in the field, the maintenance of order, and an anti-Bolshevik political stance in which the government would rely on the army as the guarantor of the power of the state. These conditions would also serve Groener's primary aims of preserving the reputation of the army by marching it home under the control of its officers and salvaging above all the General Staff from the wreckage of the empire. Ebert, dealing with the familiar Groener, entered readily into this forced alliance, because his Majority Social Democrats faced loud opposition and claims by more left-leaning Independent Socialists and communist radicals. He cabled his complete agreement to Spa the next day. Both men got what they needed from the arrangement, but Groener's bargain with a Social Democrat incurred the suspicion of a large part of the German population convinced that the monarchy had been betrayed, something that would dog him in due time.[44] From this point until his retirement from the army in September 1919, Groener influenced heavily the play of German military policy and its linkages with the German moderate political left in the turbulent postwar years.[45]

Groener saw his own and the German Army's association with other delicate developments gratifyingly limited when a civilian politician rather than a German officer dealt with the Allies on the cease-fire. German Center Party leader Matthias Erzberger had led German Catholics from an enthusiastic acceptance of the war and even the High Command's dictatorship to a formal resolution for peace in the Reichstag in 1917.[46] Erzberger, named the government member of an armistice commission that had been formed within the supreme command at Spa, now assumed leadership of the commission because of the common belief that the Allies would deal only with a civilian.[47] At noon on November 7, he led a small delegation to a meeting at the front lines to seek armistice terms from the Allied Supreme Commander, Field Marshal Ferdinand Foch. French forces were nearly as exhausted as the German, but the British Army was somewhat on the mend by late 1918, and Foch knew he was negotiating from strength with more than a million fresh American troops on the Western Front. After a harrowing trip, Erzberger eventually arrived on November 8, accompanied by Gen. Detlev von Winterfeldt, the German military attaché in Paris before the war, and German naval Captain Ernst Vanselow, at the railway car serving as Foch's headquarters in the forest of Compiègne, near Rethondes. There, after some pregnant delay, Foch produced a ready set of conditions under which the Allies would agree to an end of combat within seventy-two hours.[48] To prevent any reopening of hostilities, the Allies required a wholesale delivery of war matériel, and the recipients of the document could already sense the punitive ring in the preconditions to what was supposed to be an armistice between equal combatants. Germany was understandably called upon not only to give up territory occupied during the four and a half years of war, but, as an additional means of preventing further offensive operations, to hand over immediately 5,000 large-caliber field pieces and 30,000 machine guns. Clause 12 in the document opened the question of reparations for damages and the restitution of sequestered national properties that presaged bitter dispute through the years ahead. Clauses relating to the occupation of the Rhineland and the creation of neutral zones there struck the military members of the Erzberger delegation as so harsh that they read over them with tears in their eyes.[49]

The scope of the demands in the final document far exceeded the mere surrender of military hardware to stop the fighting. Another requirement drew Maj. Friedrich von Boetticher into the confrontation over the terms requiring delivery of large quantities of rail stocks to the Allied and Associated Powers, mainly to France. Clause 7 specifically called for the surrender of 5,000 locomotives and 150,000 rail cars within thirty-one days. All rail equipment and operating personnel in Alsace-Lorraine were to be handed over within the same thirty-one days, and all similar rail matériel in the Rhineland, scheduled for occupation by the Allies, was to be left in place and maintained until Allied troops arrived. Five thousand trucks were also to be forfeited in thirty-six days, the term of the original armistice. Further, all coal and signal equipment necessary to run the trains were to be in good order.[50]

Already posted to the Army Supreme Command at Spa on October 14, 1918, von Boetticher answered Groener's summons on November 10, the day after the kaiser was dispatched to exile in Holland. Connected immediately by telegraph to Spa and Berlin when they received the armistice conditions, the Erzberger delegation cabled the list of armistice demands to Spa. Groener ordered his protegé from the former Field Railway Directorate to Erzberger at Rethondes to advise him on the rail and transport issues raised there. Von Boetticher set out that same evening across the battle lines in rain and fog. French military patrols repeatedly stopped his car and threatened to take him prisoner. His fluent French let him talk his way through the roadblocks, but with these delays and the gathering tension, he arrived exhausted at Rethondes. Erzberger's signature was already several hours old on the armistice document.[51]

The delegation that Erzberger led to effect the cease-fire became the nucleus of what took formal existence on November 12 as the German Armistice Commission, or WAKO (the German acronym for *Waffenstillstandskommission*). Situated in Spa, this element grew continuously with the addition of other military and civilian technicians whose advice was indispensable in Germany's compliance with the terms. The WAKO was until the following spring the only designated entity through which the Allied and Associated Powers dealt with the defeated Germany.

In his continuing role at Erzberger's side, von Boetticher's close association with the events of the time unfolded. In December 1918, he began filling out the German commission's Subcommittee for Transport Affairs (*Unterausschuss für Transportwesen*). Comprising eventually four military men and twelve civilians, von Boetticher's subcommittee existed to handle the specifics of Clause 7 on railroad equipment and to negotiate whatever amelioration of the stipulations could be wrung from the Allies. Von Boetticher in the latter case presented the argument, ultimately agreed to by the Allied side, that the 3,500 locomotives and 85,000 cars the Germans had left in place on the western front as they withdrew would count toward the total amount of matériel due.[52] The remainder of the locomotives and cars would have to come from domestic German stocks. For the subcommittee, this acquiescence by the Allies engendered some hope of staving off a threatened economic collapse that would accompany the abrupt surrender a large part of the railcar inventory needed to move German goods at home, but this hope soon evaporated.

On the Allied side, German attempts to schedule deliveries so as to diminish their domestic impact had the character of deliberately subverting the intent of armistice and the commission's purpose. An

American observer at the scene noted that once the immediate shock of defeat had worn off, the German delegation showed some cockiness, and its members were now inclined to argue over the delivery of goods as required. More than that, the Germans made considerable issue over the hostile receptions that met German trainmen when they rolled into Allied territory.[53] The French especially used this sign of German intransigence to increase their demands continuously. The qualifying phrase, "in good condition," describing the matériel in the armistice document's language, also became a device to extract only the best stock from German inventories. Though von Boetticher showed himself "adroit," in Erzberger's words, at resisting these demands,[54] a second extension of the armistice ran out without complete German fulfillment of the terms, and the Allies, largely at French insistence, demanded more than 58,000 agricultural implements of all descriptions as a penalty.[55]

The sessions at Spa ended on June 4, 1919, with von Boetticher's subcommission having delivered 4,554 locomotives and 143,828 rail cars,[56] the bulk of the deliveries coming toward the end of March. Von Boetticher's reputation for technical excellence had grown with the enormity of his task, and his subcommittee changed rapidly from a lower-level executive agency into a planning body. Matthias Erzberger, as it turned out, relied on von Boetticher for services other than an adroit deflection of Allied demands.

Between Erzberger and the German political right of the time, an unbridgeable gulf had opened by reason of his presumed abject surrender of German lifeblood. Already suspect in some quarters for his leadership of the Center Party in its belated doubts about the prospects of success in the war and for his too-ready espousal of the League of Nations idea, Erzberger fell out as well with the only other formal German contact with the Allies in these days, Ambassador Ulrich von Brockdorff-Rantzau.

Without experience in diplomacy and with no talent to draw from among his Socialist Party ranks, Ebert chose this stiff aristocrat-professional, now a grudging democrat, as his foreign minister. In this capacity, Brockdorff-Rantzau was head of the German Peace Commission, or FRIKO (for *Friedenskommission*), at Paris after May 1919. His views on Germany's next course of action frequently opposed Erzberger's. He further expected normal diplomatic courtesies and protocol from the Allies; the Allies saw the FRIKO as the German agency authorized only to *accept* the peace conditions, not negotiate them. Between WAKO and FRIKO, open and bitter rivalry soon reigned, and the opportunity for treachery abounded.[57]

In each body, factions argued over the strategy governing negotiations, and emotions ran high. While the peace treaty evolved in draft form in Paris, rumors, plans, suggestions, and speculation filled the German press and official quarters. Clandestine reports or letters from commission members, secretaries, servants, and military officers at the scene swelled the torrent of passion in Germany's crucial hour. On the WAKO staff at Spa as the General Staff representative, one Maj. Theodore Düsterberg, later a national leader of the *Stahlhelm*, the German veterans' association, sent Groener reports critical of Erzberger's strategy discussions and comments reflecting his own attitude on the necessity for fulfilling armistice terms. Not specifically meant for Brockdorff-Rantzau, these reports had more currency among Erzberger's enemies and undoubtedly came to the attention of the FRIKO staff as well. Erzberger, who had stormy clashes with Brockdorff-Rantzau about the informers on their respective staffs, sent Düsterberg packing upon the discovery of this disloyalty.[58]

Von Boetticher served Erzberger loyally at Spa. Erzberger managed WAKO affairs from a separate Berlin branch office,[59] and von Boetticher continuously informed him of developments in which Germans remained face-to-face with Allied officials. From Spa and later from Versailles, von Boetticher reported on political and personal matters of interest, adding his own interpretations.[60] Probably motivated by General Groener's approval of Erzberger's role and his own full understanding of Germany's inability to reopen the war, von Boetticher nevertheless was placed at some risk by associating with a man murdered by a right-wing vengeance squad in August 1921.[61]

Because of his abiding association with Groener, von Boetticher's own analyses of events before the signing of the peace treaty reached a wider audience than Erzberger and his immediate circle. In a memorandum dated at Spa on March 25, 1919,[62] the same day von Boetticher signed over a massive delivery of equipment to the Allies, he elucidated principles to guide the German approach toward the peace treaty. "Thoughts on the Approaching Peace Negotiations" made a strong impression on Groener, and he repeated its general theses to Brockdorff-Rantzau in a conference with the new foreign minister and FRIKO head on April 4, 1919.[63]

Von Boetticher dwelt here on long- and short-term strategies in laying out his proposals. For the immediate future, Germany had to resist the fundamental basis for the enforced peace. He argued that the enemy's aim in the war—to reduce German will by arms—had failed. Despite the currents of Bolshevism, the "evangelism of new teachings coming from the east," the German people, he insisted, found new internal strength. Since the German will to self-affirmation (*Selbstbehauptung*) remained unbroken, the state remained intact; hence, ". . . We do not approach the negotiation table to confront a *Diktat*, but as a co-equal partner in the play of the forces of the world."[64]

The analysis went on to explore in depth the spiritual aspects of the peace for Germany. Von Boetticher sought to combat anything that would erode the moral basis for the continuation of the nation whose uniform he wore. The worst threat to German sovereignty in his view was the imputation of war guilt. If the future of the nation hung on its collective faith in its own rights and the belief in its cause, the Allied assertion of sole German war guilt was a direct assault on this faith, a blow designed to induce doubts among Germans and to "rob their thoughts of their convincing force."[65] Von Boetticher's tactic was not merely to adopt a defensive stance on the question, but to take the initiative. Mere exculpatory statements about an equal share of blame among all the combatants would serve to unite the enemy more in renewed and sustained accusation. The point was to attack those areas of compromise among the Allies themselves in the proposed treaty, which would in turn re-open disagreements within *their* ranks, dividing them and confounding their efforts to destroy the German nation.

As spellbinding a plan as von Boetticher spun here, and indicative as it was of his misreading of Allied resolve to enforce the peace at this stage, he was more sweeping in a long-term strategy. In his view, one nation in the world held the key to German recovery—the United States of America. Though he saw in the United States some of the moral force he spoke of in his own nation, von Boetticher's cynicism was also evident in that he regarded Wilson's program and the League of Nations as an outgrowth of American missionary imperialism and a "healthy egotism." America was now a first-ranking power, he maintained, a force that had grown from a daughter of England to a rival to British power and commerce. In the Pacific, the Japanese represented a varying threat to the United States; hence, the recommendation for a world body that could attenuate the influence of those two powers in spheres of American interest. The German course of action was then clear. Since the American political star was in the ascendant, Germany should be first to join the American-sponsored League, but as nothing less than a sovereign equal, and "then we can hope to win time for the reconstruction of our state, then we can hope to enter into close relationships with the Union [*sic*], the state from which no conflicting interests of any decisive kind separate us."[66]

If von Boetticher rightly confessed in this document to basing his analysis on some optimistic premises, his avowal of the United States was rooted in Germany's direst need, not in any attachment to American ideal or principle. A cultivation of American goodwill was for Germany an obvious expedient, but the methodical assessment of conditions of the moment prompting a German western orientation showed von Boetticher in the exercise of strategic thinking typical of the German Great Staff officer. Conditions would soon change; so would von Boetticher's assessment of German strategy.

The Social Democratic government of Friedrich Ebert, whom von Boetticher had occasion to advise on military matters,[67] had also to make the choice between east and west. Among the most pressing needs was food. To pressure the defeated Germans more, the Allied wartime naval blockade remained in place to constrict German imports while the treaty was forged. Despite unsettled conditions, some bulk Russian food shipments continued to reach central Europe after the Bolshevik upheaval in Russia in November 1918. The revolution's excesses deepened the aversion of the moderate German Majority Social Democrats toward the new Soviet government in 1919. With mass starvation confronting Germans at home, "the paltry two trainloads from Moscow were weighed against the prospect of trans-Atlantic abundance."[68] Yet the American savior of the moment would, within a year, abandon Europe to its ills. Some elements of the Foreign Office staff but, more especially, the Reichswehr, the reduced German army under General Hans von Seeckt, looked eastward for friendship in international affairs and even for more ambitious military rearmament.

By now, von Boetticher was already situated in the very center of the evolving postwar German military command and staff structure. Relieved at the WAKO in late August, on September 1, 1919, he went home to the second section of the still functioning Great German General Staff, already doomed in the deliberations at Paris. A month later, October 1, he was in the operations section of a re-named element now known as the Reichswehr.[69] From this van-tage, he continued his analyses of the confused events of early 1920, which led him to new conclusions about Germany's future.

In the wake of the failed Kapp Putsch, a botched right-wing coup attempt in late-winter Berlin, von Boetticher penned a memoran-dum on March 23, 1920, appraising "Germany's next political tasks."[70] Almost a year to the day after he described for Groener a German alignment with the United States, he had to deal with en-tirely new conditions. The American Senate had rejected Wilson's plea for an American participation in the League of Nations, leaving the League the embodiment of a local European security arrange-ment relying on the British Navy and the French Army. In eastern Europe, an imprudent attack by the new Polish state on the Soviet Union had collapsed, and rebounding Russian columns now men-aced Warsaw. These Russian successes enlarged the attraction of the revolutionary idea among some Germans, yet armed resistance to it was not feasible or wise: it would be militarily hopeless and further divide loyalties at home. The former entente, on the other hand, feared Russian advances as the triumph of Bolshevism over the cap-italist system, a threat to British dominions overseas, and a counter to French designs for splintering Europe. This anxiety von Boet-ticher hoped to use. Awaiting the outcome of the Russian operation in Poland, Germany should publicly announce that it would live in peace with Russia. This would serve notice on the Allies that any in-cursion into German territory to exact demands would drive Ger-many into the arms of the Soviet Union. Further, he wrote in this perceptive piece, the Allies would need the Germans to offset the Russians, and would have to loosen the terms of the peace to meet the unwelcome challenge from the east. If the tempo of affairs did not yet permit Germany this free a hand in countering the Allies by using the Soviet threat, von Boetticher had predicted accurately the orientation of Germany by 1922.[71]

In this season of hard choices for German authorities, von Boet-ticher's career might have stood in some jeopardy, too. For the new Reichswehr, the peace treaty, signed on June 28, 1919, required the reduction of the German officer corps from its wartime peak of

24,000 to 4,000 men by March 31 of the next year.[72] Heated debate arose as to which officers to favor as leaders of the 100,000-man police-army permitted by the treaty: the *Frontkämpfer* (front-line combat commanders) or the *Generalstäbler* (General Staff officers). Many of the front-line officers were now in the ranks of the various *Freikorps*, whole or remnant German army units that had set themselves to battling German left-wing paramilitary groups, armed rioters, and the Bolshevik menace generally. These elements were particularly active in the east. For Groener, von Seeckt, and now-Reich President Ebert, himself a labor leader, the choice was a stiff one. If Ebert's socialist convictions would not allow the *Freikorps* element to guide the new German armed forces, von Seeckt also implicitly distrusted the rowdy brawlers who flocked to their ranks, recognizing that they were not the diligent, studious, and brilliantly trained staff men needed to administer and patiently train the new Reichswehr.[73] Groener planned to rely solely on the General Staff cadre and to make of the most promising young captains and majors mobile administrators attached to no specific geographic command.[74] When Hans von Seeckt arrived as chief of the army command, in effect the commander of the Reichswehr, in March 1920 after the Kapp Putsch, the issue was irrevocably resolved in favor of the General Staff officers.[75] Von Boetticher's place in this august company was cemented by his own proven competence, but most tellingly by Groener's continued patronage. His future seemed less threatened than that of many of his brethren. For the next years, he was at the heart of the effort to keep intact a German military capability, however limited.

2

SOLDIER, SCHOLAR, DIPLOMAT, SPY

WITHIN a humbled but by no means subservient Germany, the new Reichswehr shrank toward the size required by the terms of the Versailles treaty. The German establishment nominally complied with the demands of the Allies under the eye of the Interallied Control Commission actively pursuing violations it could detect. March 31, 1920, the date by which German military strength levels were to reach the 100,000-man figure, passed, however, with actual ration count at twice that. The agendas of the international conferences in the early postwar period were heavy with inquiries about German acquiescence in treaty terms. As the United States abandoned Europe to its ills and the League of Nations to its febrile warranties of the peace, France, obsessed with guarantees of its own security, looked to the exact enforcement of the stipulations, relying nervously on the support of Great Britain. The decreasing patience of British diplomacy with French demands on Germany became one of the hallmarks of the interwar period. German diplomacy, on its side, sought leverage wherever it could perceive gains to be made in the fissures that opened between the wartime Allies.[1]

In this strained atmosphere, German soldiers remained alert to any opportunity affording open or clandestine advantage. Denied the possibility of large-scale exercises to practice coordinated activity among higher headquarters, the Reichswehr had, for the moment, to make a virtue out of its small size. Gen. Hans von Seeckt set about realizing a cadre army, a *Führerarmee*, in the German term, in which every noncommissioned officer would one day become a company or field-grade officer. It also became a maneuver army, one dedicated to mobile tactics. Limited by the necessity to conceal many of its activities, the German military moved to fill its requirements on all fronts.[2]

Von Boetticher remained a part of the central planning cell, the very intellectual middle, of the new German establishment. Article 160 of the Treaty of Versailles, coming into force on January 10, 1920, outlawed the Great Staff. Under the new Chief of the Army Command (*Chef der Heeresleitung*) was a much-reduced planning element, the *Truppenamt*. Comprising four main divisions, this innocuously named Troop Office carried on the traditional work of the old staff: Operations and Mobilization (T–1), Organization (T–2), Foreign Armies (T–3), and Troop Training and Indoctrination (T–4). A Transportation Section (T–7) rounded out the organization, which, for reasons unexplained, had no T–5 or T–6.[3] On June 1, 1920, Major von Boetticher became chief of T–3, officially the Army Statistical Section, or *Heeresstatistischeabteilung*, but also known as the Foreign Armies Office. Nominally responsible for professional evaluations of foreign armies, he was, in short, the new chief planning agent—and often the executive—for German Army intelligence operations. From his Berlin office, von Boetticher actually oversaw a host of open and clandestine activity. Vestiges of the Great Staff's functions involved in these pursuits in the past found their halting way to the T–3. New functions were incorporated; in recognition of what aircraft had become in the war, one section specialized in reporting on developments in foreign military aviation.[4] At least one part of the old Imperial German intelligence organization sought out von Boetticher in sheer desperation.

Among the footloose remnants of the German Army was a fragment of the former *Nachrichtendienst*, the military intelligence service, now struggling for existence. On a grand scale, this bureau before and during the war combined espionage abroad and more prosaic military intelligence collection activities under Col. Walther Nicolai. Nicolai's erstwhile military aide, Maj. Friedrich Gempp, kept the rump organization barely alive in spartan Berlin offices abandoned after the war by the German Navy. With nine other men, two of them officers, Gempp embarked on the self-defined mission of protecting the army from agitators within its own ranks and from other vague, presumably hostile, influences. Without patronage, he also sought the protection of a larger army component and presently found a home in von Boetticher's T–3 section. The meager reporting that he could command came to von Boetticher.[5] Gempp's appendage, christened obscurely as the Abwehr, would in due course take on a larger life of its own under an erratic naval officer, Adm. Wilhelm Canaris. During his service in Washington, von Boetticher would have reason to remember the Abwehr.

As the reception center for any military reports from abroad, von Boetticher's command suffered a marked handicap. The victorious Allies had hobbled this function from the start. The treaty had stripped the German establishment of the General Staff that assimilated military attaché reports in the past. Another of the military clauses, Article 179, was held by extension to forbid the dispatch of any German attachés at all.[6] The Allied peacemakers who had drafted it supposedly had in mind the case of Liman von Sanders, who trained and advised the Turkish armies that so embarrassed British and Australian landing forces at Gallipoli in 1915. The signatories of the peace understood the article to be consistent with the idea of disarming Germany as a precursor to world disarmament.[7] As such, the right to dispatch attachés was an implicit issue in the continued German representations in the interwar period for equality with other powers. Von Boetticher's earliest work in the T–3 section contributed to a shadow system of attachés sent abroad. As chief of the section, he emphasized especially the analysis of the close relation between political imperatives and military thought in foreign staffs. Some German diplomats were willing to supply information from foreign posts, but without training or professional military backgrounds, their value as observers was limited. They usually sent home newspaper clippings without analysis. Disguised attachés thus sent out in contravention of the treaty went mainly to Mussolini's Italy and to Spain.[8] With these men quietly deployed, and with the information coming in from Abwehr sources and the cooperation that von Boetticher could develop among traditional diplomats, the Reichswehr at least kept the institutional semblance of an attaché system.

Centered in the T–3 office, too, was the administrative machinery for something far more ambitious. In what seemed an improbable concurrence of interests, Soviet Russia and Germany began a cautious approach to each other driven by economic necessity and their common status as pariahs in international circles of the time.

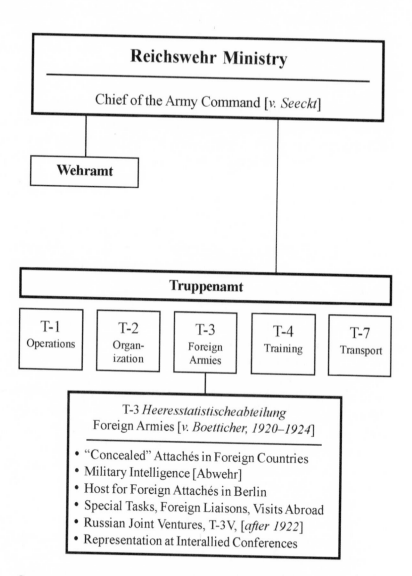

Reichswehr Ministry

Chief of the Army Command [*v. Seeckt*]

Wehramt

Truppenamt

T-1	T-2	T-3	T-4	T-7
Operations	Organ-ization	Foreign Armies	Training	Transport

T-3 *Heeresstatistischeabteilung*
Foreign Armies [*v. Boetticher, 1920–1924*]

- "Concealed" Attachés in Foreign Countries
- Military Intelligence [Abwehr]
- Host for Foreign Attachés in Berlin
- Special Tasks, Foreign Liaisons, Visits Abroad
- Russian Joint Ventures, T-3V, [*after 1922*]
- Representation at Interallied Conferences

GERMAN MILITARY INTELLIGENCE functions in the early Weimar Republic were often ad hoc arrangements. As head of the T-3 section, von Boetticher took on diplomatic assignments even as he re-established the operations of the former German *Nachrichtendienst* and the attaché system. He undertook clandestine visits to foreign capitals, played host to foreign military officers in Berlin, and advanced the German-Russian cooperation of the time.

Source: Paul Schneider, *Die Organization des Heeres*, pp. 43–45.

A Russo-German commerce treaty was signed in May 1921, and a secret economic agency had already begun the process of reopening Russian markets for German capital investment. The German share of Russian imports rose from 25 percent to 32.7 percent by 1922, and Russian cooperation had extended even to the provision of 300,000 hand grenades, which, in the hands of German municipal police, at least partly guaranteed the stability of the Weimar republic.[9] A Soviet-German treaty signed at Rapallo in April 1922 stunned the wartime allies of the time. This pact foreswore issues of war guilt and reparations between the two signatories, and a season of open political and economic cooperation began between the two European outcasts.[10]

Paralleling these political-economic developments was a covert military cooperation that lasted until the arrival of the National Socialist government in power. Von Boetticher was not part of the earliest military discussions, pursued at von Seeckt's direction by a shadowy and indistinct *Sondergruppe R* (Special Group R) within the Reichswehr already by the end of 1920.[11] In Russo-German diplomatic discussions for prisoner-of-war exchanges opened in April 1921, the two sides explored their common hostility toward the new Polish state and the possibility of cooperation in arms, though no formal alliance developed at this early date.[12] While German arms and aircraft conglomerates began their investments in Soviet military reorganization and equipment by opening manufacturing plants on Russian soil, another side of the bargain allowed for a German aviation establishment at Lipetsk, an armored warfare center at Kazan, and a gas and chemical school, codenamed TOMKA, near Saratov.

Subordinate staff sections of von Boetticher's T–3 directorate managed personnel transfers, worked through a tangle of financial arrangements, and established administrative procedures for this effort, especially in concealing the whole enterprise.[13] German officers transferred to the Russian centers dropped from the annually published rank lists in Germany. The matériel traffic moving by sea from German Baltic ports to Leningrad had to be hidden from Interallied Military Control Commission inspectors and even elements of the German population that would have found it more than strange. Financial arrangements were discreetly made for payments across international banking systems and exchange rates.

Equally delicate was the disposal of German victims of training accidents, especially aviators, whose dead bodies returned to Germany for burial sealed in crates labeled "Machine Parts."[14] In the wake of Rapallo, a T–3V section took over the functions of Special Group R.[15]

Amid all this, von Boetticher appeared again as a military-technical advisor at international conferences, probably with the intervention of Wilhelm Groener, who had, by this date, become the Weimar government's minister of transportation. Several meetings convened to continue refining the details of the general peace settlement and to pressure the German government on delivery schedules for goods and money. Little is available to document his exact contributions at these sessions, but a fortnight before his appointment as head of T–3, he was again at Spa[16] for the first post-treaty Allied attempt to reaffirm periodic German reparations payments, already behind schedule. From July 5 to 16, the Germans confronted their conquerors, who were still presenting a united front at this early date, to make their own "honest proposals" on four major issues: disarmament, war crimes trials, reparations, and coal deliveries to the Allies. On the last score, despite strong German protests on the exactions levied by the wartime Allies—the loudest from Hugo Stinnes, the German coal baron—the German delegation was forced to agree to deliveries on specified terms. Even more sensitive was the size of the German Army, still acknowledged at above 200,000 men. General von Seeckt, summoned to the meeting at British Prime Minister David Lloyd-George's insistence to answer for this, infuriated the Allied conferees. He stalked into the chamber, tall, slender, and grim, in full uniform replete with all his wartime decorations. The outcome was the same as on the coal issue: von Seeckt had to guarantee a reduction of the German Army to the 100,000-man limit cited in the treaty. Not only were these demands again made explicit; the German delegation—comprising Chancellor Konstantin Fehrenbach, German Foreign Minister Dr. Walter Simons, and Reichswehr Minister Otto Gessler—was deliberately humiliated. To emphasize the subservient position of the Germans, other delegations talked to them only during formal sessions and avoided any of the usual social engagements. Von Boetticher could only witness these failures to soften the effect of the reparations and the military limitations on

Germany.[17] His presence had no visible effect at Spa or at the London conference that continued the same work in February and March 1921. It took another year for the Allies to recognize that their payment figures and timetables were beyond the Germans' capacity to manage.[18] In the military sphere, these humiliations had the inevitable effect of driving the Germans to their connections in the east.

With his patient diligence, von Boetticher continued to impress his seniors with his demeanor and staff experience in these international meetings. The coordination of the eastern policy had required the closest cooperation by T–3 with the German Foreign Office. As a result, von Boetticher was entrusted with other discreet matters. On at least two occasions, he undertook secret, quasi-diplomatic missions for Chancellor Friedrich Ebert's government. In the fall of 1923, the Lithuanian government had approached the East Prussian German military administrative command (*Wehrkreis*) in Königsberg to request the dispatch of a German military representative. A response in this affair was coordinated between the Reichswehr Ministry and the German Foreign Office, and by late November, von Boetticher was in Kaunas, then serving as the Lithuanian capital. He was to determine what the attitude of the government there would be in the event of a Polish-German war. Tensions over the inclusion of the former great Lithuanian capital city of Vilna in Polish territory at the end of the Russo-Polish war of 1920 were still simmering,[19] and this border rectification was one of many irreconcilable disputes in the region. The feeler in 1923 was another instance of larger possibilities for Germany in the fluid politics of the east at the time, but von Boetticher's report on this occasion was such that the initiative quietly died.[20]

In von Boetticher's own assessment, Ebert's trust in the army rose after von Seeckt proved consistent, if grudging, in supporting the republic. Von Seeckt's military was steadfast in the economic collapse following a punitive Franco-Belgian military incursion into the Ruhr in January 1923, and the Reichswehr helped contain National Socialist unrest in Bavaria after the abortive Nazi coup later that year. The socialist chancellor counted on von Seeckt with other delicate approaches to foreign powers at the same time. Among the more important of these was a visit to Rome, one of a series of probes between the two governments.

From its beginnings, the Fascist government in Italy had followed a dilettante's course in foreign affairs. Given to grandiose gesture, Mussolini also resorted regularly to private, even clandestine, exchanges among foreign governments without informing his own diplomats. The often contradictory results were a feature of Fascist foreign affairs. *Il Duce* dabbled in German politics at this time by secretly sending a military emissary to Berlin (and von Boetticher was probably involved here, though no formal record of the conversations is anywhere apparent) with offers of assistance in a right-wing coup and went so far as to supply arms to radical elements. He also sought to embarrass French and British interests and the Allied administration of new League of Nations mandates in colonial areas, especially Africa, all in the name of establishing Fascist prestige and making himself a force on the international stage.[21]

Von Boetticher's meeting with the Italian dictator ran true to the latter's irregular form. Mussolini insisted on absolute secrecy. This time, the German Foreign Office contributed nothing to the project and had no inkling of von Boetticher's departure; his passport bore the name Franz von Berthelsdorfer and listed him as an art instructor. On May 26, 1924, he met Mussolini face-to-face. In von Boetticher's recollection, his host judged Germany as too unstable and threatened by radical movements for a public show of Italian support for the Ebert government. He rehearsed his grievances against the French treatment of Italian colonists in Tunisia and mused over the prospects of an Italo-French war. Both Germany and Italy should avoid this, he said, and seek to lull this common opponent.[22] Summoning his German confidante to a second intimate meeting on June 2, a more reserved Mussolini once again toured his own diplomatic horizon and made a point of Italy's unpreparedness for war.

In this exchange, von Boetticher cast himself later as no more than a minor character in a grand opera staged by the Italian dictator. Even the elaborate security precautions had a farcical side. Sightseeing in the city alone after his first encounter, von Boetticher was shocked when another German hailed him by name in the street. The man, a diplomat just transferred to Rome, had met von Boetticher just six months earlier at the German legation in Kaunas.[23] Von Boetticher reported all this at home but never perceived any result from the whole business.[24]

Of more visible consequence were developments with one group of representatives in Berlin in the early 1920s. The T–3 section was also the intermediary between foreign observers and attachés stationed in the city and the German military establishment. Official Reichswehr news releases to foreign delegations, invitations to inspect "guard" units, and schedules of social functions for foreign officers other than those in the Inter-Allied Control Commission emanated from the T–3 section. American officers throughout the period of von Boetticher's service there were among the most frequent contacts in his Statistical Section. Along lines that von Boetticher had suggested to Groener in March 1919, the German military entered into particularly fruitful relations with American officers stationed in Berlin. Von Boetticher was useful to American interests in several ways.

The American military delegate showed little preoccupation with policing the presumed German violations of the Treaty of Versailles, among the chief activities of the Control Commission. Army Lt. Col. Edward Davis, the designated American military attaché in Berlin from 1919 to 1921, as worldly an officer as the American army had at the time, was especially grateful to von Boetticher. As head of T-3, the latter gave Davis immediate and official access to every office of the Reichswehr but also made an all-important and wider social interaction a reality. In a world still governed by stiff formality, he compiled for Davis a list of names and addresses of key German officers so that the American officer could personally deliver his calling card, the first requirement before invitations could be proffered by prospective hosts.[25] Col. Creed Cox, Davis's successor in November 1921, showed much more interest in the record of German combat experience of the world war. The director of the War Plans Division in the American War Department General Staff in Washington put his authority behind the efforts of the U.S. Army War College to get copies of German field orders and after-action reports on German military operations, especially those involving American forces. Cox initially requested these from the German government. The flow of material was eventually heavy enough to warrant a more institutionalized and close affiliation with the authorities of the newly established German *Reichsarchiv*, a privilege extended to no other nation except Austria.[26] A succession of American officers was detailed to the Reichsarchiv until 1940.

The Reichsarchiv connection flowered in the presence of a tolerant German attitude for a nation that was largely indifferent to the blandishments of European powers desiring to keep Germany militarily quiescent. A fascination with American business efficiency and "modernity" became a feature of early Weimar culture, even as German intellectuals, politicians, and military ranks wrestled with their ambivalent attitudes toward the socialist parliamentary government.[27] The American occupation command headquartered at Coblenz in the German Rhineland from the end of the war until January 1923 made enough of a reputation for fairness amid the difficulties of its administration that the French suspected its troops of being pro-German.[28] In relations between Germany and the United States, in fact, what von Boetticher had advocated to Groener in 1919 prevailed among uniformed officers of the American and German armies through the period of the Weimar Republic. Military men in both countries were ahead of their political counterparts in fostering close professional exchanges. At a time when German military officers were suspect if they underwent sudden conversions to causes outside a single-minded devotion to the preservation and expansion of German armed strength, von Boetticher cultivated and later fondly remembered the friends he had made in the U.S. Army. He opened his own home in Berlin as well, where one of the American assistant observers, Capt. Allan Kimberley, was virtually a family member.[29] Details on weapons developments in the United States came to Germany in exchanges that no other nation duplicated in dealing with the defeated Reich.[30]

With another of these young officers von Boetticher may even have prevented bloodshed. The American was Capt. Truman Smith, a Yale graduate with a Columbia University master's degree in history, fluent in German, and recipient of the Silver Star Medal for his combat service with the U.S. 4th Infantry during the late war. He was also an astute observer of early Weimar politics. First assigned to the U.S. Army's Office of Civil Affairs at Coblenz, Smith was posted to the American Embassy in Berlin in June 1920. Ambassador Alanson B. Houghton dispatched him to Munich late in 1922 to interview Crown Prince Ruprecht and the forcibly retired Erich Ludendorff in attempts to assess the strength of Bavarian separatism. Colonel Davis had spoken to Ludendorff a year earlier. Almost as an afterthought, Houghton asked Smith to seek out the leader of the still-obscure National Socialist German Workers Party, headquartered in Munich. Smith failed to see Ludendorff but delivered one of the first direct American evaluations of Adolf Hitler. "A marvelous demagogue! Have rarely listened to such a logical and fanatical man," Smith wrote in his diary on November 22, 1922.[31]

Not all of Smith's German associations were as successful. In 1921, a former German senior lieutenant named Kurt Hesse had taken such opposition to Smith that he challenged the American officer to a duel. Smith and Cox appealed to von Boetticher, who subtly intervened to convince Hesse of his oversensitivity. The incident added a central element to von Boetticher's career as attaché in Washington by cementing a lifetime association between him and Truman Smith.[32]

In return for such services as these, Colonel Cox prevailed on the War Department to receive von Boetticher as an official military visitor to the United States. The Reichswehr, however, had little money to finance this undertaking, and von Boetticher certainly had no spare savings. The invitation might have been declined had not Max Warburg, head of the German branch of a Jewish banking family, intervened.[33] Von Boetticher's five-month tour of the United States in late 1922 brought him more attention from American officers, and, after his return, he replied to detailed inquiries about German wartime railroad management to American Army War College students.[34]

Throughout his service in the Truppenamt, von Boetticher could count the advantages he still enjoyed in the limited German Army. With the monetary crises that struck Germany in the wake of the news of the reparations bill in 1920, and again with the hyperinflation attending the Ruhr Crisis of 1923,[35] von Boetticher's personal fortunes dipped. He suffered the financial loss common to German civil servants at the time and watched his wherewithal diminish to a level that threatened his family of five. On the brighter side, he had a secure future with the Reichswehr, though he and von Seeckt eventually did not see eye to eye.[36] He had survived in an occupation that was reduced to a police function by the victorious Allies, but one that he had had a supportive hand in rebuilding as a serious professional army through clandestine schemes for eventual expansion. He was also heavily active in the Reichswehr's perceived need to keep alive the spirit of German arms.

Von Seeckt committed scarce funding to yet another campaign suited to his ends. In the conditions imposed on the traditional sword bearer of the German state, its defeated soldiers sought to justify still the necessity of their existence.[37] The Reichswehr quietly underwrote a flood of published material to keep before the population the sacred myth of the soldier. Not only did von Boetticher sustain the new Reichswehr by his service in intelligence and clandestine diplomatic affairs, he lent it a facile pen as well. His characterizations of events and political blueprints sent to higher authority gave von Boetticher a reputation as a strategic analyst beyond the circle of his Truppenamt contemporaries by 1920.[38] A continuing series of his memoranda and short studies circulated among the staff, and several found their way into print for wider audiences.

Von Boetticher's commentary ranged over the issues confronting the German polity of the day in ways often almost spiritual. From his position in the central planning element of von Seeckt's cadre force, he produced essay after essay—and several books—on matters of mind and heart, the realm of German national attitudes and self-identity. In his first year as intelligence chief of the new Reichswehr, his name appeared often in the early Weimar literary press, sometimes under a nom de plume. In this pursuit, his commissioned status was seldom revealed in his bylines.

His deliberate appeal was to a class of still-extant German intellectuals moved by strategic analyses and the flow of higher politics, and his message was usually meant to give heart to those awaiting a national resurgence. When Rudolf Kjellen, the Swedish father of the "science" of geopolitics, published a widely received assessment of the post–World War I crisis of Europe, von Boetticher offered this audience a subtly incredulous review of Kjellen's pessimistic predictions for Germany's future.[39] The rise of an Anglo-Saxon imperium based on the transatlantic bonds of culture and blood simultaneously marked the decline of any German national aspiration, Kjellen argued, especially in the balance of world trade. Von Boetticher's repetition of Kjellen's judgment supported his prediction that Germany, having thrown down its weapons and emasculated itself, could await neither justice nor sympathy. He summarized these ideas as a challenge to Germans to expect exactly the opposite in dealings with the peace regime.

Von Boetticher's name appeared often in a new journal devoted to strategic subjects. *Wissen und Wehr* began publication in 1920 as a purveyor of serious debate on options open to the defeated and reduced Germany. Its content appealed to students of narrow tactics as well as to those seeking a higher understanding of events. As a frequent contributor to the journal between 1920 and 1929, von Boetticher, in his themes, laid before his readers his solutions for such things as the "German Plight."[40] He again usually dwelt on the moral and spiritual concomitants of the German problem of national self-identity and will. These elements he presented as the core problem facing the German people: retaining the national self-confidence to assert itself again in the new political conditions in contemporary Europe. Never did these pieces lay out an active program of resistance or a political course of action; von Boetticher characteristically focused on the difficulties of maintaining the moral underpinnings of a national existence among the German populace.

Three more substantive published volumes also appeared under his name before his arrival in the United States. The first of these, *Frankreich: Der Kampf um den Rhein und die Weltherrschaft*, appeared in 1922. At 156 pages, it was an extended polemic with some gloss of serious history. The text treats events from the Roman Empire and some of Tacitus's more acerbic remarks on the Gallic character. Its lively style seethes with sarcastic references to pious French justifications for the strict enforcement of the Versailles settlement.[41] Von Boetticher's premise throughout was that French policy had a constant theme from the time of the earliest Germanic hero, Arminius, who fought Romans and Gauls alike to a standstill. The persistent French thirst for domination of the European continent as a prerequisite for overriding world influence has forever collided with German culture, roots, and prerogative at the river Rhine. World War I represented for him the culmination of this policy, and all of the high-sounding verbiage of the peace treaty about an ideal postwar world where arms would come under strict control served only the end of keeping a disarmed Germany incapable of fending off new French demands on the left bank of the Rhine. Viewed critically, this argument was of a recognizable frame-of-reference literature common in Germany at the time, but its central thesis also found resonance in later, more accepted, scholarly work.[42] The treaty, von

Boetticher made clear, was really an instrument of French aspiration, as all the fine theory on self-determination was contradicted by French behavior in the occupied Rhineland areas. French plans in 1916 for an independent Rhenish state and the brief appearance of such an entity in 1919 gave von Boetticher's assertions a ring of historical truth.[43] As to American participation in the war, von Boetticher appeared to follow a line of thought consistent with what he had laid out for Groener in his memorandum of March 25, 1919. Americans came to the conflict full of ideals, he said, but with little experience in European affairs and the goals of power politics.[44]

Other familiar themes of the period showed up as well in his treatment of the war-guilt question, also designed, as he saw it, to destroy what remained of German self-confidence, and his geopolitical conceptions of the problem of French revanchism. These were elements that German presses also played up incessantly after the war; von Boetticher's contribution, even as a German officer's handiwork, was more soundly based in fact, yet its imbalance is evident in that it makes no attempt to assess the propriety of the obvious German aims and ends in the short-lived Treaty of Brest-Litovsk or to appreciate the residue of hate left from the settlement of the War of 1870. His depictions of French foreign policy undoubtedly reflect much experience from the days of the WAKO at Spa, a predisposition he also carried with him to the United States eleven years later.[45]

Von Boetticher's subsequent works have another thematic thread, one that exhibits his strong attachment to the tradition of character breeding so much emphasized in German Staff training. In two biographic interpretive treatments of German heroes, von Boetticher sought to isolate a moral force that is a combination of personality, charisma, high diligence, and intelligence in a leader of men.

Friedrich der Grosse als Lehrer von Lebensweisheit und Führertum für unsere Zeit also shares much with the anti-Versailles literature of the time. Insofar as von Boetticher repeated the characterization of a voracious French foreign policy, this book continued the theme of the earlier *Frankreich . . .* , but here he offered the steadfastness of mien and the unshakable faith of Frederick as a corrective for the damage caused the German national pride and purpose by the war-guilt clause. As a means of overcoming the rot he saw setting into German consciousness with the collapse and the ignominious treatment at the hands of the traditional enemy, von Boetticher directed the attention of his countrymen to the "eternal principles" of leadership exemplified in the life of Frederick the Great.[46]

Drawing on the published works of Frederick, von Boetticher demonstrated that even in the despairing last three years of the Seven Years' War, the king remained detached and calm but competent in inspiring his subjects and his army. He had grasped the very secret of wisdom in life, that logic is not all in human endeavor and that unfathomable forces intervene in human events—the work of "his Majesty, Fortune." Frederick had mastered his fate and risen above the circumstances of his time. Similarly Germany must await events with a positive faith in renewal; it could only prevent further deterioration by adopting a state of mind such as Frederick's after his defeats at Kolin in 1757 and at Hochkirch the following year, not an attitude of pessimism, but a devotion to hard work, studying the lessons of history, and to self-sacrifice. Von Boetticher, as many Germans of the day, harked to the time when a new national leader would appear: "Only he who has trodden the thorny path of Frederick has the right to call for a leader; but he will only arise when we ourselves are worthy of him."[47]

The imagery of the Frederick piece is of a type that new scholarship has characterized as excessively romantic and indicative of certain literary and philosophical trends in Germany of the time. Von Boetticher does not fit altogether comfortably within one interpretive framework developed to examine the susceptibility of Germans to right-wing worldviews that rejected Enlightenment rationalism as a presiding force in world—and spiritual—affairs. The failure of the German polity to undergo in the course of rapid industrialization and modernization a truly bourgeois revolution from below left illiberal, antidemocratic influences that championed the romantic ideals of the Germanic past in reaction to French influence.[48] Von Boetticher never exhibited any of the mythic brooding that made up the veneer of Nazi ideology. He was, on the other hand, taken with an individual moved by what he frequently called a "divine spark."[49] A man of refined personality, intelligence, and the instinct for decisive judgment was a compelling figure for von Boetticher. The word *Führertum* in the title of the Frederick biography is in this case less than an unintended prophetic expression from the pen of a German author. His search for this sort of leadership was not confined to German examples, but he found his most compelling representatives of the divine inspiration among military men.

The theme is central to von Boetticher's first published work on Alfred von Schlieffen.[50] A printed version of a lecture von Boetticher presented on the hundredth anniversary of Schlieffen's birth, February 28, 1933, the text is further evidence of the reverence of the German Staff for Schlieffen even after World War I. Von Boetticher's contribution was only a small part of the literature on the man, a central feature of which was a remembrance of the power of von Schlieffen's presence. Groener's influence in the presentation is also clear,[51] and many of the conclusions are to be seen in Groener's earlier *Das Testament des Grafen Schlieffens*, in which von Schlieffen's military philosophy and method is contrasted with the course of German decision making in the recent war.[52] But if von Boetticher's historical researches were not necessarily original, they reveal, aside from a polished ability with the German language, a disposition to search for spiritual motive force in human event. His employment of history has that functional aspect to it—the search for lessons to be learned—that marks the utilitarian military approach to the study of the past. A more pedestrian mind derives mere tactical expedients from such a use of history; von Boetticher focused on what was best in German General Staff tradition: an anonymous, selfless service and a striving to be more than one appears to be.[53]

Never intruding on any of the biographical treatment of German military heroes was any sense that the whole intellectual basis for German strategic thinking had by 1914 become brittle and tightly formulaic. Taking on faith that the decisive battle of encirclement in the west would succeed because no one could countenance the effect of its failure, the General Staff had no contingency studies to explore what would happen if the Schlieffen conception, however modified, fell short of its grand purpose. Von Boetticher's considered assessment of von Schlieffen continued to show up in source notes in the literature on German operational and strategic planning in the late Imperial era.[54] He concentrated even later in life on identifying not the underlying flaws in the conception, but on those who had tinkered with or so weakened the execution of the Schlieffen plan as to betray its presumed original genius. He never appreciated that German higher commands almost imperceptibly moved from a strategy of deterrence bequeathed to them by the elder von Moltke to the construction of mechanistic plans governed by singular and unquestioned assumptions.[55]

Von Boetticher's advancing career meanwhile gave him a solid technical reputation among his military confreres. Leaving the *Statistische Abteilung* in the hands of his successor, Colonel Liebmann, on September 1, 1924, he reported to the 4th Artillery Regiment as head of Section III. Here he took on the additional job of revising completely the standard Reichswehr artillery manual. With the greatly reduced army, infantry tactics had to conform to the abilities of available forces, and von Boetticher, promoted to lieutenant colonel on November 1, 1924, adapted artillery tactics to von Seeckt's mobile and thoroughly professional army. The new doctrinal statement became Reichswehr standard by 1926 and won its author a decoration for the accomplishment.

The same year was one of fateful change in the international scene for Germany. The atmosphere produced by the Locarno Pact of the previous year brought the country to the doorstep of full membership in the League of Nations in March. This halting approach suffered the pangs of German domestic politics and the linkages attaching to Poland's membership at the same time as Germany's, all of which served only to postpone Germany's entry until the fall of the year.[56] But a related decision at Geneva interrupted von Boetticher's purely military career and brought him again to an international diplomatic forum.

His assignment to the League capital in June 1926 was the last and most significant in von Boetticher's career, rendering him a logical choice for later service in a foreign mission. In marked contrast to his humiliating experiences at Spa and London, he came to the Swiss center with a slightly wider framework of action, albeit in a confined area in which his technical abilities once again occasioned his presence. The convocation was a direct outgrowth of formal wording in a League Council resolution of December 12, 1925, specifically inviting several League members and several nonmembers—the United States, the Soviet Union, and Germany—to participate in the work of a general disarmament conference. The resolution, standing as the charter of the Preparatory Commission for the Disarmament Conference it called into being, also laid down seven questions to be answered as a preliminary to the general conference.[57] These questions aimed at laying out a universal definition of armaments, simple means of comparing them, and the delineation of offensive and defensive weapons and likely formulae for limiting them. More knotty was the question of limiting or even measuring the total war strength of a nation including its reserves; its war-industrial capacity; its civilian population, natural resources, communications, and transport. These considerations, tied to questions of geography, would be the basis for an equitable scheme of disarmament. The latter was at the insistence of France, still seeking regional European security arrangements for itself under the general League program of worldwide arms reductions mentioned in the disarmament clauses of the Treaty of Versailles.

France had much at stake in this meeting. The Preparatory Commission's establishment was at this juncture the latest event testifying to an anguished vacillation over France's own national security and a concern for general European disarmament as a means to that end. The French approached the subject with two minds. General disarmament would tend to defuse German demands for equal treatment in matters of arms, an argument pushed even in the moderate tones of Gustav Stresemann's foreign policy with an inarguable logic. Yet disarmament of other nations required some reduction of French arms, which would accordingly reduce French security in the face of the immense potential of a resurgent Germany. It was a position in which France found itself ever more isolated and unable to shake off the charge of militarism in its search for safety in alliances and bayonets by the number.[58]

For Germany, on the other hand, aside from the first formal recognition given it as a non-League power, the commission was an occasion for repeated insistence on a right to equality of arms with its neighbors and sophisticated argument that pointed up the French dilemma. An erstwhile German emissary in Washington, Johann Bernstorff, now represented his country at the League. In an early statement to the diplomatic members of the Preparatory Commission on May 18, 1926, he represented Germany as having already fulfilled the noble first conditions of the League's intent to maintain a peaceful world. Germany alone was within the spirit of the covenant, he declared:

So long as there are certain countries which have excessive armaments and others whose armaments are not even sufficient to provide for their own security, the working of the Covenant must be inevitably hampered by a great many difficulties. Germany, who has fulfilled her duties in the way of disarmament in so complete a fashion, may justly hope that the other nations will follow her course in such a way that both for Europeans and for the whole world there will follow a condition of enduring peace and reciprocal confidence.[59]

This introductory set the tone for the German line of reasoning in the subordinate technical meetings that followed concurrently with the sessions of the main diplomatic commission until November of that year. Bernstorff's ploy was to discredit the French argument from the start and leave the French members on the defensive.[60]

Von Boetticher carried the thrust of the German argument into the deliberations of Sub-Commission A, the body whose membership consisted of military and naval officers from all the represented countries. Sub-Commission B tackled questions of defense financing and the application of natural resources to war production. Arriving in Geneva on June 6, 1926, to relieve Col. Heinrich von Stülpnagel, von Boetticher plunged into anything but lively discussion on the relative merits of voluntary over conscript forces as laid out in a French talking paper brought before the sub-commission. A minor point, it yet divided the membership along lines of interpretation most favorable to their respective military policies at home. Von Boetticher regarded as antagonists here the two Frenchmen he faced across the table, a Col. Emmanuel Requin[61] and his aide, a Major Lucien. With Lucien he had many exchanges through the later stages of the fifty-one sessions that lasted through the autumn.

The issue of reserves proved as central to the deliberations as it was thorny. French military policy of the time was torn between the perceived need for a continued defense-in-being to meet a possible rapid attack by von Seeckt's professionals at the gates and the blandishments of the French political left, which favored a concept of a nation in arms—a strong ready reserve—instead of a large and expensive standing force with fancy equipment. The predisposition of the political left that supported a smaller standing army also demanded a shorter length of service for the conscript in the French Army, with the consequent growth of a larger French trained reserve.[62] With a standing force averaging 240,000 men, largely deployed in the French northeast or on occupation duty in German territory, the French Army relied on a forward defense of the border areas behind which the citizen army would mobilize to help stop any German thrust into the French homeland. With this basis for military organization and training, from which grew the mentality of "no offensives" and eventually the Maginot Line, the French military delegation came to the technical sessions at Geneva in 1926. The reserves, such a major consideration in the French mobilization strategy, would be excluded as a standard for evaluating the relative size and readiness of military forces.

One of von Boetticher's lines of argument ran to the heart of the French position. In late June 1926, he made a determined attempt to bring a vote on the question of putting some consideration of reserve forces within the jurisdiction of the sub-commission. Major Lucien countered with the idea that reserve figures were not a standard for comparison, because statistics on them were not complete, and in any case, too variegated, based as they were on numerous and different defense philosophies. The exchange between the two men led to some convoluted language[63] that served further to point up the philosophical differences between them. Von Boetticher continued to insist that statistics were not only available for European armies, but were complete and reliable. Only one other delegate stood with him in favor of the proposal. Later in the summer, the German delegation got no further with another point of interpretation. Most of the delegates were content to remain within the narrowly defined technical definition of the charter of the sub-commission. Again at issue with the French attempts to reduce all military affairs to matters of only comparable statistics, von Boetticher held forth in favor of "other methods, which could not be expressed in mathematical formulae, but were of greater value."[64] Quoting a speech of Joseph de Brouckere, the Belgian minister and noted mathematician who was attending the sessions of the main commission, von Boetticher asserted that the "question is not to measure, but to appreciate."[65] The Germans made no headway here either. The sub-commission would not exceed its explicit orders to consider no line of analysis other than means of quantifying national military and naval strengths.

Through the summer, von Boetticher's pique with the grinding diplomatic process in the face of French ability to control the agendas became plain. In a long letter to one of his fellow officers, he outlined the futility of the mission he was on. "You must not think that something essential is to be achieved here in the near future," he wrote.[66] Of the twenty countries represented by officers in the sub-commission, the French controlled their eastern European allies and swayed others against German positions. The group sought to resolve the questions posed in the sub-commission's charter, he reported, by "long speeches and still longer meetings." Without any illusions, he sought to make the best of his position and place in the record provisos that established the German rationale. Operating with "plenipotentiary" powers, he nevertheless felt completely alone and worried about Berlin's intentions for his future.[67] The continuing Preparatory Commission discussions again in 1928 made the convocation of a general League disarmament conference that year doubtful, something von Boetticher reported on in another of his commentaries of the time.[68]

Not only did the majority of Sub-Commission A members reject the German proposal; the body soon heard higher League pronouncements on the subject. The League's Seventh assembly, convening in September 1926, openly expressed its disappointment at the slow progress of the technical talks. Acutely aware of public scrutiny, the Assembly formally directed a rapid conclusion to the discussions on September 24, and the French delegation in the League Council moved to open the General Disarmament Conference in 1927 with no further contributions from the deadlocked military delegates. For its part, the military sub-commission now acted under a council resolution limiting the soldiers to strictly technical affairs and not to measures designed to appreciate the extent of weaponry or strength. Thus restricted, the sub-commission on November 4 issued a lame statement that contained a commitment to arms limitation and disarmament, but with all the statistics omitted.

It was not the end of League representation for von Boetticher. He stayed in Geneva until the fall of 1929, as military advisor to Ambassador Bernstorff. As head of the Reichswehr's *Völkerbund Abteilung*, he continued backing up German diplomatic efforts, commanding a staff of eight officers who channeled the advice and opinion of the German War Ministry to the diplomats.[69] Directly subordinate to the Reichswehr Ministry, von Boetticher's section came under his old friend Groener when the latter took over as Reichswehr Minister from Otto Gessler in January 1928. While in this position, von Boetticher received the epaulet pips of a full colonel on February 1, 1928.

Social life in the League's capital was active during von Boetticher's tour there but was subject to the tensions of international diplomacy. Von Boetticher, a strong believer in the efficacy of personal contact, on one occasion sought to offset the edgy confrontations by inviting Colonel Requin, his French counterpart, to dinner. Across the frequent bitterness of the talks, von Boetticher had developed a respect for Requin's cultured character, but this dinner invitation aroused the suspicion of the German senior command. The German government had regularly refused any social amenities with representatives of powers still maintaining occupying forces in Germany, and foreign attachés from those countries received no invitations to troop maneuvers. Von Boetticher, who had gotten around this practice in his earlier relations with American officers, now found himself with orders from the chief of the Truppenamt, Generalmajor Werner von Blomberg, to rescind his invitation to Requin. Though he resisted von Blomberg's reasoning, he had to give in in the end.[70] Despite this situation, von Boetticher did forge at least three other close personal relationships at the conference, with Adm. Aubrey Smith of the British naval delegation, and two American representatives, Maj. Gen. Denis Nolan and his aide, Lt. Col. George V. Strong, of whom the latter would play no small part in his experience in America.

German representation through the remainder of the disarmament negotiations clung tenaciously and without change to the principle of equality of treatment. In March 1927, French and British delegations brought in their own separate draft conventions, which were widely divergent. France eventually stood alone on the reserve question, in opposition to England, the United States, and Germany, among the major powers. Interrupted by an American-sponsored naval arms limitation conference through the summer, the Preparatory Commission reconvened as a whole later in the year. On November 30, 1927, von Boetticher presented the Reichswehr's strictly military point of view on armaments in a rationale that included the standard German argument for their effectiveness as a deterrent:

> Security is not possible without equality in arms, which delimits the danger of sudden attack, makes an attacked state capable of self-defense until the entry of the League of Nations, and finally produces the condition in which neither the single state nor a power complex united by treaties can offer successful resistance to the united forces of the same section of the globe.[71]

Requin retorted according to French lights that Germany did not need arms because its security was guaranteed by France and its allies as well as by the League of Nations. Hardly the diplomatic bon mot delivered to the face of a German officer for whom the memory of the Franco-Belgian incursion in the Ruhr was not five years old, Requin's remark more simply illustrated the gulf that separated the two antagonists even as the League's symbolic war against war moved to a tragic denouement. By 1930, the Preparatory Commission, to the disgust of the Germans, had adopted a resolution in favor of the status quo in armaments, making the German withdrawal from the conference merely a matter of time.[72] There is little wonder that the work of the League on disarmament to 1930 "gave as much satisfaction to a weary and waiting world as did the Red Queen's dry biscuit to a tired and thirsty Alice in Wonderland."[73]

Colonel von Boetticher had returned to Germany and a more strictly military command before the bitterness of the Preparatory Commission's vote overtook the *Völkerbund Abteilung*. On September 1, 1929, he became commandant of the German Army's Artillery School at the complex at Jüterbog, eighteen miles south of Berlin. At fifty-two years of age, by the following April he had already spent thirty years in the army and had performed creditably in combat and in a succession of peacetime assignments. His future, even in a status quo army, would have been secure. Promoted to brigadier general (Generalmajor) on October 1, 1930, he had probably not a hope of becoming Chief of Staff, as some of his American friends later maintained.[74] The general consensus, even among his fellow officers, was that von Boetticher would have again become chief of one of the major staff sections in the Truppenamt—and later the revived General Staff—before he left active service. He was regarded as a superb trainer of men and would have gladly served in a capacity he seemed to relish.[75]

Even the family seemed to prosper in the uncertain times of economic worry. Von Boetticher and his wife, Olga von Wirsing, had by now had three children, of whom the older two were already planning professional careers. The elder daughter, Adelheid, born in 1908, was in medical studies in Berlin, and Friedrich Heinrich looked forward to law studies at the University of Königsberg. By late 1932, life had a settled look about it at Jüterbog, and von Boetticher even claimed later that the increasing turmoil on the domestic German political scene had absolutely no effect on the artillery establishment at the school.[76]

In this atmosphere, one of the dying gasps of the disarmament wrangle in Geneva again changed the life of Friedrich von Boetticher. Through the summer of 1932, German threats to abandon the General Disarmament Conference, alternating with proposals for shorter Reichswehr terms of service and the establishment of a militia, brought French counters for a quasi-European union with commonly designed armed services, each national army with a limited number of short-service effectives. In desperate attempts to bring Germany back to a seat that remained empty after September 1932, Great Britain, France, the United States, and Italy agreed in a Five Power Declaration on December 11, 1932, to grant the Weimar government what it had so consistently bargained for. In a reversal of the original disarmament provisions of the Versailles treaty, the declaration asserted in its first clause that "one of the principles that should guide the Conference on Disarmament should be the grant to Germany . . . of equality of rights in a system which would provide security for all nations."[77]

The effect of this vague but promising wording on the Reichswehr was electric. With an alacrity that betrayed the fact that German military leadership had long awaited such an opportunity,[78] the Reichswehr Ministry drew from the grant of equality the implication that it might again send attachés abroad.[79] Within three weeks, the army's Personnel Office (*Heerespersonalamt*) had ready a list of candidates for overseas service. In fact, a partial list had existed in September 1932, and the Foreign Office had already agreed to dispatching attachés.

In his capacity as Reichswehr Minister, Gen. Wilhelm von Schleicher notified the Foreign Office of the schedule for posting men abroad. By April 1, 1933, the American capital and the major governments of Europe would receive German attachés; naval attachés would follow by October 1. Von Schleicher requested that all responsible German missions abroad be informed and that they in turn inform their host governments. His note specified seven names: von Boetticher's headed the list. By early March 1933, sixteen men were named in all.[80]

Von Boetticher shared, in large measure, the chosen qualities of character, personality, and intelligence the German Ministry sought in its representatives. Besides his proven abilities in field and staff work, his social poise and his abilities with English marked him a natural choice for his assignment. According to post-1945 reminiscences collected among German officers, the army also wanted men who could manage a household well and who had graceful wives who could present German habit and customs favorably. In short, the ideal attaché was a man whose lifestyle corresponded "to the views of the officer corps concerning simple dignity, which had been derived from Prussian history."[81] Financial stability, not necessarily wealth, was required; the government would now assume all personal expenses for operations abroad, a departure from earlier German practice that attracted only men of some means to the posts. The relatively high rank of the early German attachés also tended to guarantee standards of living suitable to their stations.

The Foreign Office began hearing some demurrers on the attachés from overseas posts. Leopold von Hoesch, the German envoy in London, at first heard only rumors as to their arrival. "Now what are they after?" he groused in a letter, "Meddling in politics, I suppose."[82] If he gave vent here to still-bitter memories of soldier-diplomat rivalries of Wilhelmine Germany, he wrote again to say that he wanted younger men who would enter into sporting events and make friends among younger British officers. Sending older, married officers smacked too much of bringing the big guns into play.[83] It took some time for the army's views to prevail. Older men were chosen for their broader view of military affairs, and, as the first German professionals sent out since 1920, they would have to concentrate on cultivating senior military staffs abroad. Germany had much routine data to catch up with, and the Reichswehr Ministry picked the best men it could muster for the jobs, since no junior officer could begin to comprehend the advances made in foreign armies over the preceding thirteen years or report on them in a comprehensive fashion.[84]

While Hoesch's suggestions were only mildly contentious, other German diplomats voiced no apparent objection to the project. State Secretary Bernhard von Bülow, in fact, immediately notified embassies involved and ordered the subsequent announcements to the entire German foreign service establishment. He counseled speed in making the notifications to host governments before the end of a recess in the Disarmament Conference.[85] From Washington, von Boetticher's prospective post, the ambassador, Friedrich von Prittwitz und Gaffron, cabled home only positive news after he sounded the American State Department on the subject. By March 1933, he reported that the idea of German attachés was protested neither in the press nor in government circles.[86]

If the prospect of sending attachés abroad was not hotly contested by German civil servants, the old bugbear of the attaché's subordination to the mission chiefs arose again from the moment von Bülow first heard of the Reichswehr's wishes in September 1932. The independence of German military attachés in the Wilhelmine Reich, in which any officer had the right of the *Immediatstellung*, or direct access to the kaiser, caused endless tension between the army and the Foreign Office.[87] For the next five months, the Foreign Office and the Reichswehr's *Ministeramt* discussed the arrangement.[88] The Foreign Office's suggestion that the officers be detached from active military duty and assigned to the Foreign Office hierarchy made sense only from the standpoint that the attachés would then not be counted toward the 4,000-man limit imposed on the number of officers in the Reichswehr by the Treaty of Versailles. For the diplomats it had the benefit of putting the military men directly and unquestionably under their control. The compromise that evolved in the "Service Instructions for Military and Naval Attachés and Their Aides Attached to German Embassies and Legations" reflected practice common to diplomatic circles in 1933, but by comparison with the last German word on the subject, Caprivi's Instructions of February 1900, the new document was a pronounced victory for the diplomats. The attachés were to be strictly subordinate to the ambassador or his representative, in any case ranking below the embassy counsel. All attaché reports had to move through the ambassador's hands, and attachés were to use the standard diplomatic code, not a military substitute, for their cable traffic. The Foreign Office, for its part, would open diplomatic pouches containing military reports as they arrived in Berlin and forward unopened the military reports to the Reichswehr Ministry, which would return a record copy of each attaché's report to the Foreign Office. Completely absent from the Service Instructions, initialed by General von Blomberg and Foreign Minister Konstantin von Neurath on February 11, 1933, was any provision for the old *Immediatstellung*, or direct access to the head of state. Though the new instruction became effective some two weeks after Hitler's arrival in power, the new Nazi government's philosophy and character had no bearing on this regulating statement, nor did the revision of the instruction in 1935 contain any hint of the oath of personal fealty to Hitler that the armed services swore on August 4, 1934, the day of President Paul von Hindenburg's state funeral.[89]

With the aura of this same Hindenburg, von Boetticher now created a solemn mandate for himself as he prepared to leave for the United States. From the days of his service as a railroad liaison on Hindenburg's staff in 1915, he had fallen under the sway of the old man's myth.[90] According to the newly appointed attaché, he approached the now-feeble Reich president for a conference just days before his departure. What supposedly followed made a profound and lasting impression on the attaché-designate, not only something he mentioned on occasion to acquaintances, but a reminiscence he referred to repeatedly until the end of his life. According to his own account of it, which became inevitably embellished to bring into play the effect that von Hindenburg's name had on American audiences, von Boetticher came to the presidential office without an appointment and received a few spare moments on the schedule from the adjutant in the anteroom. When he entered the old general's presence, conversation turned from the purely technical aspects of attaché duty to other facets of American experience, chiefly to the American Civil War, on which von Hindenburg was a fair authority. For more than two hours, von Boetticher and von Hindenburg rehearsed the details of Stonewall Jackson's movements in the Shenandoah Valley in 1862. The Reich president told of his fond wish to visit those battlefields to study the terrain and relive the events himself. Before the conference ended, von Hindenburg exhorted von Boetticher to do all in his power to establish and maintain terms of confidence between the United States and Germany.[91]

Heavily romanticized in von Boetticher's mind and memoirs as years passed, this final meeting with von Hindenburg may have really happened, but certainly not with the weight or context given it later. His daily handwritten journals, so carefully kept, even as he prepared to leave the command of the artillery school, do not mention any meeting with Hindenburg. Recorded is the telephone call from Walther von Reichenau in November 1932 that alerted him that he was to receive the new appointment. The maladroitness of then-Capt. Franz von Papen, von Boetticher's predecessor in Washington, who became persona non grata and left the United States in bad odor in 1915, came up repeatedly in the German staff's background discussions with von Boetticher, but the Reich president's name is never mentioned. The whole episode was heavily elaborated upon, but von Boetticher, to judge from the reverence with which he repeated this story to his friends in America, took his task in this light and added the luster of Hindenburg's blessing to his activities.

Von Boetticher returned to the War Ministry at the Bendlerstraße on March 1, 1933, for briefings and hasty introductions around the Foreign Office, and then set about foreclosing his affairs at Jüterbog. His thoughts ran to the possibilities of a personal mission of his own to a people whom he regarded in 1919 as separated from the Germans by no serious conflict of interest.[92]

3

A Missionary in America

GERMANY'S new military attaché arrived in the United States resolved to act upon the fancied parting request von Hindenburg had made to him. This self-assigned mandate established one of two principal motifs in von Boetticher's service in America. Within two years, in fact, it led him to cast his mission in almost religious terms. At the outset at least, American isolationist opinion offered an atmosphere in which this view of his influence among some sectors of American life could flourish. The strong suspicion of European quarrels, resulting from the inconclusive settlement of the world war, and a corresponding disbelief in German war guilt fed a wave of revisionist history and popular rhetoric and literature.[1] Yet there were also some visible strains in American public attitudes on the new Germany appearing in editorials and in official circles. The comment was critical enough to draw warning cables from the German embassy in Washington to Berlin.[2] In an all-too-infrequent occurrence, the ambassador, Friedrich von Prittwitz und Gaffron, appalled at the character of the Nazi movement and the dark promise of a Hitler regime, had already resigned his post.[3]

A potentially hostile and always capricious New York press thus awaited the new German diplomatic mission. Among the various bits of advice Prittwitz had cabled to his hastily appointed successor, former chancellor and *Reichsbank* ex-president Hans Luther, was the warning that the latter should have a thoroughly prepared statement for reporters, who were sure to meet the *Bremen*, Luther aboard, with the quarantine boat outside New York harbor on April 14, 1933.[4] In a mismanaged scene, the German consul in New York,

Otto Kiep, raced the newsmen to the incoming liner. Kiep first barricaded Luther into his stateroom and, when reporters were finally admitted, began reading a perfunctory statement. A red-faced Luther snatched the sheet from Kiep to read it himself. Gleeful descriptions of this made the next newspapers in the city and even the national weeklies.[5] An inauspicious beginning, Luther's mishap dimly presaged the gradual but steady deterioration of German-American relations ahead.

Von Boetticher avoided a potentially worse scene through Kiep's intervention. Traveling alone, he docked in Brooklyn four hours after the new ambassador had made the Manhattan piers. His advance notices were uniformly favorable,[6] and he escaped any untoward incident in his own encounter with the local press. Forewarned as Luther had been, he fielded questions on the German Army's loyalty to the new regime, ruling out the idea that the Nazi SA or SS formations would become reinforcements for the Reichswehr.[7]

More important in von Boetticher's case, the Foreign Office alerted Kiep to limit the size and the plans of another contingent awaiting von Boetticher. The New York branch of the Stahlhelm, a German national veterans' association roughly the equivalent of the American Legion, had resolved to send members to the pier in their old German Army uniforms to greet their erstwhile comrade-in-arms. Again with an eye to the impression this would make, Kiep, with incomplete success, had convinced the German veterans at least to go in civilian clothes, to keep their visibility to a minimum.[8] Von Boetticher, in civil attire, shook hands with the leaders of the German veterans delegation, who saw fit to display two banners of equal size, one with the swastika and the other the standard American stars and stripes.[9] The presence of the swastika itself opened the question of how German representation in America was to proceed under the new political auspices at home.

Von Boetticher's briefings at the Bendlerstraße and at the Foreign Office in the Wilhelmstraße before his departure from the new Reich gave him little inkling of the broad outlines of the Hitler regime's fundamental foreign policy aims. What exactly these were is still the subject of historical debate over whether Hitler pursued a deliberate "intentional" program with specific steps laid out on a definite timetable or more of a "structural" approach characterized by no real program other than an extreme tactical flexibility amounting to a crass opportunism.[10] Still highly fluid as the two German representatives made New York harbor, the direction of Hitler's foreign policy nevertheless had some discernible underlying principles more apparent as he consolidated his hold on the German state apparatus.[11] With gathering approval and even relief among the German public by the spring of 1933 at the arrival in power of a decisive hand,[12] Hitler gradually advanced over the next six years his own reputation as statesman and strategist.[13] He scoffed at the mere continued revision of the Versailles system, begun peacefully under Weimar, as subordinate to a much larger aim of vast expansion to accommodate and guarantee food resources for an increasing and racially superior German population, a drive for _Lebensraum_ that boded ill for Germany's neighbors and augured the eventual establishment of German hegemony on the Continent and the distant goal of a commanding global position as well. Hitler's intermittent prognostications on the subject were once thought to indicate his desires for an accommodation, if not an alliance, with Great Britain that would free German hands, especially in eastern Europe; despite an agreement on naval affairs in 1935, this understanding continued to elude German policy through mid-1940, when even the remotest possibility of its realization disappeared entirely.

None of this could be accomplished outright in the short term but, in another interpretation, would be realized in a series of increments that would return Germany to the status of world power and more, with a resurgent German military as a necessary part of the plan. German military officers greeted this improvement in their career prospects with quiet satisfaction; most were more sanguine about National Socialism than not. Among historians this evident purpose of expansion and the aspiration for a commanding German weight in Europe has provoked additional interpretive discussion over how much continuity was apparent in the Nazi program and how much was radical departure from the past.[14] Some elements of Hitler's diplomatic performance mirrored an earlier Bismarckian blueprint, but the ideologically driven thrust for living space had a destabilizing character unknown in the Iron Chancellor's balanced system of international relations. It also labored under the "curse of dogma,"[15] the concurrent Nazi ideological obsession with Jews and Aryan purity as a simultaneous driving force and drag anchor on Third Reich diplomacy. Between 1933 and 1936, Hitler produced a complete reversal in the international affairs of Europe in which he initiated activity to which the guarantors of the post–World War I peace could only react. By early 1938, he became the sole, indisputable author of German policy for the duration of his Reich and dictated the tempo of events on the Continent until the outbreak of war; literal control of events thereafter eluded him. If only for tactical reasons, he could arrive at a modus vivendi with Soviet Russia, that country and its political system remaining the implacable opposite of the new German idea. In this elaborate and shifting firmament, the United States remained a potential but distant enemy, one to be engaged only in later phases of action after the consolidation of a German position in Europe.[16] That some aspects of this grand scheme contradicted others, and that the method for achieving these ends soon amounted to diplomatic blackmail, were not yet wholly transparent, though it was already clear that the racial doctrines of the Nazi Party and state were basically not exportable everywhere. Von Boetticher, who had certainly contributed his own apparently fruitless efforts at undermining the Versailles settlement in his years at Geneva, had his own emphasis. For the new German military attaché in Washington, a vague Nazi grand strategy did not play much of a direct role in April 1933. His attention was on matters more concretely personal and on the effect he might have on his host army.

Reporting to Luther at the German embassy at 1439 Massachusetts Avenue, NW, on the morrow of his arrival in the American capital, von Boetticher readied himself for the round of protocol receptions ahead. By the first of May, he had rented an impressive stone-façade house at 3203 R Street, NW, just north of the capital's Georgetown district and neighboring the Dunbarton-Oaks estate. The turreted house, an easy drive from the embassy, was the scene of many social affairs expected of men of his position.[17]

From the first, von Boetticher rehearsed details of his friendly receptions for audiences at home. He usually addressed reports of his personal contacts and evaluations of American opinion directly to the Reichswehr minister, Generaloberst[18] Werner von Blomberg, and to the chief of the Truppenamt, Generaloberst Wilhelm Adam, who left that office to Generaloberst Ludwig Beck on October 1, 1933. The content of these reports is the best indication of the scope and importance von Boetticher applied to his personal representation in the United States. With his rank of Generalmajor, the equivalent of brigadier general in the American army, he almost immediately became dean of attachés in Washington because of this status and his length of service. He therefore moved in circles in which he plied his own deliberate, if loosely defined, program.

Chief among these in the early years of von Boetticher's service was the American Army chief of staff, Gen. Douglas MacArthur. Von Boetticher's position gave him routine official traffic with the U.S. Army's higher command. Introductions began with his formal presentation to the secretary of war, George Dern, and his assistant secretary, Harry Woodring, and MacArthur on April 19. Though these formalities were common for all incoming foreign emissaries and marked their entry into Washington society,[19] the new German attaché took the niceties of the moment as more than the usual courtesies extended on these occasions, especially when MacArthur repeatedly stressed his admiration for Reich President Hindenburg. Going beyond the remarks he gave the press in New York, von Boetticher characterized events in Germany for MacArthur as a great "national upswing" (*nationale Aufschwung*), which evoked a "lively understanding" among his listeners, according to his own account of the meeting.[20] Though the personage of Hindenburg as the German victor of Tannenberg in the last war was the starting point of many later private official meetings between the two, MacArthur clearly was only observing amenities before his guest in these remarks. The chief of staff's later promise to visit the German president, whom he described to von Boetticher as "the truly great man of our time,"[21] on his scheduled trip to Europe the following summer was also the gloss of diplomatic exchange. MacArthur was hardly sympathetic toward Germany. He had imbibed heavily of French military influence on the American officers corps during the close association of the two armies during the Great War. On an earlier trip to Europe in 1931, he had avoided Germany, catching sight of it only through embrasures of the still-building Maginot Line fortifications while voicing his opinion to French generals that "sooner or later Germany would try again."[22] When Blomberg visited Washington in the same year, MacArthur had refused to see him and "politely declined" an invitation to attend the German summer maneuvers in 1933 only a week before he received von

Boetticher for the first time.[23] Thus, the new attaché fell prey to the apparent warmth of his reception, for the report sent to Berlin after this first meeting also enthusiastically noted that the American army would welcome a visit from the current Reichswehr minister, who was the very same Blomberg.[24] This did not prevent some mutual respect from growing between von Boetticher and MacArthur. The chief of staff freely and frankly discussed with the German officer the wide-ranging technical and moral difficulties assailing him and the American army during the course of their two-man conferences that spanned the remainder of MacArthur's tour as head of the army. A basic conservatism, their common profession and the American officer's blind anticommunism found echo in von Boetticher's own attitudes, but von Boetticher was never the confidant of MacArthur that he intimated in his reports. He seized on MacArthur's every comment favorable to German interests, especially in the continuing disarmament talks in Geneva, as "renewed proof that leading officers in the [American] Army see relationships correctly."[25] It was his plan to use this understanding among American military officers as a basis for spreading a better view of Germany in the country at large.

This stratagem is only to be inferred from the content of his subsequent reports after he had made official visits to American military commands across the country. In accomplishing his purpose, though, he had the regular support of the American equivalent of his old T-3 section, the Foreign Liaison Office of the Intelligence Section of the War Department General Staff. The office was the center through which all foreign attachés established their official contacts, received formal invitations, submitted requests for information on the American army, and arranged visits to the staff components or military installations anywhere in the country. The head of the small bureau upon von Boetticher's arrival was Col. Charles Burnett, a cavalryman with wide international experience as American military attaché in London and Tokyo.[26] Although von Boetticher clearly overstated his influence with MacArthur, he found in Burnett his "closest friend in America," in the remembrance of the German attaché's son.[27] Acting as a matter of course as the American army's chief contact with attachés, Burnett gave von Boetticher introductions to commanders everywhere in the United States, to heads of military research installations, and to private firms producing weapons and military equipment.[28]

Von Boetticher embarked almost from the start on a personal campaign. The administration of the interwar army centered in nine corps area commands, each headquartered in a major city. In time, von Boetticher found his way to all of these, but in backwater army posts and local gatherings he found the first fertile ground for his message and reinforcement for his viewpoint. He had no difficulty in finding either. In late May, von Boetticher traveled to Fort Douglas, outside Salt Lake City, Utah, for a ceremonial unveiling of a monument to twenty-one Germans who had died in internment there during World War I. Attired in uniform, he spoke in English and German after a thirteen-gun salute in his honor. What impressed him were the "hundreds" of German emigrés who swarmed to him, many wearing their military decorations from the last war. These elements, he reported, were especially stirred by recent events in Germany. They inclined especially to the veneration of Hindenburg still common at the time at home.[29] In his first introduction to members of the American Legion, present for the unveiling, he made the acquaintance of the state legion commander and governor of Utah, Charles B. Mabey.[30] Just over two weeks later, he again perceived a welcome for things German in America when he addressed an assembly of American 3d Infantry Division war veterans in Union City, New Jersey, also attended by six active officers, one a general. There American Legion members told him that it was forbidden within the legion to describe the Germans as enemies. Again he saw evidence that the *nationale Aufschwung* gave new and older German-Americans self-confidence in their efforts to protect Germandom (*Deutschtum*) and to preserve and strengthen the German language among those who might have lost it—all within a complete loyalty to the American state, he added. His old friend Dennis Nolan, in whose corps area the meeting took place, later encouraged von Boetticher to speak to others in the same way. Bolstered by these receptions in widely scattered locations, he announced to his superiors his intentions of touring the American eastern seaboard and the middle west, delaying only to remain in Washington for the annual congressional debate on the defense budget for 1934:

I believe that on the way, the officer corps, who have friends in leading positions, can contribute much to the growth of understanding for Germany and for the collapse of the hate propaganda. . . . It is important that American personalities are at hand who can bring out their ideas in the German sense and with understanding for Germany.[31]

By late August, von Boetticher had covered the intended ground on junkets lasting up to ten days. In July, he toured the Aberdeen Proving Grounds and met the III Corps area commander, Maj. Gen. Paul B. Malone. In New York, General Nolan and the 3d Division veterans greeted him again before he left for the U.S. Military Academy at West Point, which he had first seen in 1922, and a meeting with I Corps commander Maj. Gen. Fox Conner,[32] one of the most influential American officers of the post–World War I scene. At Fort Ontario on Lake Erie, the 24th Coast Artillery Regiment, a National Guard element from New York City, enchanted von Boetticher with a parade in his honor and a firing exhibition, something he was wont to participate in directly with troops. Even more heartwarming was the large number of German Army veterans he found in American reserve ranks, again with their German military awards on display. In an area where an anti-German press campaign was in full swing, he reported that if the press could witness this, it would be more friendly.[33] By summer's end he had seen six of the nine Army Corps area headquarters, a number of Civilian Conservation Corps (CCC) camps, recently established, and had even been the special guest of Charles Dawes at a breakfast following a formal cavalry parade at the Century of Progress Exhibition in Chicago, of which Dawes was then president.[34]

Thus, by the end of the summer of 1933, von Boetticher had established himself as an indefatigable traveler in the German cause. Until international tension in late 1938 limited his absences from the embassy, he usually spent six weeks every summer on the road, visiting regular army commands and National Guard training encampments. His constant travel, in fact, raised the objections of his superiors at home, and he spent considerable time justifying his far-flung contacts and repeating his sanguine evaluations of his own influence in the United States.[35] In the process of gaining these often colored views on American life and public opinion, von Boetticher exhibited other lasting concerns connected with his mission, chief among them a counterbalancing of what he saw as an insidious French influence on the American army and on civil life.

A French appeal in American life and military practice was still evident in 1933 but was not nearly as trenchant as von Boetticher made out. American higher-staff organization borrowed much outright and absorbed some of its postwar style during its close association with the French military during the world war. The "G" system of nomenclature for military staff elements was a direct copy of the French system. American artillery throughout the interwar period retained the standard French-inspired 75-mm piece, though it was heavily modified to later American standards of mobility. More important was the American army's practice of sending young officers for training at the French Ecole de Guerre. Gen. John J. Pershing, at the close of World War I, ordered his junior field officers into as many French military schools as remained open and, as a result, diluted the former German-oriented methods and curricula in American military training. One of the more outspoken proponents of the French system avowed that it was far more compatible with the American character and need.[36] Pershing even in retirement retained an uncommon influence over American military policy, frequently deciding promotions to key American commands right through World War II. While von Boetticher was in the United States, Pershing still cultivated an especially close relationship with the French hero of World War I, Phillipe Petain.[37]

Despite these visible indications of French effect on American military thinking, German doctrine and the strategic thought of Clausewitz enjoyed a far greater resurgence in the United States in the 1920s,[38] this could not assuage von Boetticher's sensitivities on the subject. He developed sometimes elaborate arguments for his readers at home on the necessity of combating the French presence. The British attaché in Washington did not travel much and adopted a reserve toward Americans typical of his embassy in Washington,[39] but the Frenchman was more active. Von Boetticher spoke continually of the "always increasing" influence of the American army on American society through the reserve components and, more recently, through the labor organizations of the CCC. The French also recognized this, he argued, and sought to influence the higher levels of the Army with their own propaganda. Abandoning their cruder forms of rhetoric dating from the war, they were pursuing a sophisticated program based on the French contributions to the American revolutionary cause. They were heralding especially the memory of the Marquis de Lafayette in the same way that they propagated the Napoleon legend long after the death of the emperor. In the process, he fretted, they diminish the figure of Baron von Steuben. Von Boetticher pointed out that the German hero enjoyed a great image in the American army, not only because of his service as George Washington's drillmaster and inspector general, but also because he did not turn his back on America after the Revolutionary War, as did Lafayette and other figures who are considered adventurers, but lived out his life in the new country. Von Boetticher particularly resented the theme of what transpired at "Lafayette-Marne Day" on September 6, 1934, at the U.S. Military Academy. It was for him a highly transparent attempt to sway the corps of cadets with a spurious juxtaposition of Lafayette's birthday with the anniversary of the battle that turned aside the German right wing attacking through France in September 1914. Worse, Maj. Gen. Fox Conner had returned the remarks of the occasion in kind, and the whole affair struck the German attaché as an attack on German tradition, since, he maintained, West Point is the true guarantor of the thought of von Steuben and of the spirit of Frederick the Great in American military life.[40] The incident alone was serious enough, but its long-term consequences were dire:

> We stand in the middle of a struggle for the soul of the American army, which the French pursue with an undeniable finesse, clear in the recognition of the underestimated influence of the Army on the whole nation, and which is often promoted outside the realm of the press and the public. It is not a struggle in which the foremost line is carried with clumsy means of press propaganda. It is above all a spiritual battle, in which personal influence is decisive.[41]

Despite his disappointment in General Conner's performance, von Boetticher was able to catalog a number of his own successes. His connection with the commandant of the Command and General Staff School, Brig. Gen. Stuart Heintzelman, who had presented him with the school's published translation of von Schlieffen's *Cannae* and a printed collection of Civil War documentation, fell on the German side of the scale. Maj. Gen. Leon B. Kromer, the chief of cavalry, had accompanied him on a tour of the Antietam battlefield, where von Boetticher's impromptu lecture on Robert E. Lee, with analogies drawn to the command problems of Frederick the Great, won Kromer's respect and a continued social association. In this way, and not by attempting to counter the French with criticism of Lafayette, the German cause would advance. Von Boetticher was cautiously optimistic:

> It lies in the nature of things that disappointments cannot be ruled out. You must, however, judge them as minimal as you must avoid overevaluating daily events and must know what is merely the courtesy of the Americans and what is real. But many very happy experiences lead me to believe that the spiritual struggle now in train here is to be conducted successfully for Germany.[42]

With each of Hitler's strokes on the international stage, von Boetticher reported in this vein. Much of the material from the spring of 1936 through the last quarter of 1939 is not available for analysis, but his reporting on disarmament as it affected Germany culminated in a buoyant chronicle of American military opinion on the subject. In the wake of the renewal of German military conscription in March 1935, he followed through predictably. The really important officers in the War Department had told him privately that Germany had cut through all the cyclic negotiations on arms since 1926. Germany was seeking a policy of balance, they had said, and the reestablishment of German conscription emplaced a central fact around which they hoped for a clarification of the relationships of Europe. There was no danger of war by Hitler's action, but, on the contrary, a real contribution to the stabilization of power had occurred. French chagrin at this was evident from Gen. Maxime Weygand's remarks directed at the United States a week after the German announcement to the effect that American understanding for France had declined. Von Boetticher judged from reports reaching him that the State Department had greeted the German step with alarm, but that the War Department was advertising the correctness of the German viewpoint and it "may be assumed that the President and the leading political officials will be appropriately and basically advised."[43] He even allowed himself some complacency in combating the French on the conscription issue since the "attitude of leading officials of the national defense is coming around to us."[44]

Von Boetticher often measured his success by his self-perceived ascendancy over his French military rival, Lt. Col. Emmanuel Lombard, the French attaché who rose to colonel in the course of two tours in Washington, was fluent in English,[45] and represented for von Boetticher the embodiment of anti-German propaganda. Their paths crossed repeatedly and unavoidably at maneuvers and at social functions, but in one area, at least, von Boetticher justly regarded himself as having come out ahead. Since 1921, the 35th Division of the National Guard had held veterans' reunions in various cities in Kansas and Missouri. In 1933, the division invited a number of foreign attachés, the French and the German among them, to the affair, scheduled in Wichita, Kansas. Von Boetticher noted with satisfaction the speech of the mayor of Topeka, Kansas, and that of Kansas Congressman Randolph Carpenter acknowledging his presence. But long after the Frenchman had left the proceedings, people were still flocking to von Boetticher to shake his hand, bringing their children to meet him. By his report, Gold Star mothers who led the procession to the local cemetery were especially solicitous.

Von Boetticher's head start on the French influence with the 35th Division was real and lasting. It was one of his most successful efforts to maintain close ties with a military organization through which he could transmit his interpretations on German affairs. Unlike other invited attachés, he attended the reunions faithfully until at least 1940, according to the testimony of veterans and associates of the division, and visited Kansas City three or four times a year. He always dropped in on Ralph E. Truman, the division's chief of staff after 1932 and cousin to Harry S Truman, then a county judge in Jackson County, Missouri. By Ralph Truman's own account, he had had "a drink or two" before being introduced to the German attaché at the 1933 reunion in Wichita. Pumping von Boetticher's hand, Truman sang out, "We licked the hell out of you once, and we can do it again." Von Boetticher, who, for all his seriousness in currying favor for Germany, had a sense of humor, alluded to the 35th Division's battlefield debacle in the war.[46] There was an instant mutual attachment between the two.[47] Von Boetticher hardly overemphasized his reception here. In 1934, with no mention of his usual competitor Lombard at the 35th Division's celebration of that year in Joplin, Missouri, von Boetticher came away from the two-day affair an honorary vice president of the divisional veterans' association. After the usual round of speeches, a small deputation of officers took their guest to the local radio station, where he broadcast his thanks for the fact that "they saw in me, as a German officer, a true friend today." He later summed up his impressions for the staff at home, saying that "forces which are standing very close to me and which have helped me in many ways already without much display *[ohne große Worte]* have been again beneficial to the German cause in a way surprising to me."[48]

His press notices for the 1935 reunion were equally glowing; his photograph appeared in the Emporia (Kansas) *Gazette,* covering the festivities, and he stood on the reviewing stand in full uniform for the final parade.[49]

These favorable press coverages mirrored another of his concerns in the struggle for souls. The enforced caution of his arrival in New York in April 1933 left von Boetticher with a suspicion of the American press, especially of the "liberal" *New York Times,* that rivaled his animus toward France and the French attaché. In the summer of 1934, after a particularly rewarding series of swings through the West and Midwest,[50] he charted the area in which that newspaper's editorial color was visible. Only in the far and middle west was there a resistance to eastern thought. On the West Coast, he discovered a pronounced antipathy toward New York, but the "poison of agitation against Germany"[51] had spread even there. In attempting to combat this influence, von Boetticher and the embassy staff relied generally on a system of press releases of their own that attempted to counter coverage critical of German developments. Much of this was coordinated at home and cabled abroad for use by foreign emissaries. The inadequacies of this lay in the length of time it obviously took to allow Foreign Office or War Ministry officials at home to absorb the nature of allegations made and prepare a response. Even where the truth of a matter backed the German position, the timeliness of information from Germany was poor, because it could not keep up with a daily press. Von Boetticher also implied in his reports that the press attacks had a common control, because the "forces of capital" stood behind them. In laying out his earliest analysis of the problem, he revealed his own tactical philosophy on overcoming it:

> Certainly the material you send me is employed in the press and in the general work of enlightenment (*Aufklärungsarbeit*) of the embassy. But I also believe it to be a very important assignment in close cooperation with the Embassy to put right incorrect conceptions and especially to convince the leading officers—also the commanding generals in the country—through personal conversations of the rightness of the German standpoint and the ridiculousness of the propaganda against Germany.[52]

Aside from the admission of a formal German military and diplomatic effort to sway American opinion even at this early date, von Boetticher argued here for the validity of his own solution to the problem of reaching Americans. It was impossible to achieve results either through normal social channels in the American capital, successful though they might be in themselves with men like the chief of staff, or through a program of press releases. He was convinced that he would have to carry the campaign personally, a technique he felt was already proven in his case.

Events at the continuing disarmament conference in Geneva after von Boetticher's arrival in America determined much of the content of his reporting and the direction of his mission as well. By spring of the year, the Nazi program of military renewal was fairly set. Its rearmament schemes had not yet shown up in a vast new arms output, but Hitler revived old and developed new plans to further his peculiar aspirations for Germany. The German participation in the Geneva talks was purposefully governed by the resolution to continue negotiations, but to ensure that they would be barren while Hitler managed a measured expansion of the German armed forces.[53] His only real goal for the Geneva talks was to produce for Germany a right to rearm. Against this German policy, the French, the British, and the Americans ranged their proposals to no real avail. British Prime Minister Ramsay MacDonald's plan, named after him, was the center of discussion from March through June. Accepted by the American, French, and Italian delegations, it proposed, for the first time, numerical ceilings for all European land forces and limits to the air forces of Europe, the United States,

Japan, China, and Siam.[54] German rejection of the plan stemmed primarily from the vote of the Committee on Effectives to include the Nazi Party's SA and SS formations and the Stahlhelm veterans' association in the ceilings for Germany.[55]

The impasse at the conference in May brought an appeal from Franklin Roosevelt on May 16,[56] which in turn prompted a response from Hitler in a famous Reichstag address the following day, a speech full of conciliatory phrases[57] that raised hopes for success in Geneva and elsewhere. Norman Davis, the Tennessee lawyer and Roosevelt appointee, thereupon repeated the American president's proposal to eliminate all "offensive" weapons, specifically bombers and larger-caliber artillery.[58] Germany rejected thereafter a French proposal for two sequential four-year periods of disarmament: in the first France would stop all arming, and in the second it would disarm to the German level. By September the Germans planned to leave the talks and the League of Nations altogether and concerned themselves only with the timing of the stroke.[59] With German policy at this pass, von Boetticher reported on yet another meeting that sustained his belief in the eventual triumph of German policy over French.

Lt. Col. George V. Strong, another old and close acquaintance from the Disarmament Preparatory Commission of 1926, visited von Boetticher with inside news from the conference on September 9. Assigned at that moment as a technical advisor to Norman Davis,[60] Strong confidentially told von Boetticher that he could not predict peace in Europe beyond five years unless France changed its policy of obstruction at the meetings in Geneva. The French, moreover, could not trust either their own army or those of their Polish and Czech allies in eastern Europe, Strong declared; in their most recent maneuvers, French units around Strasbourg had mutinied twice. The meetings in Geneva were personally exhausting for him, for the French military delegate had accused him of representing German interests. At one point, affairs reached such a state between Strong and von Boetticher's old nemesis Col. Emmanuel Requin that other conferees had to take steps to "safeguard the dignity" of the American representative.[61]

Though von Boetticher cautioned, in his report of this conversation, that Strong's sentiments could be qualified by political forces, MacArthur confirmed for him a well-founded belief that American officers, if they thought about it at all, regarded Section V of the Versailles Treaty a gross injustice for Germany. In a tête-à-tête on October 3, the American chief of staff told the attaché that Germany was acting as it had a right to. "The difficulty lies with the behavior of France alone," von Boetticher quoted him as saying. He regarded a balance of arms as the best guarantee for peace, but the predominant factor in European politics was French fear of Germany.[62]

In his assertions on the beliefs of American military officers and their effect on the American populace, von Boetticher vastly overstated his case. American policy was clear enough in its enunciation to German representatives in Washington. Roosevelt told the visiting Hjalmar Schacht on May 6 that he insisted on the German "status quo in armaments and that we would support every possible effort to have the offensive armament of every other nation brought down to the German level." Roosevelt intimated "as strongly as possible" that the United States considered Germany the "only possible obstacle to a disarmament treaty" at Geneva.[63]

American policy maintained this critical stance in a year of deteriorating relations over an American boycott of German goods; Nazi assaults on German Jews, and even on Americans refusing to salute the swastika emblem; and the German government's finagling with interest payments on outstanding German bonds.[64]

In October, Hitler exploded a bombshell. The Geneva debate broke apart again at the beginning of the month with German rejoinders against a French two-part scheme for standardizing all European armies as a prelude to general disarmament. British Foreign Minister Sir John Simon nevertheless endorsed the French plan before the assembly on the morning of October 14. At this, Hitler decided nothing more could be gained at the conference and withdrew from the talks and the League, a coup announced to the world after noon the same day.[65]

General von Boetticher took less than a week to absorb the effect of this on his widening American constituency. His report, coming four days after the event, identified anti-German comments as coming from "French and English sources as well as from dark influences dependent on American Jewry in America itself which accuse Germany and poison public opinion." But, he insisted, his discussions with senior army and navy officers assured him that they considered Germany no threat to peace, some navy officers even pointing to a greater danger from Japan. If there was still reason for caution because of the reserve American officers practiced toward political affairs,

> I can report that I am convinced that the Armed Services among its leading officers understands the behavior of Germany and the disarmament question and acts in this sense. Already there is making itself felt a clear influence [of the army and the navy] on sections of the press.[66]

A month later, von Boetticher was still reporting on MacArthur's "warmth and concurrence" regarding Hitler's policy.[67]

Von Boetticher did have some undeniable and clear-cut successes in his mission. His reputation as a scholar gained him entry into circles within and outside the army on the basis of his uncommon familiarity with the American Civil War and with his comment on American heroes who gave evidence of the "divine spark." He was known for his impromptu speeches on historical subjects even in the field on maneuvers, and he opened his home to cultural and social gatherings for officers and selected professional friends as he transferred to American soil his earlier observances of *Friedrichsabende*—"Frederician evenings" in honor of Frederick the Great.[68]

Among the closest of the military spirits kindred to his own as a scholar was Maj. (later Lt. Col.) Joseph Marius Scammel.[69] Scammel represented a small group of military officers, academics, and public figures dedicated to the study of military history as an end in itself. Incorporated as the American Military History Foundation in 1933, the group had Scammell as secretary-treasurer in its early years, and he managed the small membership's affairs out of his hip pocket, using his office address in the Munitions Building, on the south side of Washington's Constitution Avenue, for business purposes.[70] In this capacity, Scammell became the instrument of another of von Boetticher's more notable representations of the German cause. For Scammell, one of the chief orders of business for 1935 was scheduling speakers for a foundation-sponsored session to be held jointly with the American Historical Association (AHA) at the association's 50th annual convention in Chattanooga, Tennessee, late in the year. In May 1935, Scammell wrote the program chairman for the AHA meeting, Prof. J. Fred Rippy of Duke University, proposing a joint session on military history or the interaction of force and policy as "the best means of putting the foundation on its feet and in the way of securing an endowment." He wanted to attach the Foundation's name to the larger association's and secure a "dignified, scholarly, and valuable series of papers by those whose reputations or presentations will command respect and give the society prestige."[71] But for all his efforts, Scammell could not secure commitments from either participants, a chairman, or a discussion leader for the presentations until late September, with the convention only three months off. Of the original names he forwarded to Rippy on May 16, 1935, a list that expanded and contracted through increasingly urgent correspondence all summer long, the only one still on the program when it actually transpired was von Boetticher's. Col. Arthur Conger's name appears as the chairman for the session in the program of that December, but Prof. Robert Kerner of the University of California actually presided.[72]

A copy of von Boetticher's twenty-minute address at the convention on Friday, December 27, 1935, did not survive, but Scammell's correspondence indicates that it followed the theme of yet another piece von Boetticher had simultaneously published in the official journal of the Army's Command and General Staff School at Fort Leavenworth. As an original study published in an organ usually given to surveys of current military literature, foreign and domestic, von Boetticher's lead article was a sophisticated statement on the moral factor of leadership in war. He returned to the examples of Frederick the Great's struggle against the coalition formed against the king in 1756 and against the fears and ambitions of his own lieutenants, relatives, and allies before the battle of Leuthen on December 5, 1757, a contest in which the king bested a superior force.[73] Von Boetticher pointed up again, as he had in his earlier biography of Frederick, that the steady mastery of fate and a firm hand in the midst of chaos eventually gained victory, an analogy easily applicable to George Washington's leadership in the American Revolution.[74]

An even more enduring example of where von Boetticher's historical interests got him among the ranks of American scholars was his lasting friendship with the editor of the Richmond (Virginia) *News Leader* and an undisputed dean of southern historians, Douglas Southall Freeman. The German attaché's grasp of the history of the Civil War was renowned among military men and a number of civilians somehow associated with lecture programs at War Department offices. Even the American ambassador in Germany, William E. Dodd, whose fastidious liberal tastes led him to condemn even the military attachés on his own staff, found von Boetticher "most interesting in his discussion of American military history. He knows the Civil War as no American attaché here knows German war history."[75] It was von Boetticher's view of Robert E. Lee as one of the bright lights of American history that brought the German into Freeman's circle six months after the publication of the first two volumes of Freeman's four-volume life of Lee.[76] Their relationship grew rapidly although they did not meet until, by mutual design, von Boetticher attended a memorial lecture Freeman gave at a Chancellorsville Battle reenactment on May 2, 1935.[77] Thereafter a warmhearted correspondence and frequent visits cemented a friendship that continued until Freeman's death in 1953. In June, von Boetticher visited Freeman in Richmond with his younger daughter Hildegard, and the two men often sent their daughters for visits to each others' homes afterward. He thus gained entry into a select group of Richmond first families, some of whose names remained among the controlling interests in the Virginia Historical Society through the 1970s. The field excursions, during which Freeman, usually speaking over a wad of tobacco, lectured on the battles as the group covered the ground on foot or in cars, took the collective name of the "Valley Campaign" after Stonewall Jackson's foray in the Shenandoah Valley in 1862. With its own recording secretary, the group proceeded on regular tours that combined history and social gatherings. Von Boetticher frequently made rendezvous with the "Campaign" by driving directly to the appointed battle site from Washington in his black Buick, carrying a full ration of German wines for the entire company.[78] By the end of 1935, Freeman's regard for von Boetticher ran far beyond mere southern hospitality. "Nothing that has come to me in this momentous year has been as much pleasure to me as meeting you and binding you to me."[79]

The uncontrived relationship with Freeman nevertheless appeared as a supportive element in von Boetticher's campaign to divide truth from untruth in America. It was one sign of American recovery from depression, he reported in October 1935, that great historians arise whose works are finding large markets. George Washington is as strong with them as Frederick the Great is with us. The American generals, especially Robert E. Lee, move to the foreground as examples. They certainly want to be Americans and are considering whether their participation in the world war did not go against George Washington's lessons and cause errors which were the source of the difficulties of the present.[80]

Just as his predispositions gave him access to some American opinion makers not open to other attachés, the nature of his representation in America gave von Boetticher definite ideas on his intelligence-gathering function. His chosen method of influencing what opinion he could was entirely inconsistent with the risks of clandestine intelligence and espionage. He assiduously avoided even remote contacts that could have been interpreted as vaguely shady and was as sensitive on this issue as the Foreign Office professionals who had hastily toned down his Stahlhelm reception in April 1933. Inevitably, the German military attaché was the recipient of various offers that might have involved him in exchanges that, however respectable, would prejudice his trustworthiness with men like Freeman, who often expressed his faith in von Boetticher's integrity.[81]

Von Boetticher feared the effects that any of these involvements might have on his self-ordained mission. One of these potentially hazardous approaches in 1933 brought to von Boetticher a proposal from one Fred Adolph, the owner of a cannery in New York, who claimed to have invented a small adaptor that would convert any infantry rifle into a machine gun. Von Boetticher dutifully wrote the German Army's Ordnance Office for instructions but filled the report on the matter with his own misgivings about Adolph's money motive and his worries about avoiding compromises as the military attaché.[82]

The following year brought another threat of compromise, this one more substantial and serious. In August 1934, Freiherr von Schroetter, the North American representative of the Stahlhelm, received instructions from the German national president of the league advising von Schroetter to place himself and the North American *Landesverband* (national group) of the Stahlhelm in cooperation with the German military attaché in Washington. Von Boetticher, after discouraging the proposal, reported the *Stahlhelmführer*'s intentions and asked for Reichswehrminister von Blomberg's guidance. This produced an exchange between von Boetticher and Walther von Reichenau, to whom Blomberg delegated the matter as head of the relatively new *Wehrmachtamt* within his ministry. In a letter of August 24, 1934, von Reichenau labored first under the illusion that the idea for using the Stahlhelm in North America was von Boetticher's own, but the attaché hastily corrected this, asking von Reichenau to explain to von Blomberg that "the exact opposite is the case." He repeated the objections he recorded in his original report of August 1 and concluded that "I never had the wish to place the North American *Landesgruppe* of the Stahlhelm at the disposal of the Führer, because I can serve the German cause here in much better and more effective ways."[83]

General von Boetticher carried with him to American soil a conception of attaché operations starkly different from that of his predecessor, Franz von Papen, during World War I. He wished not only to counter French influence in representing Germany, but also to establish German military tradition as the criterion among Americans for interpreting world affairs as well. More than a technician, he was an evangelist who proclaimed an identity between the United States and Germany with himself as the bridge between the two. However, he could not subsist as an attaché on these affairs of the spirit alone. Supplementing his hopeful reports on winning American souls, he supplied the *Attacheabteilung,* the General Staff's attaché section at home, with detailed and comprehensive analyses of American armed strength.

4

EVALUATING THE
AMERICAN ARMY

AS indefatigable in his technical study of the American army as he was in courting its favor, Friedrich von Boetticher compiled a cumulative and accurate commentary on the abiding issues affecting that army in the decade before World War II. He filled the diplomatic pouch from Washington in the early years of his service there with exhaustive analyses of everything from aerial signal flares and cavalry horses being readied for the 1936 Berlin Olympic Games to national defense strategy and industrial mobilization plans.

The U.S. Army reflected the American temperament in those years. Though maintaining a penchant for participation in international humanitarian endeavors, Americans retreated behind a "high wall of neutrality."[1] Enthusiastically if innocently supporting worldwide disarmament and such declarations as the Kellogg-Briand Pact outlawing war, a nation in the throes of depression with twelve million unemployed naturally gave more attention to domestic affairs than to foreign crises. Accordingly, the U.S. Army was a minuscule force of active regular soldiers with a complicated reserve structure unable to support any forceful foreign policy. Without the capability of exercising any strategic influence in world affairs, its entire importance in 1933 lay in its potential as an expansible base. Von Boetticher's evaluations of the proficiency of this cadre, its supporting reserves, its associated industrial capacity, and the evolving master plans for realizing its potential also began with his cultivation of Douglas MacArthur.

The first concern of American chiefs of staff from 1920 to 1940 was manpower to fill the units to be formed in any mobilization.

This issue was correspondingly among the earliest and most often discussed element in the German attaché reports going to Berlin. The National Defense Act of 1920 had specified a standing military strength for the country at 280,000 men and 18,000 officers. The American army fell below these levels by 1922, and at von Boetticher's arrival in Washington, the figures stood at 121,788 enlisted men and 12,314 officers.[2] The secretary of war and chief of staff reports published warnings each year on the long-term implications of continued shortages, especially among officers. In 1934, the army had only 3,000 officers and 50,000 troops assigned to tactical units that would defend the entire continental United States and its outlying territories.[3] The forces in the country, spread among nine skeletonized army divisions, "were better deployed to fight Indians than to repel invaders," as one often repeated assessment put it.[4] External dangers to the country were admittedly nonexistent at this stage of things, but any future mobilization would have to start from an adequate troop base. MacArthur and the War Department General Staff placed that minimum at about 165,000 men and 14,000 officers. On May 12, 1933, von Boetticher began his cumulative analyses of American military manpower problems by recounting MacArthur's testimony before the House Armed Services Committee. The chief of staff argued against acting on the Roosevelt program for reducing military budgets by 25 percent, portending another reduction of two to four thousand officers and 12,000 men. The report to Berlin emphasized MacArthur's testimony that he could not guarantee the defense of the country if the cuts occurred. In June, von Boetticher further underscored the issue by noting that the army had even employed the aged but popular General Pershing in radio addresses to urge restoration of the Army's strength to the limits set in 1920.[5]

MacArthur was especially reticent over the use of military talent in one of Roosevelt's great New Deal ventures, the Civilian Conservation Corps (CCC). At the time of von Boetticher's first analysis of American military manpower, the civilian conservation program had much the same effect on the army as the threatened fiscal reductions. Officers, limited in numbers, could not devote much time to troop training if assigned to duty in the woodlands. Their own professional training could only suffer if they were preoccupied with rehabilitating American forests and unemployed urban youth.

But with congressional sanction on March 28, 1933, the program's first recruits, predominantly from the larger eastern cities, began funneling through War Department supply and physical training centers on April 7. By May 12, with various aspects of the program proceeding too slowly, the army assumed control of the camps after a conference with Labor and Agriculture Department officials. Under army Col. Duncan Major, the military mobilized nearly 275,000 men into 1,300 camps, the majority of them in the western half of the country.[6]

Von Boetticher, answering frequent inquiries from home, included his own evaluations of the camps and their effect on the army. After reviewing the program's legislative origins, he declared that, as far as he could see, military officers, though complaining, had taken up the job with "great energy and skill."[7] Successive reports developed his observations on the military potential of the training and the organization of the CCC. His visits to the camps and private talks with American officers kept him well informed on the subject, and he never ceased reporting on it in favorable terms. The men were first physically hardened according to military form but engaged in no rifle drill or shooting. As comparisons between the CCC and the German Labor Front became inevitable in the world press, von Boetticher noted early that the absence of rifle training in the American program was to forestall having it said in the Geneva talks that the United States was constructing a reserve army in this manner. Work parties did find themselves organized along military lines, and von Boetticher cited with approval the mandatory divine service attendance in the camps as one of the features that tended to make the CCC a means of reclaiming youth morally as well as physically and financially.

Von Boetticher had met Col. Duncan Major in 1922. "One of the best heads of the American Army," in von Boetticher's words, Major gave him an evaluation of the army's role in the project that contrasted strongly with MacArthur's public utterances. Major estimated that 50 to 60 percent of active officers were somehow actively involved in the CCC, but despite this, the army really believed it could handle its training responsibilities for regular troops and reserve units. With the early wave of doubt having subsided, von Boetticher reported that the army considered the whole task a "school for war" and had gone at it with much strength in the conviction that especially younger officers would gain valuable experience in leadership and troop command.[8] Indeed, from the inside information he had, von Boetticher even anticipated in his reports the measure of success MacArthur finally claimed in the army's mobilization of the 275,000 by July 1, 1933. It was a performance that MacArthur justly trumpeted in his 1933 annual report, comparing it with the mobilization of 1917 and drawing the inference that the General Staff had justified itself and the stockpiling of reserve matériel from which the army had supplied most of the equipment for the mobilized men.[9] More important, the military had moved the masses of men from the East Coast to the western work sites in army-owned or leased motor vehicles and railroads. Though he received later information showing that field-grade officers were performing work usually given to company-level officers and that plans to replace young officers in CCC work with temporarily mobilized reserve officers had come to nothing, von Boetticher remained a thoroughgoing admirer of the program.[10] At no point did he attempt to analyze more cynically MacArthur's willingness to enter into Roosevelt's social action program to use the CCC as "a lever for prying funds for the Army from the President and Congress."[11]

A singular element in American military manpower policy after World War I was the reserve structure from which the regular army would draw experienced soldiers or new cadre in wartime. Its foremost component was the National Guard, formally organized into units of up to divisional size that remained under state control in peacetime. Many officers demobilized after World War I stayed in the Officers' Reserve Corps, looser in structure than the guard, but permitting its 100,000 members to advance in military education and rank through graduated schooling and periodic service with regular forces. The 6,000 annually commissioned graduates of Reserve Officer Training Corps programs in 325 colleges around the country entered the Officers' Reserve Corps instead of the army's active ranks. A reserve corps for enlisted men existed after the war also but declined in popularity and importance. A last source of officer talent was the Civilian Military Training Camps program, which gave candidates military commissions after four years of study and supplementary field training.[12]

As the chief element in this scheme and the most immediately employable in any national crisis, the guard had found increasing favor with the regular officers in the interwar period. The rivalry between the regulars and the guard officers had subsided with the regulars' recognition of the worth of the guard in the Great War. More important, the National Defense Act of 1920 had made the regular forces dependent on the guard for mobilization of any sizable American armed host and reliant upon the guard in the search for scarce defense funding. Though the regulars doubted that the reserves could be rapidly mobilized for long war service, this element was no longer a misprized militia of unkempt and ill-trained volunteers in the regulars' eyes.[13] Scheduled under the National Defense Act to number 486,000 officers and men, all guard units were to undergo sixty drill sessions annually in addition to a two-week summer field exercise. But as the army suffered in the economic squeeze and the antimilitary idealism of the period, the guard suffered also, its numbers amounting to roughly 40 percent of its allotted legal strength from 1933 to 1939.[14] In contrast to its uncertain position before World War I, however, the guard had achieved a measure of stability and popularity borne on a local community spirit. It had a presence in small towns and rural areas. It developed ties to "the chambers of commerce, the Rotary and Lions Clubs, the associations of mayor, county treasurers and other local officials."[15] In fact, the guard was everything that von Boetticher reported it to be in describing it as a vehicle for his mission.

The German staff naturally expected more than encomiums about the reserves' place in American policy. Von Boetticher's first extended report on the subject, aside from his optimistic notes on German heritage and the influence to be found in this reserve force, was on the occasion of one of the more portentous changes in its status. On June 15, 1933, new legislation changed the line of its command and enhanced the power of the president to federalize all or part of the reserve in national emergencies declared by Congress.[16] Von Boetticher brought his grasp of American history to the evaluation of this development and remarked on the accretion of presidential power and the corresponding weakening of states' rights but, more to the interest of the German General Staff, stated flatly that it increased the combat readiness of the American army. "[T]he worth of the National Guard is important. You will do well not to underestimate it," he told his readers in Berlin. Though the officers and men drilled only weekly and had an all-too-brief fourteen-day exercise in summer, von Boetticher pronounced the spirit of the various units he had thus far seen as "splendid" (herrvorragend), a phenomenon that permeated the Guard from top to bottom, and "as they are in peace, they will enter a war."[17]

Von Boetticher had more sober thoughts on the capacity of the guard as state militia forces. When he reached San Francisco after his stay in Utah, a civil crisis had arisen for Maj. Gen. Malin Craig, commanding the IX Corps Area headquartered in San Francisco. Craig was apprehensively watching the development of a dock-workers' strike in the city. Von Boetticher witnessed the mechanics of a partial call-up of the National Guard 40th Division to contain the labor unrest. However highly he regarded the troop training and discipline among the Guard, he was critical of its dual nature as national reserve and state force under a local governor's control. Combating local unrest and subversive political influences goes on at the state level, he reported, and governors must allow a situation to develop before calling in state forces. Because of the nature of provincial politics, a governor had to act not as a military commander in a situation such as the dock strike of 1934, but as a politician whose action would sooner or later be subject to electoral approval. The influence of the commanding general, whose division included troops from as many as three states, was limited, and his area of jurisdiction did not coincide with that of the political authority.[18] His generalizations on the effectiveness of Guard formations and the spirit so evident among them remained a constant feature of the military-technical reporting from America, qualified only by von Boetticher's perception of the need of these units to undergo large unit training upon mobilization to be ready for active combat.[19]

The strength of the regular army and the quality of the National Guard were only two of the yardsticks von Boetticher used to measure American combat abilities. During his first five years in America, the active army and its reserve structure remained fairly static. The German attaché in addition exhaustively chronicled the condition of all the military equipment he saw; he interested himself in the development of new weapons, the mechanization plans, and the revisions in the plans for mobilizing the whole establishment for war.

Even with his praise of some specific matériel such as light artillery, von Boetticher could see that American military equipment was at a low pass. Although military investigating boards had written of the deplorable state of American ordnance, especially heavier weaponry, already at the close of World War I, the inventory of modern weapons in the army that von Boetticher observed was still on the drawing boards or barely evident in a few prototypes.[20] The development of new arms also fell victim to depression economies and pacifist moods. Ordnance orders and plans were always "shaved down, operations were always restricted, projects were frequently stopped short of completion, all for lack of money."[21] Of a total of slightly more than $6 billion expended for the army in the fifteen years from 1925 to 1940, only $21 million went for the modernization of existing equipment and research on new matériel, an average of $1.4 million a year.[22] The early war planning of interwar years placed a large trust in the "war stocks" left over from World War I, a supply base that had served the CCC mobilization well, but that was increasingly obsolescent when it was not totally useless or inoperable. National Guard troops were traditionally more poorly equipped, because they were rarely given new gear, instead inheriting the cast-off material of the regular army. Under these constraints, the army developed an apparent reticence toward even asking for more funding; its planners exhibited some caution in depleting funds already committed to existing programs, remaining "habituated to accepting limited funds and conservative in . . . outlook toward new and expensive ideas."[23]

MacArthur would never admit to this and told his listeners in his annual pilgrimage to Capitol Hill in 1935 that the War Department could be blamed for a variety of things, but never for refusing to ask for money.[24] His willingness to seek funds from potentially new sources in 1933 in fact led to one prediction by von Boetticher late in the year that proved premature.

Conversant with the War Department budgetary processes, subject as they were to the Roosevelt administration's newly founded budget office and the hands of congressional committees, von Boetticher foretold a marked increase in army spending and a far-reaching motorization and mechanization program for the American army if talks in Geneva failed. Warning the German Staff that military budgets in and of themselves would henceforth be misleading, he conceded that publicized cuts in army budgets amounted to $55 million, but that National Recovery Act funds provided nearly $3.5 billion for work on air installations, motorization and mechanization, general construction of camps and stations, and equipment.[25] The National Recovery Act's enabling legislation had stipulated that if the nation adhered to an international arms limitation, the funds could be spent elsewhere; von Boetticher inferred from this that if the Geneva talks collapsed, as indeed they did the following autumn, the Americans would rearm heavily. What he could not reckon with immediately was the virulent biases of New Dealer and Public Works Board Administrator Harold Ickes, who almost gleefully chopped the army's requested share of National Recovery Act monies from $300 million to less than a third of that amount, and even that was to be spread over the next two years. Ickes wrung further economies from the army in requiring the closing of some smaller posts in the United States in return for the release of the money.[26] The promises of the National Recovery Act funds were thus never fully delivered upon, and though the German attaché had adequately forewarned of the use of public works funds for pump-priming military expenditures designed to aid the depression-bound American economy, his later reporting offered no news of improvement in American army paraphernalia until late 1938. Over the next two years, he estimated the current equipment of the army as "of little value"[27] despite his simultaneous anticipation of American mechanization and motorization programs for the future. In early 1935, he referred home the figures on modern American equipment: the American army had only twelve modern tanks and eighty prototypes of the new Garand M-1 semiautomatic rifle; its antiaircraft and antitank defenses were lacking, and the mainstay of the artillery was still the outmoded 75-mm piece derived from French design, neither mechanized nor particularly mobile. "As always," he declared in an analysis of the chief of staff report for that year, "the Americans are neglecting their army in peacetime."[28]

Von Boetticher even found something lurking behind the current administration's approach to military funding. According to him, the thrust of American policy at Geneva, consistent with the language of the National Recovery Act, was only to make a last effort to achieve a balance of arms favorable to the disarmed United States before rearming in earnest. Von Boetticher reduced American policy in this regard to a subtle form of blackmail by Franklin Roosevelt.

This particular interpretation was so one-sided as to be naive, but his strictly technical evaluations of American equipment were entirely accurate and represent the obvious to historians of the American army even decades later.[29]

To von Boetticher's aptly critical eye there was one major exception to the sorry state of American equipment in the airplane, which underwent considerable advance and experimentation in the ranks of the American army in the interwar period. Though not especially versed in aeronautics, von Boetticher pursued a lively interest in the American air forces, the burgeoning aircraft industry, and the preeminent technology that supported them. He was accredited air attaché in addition to his standard duties as military attaché, and aviation matters, both military and civilian, took up as much of his time as his reporting on all other facets of American military equipment combined.

The Army Air Corps spent the interwar years in hot pursuit of two main objectives: autonomy and a strategic raison d'être. The air arm of the American army had a modicum of independence conferred upon it by the defense act of 1920, but various boards and committees only confirmed the then-current command arrangements that made air power within the army a subordinate combat arm of the service with much the same representation as the infantry, the cavalry, the engineers, or the Signal Corps, the original parent of the Air Corps. Each Army Corps Area had its assigned air units directly under the commanding general in the area. Von Boetticher's service in America coincided with the partial realization by the Air Corps of its aspirations for a revision in this structure, which air enthusiasts felt stifled the use of the one weapon that would decide the outcome of the next war. A spectacular revolution in aircraft technology and advances in engine design and power occupied the decade before World War II, a phenomenon whose greatest single impetus was the naval and military aircraft market. Aided also by the romance of the conquest of the air, military fliers constantly carried their case to a fascinated public. They propagandized willing listeners on the decisiveness of the weapon that promised to shorten the next war and therefore make it more humane. American Army Air Corps doctrine in this context was not merely a methodological norm in the use of airplanes; it was also a self-justificatory statement that followed the pioneering theses represented primarily, but not exclusively, by an Italian theorist, Giulio Douhet, who advocated independent air forces administratively equal to traditional armies and navies. The object was the prosecution of war against the productive capacity of a nation far behind the front lines in campaigns designed to break rapidly the stalemate of trench warfare that so haunted the generation that survived it in World War I.[30] Air power was to have a strategic role in future war far beyond its largely tactical nature in the Great War. Its proponents agitated for greater emphasis on aerial warfare, and their claims for its future military decisiveness were the fuel of a bureaucratic insurgency against the traditional command structure of the U.S. Army of the time. From a reputedly stodgy ground army, the airmen sought nothing less than complete independence along the lines of air forces in Great Britain and the new Germany.

Von Boetticher followed his usual habits in assembling information on the burgeoning American air forces. In mid-1934, the embassy notified the American State Department that he would be the German air attaché in addition to his normal duties.[31] He subscribed to *Aviation,* the best of a number of serials on the subject, and his reports on new developments often had articles cut from that magazine appended to them. He pursued his technique of personal contact among leading American air officers, with the result that his analyses were replete with some of the contentions over air power at the time. He also relayed faithfully the financial and political publications of the use of public works funds for aircraft procurement. In his first series of trips across the United States, he stopped at Wright Field, near Dayton, Ohio, the site of research and testing facilities for military aircraft during that period. Though he claimed he had gained "fundamental technical impressions," he decided to postpone a full report until he had gathered enough insights to enable him to make basic evaluations.[32] In the same report, he noted his access to Langley Field (in Virginia), Wright Field and the Wright Aeronautical Company in Dayton, and the Pratt and Whitney Company, engine manufacturers, for Dr. Kurt Schnauffer of the Deutsche Versuchsanstalt für Luftfahrt in Berlin in the month of August 1933. Schnauffer was the first of approximately four hundred German aircraft engineers and designers to visit American plants through von Boetticher's routine requests to the American War Department between 1933 and 1938.[33] Von Boetticher also got the feel of American aircraft firsthand. One of the contributing architects of American military aviation remembered years later that he personally piloted the German attaché on several occasions. Von Boetticher responded with pleasure to invitations for jaunts in army aircraft and loved especially to add to his appreciation of American Civil War battlefields by viewing them from an aerial vantage.[34]

The major developments in the Air Corps during von Boetticher's first two years in America finally brought it to the measure of autonomy it retained within the army until its complete separation from the ground forces in 1947. In August 1933, Maj. Gen. Hugh A. Drum chaired yet another board to determine the size, the composition, and the status of an air force adequate to the defense of the nation and consistent with the strategic planning of the time. Until this, the boards and congressional committees that had met since 1920 had always recommended 1,800 planes as a number suited to the Air Corps's needs, though figures as high as 2,200 had appeared in discussions.[35] The Drum Board, in its secret report of October 1933, abandoned the earlier limit since it correctly assumed that a large proportion of the 1,800 aircraft would always be out of service at any one time, and that 1,800 planes would never cover the Air Corps's responsibilities for the defense of the United States and its overseas possessions. The board eventually raised the recommended aircraft procurement figure to 2,320 and insisted further upon a centralized headquarters to remove all air units from the control of the nine Army Corps Area commanders. Kept under wraps at the moment,[36] the Drum Board's recommendations became the unchallenged basis for the most influential decisions taken on American military aviation in the 1930s. They appeared publicly for the first time, with new stipulations for special Air Corps promotion and pay and allowances, in a draft bill before Congress in February 1934.

The German attaché obtained, for the asking, a copy of a General Staff memorandum sent to House Armed Service Committee Chairman John J. McSwain, a South Carolina Democrat, in which appeared MacArthur's views on an expanded, autonomous air force under circumstances then affecting the army. MacArthur continued to argue against the undue emphasis on the Air Corps as unsound, reported von Boetticher. Airplanes, said MacArthur, constituted one form of weapon among many and required integration into the entire armed forces for success in war. A ruthless expansion of the air arm as the draft bill envisioned would strip badly needed funds from the army as a whole. The memorandum dwelled on the limitations of air power, noting its lack of staying power and its inability to hold the ground attacked solely from the air. This reasoned counterargument prevailed. The next skirmish in the Air Corps battle for recognition had to await the outcome of yet another panel of leading civil and military aviation experts that met in the wake of an Air Corps disaster in the infamous airmail scandals of early 1934.[37]

One of the first causes célèbres in the Roosevelt administration was the cancellation of the allegedly corrupt airmail contracts through which airlines, according to one congressional investigation, had overcharged the government $47 million over four years. In an overoptimistic moment, Maj. Gen. Benjamin Foulois, then chief of the Air Corps, had promised postal directors that the Air Corps would carry on airmail service across the country. Von Boetticher kept close watch on the experiment, which killed twelve American military fliers and littered the landscape with the wreckage of forty-six crash landings in two months. From the start of the program, managed by Brig. Gen. Oscar Westover, another longtime friend of von Boetticher's, the German attaché reported on the Senate investigations into the irregularities in the contracts, the numbers of planes, and the regional commands involved in the Air Corps's attempt at airmail transport. He also reported, even after the army flights began, the difficulties that were freely, if confidentially, admitted to him: the pilots were not trained in commercial flight, nor was the military command structure suited to commercial purpose. Military aircraft, furthermore, were not meant for cargo handling and possessed no suitable instruments for navigation at night or in bad weather and fog. He also knew that the Air Corps was gambling on success against these odds in hopes of publicizing air power and thereby winning additional funding.[38] Within a month of his first intimations of the American army's overreaching itself in flying the mails, von Boetticher filled his reports with details on the political storm that broke on the issue. He roundly seconded Charles Lindbergh's public criticism that Roosevelt had been overly hasty in canceling the contracts and had acted out of political motives.[39] He warned the German Staff against negative evaluations of American military aviation in the wake of the many accidents, suggesting instead that the German press releases on the matter stress the heroism of the airmen who flew out of a disciplined sense of duty in spite of such great hazards. This would do much, he insisted, to preserve the cooperation in the German technical visits begun by Dr. Schnauffer the previous year.[40]

Interpreted by one student of the period as the event that "dented the myth of Roosevelt's invulnerability . . . and uncovered in Charles Lindbergh a man who appealed to more American hearts than anyone save Franklin Roosevelt,"[41] the airmail problems also revealed the neglect of army equipment. While the contracts with private carriers were quietly renegotiated and the Air Corps was relieved of its postal duties by May 1, Secretary of War George Dern organized a new investigative board on military aviation chaired by the able and respected Newton D. Baker, who had been the secretary of war during World War I.[42]

The Baker Board found no irremediable fault with the Air Corps. In fact, it established the basis for future expansion of the arm in its conclusion that American commercial aviation led the world, that its naval aviation was then stronger than that of any other power, and that army aviation needed only the requisite funding to raise it to a world position.[43] The board's positive report put a momentary end to the Air Corps drive for autonomy by recommending establishment of a semi-independent command called General Headquarters, Air Forces, which airpower advocates in army uniform decided to accept. GHQ, Air Forces, as the command was known, would centralize control of all army aircraft under a single general officer who was still subordinate to the army chief of staff alone. The board further recommended that the chief of the Air Corps be responsible for developing new model aircraft and for procurement and supply functions, a jurisdictional division that left the chief of the Air Corps and the yet-to-be appointed commander of the GHQ at some odds.[44] Consistent with the reflection here of the earlier Drum Board's deliberations, the Baker Board also regarded the Drum proposals for 2,320 planes as the "minimum considered necessary to meet our peacetime army requirements."[45]

Over the next year, von Boetticher supplied his readers at home with the unfolding story of the Air Corps's evolution into a separate command. He accompanied his dispatch of a copy of the Baker Board Report on July 28, 1934, with his own insights on how deep a quarrel the matter had been, affecting opinion within the Air Corps, Congress, and among the public.[46] In November 1934, he reported on the marked advances in restructuring and re-equipping the Air Corps. Reviewing the obsolescent state of the 1,475 planes then on hand in the American air forces, he listed the new contracts outstanding and the plans for building 700 planes a year until the figure of 2,320 was reached. While the fight for the independence of aviation from the army momentarily slackened, von Boetticher noted that the internal organization of the Air Corps under the new GHQ was still cloudy and rife with the same duplication that had plagued the air service in France during World War I, according to his informants among the American General Staff. In the months after the Baker Board Report, Congress had moved to the consideration not only of new aircraft for the regular army Air Corps, but also for the National Guard, to say nothing of a complete overhaul of the antiaircraft weapons in the army.[47]

With the formal establishment of the much-awaited GHQ, Air Forces, von Boetticher also saw something of a setback to MacArthur, whose arguments had not forestalled the developments at hand. The attaché was yet alive to the improvements in tactical control of American air forces. Some two weeks before the actual establishment of the GHQ on March 1, 1935, von Boetticher had collected all of the conventional wisdom on it in a seven-page report that summarized the process to that time. He documented every area jurisdiction (including that for National Guard units) in the new Air Corps command pyramid and detailed the training and promotion policies and the administrative principles governing the organization. For the immediate effect on American war-making capacity, von Boetticher advised the German staff that there is "to be created a highly maneuverable, powerful Air Force, which is capable of being assembled at any threatened point of the United States."[48]

Though its potential remained as high as von Boetticher intimated, the Air Corps never reached the levels of strength recommended in the Baker Board Report until the nation was nearly into war again. By mid-1937, the German attaché was still reporting that aviation budgets for that year would allow the Air Corps to reach the projected 2,320-airplane strength only in 1942.[49] Though this figure stood until 1939 as the Air Corps goal, argument persisted and contradictory rhetoric abounded as to whether this was a bare minimum to meet defense requirements.[50] Concentrating on heavy bomber models to conform to its prevailing doctrine of precision strategic bombardment in daylight, the Air Corps developed the admirable B-17 Flying Fortress by 1935 but neglected, for the moment, the design of a fighter plane capable of escorting the bombers on long-range missions on the theory that such protection would not be needed.[51] Von Boetticher, in fact, referred home General Foulois's judgment in late 1933 that bombardment aircraft would soon outperform fighters in speed and range and presumably would reign supreme in the air.[52] Four years later, von Boetticher had not changed his basic view of American air power. He held the Air Corps to be very good technically, tactically, and in its training.[53]

Government support of American civil aviation and the subsidization of the industry underpinning military and commercial aeronautics scarcely escaped von Boetticher. He became thoroughly familiar with the various companies producing engines and airframes, and he explored the detail of each major contract for new aircraft. The Baker Board had underscored its belief that "an adequate aircraft industry . . . is essential to national defense" and outlined how government should underwrite design and production with liberal contracts for this sector of the American economy.[54] But von Boetticher again saw something more insidious in the barely concealed attempts by the American government to use commercial airlines as instruments of foreign policy. The airmail scandals of 1934 were evidence of nearly a decade of federal encouragement of the air industry and even of a conscious government policy of industrial Darwinism among airline contractors. Nowhere was the policy so egregious as in the American expansion into overseas air travel routes and mail service, especially in extending American influence into Latin America and the Pacific islands. Although airline merger fights and empire building were common in the early 1930s under these conditions, one of the more remarkable careers in the business was that of Juan Trippe, who parlayed his early ventures in the field into an officially sponsored flag airline trading as Pan American Airways, Inc., by the time von Boetticher came on the American scene. Not only was Pan American the chosen instrument of the postmaster general for airmail contracts, but it had become, in effect, an official agent of the American government abroad.[55]

Von Boetticher mapped each overseas expansion of the airline, charting the new areas of American influence. He divined the American policy in one of his first reports on the subject, noting in October 1933 that the United States was attempting to erect a world-wide traffic through its flag line and had already "sewn up" the Latin American routes with the service begun to Buenos Aires that year. Without mentioning the War Department backing for the commercial expansion, von Boetticher discussed the sensitive issue of the Panama Canal as "of the greatest military-political signifi-cance," a question of life and death for the United States in a war.[56] China also figured prominently in the attaché reports on what von Boetticher termed American "Luftpolitik." Quoting extensively from *Aviation* magazine articles, he affirmed that Pan Am had ac-quired 45 percent of the China National Aviation Company, a child of the Chinese government, and included maps and timetables to illustrate the services offered. Though he downplayed Japanese re-ports of direct American participation in Chinese air action against Japanese forces, he sketched the training services of American pi-lots and ground crews in the Nationalist Chinese cause and enu-merated the sales of American combat and transport planes to the Chinese.[57] The name of Charles Lindbergh again cropped up as the technical advisor to Pan American, and von Boetticher chronicled the exploratory flights Lindbergh made over the next seven years in seeking possible new routes for the line.[58] While Lindbergh's flights to Europe led to the conclusion that the routes were then not feasible, von Boetticher reported on alternatives for Pan American's surmounting the Atlantic. He cautioned the Air Ministry that the American government was investigating the possibilities of con-structing five large artificial islands to accommodate planes be-tween New York and the Azores.[59] The idea apparently died, and the attaché dropped it from his reports.

Just a year after the Lindbergh flights, von Boetticher found fur-ther confirmation for his analysis of American commercial aviation policy in the report of the new Federal Aviation Commission. Formed as a regulatory agency in the wake of the airmail scandals, the commission concluded, in a report issued in January 1935, that American competition with European luxury steamships was useless, and that American efforts would center on air travel, with a program of protection to keep American carriers solvent and competitive. The commission further declared that development of overseas airlines took priority over continued domestic expansion.[60] Von Boetticher deemed this of such weight that he sent home five copies of the report with his elaboration on its intent and the direction of future American development.[61] In isolating the spread of American overseas commercial aviation as a strategic issue, the German attaché showed some prescience and a real appreciation of the viability of the American air industry. The air networks were visible if tenuous links to areas of American interest abroad and, especially in the South Pacific island chains, came to form a vital connection with the Philippine Islands garrison.[62] His evaluation of American use of aviation as a political device was wholly accurate. Though von Boetticher seemed somewhat incensed at American expansion, all the powers involved in the rush for aerial franchises gave a fair imitation of the territorial hunger that characterized a bygone imperial era.[63]

As topical as aviation developments in von Boetticher's work was the subject of American military mobilization plans. Until 1938, he developed little on the economic aspects of a mobilization though he did explore the effects of neutrality legislation on American willingness to send armaments and troops to overseas wars. He reflected primarily the concern of American planners with more purely military than industrial readiness for war.

The War Department was riveted on the issue of manpower. Military mobilization planning throughout Douglas MacArthur's tenure as chief of staff centered on expanding the military's tactical units into a mass army whenever an international crisis directly threatened American security. In mobilizing, the army thus committed itself to a laborious process in which all its units would be formed and filled out at much the same rate; the army would not be ready for action until all, or nearly all, of its units were up to strength and fully equipped. Then, various newly formed headquarters were supposed to take over troop elements that they had never seen and whose military value was unknown. MacArthur, late in 1931, opted for a two-phased alternative, eventually known as the Protective Mobilization Plan, or PMP in the professional jargon. It called for a ready and mobile ground force of regulars that could concentrate wholly or partially at any point in the nation to repulse or at least contain an invasion. Rapidly mobilized regulars and those National Guard forces deemed most fit would hold the enemy at bay until a larger, conscripted army formed behind this protective shield. A problematic exercise among army planners of the time because of the complexities of command and the various priorities necessary for the two separate reserve and regular forces, MacArthur's plan also shared the logistical weaknesses of earlier mobilization schemes.[64] The PMP in its eventual variations through 1938 relied on the hasty call-up of ill-prepared forces, many of them existing only on paper. With no real hope of equipping either the first defensive army or the second, more numerous one, it seemed to one critic to be "little more than a plan to mobilize all the regulars and National Guard in sight."[65]

For von Boetticher to have criticized the plan in these terms during his earlier tenure would have made him a very perceptive man. In fact, he consistently defended MacArthur's conception. Relying on the chief of staff's reports, he accurately delineated the plan's basis, the four field armies that were to guarantee an efficient mobilization and a structure that could be manageable by the General Headquarters to be activated in national emergencies.[66] He went into detail about the system by which each American officer, regardless of his peacetime assignment, would have a specific wartime staff or field position to fill in the great expansion of forces. In principle, the German system of expansion was to follow much the same course. The American plan would generate at least twenty-four ready divisions in the initial force and another twenty-seven infantry and six cavalry divisions in the secondary force, mobilized later.[67] While he kept a close eye on American army equipment during the various maneuvers he attended across the country, he also acquired a positive attitude on the mobilization plan. The 1935 maneuver at Pine Camp, New York, run specifically as the first major test case for the PMP, [68] convinced him that the American army could mobilize and concentrate troops in assigned areas with precision. In spite of the age and the variety of motor equipment that he noted in his report, "the approach march was, so far as my own impressions and judgments go, an unqualified success."[69]

The exercise, involving 36,000 men, two opposing corps headquarters, and five infantry divisions (one regular army and four

National Guard) from the First Army area,[70] revealed the usual weaknesses in equipment and further pointed up to the observer the "noticeable lack of initiative"[71] shown by the National Guard units. Von Boetticher nevertheless repeated his earlier judgment that the Guard was fine material, though still raw, a force that would need a moderate training and grace period in any mobilization to become proficient in war.[72]

A month after the Pine Camp maneuvers, von Boetticher summarized his observations on military readiness across the country through the past summer. Despite the economic difficulties and the clamor of church or political pacifist theorists and noisy antiadministration opinion, he had no doubts about American abilities to gather forces for defense:

> You may not take the struggles over President Roosevelt and his economic experiments and the social tensions of the United States or the problems which face various areas as appearances of weakness. In time of great political tension, the little recognized work of the Army in peacetime will move to the fore. In a surprisingly short time the United States will undergo a very strong mobilization on land and in the air. They will become a united nation, which on the basis of its riches in men and material is capable of all manner of deployments of great strength.[73]

No political dislocations would seriously disrupt the mobilization process, in von Boetticher's opinion. American officers, like their counterparts in Europe, maintained a conservative outlook and a wary eye for radical influences in the economically hobbled country, though not out of any sympathy for a business revival.[74] General MacArthur in the year before von Boetticher's arrival in America had at least two clashes with "communistic elements,"[75] and his onetime vice chief of staff, Maj. Gen. George Van Horn Moseley, had in 1930 advocated the immediate deportation of this vague but dangerous societal stratum to a semitropical island in the Hawaiian chain.[76]

Von Boetticher was less inclined to take American communism seriously. He regarded the army as the "ultima ratio" in matters in which communists were supposedly active, such as in the San Francisco dock strike of 1934.[77] Communism was everywhere in the ascendant, he noted at the time, and it was attempting to undermine the army's influence, especially in the universities where the ROTC programs were active. He blamed Jewish intellectuals for the anti-military and pacifistic feeling in schools, but while this and the labor unrest he saw had some communist backing as long as bad economic conditions persisted, the army combated it steadily. Against its influence the communist party could make little headway. He reported that many officers had told him that they saw no real danger.[78] Von Boetticher himself remained unshaken in his conviction that "communist philosophy is foreign to the American."[79]

Pacifism, if wrongly and solely associated with a native communist movement by some American military officers, contributed also to the passage of the legislation that not only limited American participation in foreign conflicts, but also prevented American commercial profit from the sale of munitions to belligerents the world over.[80] American disillusion with the result of World War I, the deep aversion to involvement in new foreign conflicts, and the popular disgust with the "munitions lobby," so luridly overplayed by the Nye Committee in 1934,[81] produced a series of neutrality laws designed to obviate future American entanglement in foreign wars by a mandatory executive fiat prohibiting exports to belligerents once a war had begun. Franklin Roosevelt, himself of isolationist persuasion during his first term in office,[82] signed the first act on August 31, 1935, some five months after the reintroduction of German military conscription and in the middle of Italian preparations for aggressive war in Africa.

The German attaché made frequent reports on the significance of the first, interim Neutrality Law of August 1935 and on its extension six months later.[83] He followed the creation of the National Munitions Control Board, established to supervise and later to license industrial exports, and listed the firms being prosecuted for not complying with its regulations. He pointed out also that the neutrality law had left a loophole because it had not specified the types of contraband goods that in World War I had been a sore issue when Great Britain had halted traffic in foodstuffs, textiles, and other raw materials as strategically important.[84] But he was also careful to note that the military circles in the United States welcomed the apparent freedom of action that the legislation gave them. Most of his American military associates reflected the civilian isolationist stance on the "Italian business" that he recorded after several trips in late summer 1935. They found in the stated policy considerable freedom to avoid the "great mistake" of 1917. American officers were against the Italians, because they did not want a war, but they would not duplicate the errors of the days before the last war, "when they were in the tow (*Schlepptau*) of England."[85] The neutrality act, in von Boetticher's view, implied, first of all, that American military policy would not have to follow the initiatives of Great Britain.

American commercial interests interpreted their freedoms even more broadly after Mussolini's troops invaded Ethiopia on October 3, 1935. Roosevelt promptly imposed the required embargo on arms and the implements of war, but as von Boetticher earlier intimated in his references to the definition of contraband, other strategic and finished goods, but chiefly oil and bauxite (the aluminum ore that Italy possessed in quantity), flowed freely and in increasing quantity to the Italian war machine from American companies. Secretary of State Cordell Hull failed in attempts to align American export policy with League sanctions, and his so-called moral embargo of strategic materials did little to slow the Italian aggression.[86] The League powers, reluctant to risk war over Italian depredations in Africa, artfully based their own willingness to ship oil to Mussolini partly on American behavior.[87] The American army, for its part, sent technical observers to both belligerents in a show of impartiality, von Boetticher typically praising the caliber of both men.[88] American trade with Ethiopia being nonexistent, the victim of Italian aggression was also the victim of the American arms embargo. By the time the neutrality law expired in February 1936 and an extension of it took effect, von Boetticher reported that the War Department felt constrained to stay out of foreign wars, but Ethiopia's fate, still being played out, had induced some second thoughts on the effect of a military or moral embargo on weaker states, especially those in the American hemisphere that might find themselves at war with a European or an Asian power. The neutrality extension, said the attaché, therefore included a provision that arms embargoes against Latin American nations would be inconsistent with the Monroe Doctrine, but that in future wars affecting territories outside the Americas, the United States would still shut off arms, credit, and strategic materials and refuse to allow American ships to transport materials to foreign war zones.[89] Von Boetticher took some personal satisfaction in the American refusal to stand with Britain against Italy in late 1935, but the situation was more complex. Tacit American acquiescence in an inevitable if delayed defeat for Ethiopia was one of the by-products of grave American inhibitions on involvements in Europe. At the same time, the American government accepted on exalted moral grounds a responsibility for events in Asian politics.[90]

Japan, and not any European power, was the overriding concern of the moment for American military and naval authorities. Relations declined further on such long-standing and heated issues of Chinese and Japanese immigration to the United States before 1920. In its annexation of Manchuria in 1931, Japan ignored American attempts at moral suasion[91] and disdained the League of Nations, in fact abandoning membership in that body two years later. Acting from motives of "poverty and pride," Japan sought to avoid the effects of overpopulation and the economic factors threatening to drive it back to the ranks of the second-rate powers. At the same time, Japan strove to have recognized the principle that it should have rights to dominate its immediate global neighborhood.[92] Japanese aspirations ran fully counter to the perceptions that American professional officers had of their national policy in the Far East, namely, a maintenance of the status quo in the western Pacific and of the integrity of China consistent with the old Open Door Policy.[93] Von Boetticher understood also the greater American attention to events in the Far East than to those in Africa: "It is significant [he wrote with the invasion of Ethiopia one month old] that in confidential conversations with the men of the General Staff, it is not the map of Abyssinia or the Mediterranean that comes out, but the map of the Chinese empire."[94]

Von Boetticher repeated in various detail the elements of the contradiction in American opposition to Japanese ambitions and the neutrality policy. Isolationist sentiment kept the United States even from arrangements with the enemy of its enemy in the Far East. The Roosevelt administration gently refused involvement in a proffered Russian nonaggression pact after the recognition of the

Soviet Union in November 1933, and it turned a deaf ear to Ambassador Litvinov's entreaties for just the semblance of an understanding intended to produce a Japanese belief that the United States was ready to cooperate with the Soviet Union.[95] When the American diplomatic recognition of the Soviet Union was still under wraps, von Boetticher downplayed the possibility of any such cooperation against Japan: "The present power and military policy of the United States is based on the maintenance of peace. From the standpoint of the economy as well as in view of the long-standing insufficient equipping of the United States, any other policy is impossible."[96]

Even after bloody border incidents between Japanese and Russian troops in Manchuria and Mongolia, von Boetticher correctly related that neither side was interested in an open conflict. The American role would be passive, to the extent of acting as a referee.[97] Under the influence of Colonel Burnett in his evaluations, he regarded Japanese arms as poor, even below the Russian,[98] but until a real national emergency was at hand, American military force was powerless to thwart even the flawed Japanese machine.

This, too, was correct. So powerless was the American military establishment that the Army at that very moment was planning withdrawal from the citadel of American influence in the western Pacific. The original Plan ORANGE, the American war contingency plan for hostilities against Japan dating from the turn of the century, underwent continual change and updating between the two world wars. From 1928 on, an increasingly vocal faction in the army favored a drastic revision in its basic element, the ground defense of the Philippines. In late 1935, as Mussolini pushed into Ethiopia, the American War and Navy Departments appealed to Cordell Hull for help in a reappraisal of the weakened American defense position in the Far East that offered not even a scant hope of success in a war against Japan.[99]

A new army plan attempted to take the reality of the power balances into account. According to the earlier plans, the army garrison in the Philippines was to hold at least the Bay of Manila and the island of Corregidor at its mouth until the arrival of a powerful naval squadron that would fight its way across 5,000 miles of ocean and land reinforcements to oust the "Orange" (Japanese) forces from the islands. In the repeated revisions in the ORANGE plan before 1935, the estimates of the length of time it would take before the American navy could achieve control of the sea lanes necessary to guarantee the undertaking extended to as much as three years, which meant that the American garrison in the Philippines was, in effect, to be sacrificed.[100] The Army General Staff's War Plans Division, then under Maj. Gen. Stanley D. Embick, in 1935 insisted on abandoning the defense of the islands, especially since their independence had already been legislated in 1934, in favor of a more realistic strategic defense in the eastern Pacific. Von Boetticher, privy to none of the alterations in the plans, judging from his lack of discussion of them in his reports, nevertheless appreciated the strategic value placed on the Philippines by the United States. He wrote a very positive summation on MacArthur's departure from the chief of staff's post in October 1935 and emphasized the importance of MacArthur's appointment, with a field marshal's rank, as advisor to the president of the new Philippine Republic, still under American colonial rule.[101] If von Boetticher did not have all of the details of General Embick's proposals for a completely new defense plan in the Pacific, he yet grasped the realities facing the understrength American army and navy forces in far-flung garrisons. On the occasion of a much touted flight of ten American army bombers to Alaska in August 1934, a year before the State, War, and Navy Department conferences on Plan ORANGE, von Boetticher's musings over the map of the area moved him to the conclusion that Alaska was of equally critical importance to American defense. He delineated a strategic zone, which the Americans would have to command, running from Panama to Hawaii in the south and in the north out along the arm of the Aleutian Island chain.[102] Thus, he identified the fundamental basis of the new Embick Plan, which embraced a strategy relying on a naval and military *defense* of a massive triangle with its legs running from Panama to Hawaii, from Hawaii to Alaska, and from there back to Panama. The garrisons in the Philippines, on Wake Island, and on Guam fell outside this area, though no one would act as if that mattered.

Friedrich von Boetticher's technical military reporting from the United States had the breadth and scope evident only in a keen and dedicated observer of events. His research and his ability to confirm many of his conclusions with members of the American General Staff were the basis of sound evaluations of American defense capacities in the mid-1930s. He was under no illusions about the current weaknesses of the U.S. Army, but contrary to his prevailing image in historical literature, he was never prone to demean the potential of that force; in fact, he was more optimistic about its abilities than some of the American officers responsible for its efficiency and potential. He was consistently positive, especially about the quality of the army's leadership, and remained convinced that in an emergency it would meet any test. The cumulative picture that he provided the German staff was accurate in detail, and even in reflecting the grand hopes for airpower, he echoed assumptions that were common in other countries in the same period, most notably Great Britain.

By late 1936, von Boetticher had also a second line of communication open to the German staff at home. Then-Col. Kurt von Tippelskirch, who ran the German Army Staff's Attachéabteilung from 1936 to 1939, initiated the exchange by summarizing for von Boetticher the minutes of a ten-day attaché conference of December 1936 that the latter could not attend. This "backchannel," in bureaucratic jargon, allowed him even more personal observations on individual American officers and a semiprivate means of appealing to his support network for what he needed to help influence the American military opinion that he continually sought to shape to his own liking. Amounting to a private correspondence between the attaché and the head of the attaché group at home, the arrangement did not violate the strict precedence in the embassy according to which all military reports had to be submitted to the ambassador. This demonstrates that von Boetticher never pursued one line of reporting in the private backchannels while maintaining another, contradictory one in his official submissions.[103] In the course of events, the contents of his correspondence also shed some light on the extent and character of von Boetticher's anti-Semitism.

The missionary frame of mind that drove von Boetticher in his struggle for souls and the technical competence of his reports produced a decided dualism in his service. As yet, these two elements did not conflict with each other, nor did either aspect draw noticeable comment from the embassy chiefs under whom von Boetticher served at this stage: Hans Luther and Dr. Hans Heinrich Dieckhoff. Despite his occasional anti-Semitic references to influences in American life opposing current German policy, von Boetticher does not appear as pro- or anti-Nazi in his reports, but apolitical. The Hitler regime would soon make it difficult for him personally and officially to follow his instincts.

5

DISTANT THUNDER

THE interval between April 1936 and the beginning of war in Europe saw the continuing deterioration of the international order in the European and Pacific arenas. Japan, linked to the Nazi dictatorship by its adherence to an anticommunist pact aimed at Soviet Russia in November 1936, revived offensive operations in China in July 1937. Franklin Roosevelt cautiously but fruitlessly tested the American electorate's reaction to the possibility of a harder policy toward Japan in his famous Quarantine Speech in Chicago in October. Japanese aviators provoked a brief American outcry by sinking an aged U.S. Navy gunboat in the Yangtze River in December. The feeble American response to the attack deliberately shied away from even placing limits on American exports of potential war matériel, including scrap metal, to Japan. With the president's hasty retreat from his proposed actions against aggressors then, he lost his last good chance to resolve the Sino-Japanese conflict and to forestall a later American embroilment in that theater.[1] Only after the Munich Accords of 1938 did the American populace accelerate a reluctant withdrawal from its general commitment to near-total isolation and neutrality. With the electorate more inclined on the whole to the latter, American military preparedness still scarcely reflected any real external threat.[2]

As international tension grew, von Boetticher's observations of American defense measures focused accordingly. The American War Department began seriously to prepare industrial mobilization plans, and the attaché reports on these developments flowed to the same general headquarters in Berlin, redesignated the *Reichs-*

kriegsministerium (War Ministry) in March 1935, with a newly emergent General Staff soon growing out of the Truppenamt.[3] Within the German Staff, the new *Attachéabteilung* (Attaché Section), under then-Maj. Horst von Mellenthin, received and distributed von Boetticher's reports to those staff elements interested in the information that they contained.[4] No available evidence shows that Hitler consistently read any of these attaché reports from Washington (or other capitals) until mid- or late 1939. Unfortunately, much of von Boetticher's reporting for this period of April 1936 to September 1939 was also lost in the war. A series of fires in German military archival repositories and one particularly destructive Allied air raid in February 1945 destroyed the *Heeresarchiv* at Potsdam and sent most of these dispatches up in smoke.[5] Enough remains to permit generalization on his activity and his undiminished energy in following American military affairs.

Signal events of the time proved von Boetticher's value to the Embassy. As one representative of the German cause in the United States amidst Hitler's coups d'oeil, the attaché's continuing entrée with American General Staff officers ensured him an audience at the highest levels of the War Department. When Germany flagrantly disavowed the Locarno Pact of 1925 and risked a few battalions to reoccupy the Rhineland on March 7, 1936, Ambassador Luther reported that the United States would not concern itself with the issue, "since no foreign power had appealed to the American government for support."[6] Von Boetticher carried his own message on the German move to the War Department and spoke from what he called the "military-political standpoint." He proposed among his listeners the idea that Germany hardly represented any warlike threat but insisted that Germany itself was threatened. He cited comparative tables, which he had also seen in American newspapers, showing the French alliance system capable of mustering twenty-seven million men against Germany's two-and-a-half million.[7] He did not comment further on the new position of France, now separated from her allies in the east by the prospect of German fortifications on the Rhine, the real strategic significance of the event.[8]

Among the reports destroyed in the war were those that von Boetticher turned in on the loss of the German airship *Hindenburg*. The attaché played a minor role in the aftermath of the still-unexplained fiery destruction of the great airship as it approached the mooring mast at the Lakehurst Naval Air Station in New Jersey on the evening of May 6, 1937. At nearly three o'clock in the morning of the seventh, von Boetticher and Luther, in one of the latter's last acts as ambassador, flew to Lakehurst in a specially chartered airliner.[9] While Luther traveled to New York to comfort the *Hindenburg*'s survivors in hospitals there, von Boetticher immediately began arrangements to accommodate a German technical team that was already formed to investigate the accident. Dr. Hugo Eckener, one of the pioneers of German zeppelin aviation and the company's leading figure, arrived at Lakehurst within the week. Conducted under the auspices of the Bureau of Air Commerce and the navy, the inquest adjourned on May 28 without isolating a definite cause for the immolation of the hydrogen-filled ship. Von Boetticher's role, as it appears in the final report of the commission, was that of an observer.[10] The unexplained end of the airship has invited plausible speculation to this day that the airship was the victim of sabotage,[11] a possibility emphatically ruled out in Luftwaffe Gen. Hermann Goering's attempts to convince the world that only an act of God could so damage Reich interests. Von Boetticher echoed the German official line while at Lakehurst and held to the end of his life that the Bureau of Air Commerce had conducted "an excellent investigation."[12] Though criticized for this, von Boetticher maintained a view identical to that also held to his death by another key witness to the event, Vice Adm. Charles E. Rosendahl, the commander of the naval air station at the time. Rosendahl affirmed that von Boetticher's position gave the attaché no opportunity to sidetrack the investigation or interfere with the work. On the strength of their acquaintance at this time, von Boetticher and, through him, Capt. Robert Witthoeft, the German naval attaché, visited Rosendahl frequently over the next two years.[13]

Even as Hans Luther saw to the humanitarian requirements of the *Hindenburg* victims, his relief was in sight. On May 18, 1937, his successor, Hans Heinrich Dieckhoff, arrived to begin what turned into a foreshortened eighteen-month tour in Washington. He came on the Washington scene with positive advance notices from American officials in Germany, especially for his reputed anti-Nazi attitude.[14] The general view in Berlin was that Luther had not been able to counteract visible anti-German developments in the United States and that an energetic hand might improve things. The new

German ambassador identified four specific problem areas for German policy in Washington. The first, the blood and cultural-intellectual ties between Britain and the United States, was of long standing and now unalterable, a phenomenon that could only be monitored. The remaining dilemmas were all directly attributable to National Socialism itself: anti-Semitism, Nazi-Catholic enmity, and the much touted existence of a German-American Bund on American soil.[15] He was particularly insistent on the deleterious effect of the Bund and importuned Berlin continually on this question. No champion of Jews himself, he could see the impasse that anti-Semitism created for Germany in Washington; Nazi racial fanaticism would cut his mission short in due course. Dieckhoff's instincts in these matters generally found resonance with his military attaché. Barely two weeks after his arrival, the new ambassador was quick to remark upon von Boetticher's "valuable position of confidence" with American military officers when the latter had explained the German side of an incident in the Spanish Civil War in which German naval units bombarded a Spanish coastal town in retaliation for an attack on the German pocket battleship *Deutschland*. Even the ambassador convinced himself of the calming influence exercised by the American army on leading political circles after von Boetticher's visits.[16]

Von Boetticher's influence was even apparent in administrative affairs in the American army by this time. As the highest-ranking foreign military officer in the city[17] and the dean of the Attaché Corps, he was the arbiter of protocol in Washington social affairs involving attachés for the eight years of his service. His name figured frequently in American officers' duty assignments to Germany as well. When Colonel Burnett, head of the Foreign Liaison Branch, sought a replacement for the retiring American attaché in Berlin, Col. Jacob Wuest, he begged Maj. Truman Smith to take the "most important post in Europe now."[18] Burnett used the German attaché's name in his entreaty to Smith, who was then commanding a battalion of the 27th Infantry in Hawaii: "General von Boetticher would be highly pleased if he knew you were going to Germany."[19] Von Boetticher sent home elaborate recommendations on Smith once Smith had accepted the job and had arrived in Washington for briefings before going to the German capital. He also sent ahead extensive introductions for Capt. Albert C. Wedemeyer, who began a two-year course at the Kriegsakademie in 1936.[21] Through these recommendations, in fact, von Boetticher was not just cultivating friendships and influence among Americans, but serving also the elaborate quid-pro-quo system that governed his work as an attaché. He repeatedly sought to have Americans in Berlin accorded the same treatment and privileges that he received in Washington. Wedemeyer's study in Berlin followed the similar education of several younger German officers in the United States.[22]

By this time, both Smith and Wedemeyer were already among the more vocal representatives of a demonstrable attitude on foreign influences in the United States. From at least the turn of the century, American officers had imbibed the various forms of "scientific" racism, social Darwinism, and heavy suspicion of aliens rampant among even the intelligentsia in the country. From the 1920s, American military intelligence officers in particular adopted a hostile stance toward certain categories of immigrants. They reflected common class prejudices of the era in differentiating between vague "types" of people who were categorized as desirable or undesirable as additions to the population of the United States. Above all, this line of thinking despised and feared eastern European Jews, who supposedly carried with them the bacillus of political radicalism that promoted labor strife and left-wing causes.[23] It also mirrored heavily the apprehensive state of mind about these social elements in the imperial army in which von Boetticher had spent his years as a company officer. The approved philosophy on race within the U.S. Army's prestigious War College in Washington had the institution hosting speakers who openly avowed anti-Jewish social policy, exclusionary immigration laws, and accommodation with Germany even after the Czech crisis two years later.[24] As a matter of course, von Boetticher had daily contact with these men, whose ethnic, class, and racial attitudes colored their everyday discourse with the German officer as well. Von Boetticher reflected this atmosphere in his reporting over the next half decade.

For all the benefit he could derive from this verifiable goodwill and resonance between American and German army officers, von Boetticher's personal life lay clouded, at this time, by the fate of his own son under the Nazi regime. In what seemed a prosperous existence in Washington, he hosted Gertrud Beck, the daughter of the

German chief of staff, in his home for a full year. In June 1937, his own older daughter, Adelheid, married her classmate in medical studies, David K. Miller, in the city.[25] But his son in the same year had barely escaped Nazi justice.

By 1935, Friedrich Heinrich had a year's service behind him in the Prussian *Kammergericht* as a *Referendar*, a barrister at the first levels of the Prussian civil service. The atmosphere in the Prussian judiciary was already taut with the crusade of the senior justice, Roland Freisler, to Nazify the court system. The younger von Boetticher's uncle, the attaché's brother and a practicing jurist, had joined the Nazi Party before 1933.[26] When Friedrich Heinrich was called for one year's compulsory military service in 1935, he was already in open disagreement with the National Socialist regime. Even in uniform, his unguarded public remarks in Berlin bistros—where he often read thinly veiled political verse—made him the object of Gestapo attention. The police intercepted his frank correspondence with other young friends who had emigrated to Switzerland after futile protest against the regime. In February 1936, the government indicted him, citing "preparation for treason." Without benefit of counsel, the attaché's son spent a half year under this charge, until it was quashed in August. His father spent over a month in Germany, from late May to early July 1936, to all appearances on official business, but also intervening in the case.[27] Another government decree against the young man immediately thereafter ordered him to report for compulsory sterilization.[28] With the help of his older sister, then still in medical studies in Berlin, he sailed in March 1937 for New York and permanent residency in the United States.[29] The effect of this on the senior von Boetticher and on his ability to represent Germany can only be surmised. No reference to the episode appears in von Boetticher's official reports. If a part of him felt compelled to react against the regime he served, he apparently subordinated this to his highly developed sense of duty.

The resurgent German Army's need for experienced manpower led von Boetticher to at least one recorded instance of recruiting on American soil. His attitudes on clandestine German intelligence and the open propagation of Nazi ideas among German immigrants in the United States were as negative as those of the senior embassy staff, but he had no compunctions about channeling former officers home for the Reichswehr. Nikolaus Ritter, one of these veterans, was working in a textile company when a German consular official he had approached in New York suggested his return to Germany and a military commission in 1935. After nearly a year, von Boetticher met Ritter in Washington to pass on the German Army's approval of his return. He got no troop command as he had thought, but took up, with rank of major, a promising career in the Abwehr under Rear Adm. Wilhelm Canaris. Ritter at first controlled a number of agents sent to England but was most concerned with a section that collected aviation intelligence. With Canaris's reluctant permission, Ritter later came back to New York for espionage work, but with his chief's strict warning against any intercourse whatever with the official German representatives in the United States. Canaris unofficially enjoined his talking to von Boetticher. "Under no circumstances report to the German Military Attaché. General von Boetticher has no understanding for the Secret Service. He believes he can do it better alone. Stay away from him and all German representatives."[30]

With Canaris's separation of his agents from German officialdom in America, von Boetticher was spared knowledge of Ritter's further exploits there. In 1938, he obtained rough plans from which German technicians supposedly constructed an unproved version of the secret Norden bombsight being developed for American bombardment planes. Canaris's view of von Boetticher's purpose as antithetical to his own remained unchanged throughout the period of von Boetticher's service in Washington, producing a rift between the open and covert agents of German intelligence in the United States. The clandestine elements were a continuing source of embarrassment to the attaché and to German diplomacy in America. As Abwehr interest in plans for destroying segments of American industry or stealing its secrets grew, the German Army likewise established other agencies for collecting data on industrial and economic mobilization plans for various countries. Beginning in 1934, the Reichswehr Ministry created a *Wehrwirtschafts und Rüstungsamt*, or Defense Economic and Armaments Office, in the first of several successive reorganizations to centralize and rationalize German arms production and procurement.[31] In the course of things, this office also absorbed intelligence summaries on foreign planning in increasing number. The memory of American human and material wealth and its effect on the outcome of World War I weighed heavily in German deliberations. Even Hitler's appreciation of American productive capacity was not lacking in his earlier musings,[32] though he disclaimed any consistent thought on the United States after 1934 due to the press of business at home.[33] By 1936, world developments had led to ambitious revisions in war plans for American industry. Consequently, industrial mobilization increasingly became the subject of the German attaché reports from Washington.

Two purported wartime miracles by American industry in the twentieth century have predisposed many to heroic images of an indomitable production base churning out the stuff of American victory. The undeniable achievements in gearing up American industry in 1917 and after 1941 obscure somewhat the hectic and ad hoc arrangements that governed the mobilization of industry before the country's actual involvement in both world wars. The dependence of the United States on Allied manufacture as the American Expeditionary Force arrived in France in 1917 was generally overlooked in the flush of victory. Organizing the administrative machinery of wartime production and imbuing it with centralized powers that often conflicted with instinctive American feelings about governmental authority was a process nearly as bitter as some of the battles fought in the field. The period between the two world wars, and especially the interval after 1936, saw a fitful campaign for readiness driven by the conviction that in any future conflict the "delay and improvisation which had characterized our early World War One efforts would be costly and could be fatal."[34] Bernard Baruch, the head of the War Industries Board in World War I, remained a consultant on the war-industrial planning process in the War Department before World War II.[35] At one point, Von Boetticher paid tribute to the man's influence as a vocal critic. Bridling at one of Baruch's speeches reproduced in an army-associated journal, the attaché registered a formal complaint with the War Department on Baruch's arguments for American readiness because of the very contradiction between the terms "Hitler" and "peace."[36] Baruch's continuing invective drew attention to the woeful state of American mobilization machinery in the face of the German comeback.

Within the War Department, the highest legal authority in industrial mobilization planning at this time was the assistant secretary of war, Harry Woodring, and the Planning Branch under his

control. Charged under the National Defense Act of 1920 with supervision of all military supply procurement and the mobilization
of matériel and industrial organizations essential to wartime needs,
the assistant secretary had to coordinate his work with the General
Staff's plans for troop mobilization under the MacArthur Four
Army Plan with its Initial Protective Force dating from 1931 and its
subsequent revisions. Required were constant surveys of industrial
capacity, real and potential; estimates for constructing new manufacturing plants; current computations of the requirements to support the number of troops to be mobilized; and the maintenance of
standardization studies for items to be brought into mass production. The Planning Branch also outlined the allocation of industrial
orders and coordinated their distribution to industry so that an
emergency demand would not suddenly descend on a few specialized sectors of the economy. The actual purchasing power for army
equipment and supply in the prewar years remained with the
seven traditional technical services and the new Air Corps, though
their activities had to proceed within the initiatives, regulations,
and restraints laid down by the Planning Branch. Each plant involved in war work had a definite assignment with production
schedules agreed to in advance.[37] The obvious implication of the
marriage of industrial and military mobilization was that "every
revision of the military mobilization plan necessitates the Herculean task of recomputing requirements."[38] New technological developments and the need to import raw materials that were in short
supply in the country also fell under the aegis of the assistant secretary. In February 1924, the army also established its Industrial College, which trained officers from all services in dealing with the
civilian economy for munitions production.

The last major organizational element for industrial mobilization between the wars united army and navy interests in a single
body. The Army-Navy Munitions Board led a one-sided existence
from its inception in June 1922. The navy was a diffident member of
this joint entity, tending to remain in large part ready for war on
its own schedule as the nation's first line of defense. It regarded
wartime expansion as a matter of giving more shipbuilding contracts to existing yards.[39] As planning expanded, especially after
1936, the board came more to live up to its billing as the seniormost
agency for planning industrial mobilization during peacetime.[40] It

subsumed the overall authority for plant allocation; eventually compiled lists of strategic raw materials; and, later, managed to acquire funds to stockpile or import scarce supplies. Consisting of members from naval procurement agencies and of the entire Planning Branch of the Office of the Assistant Secretary of War for the army, the board was also the interim agency that would run things until the full establishment of a civilian superagency designed to coordinate all American civilian and military economic affairs in a full-fledged war.[41] If these measures began to centralize control of needed procurement at the joint level of the two services, true national direction of the war effort from the president's level did not emerge until 1943 and the existence of the Office of War Mobilization under James Byrnes.[42] Only then did all necessary price and wage controls, central resource and labor allocation, and administration of the civilian economy in war come into full play.

Von Boetticher began noticing the results of the Army-Navy Munition Board's work in articles on critical raw materials appearing in professional military literature in the spring of 1936. Citing a major study in two consecutive issues of the army's *Quartermaster Review*, he relayed the conclusions of the piece home, adding emphasis to the fact that the United States was then considered self-sufficient in food with the minor exceptions of coffee and sugar.[43] The twenty-four other natural resources listed as being in short supply in the United States included manganese, chrome, tin, nickel, wolfram, rubber, and silk, all necessary to munitions production, and quinine, then the only known effective antimalarial drug. The article's author portrayed the United States as the best endowed nation in resources despite some shortages; Germany was second on the scale, but a poor second by comparison.[44] A year and a half later, von Boetticher's estimates had not changed. He reported that most of the raw materials that America needed could be gotten from areas where political connections were fairly certain. The United States could get tin from Bolivia, manganese from Brazil, and nickel from Canada in wartime, but, as von Boetticher perceived, two years was the maximum that American industry could operate without American control of the seas. In fact, he found that American planning proceeded on this assumption, and a two-year raw material stockpile was called for.[45] Revised American studies whose results came to his ears reconfirmed his estimates in October 1937. The necessity to import much of the required material from Latin America, he insisted in late 1938, also underlay in part the American program for hemispheric solidarity that Cordell Hull laid before the Lima Conference in November of that year.[46] Though the American government was more concerned with the larger issues of Axis domination of the American sector of the world at that time,[47] and never included guarantees for materials supply in the high-toned language of the declaration, von Boetticher's inference here was well within the spirit of the document.[48]

By late 1938, he had referred home analyses of each element subordinate to the Army-Navy Munitions Board in which he correctly assessed it as the highest peacetime authority for the preparation of industrial production in war and catalogued its powers. He thoroughly understood its subordination to the temporary wartime emergency civilian agency, the War Resources Board, through which, as he put it, "the president exercises dictatorial powers granted him to mobilize the economy totally."[49] He also examined the system of so-called educational orders, under which the board sought to have plants with allocated war production quotas get some experience by producing their assigned items in limited quantities. After debating similar schemes as early as 1927, Congress, in the spring of 1938, voted an Educational Orders Act on June 16, whereby the War Department would spend $2 million a year over five years beginning with fiscal year 1939, that is, July 1, 1938 to June 30, 1939. When the program began after the president's hasty approval of the board of officers to administer it on September 1, 1938, and his addition of another $2 million to the project, six companies started work on the practice contracts.[50] The amounts of material involved were not large, the biggest single contract being with the Winchester Arms Company for 500 of the new semiautomatic M-1 Garand rifles, hardly enough to equip a battalion in the American army's divisional organization of the day. Von Boetticher listed the fruits of this exercise, including the other orders for gas masks, searchlights, artillery shells, and three-inch antiaircraft gun recoil mechanisms.[51] For all of this detail and his regular notice of new developments, von Boetticher also dealt repeatedly with estimates of the time it would take to have a mass American army ready and equipped for overseas field use.

Crucial in both military and industrial spheres was the element of time. Von Boetticher's appreciation of this coincided with the concerns of MacArthur's successor as chief of staff, Gen. Malin Craig; of Woodring, who became acting secretary of war upon the death of George Dern in August 1936; and of Woodring's successor as assistant secretary, Louis A. Johnson.[52] Though each of these men annually reported the progress toward increased readiness in his particular jurisdiction, the Army remained throughout this period, in Craig's words, "an unfinished and unassembled machine. Some of its parts are not in existence, some exist as rough forgings, others in semifinished form. Only a few are in a condition for immediate use."[53]

Getting an army (and a navy) assembled in a condition to have it taken seriously by foreign powers was the task of a period immediately following the announcement of "M-day," the actual declaration of war or national emergency. With M-day, the plans for industrial and military unit mobilization were to go into effect. MacArthur's earlier Four Army Plan visualized the call-up of 4,500,000 men in twelve months, something the General Staff came to regard as possible by 1936. Under General Craig's new Protective Mobilization Plan (PMP), more realistic figures began appearing. The army, with a threat of war in Europe more real, received congressional funding for the necessary strength of 165,000 men required to stage a mobilization. The 1938 version of the PMP, cast in the spring of the year, called for 730,000 regular army and National Guard officers and men to be in the ranks four months after M-day. Fifteen months after M-day, conscription would swell the force to a million men.[54] The new mobilization plans still received only grudging support in the American legislature. The army needed $160 million to equip just the initial protective force but could not wring this amount for ground forces from an administration whose priorities after 1934 were in naval and aircraft expenditures.[55]

The German attaché's reports dwelling on these eventualities were general in nature, mildly if aptly critical, but on the whole optimistic for the complete success of American military measures in a war. They emphasized unceasingly the element of time under which General Craig labored. During the military budget wrangles in the spring of 1938, von Boetticher laid out the particulars of the 1938 PMP. He identified the shifting character of American defense planning after 1937 from MacArthur's concentration on manpower and the 165,000 minimum army to Craig's increasing concern with the production of matériel to equip and sustain a modern mass army. The major problem was no longer in reaching the projected troop strengths, declared von Boetticher, but in the fact that the country did not stock enough war materials in peacetime and relied upon their production on the outbreak of war: "A large part of the war material such as antiaircraft guns, tanks and so forth requires considerable time in spite of all the capability of industry."[56]

Six weeks after these words were written, the mobilization of the Czech Army electrified Europe. Von Boetticher noted of the American plans, "They are clear on one thing, that the winning of time in an industrial mobilization is a basic factor."[57] The Americans could, he estimated in June 1938, equip a total of "fifty-two infantry and twelve cavalry divisions in half the time it took in 1917 and 1918."[58] In November, after the Munich Accord had taken place, he defined the "take off time" of the American arms industry supporting fifty to sixty divisions as six months, a highly optimistic estimate. The end of the year saw him even more soberly assessing the need for time. Reviewing the entire industrial mobilization picture on the occasion of his comment on the annual assistant secretary of war's report for 1938, which featured a wide-ranging critique of problems and accomplishments, von Boetticher especially pointed up Assistant Secretary of War Johnson's words about the various weaknesses in the purchasing program then in train. Standardization of military vehicles alone became a nightmare with the army's fleet of 10,000 cars and trucks in which 28 separate models of automobiles and 143 different truck models appeared.[59] He continued to affirm late in 1938 that American rearmament was evolving reliably and that the program would take only half the time of the American mobilization of World War I.

A new and more strident tone had crept into his reports in late 1938, evidence of the slowly changing tides in the isolationist-interventionist battle in America as well as the recognition of unfolding difficulties in the rearmament program, which after November 1938, proceeded not at all according to the carefully drawn plans, but according to Franklin Roosevelt's ad hoc arrangements dictated by political necessities and the president's own curious bureaucratic style.

The year of Munich brought portentous changes in German diplomatic reporting from America. In the wake of the Roosevelt Quarantine Speech in Chicago on October 5, 1937, Ambassador Hans Dieckhoff found, through von Boetticher's gleanings at the War Department, that the speech had been as much a surprise to the American military as to the populace that reacted so strongly against it.[60] In December, the ambassador characterized American policy as having a dialectic nature, moving alternately through the isolationist thesis and the interventionist antithesis strongly represented in editorials in the *New York Times*.[61] But Dieckhoff also repeated in the following months his conclusion that American isolation was a weak reed, repeating it so often, in fact, that he feared he was becoming a bore in Berlin. After the forcible German *Anschluss* with Austria in March, he perceived an administration-backed "Wake Up, America!" campaign in the country and that if it came to war, "the United States would not hesitate to range itself on the British side."[62] Among a number of themes in Dieckhoff's analyses, this conviction became a tenet of von Boetticher's reporting at the time also, and it was particularly meaningful as British and French purchasing commissions began appearing in the United States in early 1938 seeking to place orders for American planes.[63] Thus, von Boetticher seconded Dieckhoff's interpretation that American neutrality was, in large measure, dependent on the fate of Britain. Yet isolation prevailed for the moment. When Hitler wrung large tracts of Czech borderland from the appeasing western Allies at the Munich Conference, the American population loudly condemned the agreement and Nazism generally, but it was also clear that there would be no American intervention in the event of a war over Czechoslovakia.[64]

Of more immediate moment to von Boetticher as a member of the embassy staff was Dieckhoff's departure following the worst Nazi pogrom to that time. On November 7, 1938, a young Jew named Herschel Grynspan entered the German embassy in Paris bent on assassinating the German ambassador to avenge the Nazi treatment of Jews and especially that of his own father in Germany. Failing to find the ambassador, he gunned down the next available legation official, Ernst vom Rath. The Nazi government, under Hermann Goering's direction, orchestrated a week of anti-Semitic demonstrations in Berlin, beginning on November 9. SA and SS thugs wrecked Jewish shops, burned residences and synagogues, and summarily arrested some 20,000 Jews in what became known as *Kristallnacht*, for the broken glass that littered German city streets. Hitler imposed a 1 billion mark fine on the Jewish population of Germany. Roosevelt, over State Department objections, called American Ambassador Hugh Wilson home "for consultation" on November 15, a course that stung the German government to similar response. On November 23, Dieckhoff left the United States. Though he continued to act as designated ambassador to Washington until the outbreak of war, Germany went without a representative of full ambassadorial rank in the American capital until 1955.[65] Short of a complete rupture in relations, the mutual recall of ambassadors left the German embassy in Washington under Hans Thomsen, a Foreign Office professional whose earlier service as the Foreign Office liaison to the Nazi Reichschancellery had brought him to Hitler's attention. Having served in the United States since 1936, Thomsen was one of the bright, cultured young men of the German diplomatic corps, with a mastery of several languages, but whose genuine distaste for the Nazi regime was evident to his close associates.[66] He was called home to accompany Hitler on the much-touted visit to Rome in May 1938. He now replaced Dieckhoff as the senior political authority in the mission. With his rank of chargé d'affaires, indicating a temporary assignment, he still had all the prerogatives of the ambassador vis-à-vis his military attaché. Thomsen in fact fell below von Boetticher in the German civil service scheme of things. The attaché, a major general with thirty-eight years in uniform, overshadowed the thirty-nine-year-old Thomsen in rank and length of service. Still, the *Dienstanweisung*[67] governing their relations in the embassy forced von Boetticher to remain subordinate to the chargé. This caused no immediate difficulty, and the initially jittery Thomsen[68] found some comfort in von Boetticher's assurances that the American rearmament measures then current were not in direct response to the German demands on the Czech government.[69]

The very negative American reaction to the Czech crisis and the *Kristallnacht* six weeks later privately alarmed von Boetticher but failed to change his view of the American staff and his circle of friends connected with it. In a backchannel message, he described the latest public outcry against Germany as something he had never experienced. "I find it good that I am here in times of tense re-lations," he confided to Tippelskirch, with Dieckhoff leaving the country the next day.[70] He continued to regard the chief of staff, Gen. Malin Craig, as the "composed, clear, independent, and warmhearted personality" that he had described in 1935, when the latter succeeded MacArthur.[71] He also frequently credited Craig with a deep understanding of Germany and with keeping politics out of the American army and vice versa,[72] something critical to the attaché's ability to retain an influence on American opinion through the country's military structure. By September 1938, with war apparently imminent in Europe, the General Staff in America was more than a conduit of the "correct" German views he had supplied for the American people. It had become for von Boetticher the single most trustworthy element that understood German de-mands on Czechoslovakia and combated the political forces that "want to come to a reckoning with Germany."[73] This interpretation provides one major theme of von Boetticher's last three years in America, and one that led him to burgeoning differences with Thomsen as pressure on the embassy increased. The dualism in his reporting became more evident with the increasing tension be-tween American policy and German behavior. From the latter days of 1938, he supplied keen observations on the American rearma-ment program, which obviously went ahead in response to a clear danger from the Axis powers, while continuing to insist on the ef-fect his influence had on his American listeners.

The close relationship the German attaché had with historian Douglas Freeman changed not at all in light of the events of late 1938. This noted historian and journalist, who had earlier brought into play his considerable influence in an attempt to get von Boet-ticher's younger daughter accepted at Vassar College, now offered the young lady a home with his own family so that she could finish her education should her father have to return to Germany to fight.[74] By now thoroughly taken with her American surroundings, Hilde-gard von Boetticher had attended the prestigious Sidwell Friends School in Washington for her secondary education and had entered Randolph-Macon Woman's College in Lynchburg, Virginia, in Sep-tember 1938, as a member of the class of 1942. Her plans for a jour-nalism career were to take unforeseen turns before she could com-plete her term at the college.[75]

In the crisis atmosphere prevailing through the summer of 1938, and with the promise of an enlarged American air force, von Boetticher had also acquired a real technical expert as an addition to his attaché staff. In addition to a regular executive secretary, that staff employed at least one engineer, Wilhelm Wolff, for technical assessments, and a second member, Heinz Haehn, as a more general analyst of American military affairs.[76] Often this trio was heavily employed in clipping newspaper articles or pursuing copies of routine American government statistical publications that were referred home as evidence of larger developments in American munitions, aircraft sales abroad, or preparedness for a potential mobilization at home. Though accredited as air attaché in July 1934,[77] von Boetticher had no deep knowledge of aeronautics or the industry and the engineering applications underpinning it in the United States. In 1938, von Boetticher added to the technical breadth of his embassy staff with a man of surpassing reputation and real ability in aviation, but also one of complicated and contradictory character.

Peter Riedel was among a small but celebrated group of German soaring enthusiasts who had established world records in distance and time trials after World War I. In 1920, the fourteen-year-old Riedel had constructed his own motorless biplane and successfully flown it from the 960-meter hill formation known as the Wasserkuppe in the Rhön mountain range outside Fulda in central Germany. He returned there year by year as one of the leading "Rhön Indians" with other devotees such as Oscar Ursinus, the beloved *Rhönvater*, and the legendary Wolf Hirth to experiment with new techniques and glider designs stretching the theoretical and practical boundaries of their craft. Riedel gained experience in powered flight during 1924 and 1925 at the Sportflug Company in Magdeburg.[78] With his family's financing, he began work on a degree at the Darmstadt Technische Hochschule, only to break off for a stint at the German air transport school in Braunschweig in 1928. A year's study gave him the German Professional Pilot's B Licence, but no prospects of a job with an airline. With nothing else in view, he returned to the Hochschule as depression overtook the German economy. An indifferent student by his own account, he nevertheless graduated a *diplom ingenieur* with an aviation specialty in September 1932.[79] While still a student, he made ends meet by becoming a technical manager and test pilot with the Meteorological

Institute of the Rhön-Rossitten Company, also headquartered in Darmstadt. The institute was headed by Dr. Walter Georgii, already a leading aeronautical authority. Riedel's experiments and demonstrations with towed starts for gliders and his mastery of particularly unstable sailplane designs earned him the 7th Silver C badge issued by the international soaring society Istus in May 1932. Riedel thereafter went international in his search for new distinction in the air. In June 1933, he set an unofficial distance record of 228 kilometers, starting in Germany and landing in France. In August came his most celebrated accomplishment yet. He took first place in the annual week-long Rhön soaring competition and was an instant celebrity. The German Sailplane Museum at the Wasserkuppe still carries his records prominently on it walls.

Riedel's politics seem tinged with more than a modicum of opportunism. In later years, he proved a careful dissembler in matters of his association with events in Germany after 1930. To his collaborator-biographer, he admitted only to voting once for the Nazi Party in 1933. Though he briefly considered a party membership, he maintained sixty years later, he never joined.[80] His sailplaning triumph in 1933 came just as the whole flying enterprise at the Wasserkuppe fell under the aegis of Hitler's Reich. Among the first acts of the new government was the organization of a Reich Air Ministry to establish closer control of the entire German aviation industry and, by extension, gliding activity in the Rhön. Whether Riedel advanced any of this activity remains open, but available evidence contradicts his story on his political affiliation.

Nazi Party membership files conclusively establish that he joined the party, not once, but twice, and retained some connection to the movement even when his adherence to it was apparently dormant. In each case, he abandoned the party again within a year. His first entry was on March 1, 1931, as Member No. 494110 in Darmstadt (Gau Hessen); the record shows he departed as of September 30, 1931. Gau Berlin then reopened his membership as No. 2601567 on May 1, 1933, with another lapse after September that year. Other files indicate that the party considered him in active status as late as mid-1940.[81] An extant photograph shows Riedel in what appears to be SS uniform at a glider event apparently dating from the early 1930s. It is not clear that Riedel donned Nazi uniform out of principle; his detached personality turned him away from mass movements with unthinking adherence to a demanding leader.[82] The party was an enthusiastic supporter of aviation in all its forms, however, and its endorsement of flying put money behind these heroes of the air.

In spring 1934, Georgii headed an expedition to South America to explore meteorological conditions there. Riedel, with three of the best German soaring pilots of the time, contributed to this scientific work. The group also found Andean topography particularly suited to their business. Hanna Reitsch, Heini Dittmar, Wolf Hirth, and Riedel found thermals conducive to long-distance flight and audiences thrilled by their exploits.[83] Riedel returned after four months much taken with South America. It gave him a first chance to view German politics from a distance, "postage-stamp size," he said, and it played to his own personality that yearned for more limitless horizons. He discovered, too, that his essential attractiveness to women was unchanged below the equator. At the expedition's homecoming, Riedel was also honored in May 1934 with the Hindenburg Trophy for the South American tour and for his performance in the Rhön competitions of the previous year.

On the same day that he received his latest recognition, Riedel realized an earlier dream and became a commercial pilot for the German national airline, Lufthansa. After 1926, it had overcome the resistance of the wartime Allies to the development of German commercial airlines, merged several local feeder lines, and become the government-subsidized flag carrier of Germany. At the time Riedel joined it, the company was among the world's most successful, carrying about 20 percent of all airline traffic on a service net with routes running from Lisbon to Shanghai and Canton.[84] Riedel was also introduced to Lufthansa's compulsory instrument training for its pilots, this in an age when most distance navigation was still by dead reckoning and seat of the pants.[85]

Within two years, the restless flier had enough of the company regime. His clear technical talent and the standardization that guaranteed commercial success and safety had Riedel slated for an engineering position at home—a desk job—despite his repeated applications for assignment overseas. He escaped the routine with yet more soaring feats, among them exhibitions from the Alpine Jungfrau with Ernst Udet, Germany's leading World War I ace, holder of the *Pour le Mérite*, and a colorful barnstormer. He staged more demonstrations from the frozen ice-skating rink at Garmisch in Bavaria during the Winter Olympics of 1936. When an obscure airline in South America offered him a contract the following November, he jumped at the chance to move on. A disappointed Lufthansa director groused at him as he came to say good-bye. At Tempelhof, his friends accused him of joining the Foreign Legion.[86]

The Sociedad Colombo-Alemana de Transportes Aéreos operated under its trade name SCADTA from a headquarters in the Colombian coastal city of Barranquilla after its founding in December 1919. Advertising itself as the oldest airline in the Americas, it immediately reduced the overland trip from the coast to the Colombian capital at Bogota from a two-week boat-and-mule trek up the Magdalena River to a one-hour flight. Its German connections were obvious in the aircraft it flew, among them the first all-metal Junkers F-13 transport, fitted with either wheels or floats, the latter for landings on the Magdalena. By 1929, the line had service as far south as Peru and westward into Panama. There, German pilots flew into fields at either end of the American-owned and -operated canal, a fact that later raised increasing alarm among American military aviators. With the reserve of German talent and commercial interest that existed in SCADTA, it became suspect as one element the Nazi regime could presumably use as part of a "fifth column" in the Western Hemisphere.[87]

Riedel's service with SCADTA was a step backward for a pilot in a developing airline world, but one toward more far-flung international possibilities for him. When not flying regular routes, he returned to soaring around South America. He ordered a glider shipped to Barranquilla from the Schweyer firm in Mannheim and apparently became an unofficial sales representative for the company in the region.[88] There was enough slack in his company duties that Riedel, from his base in Colombia, joined the American Soaring Society in June 1937,[89] with the object of entering the annual meet at Elmira, New York, that year. Von Boetticher clearly had advice from home, most probably from the level of Ernst Udet, by then a colonel in the Reich Air Ministry, that the flier would be in the United States for the American national soaring events climaxing in early July. The fact that the German Aero Sport Club was sponsoring a German Sperber *Senior* glider for Riedel's use in the United States was no secret among the German pilots at home.

Riedel was already known among gliding pilots in the United States. In late June, he flew the *Senior* over the city of New York, starting from a field on Long Island. Universally favorable press notices hailed his appearance over Manhattan. In the two weeks of activities centered on Harris Hill, the American equivalent of the Wasserkuppe outside Elmira, Riedel achieved even greater renown and a following in America with the best distance flight—113 miles—in the competition.[90] His lasting friendships thereafter included Richard duPont, one of America's aristocrats and president of the Soaring Society the following year. The organization's eighth annual show had given Riedel his first taste of the United States. The attractions of the informal American style and the camaraderie of the fliers he had just met influenced his decision when Friedrich von Boetticher subtly opened an interview with the bemused flier in Elmira's Mark Twain Hotel on July 11, a warm Sunday.

Confronting a figure he thought more reminiscent of a bishop than a soldier, Riedel dutifully answered the general's polite inquiries on his technical background, his family, and his attitudes toward the Nazi government and the führer's policies. When von Boetticher came to the point and offered Riedel a position as his assistant for aviation matters in the embassy, the surprised flier dismissed the idea of yet another confining desk job practically out of hand. He also had to attend to an invitation for a few days with the duPonts. Riedel had reached Miami on the sixteenth and sat waiting for a flight back to Barranquilla when the lost opportunity to stay in the country overtook him. He penned a hasty note on hotel stationery to tell von Boetticher that he had changed his mind and would accept.

Months passed. Only in December did Riedel hear from Germany, and it proved to be Udet, once again confirming Riedel for the position in the Washington embassy. The Air Ministry was buying Riedel out of his SCADTA contract, but he still had to await a replacement from Germany. Only in February 1938 did he leave Colombia and travel up the American east coast, bound for Germany and the administrative routine at home that would prepare him for his new post. The Austrian-born head of SCADTA, Peter Paul von Baur, blew hot and cold on the loss of Riedel when an American consular official interviewed him in Bogota.[91] Von Boetticher marked this brief transit with a grave lecture on the evils of

German espionage in the United States and emphasized his own strictures on using the embassy as a tool of the Abwehr. Making Southampton in England on March 11, Riedel endured the glares of British officials eyeing his passport. Hitler that day had sent German forces into Austria to unify it with the German Reich.

Udet's sponsorship of his case notwithstanding, the paperwork employing Riedel as a civilian engineer with the Air Ministry detailed to the Washington embassy ran on until June 1938. His reputation as a soaring pilot counted for little in a bureaucracy dominated by uniforms and mutual back stabbing, and he found his friend Udet distracted, a distant remnant of his earlier dashing self. Surrounded by indifference or outright hostility, Riedel welcomed renewed acquaintance at the ministry with an old colleague, flight engineer Fritz Grosskopf, who had been at the air transport school with him in 1928. Grosskopf alluded to certain connections he had, then took Riedel for an obviously prearranged interview with functionaries at the Tirpitzufer address of the Abwehr. The stiffer formality of the occasion was interrupted by an exquisite lunch for eight at Horcher's, a renowned Berlin restaurant. Five Abwehr officials joined Riedel and Grosskopf. The remaining empty chair at the table soon had another occupant—Adm. Wilhelm Canaris himself, enigmatic head of the agency. Flattered at the uncommon attention, Riedel—by his own account—promptly rejected the approaches of the German military intelligence organ to work quietly for it while employed in the embassy.[92] For the Abwehr, courting Riedel probably had wider implications. The military intelligence organization was by this time locked in a bitter contest with Heinrich Himmler's growing SS police empire in the Nazi hierarchy. By 1936, one of Himmler's lieutenants, Reinhard Heydrich, among the more fearsome of the Nazi inner circle, had made a name for himself and his *Sicherheitsdienst* (the SD, or Security Service, a subordinate element of the SS). He fed information and documents to Russian operatives that caused the demise of Marshal Mikhail Tukhachevsky in the beginnings of the great purges that wracked lead elements of the Red Army in 1937 and 1938. This coup put the SD in the ascendant and in direct competition with the Abwehr.[93] Having a man of its own in the legation in Washington might have offset the presence of Ulrich von Gienanth, known as the SD's agent in Washington. The flier prepared for his return to the United States but had another errand before reporting to the embassy.

Riedel's return to Elmira in 1938 was an even more heady affair, an interlude to be followed by more sober reality. At Harris Hill for the 9th Annual National Soaring Contest, he was among friends again for two weeks. More important, on July 3, he left the hill with the announced goal of making Washington, D.C., by unpowered flight. Airborne seven hours and nineteen minutes, he covered the distance of 225 miles, skimmed the Washington Monument with 200 feet to spare, executed a series of aerobatics above gathering preparations for Independence Day on the Mall, and touched down at Hoover Airport, across the Potomac River from the city and on the site of the Pentagon today. He had established not just an American mark, but a new world record. Hauled back to the Elmira start point, he and his glider repeated the performance two days later by running 196 miles to Roosevelt Field on Long Island in nearly seven hours. In an era when soaring distance records were about 125 miles, Riedel had shown himself the master of his trade. Only his lack of American citizenship prevented his being declared the national champion. Von Boetticher, on the scene for his new junior attaché's latest exploit, made a short speech on the last day of the meet.[94] Work—the drudgery of office routine—now beckoned.

In recollections that often attempt to distance himself from von Boetticher, Riedel remarks that the man was now less affable, and had turned into someone "sober, solemn, [a] rigid Prussian soldier, moody, often unreasonable, humorless, disagreeable, and pompous."[95] Von Boetticher, for his part, had waited a year for the arrival of his assistant. The fact loomed that the two were men of radically different temperament and outlook, but now mutually dependent. The general, by tradition and inclination a faceless staff officer who shunned publicity, and the flier, a brilliant technician at ease in the limelight, between them constructed the analytic content of military reporting flowing to Berlin from Washington. Anything pertaining to aviation in the transmissions from July 1938 until the United States entered the war came first from Riedel's hand. Von Boetticher could not have kept adequately abreast of American military and naval aeronautical developments without this assistance, and the coverage was extensive and well informed. For Riedel, the paying job at the embassy offered a means of staying in the United States, and he often swallowed his anger at von Boetticher's sometimes arbitrary influence in his life. At the same time, he seemed always to have enough free time for flying and social activities in his host country. Whether Abwehr funds actually financed some of this activity remains an open question. The general recognized the positive effect of Riedel's easy style on younger American colleagues and the benefits of his genuine entrée among acquaintances in the aviation industry in the United States. Riedel later also admitted his patriotic feelings as a German as a factor keeping him at his tasks in the face of the rising unpopularity of Hitler's tactics in Europe. Among several Americans who knew him at the time, he never quite escaped the suspicions of Nazi sympathies.

German demands against Czechoslovakia through the spring and summer after Riedel's arrival raised the stakes for the embassy. The initial attempts to form estimates of American aviation potential were largely inductive for Riedel's first six months in his new position. The information was easily obtained but still came from a more passive collection of clippings from American newspaper and magazine sources that the attaché had compiled since early 1934. Riedel worked on the undifferentiated files with the help of one secretary, but only with specific direction on procedures from his chief. With little initiative required, he found the work limited— and limiting—and von Boetticher's supervision hypersensitive to problems and difficulties.[96] He managed at least occasional escape from Washington under the guise of other duties.

"Arriving New York with Habicht on Bremen on 22d," read Hanna Reitsch's cable to Riedel at the embassy in mid-August. "Please pick me up."[97] She and two other German pilots were on their way to the Cleveland Air Races held annually for the two weeks surrounding Labor Day. Riedel, who had engineered the invitation to the German team from the organizers of the events, accompanied his colleague there and spent some carefree days in the company of aviators. If von Boetticher objected to this diversion from embassy duties, he could not do so too loudly, for the skill of German fliers still gave some offsetting publicity to events in Europe. Riedel soon gave the general other concerns.

In another of his deliberate distractions from bureaucratic routine, Riedel took up horseback riding in the late summer of 1938. Naturally athletic as a pilot, he confessed to having to master the skill of staying aboard a mount and making it do his will. He succumbed to the easy notion of bribing the usually docile animals from the stables in Washington's Rock Creek Park with sugar cubes to keep them going. On one ride, he ran out of these inducements before getting back to the barn and was reduced to begging for more from a young woman rider passing by.

Helen Klug was at this time a twenty-seven-year-old art instructor in the District of Columbia public schools. The eldest daughter of a large Catholic family in Terre Haute, Indiana, she had a struggling existence there after graduating the John Herron Art Institute in Indianapolis. With the offer of a teaching position at a small Catholic girls' school in the nation's capital, she struck out alone for Washington. She had also finished an advanced art degree from New York's Columbia University at the time of the chance equestrian meeting with Riedel. Though her family descended from Alsatian immigrants, she knew no German. Within a few months, though, the couple was discussing marriage. The principal obstacle to this, in Riedel's account, was General von Boetticher. The presumed complications of such a German-American connection no doubt troubled him, but the abstemious attaché's reaction to Riedel's eventual decision to begin living together with his strongly independent-minded companion[98] can only be imagined.

The gathering crisis over Czech borderlands and the sacrifice of Czech territory at Munich in late September 1938 gave no small impetus to American arms building but also produced, in the words of an official historian, "a confusion of aims."[99] As the tension grew, Charles Lindbergh's travels in European capitals and his assessment of the relative strengths of the air forces of the Continent made for sober reading among American diplomatic staffs. U.S. ambassador in London Joseph P. Kennedy, himself a rival and visceral critic of Roosevelt, repeated Lindbergh's judgment that Germany could destroy Europe's major cities, that war should be avoided at any cost because it would result in disaster and the spread of communism in Europe, and that Germany should be encouraged to expand to its east.[100]

The perception of this imbalance in military aviation strengths moved the American government to hasty countermeasures. Evidence of an American resolve to promote rearmament appeared at a White House conference called by Roosevelt on November 14, 1938. The president proposed to his military service chiefs a massive increase in air strength and asked the army to draw up a two-year plan for 10,000 new aircraft, mentioning an outlay of $500 million. Then–Maj. Gen. Henry Arnold, chief of the Army Air Corps, looked back on this session as the Magna Carta for his branch of the service. The windfall for the American army aviators was supposed to begin matching the strength of the German Luftwaffe, which then had a program for more than 8,000 aircraft, but had an advertised production capacity of 12,000 airframes per year. Roosevelt saw the planes as suited to the defense of the Western Hemisphere, but also for the purpose of sale or loan to the British and French governments,[101] then at a loss to match German production. They could be built in quantity faster and more cheaply than naval ships and then quickly deployed as ready statements of American political will. When Arnold left the White House and returned to his office that day, his aides protested that American industry could not begin to match German production; the bureaucratically shrewd Air Corps leader agreed but slyly reminded them that at least they now had marching orders to build an air force.[102]

Assistant Secretary of War Louis Johnson was busy seizing opportunity on the morrow of the White House meeting. He hastily directed the Army chief of staff to prepare a two-year plan not only for producing the 10,000 aircraft but also for acquiring or constructing seven government factories to build them. He also wanted ready plans to re-equip completely the regular and National Guard forces scheduled to be called into federal service in the Initial Protective Force, for funding the rest of the educational orders program, new munitions-making machinery for government arsenals, and orders for critical supplies; for accelerating the industrial mobilization surveys and specification studies then ongoing; and for purchasing new stockpiles of strategic raw materials. The General Staff continued to whittle away at the president's aircraft proposals through December 1938 in favor of a more balanced program that included not just combat planes, but also training craft to school American pilots and allocations for expanding the existing ground forces and the National Guard. Roosevelt finally accepted the necessity for more diversity in armaments, and a more variegated purchasing scheme appeared in his expanded budget message to Congress on January 12, 1939, with a price tag of $525 million exclusive of supplementary naval allocations for the year.[103] Approved in segments by May 2, the supplementary arms program called forth some premature gloating in army quarters: "The country has become defense minded in a big way! No longer is serious attention paid to those nit-wit forces which only four years ago seemed well on the road to make us a nation of left-wing pacifists."[104]

But as much as the allocation of money was an expression of intent, it was a matter of months, even years, before a full complement of modern equipment would be in the hands of the troops of an expanded army. The rearmament began with no clear objective. The M-day concept never took effect. Without a declaration of war or national emergency, no civilian czar appeared under Roosevelt's direct command, as called for in the industrial mobilization plans, to direct all aspects of a coherent national effort. Though the armed services had headed off the wholesale and one-sided commitment to aircraft construction, limiting it to a goal of 5,500 machines, it was clear that the president was determined to share American war production with foreign governments to stiffen their defenses against Hitler, something never envisioned in the mobilization plan. Roosevelt's political strategy had other consequences as well.

The entire sequence of events inflamed a bitter feud in the War Department between Harry Woodring and Louis Johnson. Woodring, a proponent of readiness but not of widespread aid to European armies at the expense of American preparedness, was not invited to the meeting on November 14. He had already argued with the president over arms sales abroad and the question of neutrality. Johnson, a man of overweening ambition who coveted Woodring's job, took a broader, interventionist view. Roosevelt even kept Woodring ignorant of the arrival of a French air mission in December 1938, advising the delegation, which was in the country to test a new American aircraft for use with the French air force, to work through the office of the more reliable secretary of the treasury, Henry Morgenthau.[105] Roosevelt tended, in his often deliberately contradictory administrative style, to vacillate in his support for one man and then the other, entertaining Johnson's habit of going around his superior Woodring when it suited presidential policy to do so. The General Staff also tended to split into Woodring men, represented more heavily among the land forces officers, and Johnson adherents, found largely among air corps officers, causing political headaches for Craig and his successor Marshall.[106] Technical problems involving the coordination of the entire production effort showed up almost immediately. In the publicity that accompanied the news of the arms program, von Boetticher found the usual suspect influences, but also visible evidence of the working of the circle close to him in the General Staff.

The German service attachés took the news of the new expenditures calmly. Von Boetticher and Witthoeft sent home a joint review of the President's requests for arms. They emphasized Roosevelt's warnings against a war hysteria and his declaration that rearmament gave no indication of an American willingness to send troops to Europe. In all, the report concluded buoyantly, the new program had actually retreated from

> the extravagant and provocative rearmament campaign of recent weeks, and is especially in regard to the air arm less far reaching than certain parties would wish. It signifies a clear victory for the circles advising moderation and should reflect the views of the Armed Services.[107]

A similar report from von Boetticher brought the revelation that among the "certain parties" cited earlier were his old nemesis, Bernard Baruch, and the Jewish circle around the president, who nevertheless were even then opposed in the press and by public opinion, which "would not follow the President and his Jewish friends in their boundless armament plans and their attempts to paint a German specter on the wall." He reasserted that six months' time was still necessary to mobilize an American army of fifty to sixty divisions and another six months before the country could commit forces overseas.[108] These still-optimistic projections did not change when, two months later, Hitler wrote the end of appeasement in Europe by occupying the rump Czech state left by the Munich Agreement.

The continued publicity on American rearmament in the sensitive atmosphere following the end of Czech independence no doubt galled von Boetticher. He lashed out at what he saw as the pretense of the campaign, citing in particular an article in the April issue of the journal *Foreign Affairs*.[109] In a comprehensive and astute report entitled "The American Rearmaments: Propaganda and Fact," he ridiculed the general impression being conveyed that

America was a highly armed state, an idea, he insisted, that was meant to convince smaller Latin American states to stay loyal to the United States and to underscore the validity of American promises of aid to England and France. He reviewed the emphasis on the navy after 1934 and especially the supplementary allocation of 1938 as an effort to acquire a two-ocean fleet that could match Japanese might in the Pacific. The active army, on which the first part of a mobilization depended, would reap only $110 million of the $500 million program to re-equip itself. As the attaché aptly noted, American artillery, much of it still left over from French stocks bought in World War I, was all obsolete; most of the pieces were not really mobile. The American army had no light field howitzers, no antitank weapons, and few antiaircraft guns. Only 10 percent of its projected needs in combat vehicles were then in existence. The figures mentioned would not even begin to re-equip the second wave of the projected troop mobilization in wartime. As to industrial mobilization, von Boetticher cited the testimony of the American chief of ordnance, Maj. Gen. Charles M. Wesson, before the House Military Affairs Committee. Wesson admitted that munitions production skills were, at that moment, concentrated in six government arsenals and that a whole series of industries would have to be trained to meet the demands of the current program. The Air Corps was in a similarly less optimistic condition than implied, expecting to have a total of 1,096 planes by June 30, 1939, not even half the recommended total the Baker Board had given out in 1934. Plans called for 6,000 aircraft by June 30, 1941. The 1939 rearmament campaign, he stressed, as he dealt with each segment of the American defense establishment, was a two-year one, and he named June 30, 1941, as the date of its completion. If he anticipated the conclusions of the staff men working on the Protective Mobilization Plan of 1939 in his recognition that, with its imbalances, the U.S. Army was not yet a real fighting force,[110] von Boetticher was as yet without delusion:

In all it is to be realized that the Army and the Air Corps find themselves in a development which should be finished by the middle of 1941, that at the moment, however, there is no reckoning with the introduction of considerable parts of the Air Corps into a European theater of war.

But also:

The depicted weaknesses of the armed forces and the industrial mobilization must not lead to an underestimation of the armed forces and the energy and capability of development in the American people.[111]

The American grand strategy of the moment projected a concentration on the defense of the hemisphere, especially the Panama Canal, he declared. Japan's behavior limited much of American freedom of action, as von Boetticher effectively pointed out in comparing American options in World War I, when British and French industry had equipped the American Expeditionary Force, and an acquiescent Japan did not threaten the United States in the Pacific.[112] The April 18 report played upon themes he returned to later, but central to the appreciation of von Boetticher's analyses of American readiness in 1939 was his constant repetition of the date June 30, 1941. From early 1939 on, he stressed it as a juncture at which American industry's capabilities and the army's demands would be in balance. The shortages of such skilled workers as toolmakers already showing up in 1939 in the attaché reports were real[113] and signified no underestimation or denigration of American industry. He knew what that industry was capable of, but he was also simply repeating what American military procurement officials themselves understood, that it would take the American military economy two years to achieve its full potential.[114] The supplemental military outlay of 1939 was not enough. The allocation of the money did not automatically call necessary arms and equipment into being; the critical factor now was time.

One less-publicized aspect of typically National Socialist diplomatic style worked somewhat to von Boetticher's advantage after January 1939. Over the preceding year, Joachim Ribbentrop, erstwhile German ambassador in England, had consolidated a hold over the Nazi government's foreign ministry. He had succeeded Konstantin von Neurath in the position as part of Hitler's shake-up of February 1938 in which Hitler dismissed Gen. Werner von Blomberg as defense minister and added the powers of that office to his own as führer; he further cashiered Gen. Werner von Fritsch, commander in chief of the Reichswehr, on trumped-up morals charges. Ribbentrop thereafter turned his professional establishment into "little more than a stenographic bureau."[115] Reacting to Roosevelt's critical remarks on dictatorships in the president's annual message to Congress on January 4, 1939,[116] Ribbentrop imposed a social boycott on the American embassy in Berlin and extended the prohibition on similar intercourse with Americans to Thomsen's staff in Washington.[117] By the fall of the year, Thomsen was cataloging the reasons for lifting the restriction. He especially protested the paradox in which his armed service attachés had more regular and frequent informal contact with American State Department officials than he or his political staff could enjoy under the self-imposed sanction.[118] Von Boetticher's close relations with the American General Staff that Dieckhoff had attested to in his reports during the Spanish Civil War extended now at least to some members of the State Department as well. Thus, from January 1939 through the entry of the United States into the war, the German military attaché had open and informal entrée into American governmental channels often denied to the chargé d'affaires operating on a more strict protocol and answering now to Ribbentrop. As if to add to the tension, a public row arose over the existence of a pro-Hitler movement in the country.

Von Boetticher's often exaggerated sensibilities on overt manifestations of Nazi sympathies in the United States were proven correct in one instance in early 1939. A nascent German-American Bund, under a self-styled American führer, had made headlines, though it manifested more comic opera than serious threat to American security. At its high tide, it staged a mass rally of 20,000 adherents in New York's Madison Square Garden on February 20, 1939, in an attempt to link a demonstration of American National Socialism with the observance of George Washington's birthday. As the participants left the sports arena, though, a crowd outside estimated at 100,000 shouted its disdain for the American Nazis. Some 2,000 New York police, mobilized for the occasion, kept the vast crowd from attacking anyone wearing a swastika. The occasion still left an impression that the Bund was a highly organized pro-German faction within the country, but its leader was shortly thereafter imprisoned for embezzlement and the movement withered.[119]

Other events came closer to home for the attaché. He was, in the atmosphere of the time, prone to socially embarrassing situations, an example of which occurred in the tense days after Munich. Von Boetticher had an especially close association with George S. Patton, Jr., already a flamboyant American major general who was commandant at the foremost army social and ceremonial post of Fort Myer in Arlington, Virginia, from December 1938 to July 1940.[120] The two men probably met during one of the innumerable affairs at the post to which foreign attachés were routinely invited, and von Boetticher was a frequent guest at the Patton table. They shared a mutual passion for the history of the American Civil War, and the enthusiastic Patton children participated in history field trips to local battlefields in which von Boetticher and Patton vividly re-created the action. Their dinnertime socializing ended, however, when, during one of these formal affairs, a local Jewish business-man became increasingly vocal about Nazi pogroms in Europe in von Boetticher's silent presence. The speaker grew louder as the German attaché and his wife wordlessly left the room. Mrs. Beat-rice Patton called von Boetticher the next day with profuse apolo-gies. He gently put her off, saying that in the interests of Patton's career, the general should perhaps no longer entertain the von Boet-tichers. The amenities of issuing invitations persisted, but the Ger-man attaché never returned to dinner at the Pattons'. The battle-field excursions, however, continued until Patton's transfer in mid-1940.[121]

In February 1939, von Boetticher reached an apparent turning point in his attitude toward the regime he served. It remains diffi-cult to assess the degree of a conversion, given the conflicting ac-counts bearing on his thoughts at the time. He had returned to Ger-many the previous month to attend the annual attaché conference in Berlin. Here, for the second time, he came face-to-face with Hitler himself. Von Boetticher later represented the occasion as one in-volving a formal luncheon. He sat at Hitler's right while Gen. Ernst Köstring, the German attaché in Moscow, on Hitler's left, held the führer's attention with Russian affairs. When Hitler at last turned to him, von Boetticher attests, it was to say that he intended to strike a lasting blow against Roosevelt by revealing to the world that the American president had Jewish ancestors.[122]

Given the decidedly different description that von Boetticher constructed of this event after the war, Riedel's reflections on the scene in the embassy after the general's return offer somber testi-mony to Hitler's legendary power to enthrall his audiences. Riedel found his superior awed by his experience with Hitler, wishing that his assistant could have had "the same opportunity to look into his deep blue eyes and feel the magnetic power of his personality."[123] For Riedel, who had only heard of the attaché's anti-Nazi stance in the past,[124] this was a marked change. This was a prelude to the revelation of an "order" von Boetticher had received, Riedel reported, one that meant for both of them a deep responsibility. It revolved around a question: When could the United States intervene if a war should break out in Europe in 1939? The singular inquiry drove much of the military analysis in the embassy over the next months.

Von Boetticher's account of these events was diametrically at odds with Riedel's recollection. He reported his two-month sojourn in Germany in January and February 1939 as filled with a round of quiet conferences with his brother-officer contemporaries. He describes the small-scale dinners with the disgraced Werner von Fritsch, whom he regarded highly. He closeted himself as well with Ludwig Beck, who had hoped to galvanize his colleagues with a dramatic resignation as chief of staff in late August 1938, only to find the impact of this gesture lost in the euphoria over the end of the Czech crisis. Ernst von Weizsäcker, state secretary at the Foreign Office, confided to von Boetticher his fears about an approaching war that very year. The German Army's old guard and the professional diplomats were in retreat and disarray, trading in wishful thinking. Beck and von Fritsch particularly distrusted Walther von Brauchitsch, von Fritsch's successor as commander in chief of the army. The tone of all his discussions was decidedly guarded, as von Boetticher recounts them. Everyone hoped that with the Czech business over, reasonable elements among the National Socialists would prevail.[125] For his own part, when an unnamed foreign ministry official begged him to begin reporting as soon as he returned to the United States that the Americans would intervene immediately in a war and place their enormous productive capacity on the side opposing Germany, von Boetticher refused outright.[126] He could not bring himself as a German staff officer to engage in such holy subterfuge even to help curb Hitler's bent for war.

What the attaché could have achieved with this proposed shading of his reports is doubtful in any case. In this recollection, von Boetticher carefully skirts the realities of what had happened to the senior elements of the German army command and the General

Staff. By the time of these unobtrusive dinners, the senior generals were portraying themselves as victims of the Nazi regime, a fiction maintained into postwar Germany as well. Hitler had completely reversed the party-army relationships that prevailed after various arrangements in 1935 had drawn careful boundaries around the functions of both organizations and limited party influence within the armed services.[127] The events of February 1938 in which Hitler eliminated the War Ministry and took this function to himself as the Oberkommando der Wehrmacht reduced the military's position from a political one to a mere functional one.[128] The generals no longer contributed to the formulation of strategy and national policy as they traditionally had, except to second what was directed from above. Despite their protests and inability to resist, the generals had also been willingly led to their impasse. Von Brauchitsch was a pliable man with no independence of mind. Hitler further corrupted him and others of the military elite with bribes.[129] If the basic hierarchies and functions of field command remained in place, and senior service officers consulted directly with Hitler, the assessment of German options and reaction abroad were essentially confined to him. The structures contributing to the weakness and cross-purpose in German intelligence assessments after 1938 were already in place as von Boetticher consulted with his colleagues.[130] The data from Washington reached mixed audiences at home.

Peter Riedel's work at the German embassy had done much to expand on von Boetticher's appreciation of American potential in aviation. By early 1939, Riedel had broadened and deepened the inductive file keeping on all the major producers of airframes, engines, and propellers, and most of the minor producers of the subassemblies that made up this specialized American industry. He now added real focus to the earlier passive collection of news clippings by not only applying his engineering acumen to evaluating the industry, but also devising simple ways of deducing production from public financial information required from any corporation whose paper traded on the New York Stock Exchange. Public as well were the succession of contract orders let by the war and navy departments, complete with total numbers of aircraft ordered and the cost of each contract. Publications such as the *American Aviation Yearbook* offered reliable cost data, and Riedel devoured back issues. He likened the problem to a schoolboy exercise in which young students have to compute how many eggs a farmer sells if the gross receipts and the price of a single egg are known. "Eggs or airplanes, there isn't much difference," he related in recollections drafted six years later.[131] By the Easter weekend, he had passed to a grateful and unquestioning von Boetticher the judgment that it would require two years of concentrated mobilization for American aviation output to influence events on the Continent. This estimate was entirely consistent with von Boetticher's own assessments on ground forces. This made mid-1941 the time of reckoning for German strategy.

As the attaché's office forged its own assessments of American preparedness, Hitler continued with his program. With the removal of the independent Czech state from the map of Europe, German troops established a "protectorate" in Prague and directly ruled the country—minus its eastern Slovakian provinces—for the next six years. The führer then turned his attention to the Poles. As the next European crisis simmered, Riedel, with von Boetticher's willing acquiescence, took a six-week tour of the American west, a circuit divided between gliding adventures and exhibitions[132] and real work looking into American aircraft factories located in California and Washington. By the end of his travels in July, he had inspected, usually by invitation and with the War Department's express permission, the plants belonging to the larger American producers: Douglas Aircraft, Consolidated, Lockheed, Vultee, Ryan, and North American. Only the massive Boeing works in Seattle failed to answer his polite request for a visit. This he later reported as an oversight, and with his established system and published reports in local newspapers, he could easily estimate the limited production there of the newest heavy bomber in the American inventory, the B–17 Flying Fortress. Wherever he went, he confirmed the lack of serial production either for the American Army Air Forces or for British and French forces. After visiting other plants in Wichita, Kansas, and St. Louis, Missouri, he could say that "there was not the slightest indication of preparing for war."[133]

Threats proliferated in Europe through the summer of 1939 as Hitler raised his demands for the settlement of the question of Danzig and the Polish Corridor. Geared to these events, Roosevelt attempted some halting but, as it turned out, ineffective steps to prepare for a coordinated wartime economy. On July 5, 1939, he subordinated the Army-Navy Munitions Board directly to himself, a move that indicated his concern over armaments, but affected an agency involved in too much technical detail to warrant such direct presidential supervision.[134] It further disjointed the planning process for mobilization by changing the relationship of the board with the civilian secretaries in the War Department. With the 1939 version of the Industrial Mobilization Plan complete, Louis Johnson pressed his latest request for a board of distinguished civilian business overseers to the War Department's current procurement and future plans, a panel that would evolve, in his own scheme of things, into the civilian superagency contemplated in the war planning. Roosevelt acceded to this on August 5, 1939, creating the War Resources Board, and setting off another storm from defenders of isolation and neutrality, who saw it as a step toward war. The board never functioned as envisaged, met with the president only once, and was still wrestling with its organizational charter as war engulfed eastern Europe.[135]

With documentation on his reaction to those eventualities lacking, it is unknown whether von Boetticher viewed them with any alarm. Concentrating on the logistical elements that are the limiting factors to any strategy, he generalized only in passing on the shift in American strategic thinking from a passive to an active defense and definite planning for acquiring bases in Latin America after January 1939. In 1939, the army's contingency planning reflected the new realities, and the individual color-coded plans outlining war strategies against single foreign powers coalesced into the RAINBOW plans that presumed that war would more likely involve hostilities by a coalition of allies against a coalition Axis.[136] Evidence of this showed up already in 1938 in von Boetticher's reports as intermittent comment on American policy for defending only the hemisphere.[137] The existence of a Standing Liaison Committee, convened first on January 10, 1938, to coordinate Navy, Army, and State Department policy and strategy received no extended analysis; the committee appears in no extant report. Even when he decided that the United States was assuming that it might have to fight a two-front war, von Boetticher divined from maneuvers he attended that American strategy would be defensive, the army thwarting any foreign thrust against the East Coast, while the Navy fought off any aggressor threatening the West and Hawaii.[138] The demands of an active, as opposed to a passive, defense themselves were barely consistent with the mood of the country. If American faith in isolation and neutrality began its slow decline by late summer 1939, the majority would also not stomach any more than a commitment to defending the hemisphere. Neutrality in the event of a European war was still a fond hope, and for one of the last great influences on von Boetticher, it was a positive necessity.

Lt. Col. Truman Smith returned from his three and a half years in Berlin a sick man in April 1939. Diabetes threatened to end his career at this point, but the direct intervention of the deputy chief of staff, Brig. Gen. George C. Marshall, banished the possibility of a disability retirement.[139] Smith had served well, even brilliantly, in Berlin, but his work there was often an uphill struggle. Functioning under the ineffectual Ambassador William E. Dodd, a University of Chicago history professor and Jeffersonian purist who thought he was at the post "as a living sermon on democracy,"[140] had been a trial that Smith was hard put to conceal.[141] He had turned in penetrating evaluations of German military expansion but, as did von Boetticher in Washington, sought help on the rapid evolution of German aviation. His highly astute and assertive wife, Katherine, remarked on a news article from Paris describing the visit by Charles Lindbergh to a French aircraft factory in May 1936. Smith seized the opportunity to engineer an invitation to Lindbergh from the German government to examine German aviation progress under the Nazi regime.[142] During six separate visits to Germany from July 1936 to January 1939, Lindbergh immeasurably improved American attaché reporting from Berlin by his direct observations and by training Smith's staff to evaluate new aircraft designs and to estimate productive capacities of factories in detail. That Smith could summon Lindbergh in this way also raised his stock considerably with the Germans.[143] But during the third of these trips, Gen. Hermann Goering, procreator of the burgeoning German Luftwaffe, surprised the unsuspecting American hero with a presentation of the Service Cross of the German Eagle with Star on October 19, 1938. Though the honorific seemed hardly noteworthy to Lindbergh then, his enemies turned it into a symbol of the flier's presumed Nazi sympathies, consistent with his "polite" anti-Semitism and later isolationist, "America First" stance.[144] Smith, who became an intimate friend of the flier, also confirmed in his association with Lindbergh ideas about Germany's unprecedented ability to destroy any major city in Europe and the helplessness of England and France to defend themselves from air attack. These ideas, current in the English and French capitals, still made it essential to avoid war at almost any cost.

Smith further nourished an obsessive enmity for Franklin Roosevelt as well. Because his memoirs do more to conceal than reveal his motivation for this, it is difficult to fathom his reasoning, but he was no pacifist or isolationist from moral conviction. He more likely feared an American involvement in a war between Germany and the European democracies because of the odds against the Atlantic powers. Thus, he too favored isolation or neutrality, a policy that paralleled the German policy of giving the United States no reason for intervention.[145] One popular, if flawed, chronicler of German espionage in this period claimed that Smith became the "spiritus rector" of a crabbed and dangerous anti-Roosevelt cabal of which von Boetticher became a member.[146]

The story was more subtle. Smith returned to work at Marshall's order in the summer of 1939 in the European section of the flaccid War Department Military Intelligence Division, the G–2, then under Brig. Gen. Sherman Miles. Here he was among the leading and most sympathetic contacts for the German attaché in von Boetticher's attempts to channel timely information on German field operations to receptive American authorities. Smith was for von Boetticher the paragon of that reliable cadre of military men who calmly received such news as that of the pact concluded between Nazi Germany and the Soviet Union on August 23. Within G–2 were other officers with whom von Boetticher had associated for years. Col. E. R. Warner McCabe, still at his post in the division, had been von Boetticher's principal War Department contact during his five-month visit in 1922. Smith, however, was unquestionably the bastion against those "political and Jewish forces" von Boetticher always described as seeking "decisive influence over the armed forces, especially over the Army command which is still today the stronghold of all that is best in American life and thinks independently."[147]

Thomsen could still rely on his attaché's views in late August, when he restated the evaluation that American intervention in Europe was very unlikely for a year or more.[148] Not two days after these assurances to Berlin, however, European affairs took a violent turn. American Ambassador William Bullitt awakened the president at ten minutes to three in the morning of September 1, 1939, with a transatlantic call from Paris announcing that German bombs were raining on Polish cities.[149]

German ground forces shortly crossed their eastern frontier. Two days later, Great Britain and France, honoring their guarantees on Polish territorial integrity, made the conflict a general European war.

6

A CONFUSION OF AIMS

WHEN war broke out in Europe, American politics remained a paradox. A stronger groundswell of opinion still favored a sacrosanct neutrality, even if tempered with sympathy for the opponents of Hitler. A second, and growing, movement began to promote the notion of more active aid to the western Allies and the necessity of eventual intervention. President Franklin Roosevelt played to both sides of this phenomenon. In his first public pronouncements, he promised to remain neutral[1] after Britain and France declared war on Germany on September 3.[2] Concurrently with his legally required declaration of American neutrality on September 5, Roosevelt began marshaling forces for the repeal of the arms embargo clauses of earlier neutrality legislation. The president's carefully orchestrated campaign resulted in the revised law of 1939. Though it nodded to isolationist principle by forbidding American ships to enter the war zone, the new enactment also overturned the embargo on arms sales to belligerents in wartime as long as they carried the goods away in their own or hired bottoms. Ambivalent in purpose, the legislation more than vaguely favored the European democracies with their fair-sized merchant fleets and better access to the Atlantic, while German merchant ships were prey to the more numerous British fleet. The American public saw no particular inconsistency in the 300-mile neutrality zone drawn around the American hemisphere in September at the Panama Conference with the attendant notices that the American navy would patrol those seas.[3] Even from these only moderately active American responses to war in Europe, it was clear that Hitler had reached the end of his string of diplomatic successes and was confronting new conditions involving far more complex risks for Germany.[4] One historian remarks that the German attack on Poland was "the great failure of his [Hitler's] statesmanship that was inseparable from the faults of his character." His miscalculation about British and French resolve stemmed not from ideological fanaticism but from his haste to achieve an impregnable German position in Europe by 1943.[5]

German suspicions of the American president's intention to interpret neutrality in wartime one-sidedly and to seek every means to change existing neutrality law filled the exchanges between the Wilhelmstrasse and Thomsen's embassy through the outbreak of the war. In agreeing with the contents of von Boetticher's views on the weaknesses of the American army evident in late August, Thomsen nevertheless predicted a number of conditions affecting American behavior in the event of war. Roosevelt, he argued, considered neutrality despicable and would ruthlessly bring the country to a state of mind ready for intervention when the time came. Again reflecting von Boetticher's opinion, he said that the appearance of an American military force in Europe in less than a year was impossible.[6] Though the Foreign Office in the person of Hans Dieckhoff agreed with Thomsen's analysis, neither could rest assured that they had perceived Roosevelt's inmost thoughts correctly.[7]

One of Hitler's fundamental policies of the moment was to keep the United States neutral so that he could confine the war to European battlefields and waters.[8] Overt anti-American, but especially anti-Roosevelt, propaganda descended to a whisper. On September 3, with the torpedoing of the liner *Athenia* and the loss of twenty-eight American lives, he specifically forbade German submarines to attack American shipping even if it were found in the war zones around the Continent. As time progressed, he increased the stringency of his restrictions on his U-boat crews, though the Roosevelt administration's "measures short of war" gave him ever less reason to observe any restraint at all. Supplementary to the policy of extreme caution toward the United States, Germany later pursued an elusive Japanese connection that would occupy American minds and sap British power in the Far East.[9] Any great achievement in this area lay a year in the future. As the war in Europe began, Japan took a distinctly independent stance toward it.[10] The Rising Sun ignored Hitler's entreaties to move on Singapore.[11]

In Washington, the German diplomatic mission had a quietly active supporting role in this strategy. Once the Senate passed the new neutrality bill on October 24, Thomsen assessed again the mood of the country as fundamentally anti-Nazi.[12] On November 4, when Roosevelt signed the bill into law, German diplomacy in America was "hamstrung and without real initiative."[13] But this circumstance did not prevent Thomsen from raising the level of propaganda activities directed from the embassy. With the war just two months old, he replied to a Foreign Office query as to his propaganda work with an impressive list. The German *Transozean* (TO) news agency was having unexpected if indirect success in getting German viewpoints into American wire service nets; a new German-subsidized English language weekly, *Facts in Review*, had begun publication with 20,000 subscribers; and the German Library of Information in New York had become a "propaganda institute," with German-sponsored material being disseminated through all German consular offices, the German Railway Office, and tourist bureaus throughout the country. He urged Berlin to make the greatest use of American newsmen in the German capital to pass on desired interpretations through the pens of American journalists.[14] Thomsen geared up the German mission and various subordinate offices in the country for the support of the scattered forces favoring isolation. Not the least of his efforts was directed at keeping Franklin Roosevelt from a third term as president.[15] Inexplicably left out of this catalog of his preparations were the activities of Thomsen's military attaché.

Von Boetticher unquestionably performed valiantly to further the ends of the embassy, at least as he interpreted them. In an evident quickening of pace, much of the German military reporting switched to a more rapid cable dispatch in place of the pouch, no doubt at the insistence of military authorities at home. Once again the attaché subordinated his personal feelings to the business at hand, and official reports show none of his obvious concern for his wife and daughter, caught on the high seas aboard a German liner less than a week before war began.[16] To American friends, he presented a sober, objective, and businesslike mien. Douglas Freeman, who visited him at the embassy on September 19, saw a "very un-happy" man.[17] In later statements to American officers, von Boet-ticher found the 40,000 German casualties during the Polish cam-paign unconscionable.[18] Yet, at the same time, the tone and the mood of his reports remained quietly reassuring to readers in Berlin.

In "propagandizing" the American military echelons closest to him, von Boetticher had another advantage over the chargé d'af-faires. Unlike the diplomat, the attaché had an audience obviously impressed with German military performance, and he could let German successes speak for themselves. As Warsaw fell to German forces on September 27, he repeated his requests for detailed mate-rial to pass on to the American General Staff:

> My visits are all the more welcome since the Allied Powers inform them only from the propaganda standpoint and therefore very inade-quately from the military standpoint and since my previous state-ments have been confirmed by the outcome of the Polish campaign.[19]

All the senior German troop commanders then active in Poland were von Boetticher's contemporaries, and his nearly daily discus-sions with American officers had the appeal that his closeness to those officers could add. Still, he wanted more than the usual com-muniqués intended for German press and radio. The more confi-dential revelations would enhance his own prestige in his cultiva-tion of the influential staff. He expected his words to reach the hostile State Department and even the president himself.[20] In this he was not entirely mistaken, for as Sumner Welles noted later, the Intelligence Division in the War Department prepared continual situation briefings for diplomats in this period, and the G-2 sum-mary conferences in Cordell Hull's offices were daily occurrences in the desperate days of the following spring.[21] With immediate and detailed orientations from home, von Boetticher felt he could effectively help the American staff prevail over the politicians. In late November, when the war in western Europe had settled into desultory air actions and small raiding operations on the ground, he continued to beg the Luftwaffe Operations Staff at home for Leica projection slides of aerial engagements and any other ad-vance material he could hand directly to his contacts.[22] The first of many demands upon the Luftwaffe, this request got him excellent and detailed pictures. He also knew what appealed to Americans. When he received footlockers full of books and magazines more suited to the German temperament than to the American, he made bonfires of the lot in the courtyard behind the embassy.[23] Oddly enough, developments in this reciprocal system had von Boetticher trafficking in some of the same refuse arriving through unexpected channels later in the year.

In the interests of preserving this system once war had overtaken Europe, von Boetticher repeatedly tried to enhance a faltering German cooperation with American officers in Berlin. On September 7, 1939, he learned that Maj. Percy Black, Truman Smith's interim successor in Berlin, would ask the German government to approve the dispatch of an American military field team to study the war firsthand. In lobbying for the acceptance of this idea, von Boetticher cited the American staff's continued relationship of trust with him in spite of English hate propaganda. For the newly appointed American attaché, Col. Bernard Peyton, arriving in Berlin the same day, he recommended "a similar accommodation . . . , as I find here."[24] Von Boetticher's entreaties wrung no concessions from the German High Command for the American officers in Berlin. Peyton received the same treatment as did the other military attachés there, including the Japanese. All of them were first restricted to the territory within fifty miles of the capital, but later, when the German Army had organized things and established tours to show off its accomplishments, foreign attachés could visit the eastern battlefields. Air attachés were an especially suspect group and could not visit installations even within the Berlin suburbs. Peyton reported that the flow of information had declined due to the war, that no technical news was available at all, and that the few remaining valuable German contacts not on field duty had become "absolutely noncommunicative" due to the espionage laws.[25] He later learned that Hitler himself had forbidden attaché visits to the West Wall. The Air Ministry stopped regular briefings for foreign attachés; the War Ministry gave out only trivia.[26] While this seemed to limit the free and informal trade of military information for American attachés in Germany, von Boetticher retained his channels in Washington and was also the beneficiary of other largesse at the hands of Colonel Peyton.

Peyton's office routinely received German promotional literature through Col. Horst von Mellenthin, still chief of the German
Army's Attacheabteilung. The American attaché deemed much of
the material useful despite its propaganda value to Germany. Since
he was shipping wholesale lots of it home under diplomatic auspices, he saw no reason not to include consignments for General
von Boetticher in his own packing cases. The system occasioned no
complaint as long as the boxes went direct from Berlin to the G-2 offices in Washington via German ports, but in April 1940, a furor
arose when Peyton routed one of these huge loads through the
American attaché in Paris, Lt. Col. Sumner Waite. Waite immediately brought it to the attention of Ambassador William Bullitt. An
ardent champion of the European democracies, Bullitt was at that
moment sharing the French government's distress at the lightning
German stroke that had fallen on Denmark and Norway. Despite
his protests, the shipment proceeded to the United States, where
the State Department's Undersecretary Sumner Welles argued so
hard with Army Chief of Staff Gen. George C. Marshall that the War
Department dispatched an officer who returned to Paris with the
entire shipment a month later.[27] War Department apologies offered
suitable contrition for the fact that the material included highly
flammable cellulose nitrate motion picture film, and Peyton eventually received a slap on the wrist for contravening regulations.[28] If
this ended the American transmission of propaganda material to
von Boetticher, the foreclosure of the service did little to limit his
ability to advertise his cause. With the exception of the sound films
delivered, the cargoes usually consisted of the heavy-handed stuff
he discarded summarily. The episode thus serves only as an indication of the degree of cooperation a now one-sided quid-pro-quo
system produced before an active American involvement in the
war. Peyton continued to send such material home despite the State
Department's protest. In September 1940, he was arranging for the
shipment of 500 pounds of it through American agencies in
Lisbon.[29] Even with this sort of help, though, there was already evidence of some limits to von Boetticher's influence on the upper-
most strata of the U.S. Army.

These limits were evident on social and official levels. Albert
Wedemeyer, who had returned from his Kriegsakademie tour in
1938, remembered that it became impolitic to entertain too close a

relationship with the German attaché after his own assignment to the General Staff War Plans Division.[30] Wedemeyer's case might seem special in that he did occupy a sensitive position in a highly secretive planning office, but the von Boetticher family also noticed that other regular social contacts among American officers began slacking off.[31] Even more telling perhaps was the lack of mention of a strong and confidential relationship with the American chief of staff that von Boetticher had always claimed in the past. General Marshall had taken over as acting chief on the departure of the ailing Malin Craig on July 1, 1939. Wedemeyer remembered that Marshall, who met routinely with von Boetticher, if only because the latter was dean of attachés, liked and admired the German officer. Yet, in all of the hundreds of messages he sent to the German staff between September 1939 and December 1941, many dealing with the great influence of the American staff on politics in America and his own influence upon it, von Boetticher only rarely mentioned Marshall by name.

Another incident in late 1939 indicated the tightening ambiance in which German officialdom in the United States was now operating. Peter Riedel's aerial exploits in the country continued to make him new acquaintances, and his soaring activities based at Washington's smaller airports were widely supported by American friends. On November 14, he drove to a garage on Washington's 10th Street, NE, owned by a Father Paul Shulte, billed as "The Flying Priest." Riedel's object was to borrow Shulte's automobile, equipped with a tow hook and trailer, with which to retrieve a glider from a soaring site in central Virginia. While about this legitimate business, Riedel was accosted by a neighbor for reasons uncertain. The police blotter described a Frank Werner, his wife, and a "Mexican lad" as variously involved in a physical altercation that left Riedel with visible bruises on his face and a nasty cut above one eye. The report mentioned that he was temporarily unfit for duty at the embassy. Three days later the German legation was still considering legal action with a city police increasingly disinterested, because there was to be no court appearance for Riedel.[32] The Washington press corps in September had taken special notice of Thomsen's wife, Bébé, in her voluble but transparent utterances of sympathy on the capital's cocktail circuit for the recently vanquished Poles. By the next spring, the Germans were diplomatically and socially isolated in the

American capital.[33] In this atmosphere, Riedel's plight would only have offered more unfavorable news copy, and the case quietly dropped.

The same Brig. Gen. George C. Marshall who met von Boetticher as a matter of formal course was now presiding over plans for the continued reconstruction of the American army and the new strategic planning efforts of the General Staff. While the president began his campaign for the revision of the neutrality act, he also issued an executive order on September 8, 1939, declaring a limited national emergency and authorizing an increase of the American army from 210,000 to 227,000 men and the purchase of $12 million in motor vehicles. Authorized National Guard strengths likewise increased from 200,000 to 235,000 men, and paid drill sessions went from forty-eight to sixty in a year.[34] But the stated raw numbers were illusory. Executive orders could not call men and equipment into being overnight. The active Regular Army only grew from 187,983 officers and men on June 30, 1939, to 200,893 on November 30 of the same year, an expansion of a meager 6 percent.[35] Obsolete equipment still abounded among the ranks, though orders on industry were introducing new material at a growing pace. The authorized 17,000-man increase for the ground forces permitted the General Staff a number of new programs, among them the reorganization of additional infantry divisions along the modern "triangular" lines,[36] but grave errors in developing equipment offset some of the progress in other areas. The Ordnance Department, in one glaring example, continued to push an American near-copy of the German Rheinmetall 37-mm antitank gun in the face of warnings from observers in Europe that the piece was already incapable of penetrating some of the tanks then in use in European armies.[37] The executive order seemed to some to be the point at which American rearmament became a mobilization,[38] but Marshall was still inclined to see the American army as a third-rate force.[39]

None of this changed Friedrich von Boetticher's assessments of American readiness. He knew that the 227,000-man authorization had disappointed the War Department, which had set its sights on a strength of 280,000, the figure mentioned as the minimum emergency strength in the revised divisional organizations. He scarcely analyzed at all the triangular concept that promised to give at least five American regular units the flexibility demanded in blitzkrieg, or maneuver, warfare. The changeover would be gradual, he noted, and no completion date was set. Recruiting for all forces was slow, he decided in October 1939. "The youth is little inclined to war service," was his comment of the moment, and in the absence of an American conscription law, still a year in the future, his remark was quite accurate.[40]

Von Boetticher's statistics on industrial expansion at this time were a broad selection to show the gradual expansion of the nation's production base. He drew no conclusions on the weak, advisory Office of Emergency Management that Roosevelt's executive order had also established on the White House Staff. Developments under the "limited" emergency still proceeded without the organizational elements envisaged in the last Industrial Mobilization Plan, and Roosevelt's ad hoc creations made it less likely that the plan would go into effect in the near future. Bernard Baruch implored the president to begin emplacing the projected managerial machinery for war production. Roosevelt only angered his long-time friend by erecting new interim agencies that would only compete with the ones called for in the grand mobilization plans.[41] Von Boetticher nevertheless found that in mid-September, visitors were barred from certain plants and that heavy orders for tool and die machines, to say nothing of demands for finished warplanes, had come from the French, and, to a much lesser extent, from the British, who were anticipating the repeal of the embargo.[42] The demand for steel alone fired up so many cold ovens that the proportion of total American steel capacity in use rose from 62 percent to 79 percent in a single month.[43] Yet in mid-October, von Boetticher reassured his readers in Berlin that the General Staff had again admitted American weaknesses to him. The procurement of weapons for five new divisions to bring the army to a strength of 280,000 in the future would take at least until the beginning of 1941 at the current pace, and a mobilization of existing forces would still require an industrial lead time of eight or nine months. Some entertained hopes of equipping the five divisions by May 1940; the 8,000 trucks for this could be delivered in the next six months, but even the infamous 37-mm antitank gun was still not in the hands of the troops. Getting 165,000 of the M-1 Garand rifles and 329 modern 12-ton tanks for the Regular Army alone was a process that would run at least into the year 1941 at present rates of delivery.[44]

Even as Roosevelt prepared to sign the Neutrality Law of 1939, von Boetticher reflected the uncertainty and the great secrecy surrounding deliveries on actual orders coming from England and France. By November 3, he reported that a six- to eight-month expansion program would produce a marked increase in output, but that already the combined orders of the U.S. Army Air Forces and the Allies exceeded the capacity of American industry at that moment. "A heavy delivery of . . . production to the allies will not enter the scales unless the American armed forces cut back their orders," he wrote. On just this issue, the decision on the priorities for Allied purchases versus the requirements of the American air forces, the bitterest intramural battle of the Woodring-Johnson duel was to be fought over the next few months. After the expiration of the specified lead time, von Boetticher yet cautioned his OKW addressees, "You may expect constantly increasing and very highly rated accomplishments."[45]

As 1939 drew to a close, von Boetticher took some pride in the fact that his educated estimates of the prewar period had proven accurate in the first three months of the war. On December 1, he ticked off the reasons for his continued belief that America would not intervene in the war in the foreseeable future. There were still not enough American military and air units to make intervention feasible. The American fleet was still tied to the Pacific, and a fear of becoming an opponent of Japan forced even the "warmongers" to wait and see what the situation in the Far East would bring. The United States had no formal alliances with the European Allies and even had begun doubting the validity of the British program of starving Germany economically with a naval blockade. His host country, he reasoned, was coming to an understanding of the limits of its own power. He based his attitudes on the men of the American General Staff, who in their collective professional opinion, stood against involvement and therefore opposed the "sterile politics of hate of the State Department"[46] in its understanding for Germany and its appreciation of German military leadership. Von Boetticher had also reversed completely his former agreement with Hans Dieckhoff in 1938 that the United States would certainly act if England's fate were at stake. He now saw the American buildup as support only for a hemispheric defense policy. As a final proof of his contention, he cited the apparent lack of aircraft orders from the

Allies at the end of the year.[47] Though the French were prepared to buy large stocks, the lackadaisical transmittal of British purchase orders thus far led von Boetticher to the premature conclusion that the repeal of the embargo had not had its desired effect. By the first of 1940, French orders for 2,095 planes had resulted in 617 deliveries, "and British demands for 1,450 machines had netted them 650."[48] The French government was already writing orders for 10,000 planes in November,[49] but von Boetticher was confidently betting that the demand would exceed the American ability to produce planes for the more than year-long grace period he continued to emphasize. In his best judgment, no real American strategic weight would enter the international arena before the late summer of 1940, if then.

Von Boetticher's view also coincided with that of a large number of American officers in Washington headquarters. In his world of interlocking strategic conceptions, von Boetticher had plumbed a central element in the secret series of advance American war plans in train in early 1939. The American series now reached its last variation, RAINBOW 5, approved in mid-1939, which envisaged the dispatch of American armed forces to Europe or to North Africa to defeat Germany or Italy (or both) in concert with French and British military efforts.[50] The most ambitious statement of American strategic intent, the plan required, as did the four earlier versions, the absolute security of the American hemisphere as a precondition to projects further afield. Von Boetticher correctly asserted that these could not be supported for another year and a half. Freely available to the German attaché, open admissions of material weaknesses that prevented such plans from being at all feasible in the near future were common even in military professional digests of the time. One aging hero, Brig. Gen. Henry J. Reilly, wrote somberly that the country could not even resist the type of war that the Germans had mastered and that it was actually possible for a lesser industrial power to overcome a larger one if the latter were ill prepared.[51] Aside from political sentiment, the yawning gulf between American obligations accepted in the strategic plans and the current condition of the American army formed the basis for the opinion among a sizeable proportion of even General Staff officers that the United States should stay clear of war in Europe. Many of von Boetticher's confidants in the War Department G-2, but especially

Truman Smith, shared the outlook Reilly enunciated here. By the fall of 1940, it left many officers in sympathy with the aims of the new and vocal opposition to the Roosevelt administration, the America First Committee.[52] Smith had in fact taken a more active role in resisting the gradual movement toward an interventionist opinion. By late 1939, he had begun publishing articles under the pseudonym *Strategicus*, something the White House inevitably noted with due displeasure. Though these columns appeared in such quasi-official serials as the *Army and Navy Journal,* he also lent his military acumen to the editorial board of *Reader's Digest,* itself a vocal proponent of nonintervention.

Japan fitted into this complicated framework as another counterbalance to American intervention in Europe. Japanese behavior through the course of 1939 aggravated American fears and prompted countermeasures. Thrusting in a new direction, Japan had taken Hainan Island, off China's south coast, and then moved to the Spratly Islands, within easy striking distance of Manila. In July 1939, the United States government unilaterally gave notice of intent to abrogate its long-standing commercial and navigation treaty with Japan by January 1940, a step that made a wide-ranging embargo seem likely. When von Boetticher reviewed American relations with Japan in early October 1939, the Japanese menace had occasioned American action to reinforce Pacific defenses "in deep echelon." With some fanfare, fourteen B-17 bombers went to Manila, and the vanguard of the U.S. Navy battle fleet had stayed at Hawaii instead of returning to the American west coast after its maneuvers in April. Air base construction began at Fairbanks, Alaska. The five new divisions mentioned in the latest news of army expansions would remain on the west coast.[53] Despite tensions over administration initiatives to embargo strategic materials going to Japan through August, the Japanese announced their resolve to stay out of the European conflict on September 3. Von Boetticher reported that the American General Staff was counseling a "sense of understanding" with Japan. He predicted that even a success in American-Japanese contacts over commercial affairs would not permit an American policy against Germany until at least mid-1940.[54] That any success in this direction would be forthcoming was doubtful, for any American inclination to compromise with Japan was low, despite voices in the State Department that were as cautionary as those von Boetticher reported in the General Staff.[55]

In an unexpected occurrence at this point, von Boetticher found himself briefly discussing German-Japanese cooperation with one of the more influential Japanese figures of the period. Hiroshi Oshima left his post as Japanese ambassador in Berlin in early November and traveled home via the United States, where he spent several weeks.[56] Upon Oshima's arrival in Washington, the normally very reserved Japanese attaché in the city organized a private banquet so that Oshima could consult with von Boetticher. Although the two discussed the necessity for cooperation and the importance to Germany of keeping the American fleet in Pacific waters, von Boetticher's report noted that Oshima gave no further details as to how to accomplish this. Of more concern, apparently, were the possibilities of an American naval attack on Japan and of the threat of embargoes against Japan once the commercial treaty expired in January 1940. Beyond this, Oshima made only general remarks about his tours of Polish battlefields and a single sanctioned visit to the West Wall fortifications in Germany.[57] Inconclusive as it was, the Oshima–von Boetticher conversation of November 21, 1939, mirrored well the condition of German-Japanese relations in this interim: approaches and exchanges with little substantive result between two supposed allies.

With the outbreak of war in Europe, von Boetticher focused on the host of strategic and moral factors that would govern eventual German success. Chief among these were conditions affecting the American ability to deliver munitions, but especially aircraft, to the Allies, and a concurrent propaganda campaign that the attaché repeatedly sought to counterbalance with his personal ministrations to his contacts among the General Staff. It is also through his performance from this time forward that he is critically represented in historical literature.

By this point, it is certain that von Boetticher had some effect on Hitler's war plans. With the outbreak of war, the attaché's cabled reports were proceeding not only to the German Army staff offices as before, but also to the OKW and its chief of staff, Gen. Wilhelm Keitel, who laid them, at least in abstracted form, before the führer. It would be extreme to blame the initiation of the hostilities in some measure on von Boetticher's direct advice, but his reports can be seen as influencing timetables in Berlin. While echoing distinctly Nazi phraseology designed to appeal to Hitler and his coterie,[58] von Boetticher seemed captivated by the possibility that Hitler would indeed fulfill German aspirations of the past twenty years, a matter confirmed by men in positions to observe him at the time.[59] Estimates in von Boetticher's reports after September 1939, however, contributed heavily to the conclusions of a major staff study compiled by the OKW Defense Economics Staff (OKW Wehrwirtschaftsstab) under Gen. Georg Thomas by December of that year. The United States would need a year to retool its industry for mobilization, but in another six months thereafter would far outstrip the output of any other countries.[60] His reports are too consistent on this same time element to support the idea of such a radical change in his mood toward a pessimism simplistically depicted in him by one leading German historian.[61] Rather, a detectable buoyancy in his cables arose from the way events tended so strikingly to confirm his earlier analyses. This passes too for the Herculean calm that a General Staff officer was supposed to exhibit in the midst of crisis. Hitler, at this moment, also spoke his praise for von Boetticher's understanding of the American mentality.[62] Still, the expert on the United States within the German Foreign Office at the time, Hans Dieckhoff, continued penning assessments to counter von Boetticher's forecasts: the United States would do everything to circumvent the neutrality acts and send material especially through Canada.[63] Hitler preferred reading his attaché's commentaries instead.[64]

The essence of the situation by the beginning of 1940 still hinged on the answer to the same question Hitler had purportedly put to von Boetticher in February 1939: How soon would the United States provide a measure of support to England and France that would forestall a decisive German stroke in Europe? Even if American output began to portend a shift in the balance for the two western European allies, the necessity under the Neutrality Law of 1939 for paying cash for munitions forced England and France to husband their dwindling liquid reserves. Only fifteen months later, with France already occupied, did Lend Lease relax for embattled Britain the financial requirements for the delivery of war goods.[65]

If von Boetticher never assayed the financial problems involved in Allied orders, he fully appreciated the dilemma of American policy. The captains of industry and some military planners regarded the larger overseas bids as a welcome substitute for the minimal educational orders subsidized by American government funds. The American General Staff found, however, that they also cut heavily into attempts to build the 5,500-plane air force for the army and run a coherent ground-force buildup. Roosevelt after January 1940 pushed deliveries to the Allies of the latest types of aircraft, regardless of the sensitive new equipment they carried, and he wanted spare engines in quantity to accompany them. The president and Treasury Secretary Morgenthau ran into such heavy resistance from Woodring, Johnson, and General Arnold, chief of the Army Air Corps, that on March 12, Roosevelt swore that he would tolerate no more leaks to the isolationist press on the subject from this trio. He threatened Arnold with extended duty on the island of Guam if he did not change his attitude.[66]

Von Boetticher easily took the measure of contradictions in the program of aircraft production for American forces and for the Allied powers in Europe. Basing his reports on Riedel's exhaustive research, he leveled his own often sardonic conclusions. He portrayed the acrimony among senior American officials over the division of production. There were no immediately usable reserves of aircraft, he reported on March 20, and the country could not at the moment equip squadrons meant to defend Alaska, Puerto Rico, and the Panama Canal. Any deliveries to France and England would correspondingly diminish American rearmament. In light of these realities, he scoffed at British claims he found current in the American press that German aerial supremacy would be overcome in mid-1940 with American help.[67] By early April, he was discounting Louis Johnson's predictions in military appropriations hearings before Congress that the United States would produce at year's end as many as 3,300 planes a month, an annual production of 40,000. Secretary of War Woodring, on the other hand, named a more realistic total of 2,200 aircraft expected in American inventories by early 1941. The expansion of a balanced air force was one of three concerns that the latter had written into his annual report to the president for 1939. His program for the entire army, laid before Congress in the spring of 1940, asked for $835 million, about half the $1.5 billion his military chiefs had requested for the fiscal year from July 1940 to June 1941. Under the complacency that had set in once the war had settled into what looked like a standoff, the House cut the figure in the first week in April to $735 million.[68] Armed with this information, von Boetticher, though admitting the likelihood of a 30 percent increase in aircraft production by the end of 1940, could nevertheless label Johnson's testimony pure propaganda.[69] By now he could also approximate the maximum help to the Allies from American sources as 1,250 bombers from a production of 2,150 and 900 fighter aircraft from a total of 2,000 constructed in the current year. As of January and February, as Riedel could ascertain from open sources, the European allies had received only 242 bombers and 12 trainers, but no fighters. Von Boetticher wanted this obviously critical revelation kept out of the German news organs. "Jewish propaganda" in America would use any German exposures of this sort as a spur to the domestic competitive spirit in the aircraft industry and contribute to rapid settlement of thorny price negotiations then in progress.[70] A mere six days after he dispatched this, von Boetticher received news that demonstrated for him the continued superiority of German armed forces.

On April 9, on the pretext of protecting Scandinavian neutrality,[71] Germany secured its northern flank in preparation for operations in western Europe by occupying Denmark and Norway in Operation *Weserübung*, an undertaking of some three weeks.[72] The effect of these events was equally profound for von Boetticher and his audience among the General Staff in Washington. His conference with American officers on the Tuesday morning of the invasion yielded

a notably insightful and basic evaluation which follows the German viewpoint.

They spoke especially with great understanding of the necessity for Germany to insure a continued import of ore. England will be heavily struck by the cut-off of wood and ore. Again the warmest admiration for the accomplishments of the German Wehrmacht. . . . Generally there was little sympathy for England. Very coolly they weighed the way in which the war situation changed in favor of Germany and what chances now exist for a decisive stroke against the British Isles themselves. In the American General Staff, no preparations for the purpose of helping England have been entered into.[73]

American military policy still centers on hemispheric defense, and he could change nothing in his earlier reports, declared the attaché.

By the opening of *Weserübung*, the German staff was also convinced of the value of informing the American military fully and freely of German successes, precisely to defuse the possibility that British misstatements would gain credence among American officers. Not only descriptions of Luftwaffe operations in detail came to von Boetticher, but now the most elementary maneuvers of the German forces in Norway filled the cables to Washington. During the campaign, Gen. Franz Halder, German chief of staff, specifically ordered the German attaché section in Berlin to give top priority to notifying von Boetticher even of such minor tactical events as the fall of individual villages and towns.[74]

The interpretive consistency of von Boetticher's reports persisted into the next phase of the war, in which the Wehrmacht knifed through the Netherlands and Belgium, smashing the French Army and the British Expeditionary Force in six weeks. Suddenly all the assumptions of even the moderate isolationist position in the United States fell in shambles.

> The Maginot Line, which had been basic to the argument that this war could not be fought out to a decision, was swept away and became no more germane than the Macedonian phalanx. The war was going to a decision, and it was going with unbelievable speed and the decision looked as if it would be one we could not live with.[75]

On the morrow of the German assault into Holland, von Boetticher learned from the responsible commanders of the army and navy who advise the State Department and the President that "an early entry into the war by the United States . . . can be ruled out as long as the western hemisphere is not directly threatened," confirming for him again that England's fate was secondary; American statements on England were merely slogans to affect policy. Conceding that his American advisors feared a "substantial deterioration in the general attitude toward Germany," he nevertheless cited the American assumption of England's imminent downfall.[76] When Franklin Roosevelt stood before Congress on May 16 to ask for $1 billion in

military appropriations for equipment and an aircraft program producing 50,000 machines a year, von Boetticher dispatched two cables
in which he reduced all of the president's words to propaganda. The
facts had not changed, and the May 16 address did nothing to alter
his opinion. Americans were even then admitting to themselves that
they could not hope to intervene anywhere overseas until mid-1941,
and any American adventures in Europe would be held in check by
Japan.[77] Any expansion of the air industry on the scale Roosevelt proposed would entail employing five times as many skilled technical
workers as it now had and a tenfold increase in the number of aviators and ground maintenance crews in the army and the navy.[78] This
assessment, too, came from Riedel's by now intimate knowledge of
factory capacity in the American aviation industry.

In the roughly two months between the capture of Denmark
and Norway and the collapse of all French resistance in June 1940,
the continuing themes in von Boetticher's reporting became all the
more sharply defined. His impressive knowledge of the American
army enabled him to recount repeatedly and accurately the incon-
sistencies of the burgeoning rearmament program and the period
required for its realization. On the other hand, his reliance on the
vague circle of friends, many of Anglophobic conviction, in the War
Department was the last vestige of the missionary persuasion that
he had carried with him to the United States. That he took whole
the private political opinion of the members of this group along
with their aptly realistic professional and technical evaluations in-
fused his cables with a prophetic reality on technical subjects but a
narrow political myopia. He believed that their viewpoint would
be the one the American government would perforce adopt in the
face of German faits accomplis in Europe. As the German campaign
in France continued its breathtaking course, von Boetticher's "military-political" summations exuded the confidence that Roosevelt
would not drag his country into the war even if the Anglo-French
coalition could not stop Germany: "In coming decisions, the representatives of the General Staff will influence the President toward
an independent attitude toward the Allies, as long as they think
that Germany has no plans up her sleeve against the United
States."[79]

His caveat about plan-filled sleeves addressed the sensitivity
about another problem of moment in German diplomacy in Amer-

ica: the Abwehr and its agents in the country. For his adamant refusal to countenance their presence in the United States, von Boetticher had already received a telegram on March 15, 1940, accusing
him of failing to further Reich interests at his post. Struck to the
quick, he sent back a handwritten letter to General Halder begging
the chief of staff's intercession and protesting the slur on his performance.[80] He followed this with a series of warnings against subversive activities.[81] Now, in another synopsis, he seconded Thomsen's urgent pleas for restraint upon the latter's discovery of one of
these shadowy creatures in New York, who supposedly worked
under a Maj. Ulrich von der Osten, one of Abwehr's five main spy-
masters in the United States. The man was turning to the embassy
for funds and claimed to have a network of subagents and to have
sunk a steamship in Baltimore harbor.[82] While the Abwehr played
innocent with Foreign Office officials at home,[83] von Boetticher
added his voice to Thomsen's. The balance of opinion in Germany's
favor among the General Staff was delicate enough that this sort of
behavior would destroy everything he had been able to rebuild
since the American Congress had begun investigations into German espionage in 1938, he wrote. Even American news media asserted that these German efforts damaged German interests in
America more than American property. Citing the long list of German technicians that had visited secret American arms and aircraft
factories through his intervention since 1934, he argued that this
was possible only through his frank and aboveboard personal contacts, not through subterfuge. Trust had returned only through his
efforts:

> I personally warned about this during my visits in Germany in 1936
> and 1937 and am doing so again. The Jews and Freemasons [sic] who
> used the trial of 1938 against Germany are again at work to create a
> rift, and with that to play as a tool for the re-election of Roosevelt and
> for the destruction of the influence of Americans valuable to us.[84]

These valuable Americans now included not only his contacts on
the General Staff, but new names. Alford J. Williams, an ex–Marine
Corps pilot who wrote aviation columns for the Scripps-Howard
newspaper chain, came to von Boetticher's attention for his frank-
ness on British and American weaknesses. Baldwin hammered

against foreign propaganda on a lack of German oil reserves, and last, Charles Lindbergh had emerged since the past September as a magnetic orator[85] who had destroyed the administration's position on the German threat to the Americas. Even slight agent activities, when revealed, would "dash from out of the hands" the moral weapons these men held."[86] More than that, they would cripple von Boetticher's influence with the American army, which, because of the Wehrmacht's victories in Europe, had grown accordingly: "It is just as if a fresh wind of German spirit has blown over from the battlefields of northern France and Belgium to America."[87]

In attempting to preserve their own room for maneuver and a sense of confidence in their contacts, Thomsen and von Boetticher were at one in demanding a halt to Abwehr activities within their own preserve, but the "fresh wind" of von Boetticher's imagery blew through a notable rift between the interpretive positions of the two men on other matters. The strong, tonic impression made by German victories on American professional soldiers had a reverse effect in the State Department, and Thomsen's statements there drew anything but warmth. On April 10, Thomsen took a view of the effect of the German operations in Scandinavia that was the exact opposite of von Boetticher's. Roosevelt's chances for re-election were thereby heightened, and the isolationists would "see part of their argument shattered."[88] The German Foreign Office, corroborating Thomsen's reports with news from other sources, accepted the chargé's version of the situation in America. State Secretary Ernst von Weizsäcker sent a testy, "eyes-only" cable to Thomsen directing him to ensure that attaché reports touching on political affairs were thoroughly coordinated with the chargé d'affaires.[89]

Thomsen's somewhat plaintive response to this on April 24 shows how delicate his position was. Protesting that he had only harmonious relations with von Boetticher, Thomsen admitted to differences of opinion that were heightened by the attaché's "extraordinarily sensitive personality." Von Boetticher was inclined to evaluate highly his sources and their effect on the formation of American policy, and although he accurately reflected the mood of the General Staff, he ignored more decisive factors in American politics. Thomsen explained to von Weizsäcker that he attempted to counterbalance this in his own reports. His lesser rank became a limitation in this, insisted Thomsen; were he von Boetticher's equal, he would risk a conflict. The general regarded his position as greatly increased since the war broke out, Thomsen said, and Hitler indirectly sustained von Boetticher in this by sending a personal congratulatory telegram to mark the general's fortieth year in the army. Despite this, Thomsen also acknowledged that the attaché upheld him in everything, including embassy routine. He retained relations with American soldiers "as excellent as one can possibly imagine," which was "a political asset whose significance is not to be underestimated."[90] Five years later, amid the wreckage of the Reich, other Foreign Office members would be far more critical of von Boetticher.

Despite Thomsen's apt criticism of von Boetticher's fixation with the influence of American military officers, the logistical and technical aspects of the attaché's opinion were overwhelmingly borne out by the summer of 1940. The thought no doubt sustained him as it did Adolf Hitler on June 22 after receiving the French surrender that the war had been won before American intervention was feasible. The Russo-German alliance still intact, Germany was supreme on the Continent, and England stood alone, albeit with the minor triumph of the evacuation of Dunkirk behind it. With little hope of American help before the year was out, the British could either accept a peace bid or continue a suicidal battle for survival. Roosevelt was already gravely worried over the fate not only of the British people, but also of the British fleet, now that the French Navy was under German control at Toulon. The president despaired briefly at the possibility that the German Luftwaffe would hold the British civilian population hostage to demand the return of any ships that took refuge in British dominions around the world or in American harbors.[91]

Von Boetticher in these circumstances countered each development in the United States that would give hope for England with hard strategic and logistical truths. Congressional reaction to Roosevelt's speech of May 16 produced $500 million more than the president had asked for, and supplementary appropriations at the end of June had raised the total of regular and special funds in 1941 to nearly $3 million.[92] Von Boetticher applied his practiced eye to the possibilities ahead and changed nothing in his estimates. The army's projected expansion to 280,000 men was an old plan, he remarked on June 1, and the million-man host rumored in the press could not arise until mid-1941. Aircraft production would create

3,609 front-line craft and 4,310 trainers by the end of 1940. Most significant was his examination of the large-scale shortages in machine tools and skilled men to operate them that became apparent at this time. No amount of sudden defense appropriations could produce trained mechanics overnight. Yet, he warned, even with Roosevelt's "laughable and misleading" talk of an attack on the hemisphere, the majority of the nation was now behind the president's armament plans.[93] Aid for the Allies at this point confined itself to shipments of World War I British Lee-Enfield rifles from American arsenals and French 75-mm field guns scheduled for the French Army.[94] Despite a "hysterical willingness" to help, von Boetticher wrote on June 9, "they see that they can vote money in a few minutes, but can create weapons and arms only in months and years."[95] And on June 13, after reviewing again a catalog of material promised to the fighting fronts in Europe, von Boetticher relayed the news that even in the American War Department it was common knowledge that French officers were talking about a just peace. The Americans could make no decisive contribution to the war in 1940; their arms program would bear fruit only in the first half of 1941. With a certain finality, he added: "Miracles cannot happen."[96]

There were still, at this point, ominous signs that the United States, for the existence of an increasingly vocal isolationist faction, was ready to gird for war, and that the political will of the country was considerably more cosmopolitan in the summer of 1940. The Republican Party's national convention in late June chose an internationally minded candidate for the presidency in Wendell Willkie, enabling the Roosevelt administration to continue subtly pushing for aid to England without fear that it would become the decisive issue of the fall campaign.[97] In England, the new prime minister since May 10, Winston Churchill, refused even to make plans to evacuate the British government and, on June 8, spoke movingly of fighting on the beaches, in fields, and in streets to defend his "beloved Island." Roosevelt courted political suicide in the minds of some of his advisors by replying in similar vein on June 10 at Charlottesville, Virginia, when he castigated the stab in the back Mussolini delivered to the already defeated French nation two days earlier by declaring war against France. He further acted to speed the delivery from American sources of a half million Lee-Enfields, 800,000 machine guns, 130 million cartridges, 900 75-mm guns, over a million shells, bombs, and powder, all rushed to defensive positions when they reached England later in the summer and fall.[98]

More to von Boetticher's alarm was Roosevelt's dismissal of Harry Woodring on June 20 and the succession to the post of Secretary of War of Henry L. Stimson, a lifelong Republican, but a man of pronounced international outlook and sympathy for England.[99] Roosevelt at the same time installed a man of similar outlook, Frank Knox, at the Navy Department. After Stimson's confirmation hearings ended in late July, von Boetticher resigned himself to the fact that

> the Jewish element now controls key positions in the American armed forces, . . . having in the last weeks filled the posts of Secretary of War, Assistant Secretary of War, and Secretary of the Navy with subservient individuals and attached a leading and very influential Jew, "Colonel" Julius Ochs Adler, as secretary to the Secretary of War.[100]

The general purge of isolationists from the Roosevelt cabinet in June 1940 nearly caught up Truman Smith as well. Smith had remained close to Lindbergh and now found that Treasury Secretary Morgenthau was calling for his head.[101] Von Boetticher cryptically reported home on June 11 that Roosevelt, not shrinking from any means to silence his enemies, had succeeded in eliminating an influential friend of Lindbergh from the General Staff.[102] Marshall, protecting the most knowledgeable analyst of German military affairs he had in the G-2, sent Smith out of town for several weeks until the storm blew over. Thus, von Boetticher's chief contact in the War Department went into temporary and troubled exile at Fort Benning, Georgia, where he and his wife stayed in a house owned by the Wedemeyers in an enforced hiding.[103]

All in all, Britain stood on the brink of defeat in those days, and von Boetticher's personal triumph was of nearly full measure.

7

TIME RUNS OUT

IN the last year and a half of General von Boetticher's service in the United States, events increasingly crowded him. The English made their will to resist unmistakable to American officials and the world in early July 1940 when Churchill ordered the capture or destruction of French fleet units at Oran. The exasperated German attaché freely railed at the willful American political minds that seemed to encourage England's fruitless struggle with grandiose promises. He championed the isolationist cause even as German victories made it the more untenable. He perceived subtle shifts in the role England was to play in a self-serving American strategy that sought to prolong the war rather than concede a German victory. Yet, the longer England held on, the closer approached the midpoint of 1941, at which, by his own analysis, American defense production would begin to match the mobilization demands of the army and the navy. The possibility of an American entry would then increase accordingly, and von Boetticher divined Roosevelt's behavior as meant to introduce the will to combat into the American people who otherwise rejected the prospect of American boys in a foreign war.

Von Boetticher's representations to his Berlin readers in early summer 1940 came amid a marked upswing of vocal opinion, some of it hysterical enough even to endanger civil rights in the United States.[1] On a calmer plane was the rapidly successful establishment of more than 600 local chapters of the Committee to Defend America by Aiding the Allies, headed by the editor of the *Emporia Gazette*, William Allen White. Under the committee's loose auspices, a widespread campaign began to complement Roosevelt's careful cultivation of American awareness of the country's peril, and through August 1940, a variety of talent, civilian and uniformed (but mostly naval officers), argued for all possible succor for England. They lobbied especially for the release of fifty overage American destroyers to replace those Britain had already lost to sustain the Royal Navy in antisubmarine warfare and convoy escort duties.[2]

Without analyzing the constituents of this burgeoning popular movement, von Boetticher placed his faith in its opponents, who he insisted would prevail. In the tension of the period, he also hotly defended Charles Lindbergh, whom the attaché unquestionably regarded as the most intelligent and effective spokesman for common sense in America. Lindbergh conceded that he might have met von Boetticher at some formal function in the United States or Germany,[3] but the two never had any more informal contact. Von Boetticher in fact recorded only a brief encounter with Lindbergh as both of them were being introduced to Orville Wright in 1938.[4] The discovery of any close cooperation between them would have confirmed an ill-founded public criticism and private suspicion of Nazi sympathies on Lindbergh's part and identified the attaché publicly as a supporter of American isolationism. For von Boetticher, the moral value of Lindbergh's message lay in his independent reflection of Hitler's policy statements on America contradicting Roosevelt's projection of the German threat. While Hans Thomsen pursued his own audience in 1940 and 1941 with subsidized copies of carefully selected Polish diplomatic and military documents recovered from Warsaw's ruined government quarter, liberal bribes to American politicians, and extensive support for books favoring the isolationist viewpoint, von Boetticher concentrated on his more narrowly defined group for which the hero became in his eyes the purest and best spokesman:

> Persons close to me and in close contact with Lindbergh believe that Lindbergh's influence can be very significant for the future. He will be evaluated as a person of the greatest importance, is independent of the Freemasons and Jews. Therefore the circle around Roosevelt hates and fears him.[5]

Roosevelt's system, von Boetticher decided in mid-July, echoing a "close friend of mine and a mortal enemy of Roosevelt," now consisted in letting other countries, namely England, fight for his cause.[6] The intervention-minded movement had in fact made England the first line of American defense since May.[7] Von Boetticher maintained that the strategy was dictated not out of a concern for American safety, but purely out of Roosevelt's refusal to admit a German triumph. According to him, the president even scorned the will of his own party, expressed in the platform of 1940. His acceptance of the Democratic nomination for a third term, broadcast from the White House,[8] breathed his opposition to a peaceable understanding with Hitler. Von Boetticher found Lindbergh trying to impede this fatal "Jewish control" of American policy and hoping that Wendell Willkie as the Republican candidate could avoid the same bondage that Roosevelt, the "exponent of the Jews," had fallen into. He had been asked to tell his superiors that Mrs. Paul E. Pihl, Willkie's sister and the wife of the American naval attaché in Berlin, had definite pro-German sympathies and could influence her brother.[9]

At the height of the summer, von Boetticher further described the effect of Lindbergh's speech at Soldier Field in Chicago on August 4.[10] He quoted from the talk at length to reaffirm his judgment of Lindbergh's spiritual superiority and purity. Among other things, the speech ridiculed the possibility of the establishment of German air bases on Greenland, but it also struck themes of cooperation with a triumphant Germany that invited attack on him as a fifth columnist. Even the aged General Pershing had swung into the administration's camp, reported von Boetticher, and had advocated the dispatch of the disputed fifty destroyers to England and the adoption of universal military training. On the latter issue, von Boetticher also noted that the old general had spoken for the General Staff, which favored a conscription law, but that the "war-hysterical" element sought to use a large standing army as a means of controlling the people.[11]

Von Boetticher approximated very well the galvanic role that Lindbergh played among the often dispirited isolationists and captured the essence of the Roosevelt campaigns against the flier. Lindbergh frequently bolstered the morale especially of American isolationist legislators in the summer of 1940, before a counterweight to the White Committee to Aid the Allies finally coalesced as the America First Committee in September. His effect with the public was such that Roosevelt began an attempt to appease him with a vague promise of a cabinet-level secretaryship for aviation matters, then followed with genteel reminders that he could lift Lindbergh's reserve colonelcy in the Air Corps. He later harassed his opponent with income tax return audits as well.[12]

None of this dissuaded Lindbergh from regularly contradicting the president's published statements on world affairs. Von Boetticher usually followed with glowing commendations on the flier's "commanding spirit" and his growing influence on the country. His continued and perfervid recommendations of Lindbergh led at last to another of Ernst von Weizsäcker's icy warnings to Thomsen to "see that the precedence of the Embassy is maintained" when the attaché's analysis strayed into political areas.[13]

If the Foreign Office faulted von Boetticher for his frequent zeal, the counterespionage agencies in his host countries could not. He continually begged Berlin to keep his revelations on Lindbergh out of official pronouncements and the German press, a rule that governed Nazi propaganda in any case.[14] In June 1940, he rejected the offer of another assistant to work under him at the German consulate in Mexico City and put off firmly the requests from the German Consul there for him to visit the Mexican capital. No hint of scandal attached to his name to the end of his service. In fact, the informants of the American Federal Bureau of Investigation could report no evidence of wrongdoing by von Boetticher or Robert Witthoeft, the naval attaché. Both were "conducting their affairs above board."[15] But this did not preclude efforts to add whatever weight he could to the isolationist argument in another way.

For a full year, from August 1940 to August 1941, von Boetticher supplied the War Department with detailed reports on German air operations, aircraft strengths, and bomb damage assessments. In the week after August 15, the date of the so-called *Adlerangriff* signaling the opening of the aerial Battle of Britain, cables from the Luftwaffe Operations Staff reached the German attaché in a steady stream. Each of them summarized German aerial operations of one or two days at a time, giving the targeted cities, individual installations hit, and meteorological conditions affecting the operations. Also important from von Boetticher's point of view was the accurate count of German planes lost or damaged and German claims of English planes destroyed. He took the cables to the War Department as he received them, and Truman Smith abstracted them himself, producing a thick file entitled "Digest of Telegrams Sent by the Air Ministry in Berlin to the German Military Attaché in Washington."[16]

The arrangement had a diverse effect. It certainly added to von Boetticher's reputation among American officers. He became so valuable an informant to American intelligence work that the bundles of wall maps and cables he carried in and out of the G–2 offices in the old Munitions Building on Constitution Avenue eventually were exempted from security searches.[17] The material he handed over balanced from the German side the daily war situation dispatches that Churchill furnished the White House through the British Embassy after May 19, 1940.[18] As his cabled dispatches make clear, the German attaché retained his position of confidence with G–2 in partial return for these services, and he received confirmation and elaboration on what he could read about American preparedness in open newspaper sources. The collection gave further bureaucratic weight as well to the G–2, which, though growing rapidly at this time, still had a sour reputation.[19] The exchange also confirmed Truman Smith's value and General Marshall's trust in him.[20]

At the same time, von Boetticher's relayed Luftwaffe cables cast doubt on those reports sent in from two American military attachés in London, especially when they cited estimates of German air strength in the winter of 1940–1941. Of the two men there, Lt. Col. Martin Scanlon, the air attaché, and Col. (later Brig. Gen.) Raymond E. Lee, the senior man at the London Embassy, Lee was by far the more engaging. Urbane, cultured, and handsome, Lee raised morale among his English friends by his jaunty appearances in a straw boater in the streets of London at the height of the blitz. A thorough Anglophile, he had the same privilege and free access to the offices of British intelligence as did von Boetticher in the realm of the American G–2.[21] If British intelligence was inclined to overestimate German air strength after some of Lindbergh's pronouncements on the subject in 1938,[22] the staff of the Military Intelligence Division found by comparing Lee's submissions with von Boetticher's that their British counterparts were seriously underestimating German air resources in 1940. Whether senior G–2 officers suspected this as purposeful or not in attempts to influence American official decisions by projecting better odds for Britain is unclear, but Scanlon added his own conviction that "the strength of the German Air

Force has been greatly exaggerated."[23] Through the following spring there was a running exchange between General Miles and Lee. American military attaché reports from Berlin estimated German production at 2,600 planes a month in early 1941, while the London attachés would only admit 1,800. In March 1941, Miles directed Lee to report on what bases the British were making their estimates since Gen. Sir John Slessor, head of R.A.F. Coastal Command, had already allowed that British intelligence on German airpower was little more than guesswork based on the units identified over England. Miles cited his own sources, one of them being von Boetticher, as indicating figures almost double those the British Air Ministry was handing Lee and Scanlon.[24]

Unusual as von Boetticher's trade-off was insofar as its content was ordinarily secret operational material,[25] the arguments it generated showed merit and error on both sides. Lee and Scanlon were obviously accepting at face value British statements on German losses. Yet they also knew that under Lord Beaverbrook's whip cracking, British plants were producing up to 490 aircraft a month by September and showed signs of continued improvement. The Luftwaffe, on the other hand, began the battle with 2,287 aircraft of all types against a Royal Air Force (RAF) of 704 fighters.[26] German production, itself not fully mobilized at this stage of the war, was actually even with British output as the aerial engagements began.[27] The opening skirmishes also revealed some glaring German technological weaknesses. Certainly not the least of the factors operating against the Germans was the ULTRA intelligence system that provided Britain with access to German radio messages passing from higher German headquarters to the field. With this advantage, the British defenders could often divine the Luftwaffe's strategy for the air battle and for the projected but aborted Operation SEA LION, which called for an invasion of the British Isles once the R.A.F. was destroyed.[28] The argument over statistics von Boetticher contributed to served his purpose in keeping German strengths before his listeners, but it was a poor reflection of the ebb and flow of the close-run battle. Among German aircraft, the heretofore feared but slow Ju 87 Stuka was easy prey for the RAF and was withdrawn early, to see only intermittent service thereafter over Britain. The standard first-line German fighter, the Bf 109, with a slight edge over the standard British Spitfire in combat, still lacked the range for escorting German bombers to targets in England. British radar developments, the central tactical control of forces, and the ability of British science to deflect German radio beams used to guide Luftwaffe planes at night all reduced the odds against Churchill's famous "few."[29] The comprehensive British radar network also proved a crucial element of the battle, since the relative size and direction of the attacking German waves were evident as they assembled in the air over the French coast. The RAF could hold its forces on the ground, conserving fuel, until the targets were clear, then counterattack with economy and effect. Moreover, any German pilot bailing out of a crippled aircraft over England or surviving a forced landing went into the prisoners' bag, lost to the German war effort,

Von Boetticher, though duly assigning some weight to these observable tactical factors,[30] never ceased to regard Great Britain as a dead man who refused to lie down and act the role. Most of his reporting in the year before the Wehrmacht's attack on the Soviet Union carries the often stated assumption that Britain's downfall was a mere matter of time, time in which it was impossible for American aid to have any effect. His considerable familiarity with American difficulties in industrial mobilization therefore produced in his reports of the time a not necessarily unwarranted predilection to regard the signal events of the year as less than helpful. The famous but decidedly unneutral destroyer deal of September 2, 1940, in which Roosevelt finally, after overcoming nearly insuperable odds and political and naval opposition, traded fifty old destroyers for several British bases in the Western Hemisphere, drew predictions of a Roosevelt dictatorship from chargé d'affaires Thomsen to match the outraged American reaction against the "executive agreement" forged without congressional approval.[31] Though the exchange made the United States the virtual ally of England, von Boetticher confined himself to remarking that it was all in the realm of the official propaganda deluding the American public into thinking that Britain could hold out a long time.[32] Calling attention to the wide divergence between British orders, amounting to over $2 billion in the second half of 1940 alone, and the slow American delivery of the purchases,[33] von Boetticher characterized well the fact that American supply, after the dispatch of the existing stocks of World War I ammunition and the fifty destroyers, was very limited. As one study put it:

> The six months from October to March were spent in marking time, at least as regards any serious expansion of supply from the United States. The six months were spent—as the preceding six months had more or less been spent—in piling programme on programme, with seemingly endless revisions.[34]

By late May 1940, von Boetticher's reports were read at home as being more optimistic on Germany's chances, since most American staff officers observing the incipient French collapse were predicting an imminent British one as well.[35] By September, when Hitler was still considering an optimal date for an invasion of Britain, von Boetticher's reports on the prospects of England's survival added to the führer's deliberations. Altogether, concluded German historian Andreas Hillgruber, von Boetticher, though well informed, failed to integrate his acquired information with political realities, an imbalance that Thomsen could not rectify in Washington.[36]

Through summer and fall 1940, the attaché continued in the same vein on the arrival of the desperately needed supplies. On November 7, von Boetticher further reported that American export to England suffered the lack of cargo vessels to carry it to its destination. British losses, 430,000 tons of shipping the victim of German submarines in the North Atlantic in September and October alone, made shipbuilding the decisive issue of the moment after munitions.[37] On the same day, in fact, Roosevelt was discussing with Lord Lothian, the British ambassador, an American program to build 60 cargo vessels immediately, to recondition 70 older ones, and eventually to construct 300 additional ships to offset German U-boat destruction of British transports. Yet American yards were just beginning to expand; production in 1939 was twenty-nine ships; in 1940, fifty-three bottoms slid down the ways. British orders for ocean transports in 1940 netted five ships that year, with the sixty new ones expected only at the end of 1941. The two yards that the British financed to build the ships did not yet exist.[38] The shipbuilding question further exacerbated the financial drain for England, and testy words passed between Lothian and Roosevelt on the subject.[39]

A series of visits by American officers to London during the blitz lent weight to the administration's faith in Britain's viability in the long term, despite some private misgivings. Among these men was von Boetticher's old friend from Geneva days in 1926, George V. Strong, now a brigadier general and chief of the War Plans Division of the General Staff.[40] A week before the German *Adlertag*, he led a mission to London ostensibly to survey the effects of Luftwaffe bombing.

In reality, the party, which included Navy and Air Corps members, furthered Anglo-American cooperation by discussing the standardization of American and British munitions production and by presaging the full combined staff conversations that took place in Washington the following spring.[41] Von Boetticher had fairly exulted when he learned of Strong's presence in the group: he "has stood close to me for fifteen years and will report independently."[42] When Strong returned to New York on September 19, he destroyed the attaché's faith in him by publicly asserting that the Luftwaffe had made "no serious inroad in the strength of the R.A.F., that the military damage done by air bombardment has been relatively small, and that British claims of German aircraft losses were 'on the conservative side.'"[43]

Appalled at this, von Boetticher could only say that the Strong statement was universally doubted and that his former friend had "behaved and negotiated basically on orders from and as an organ of Roosevelt, his superior."[44] He similarly dismissed the public statements of the next head of a formalized observer mission, Maj. Gen. James E. Chaney, on November 23.[45]

Strong, in fact, had gone far beyond the advertised purpose of the observer mission to London. With no clear authority for doing so, but most probably prompted by the White House, he offered his British counterparts access to U.S. deciphering methods and accomplishments in penetrating Japanese coded message traffic thus far under the cover names MAGIC and PURPLE. His uncertain U.S. Navy fellow observer seconded the proposed exchange, which placed the Japanese JN-25 codes on the table as well. On September 5, Strong cabled the War Department inquiring whether American authorities were ready to exchange "full information on all German, Italian, and Japanese code and cryptographic information. . . ."[46] This initiative marked the beginning of the unlimited sharing of signals data by British and American intelligence operatives and brought American military and naval establishments into the British ULTRA system of interception and decryption of German strategic radio traffic.

Von Boetticher retained his credibility in other small accomplishments in which he was the sole source of information for his hearers. Among the more humanitarian of these was his part in the German High Command's proposal of a Christmas truce in 1940. Though the embassy in Washington was only the recipient of the plan made in Berlin, Thomsen permitted von Boetticher to carry the announcement to the American General Staff. The attaché added a touch of drama to his tidings by dispatching a small white heather tree to Truman Smith's home on the evening of December 24 with a cryptic note to the effect that he had important news. At the same time, he and Thomsen composed the gist of a radio announcement, which went to a local station and was broadcast on Christmas Day.[47] Perhaps of only slightly more lasting effect was the advantage that the attaché and the embassy euchred from the sudden appearance in the United States of a flamboyant German hero of the moment.

Luftwaffe Oberleutnant (Sr. Lieut.) Franz von Werra was one of the knights of the air whose exploits made the battle of Britain such a gripping contest. On September 5, three weeks into the Luftwaffe's full-scale attempt to force a British defeat solely from the air, he rode a crippled Messerschmitt Bf 109 fighter to a belly landing on English soil. The yeomen of the Home Guard ushered him off to interrogation and captivity, but he would not be held. After two colorful escapades that came close to his getaway, the British shipped von Werra off to internment in Canada, where he could be battened down for good.[48] On a slowly moving train carrying more than 200 captive German airmen from Nova Scotia to the Canadian west, von Werra prized open a frozen double-paned rail car window and dove out head first into a subzero night. Hitchhiking south by dead reckoning, he reached the St. Lawrence River. A stolen rowboat got him across the current to Ogdensburg, New York, in late January 1941. Only days later in New York, he was an instant celebrity.

The subject of German prisoners in Canada had already entered von Boetticher's cables even as von Werra made his break.[49] In his

case, embassy officials were immediately concerned with controlling the flow of military information and wildly ebullient war stories von Werra gave out in press conferences as they were with preventing the United States from extraditing or deporting the man.
Once he was safely in the home of a German vice consul in New
York, von Werra's statements were momentarily more guarded, but
he remained a press sensation and much in demand in New York
City's society. Hitler awarded him the Knight's Cross, Nazi Germany's highest decoration for combat valor, while the pilot was in
the city, the announcement of which occasioned a victory party for
him.[50] Von Boetticher shuttled this hero to Washington several
times to meet leading American General Staff members and army
fliers "in order to present them a living impression of a German flying hero, but caution him on what to say beforehand."[51] At von
Boetticher's request, von Werra also wrote a preliminary report on
British interrogation techniques that proved to be of value to the
Luftwaffe.[52] The attaché sent the entire reminiscence home in the
pouch, and the Luftwaffe used it to tighten up security among its
aircrews and inform them on what to expect if they were captured.
     What looked here like a relatively low-level German intelli-
gence coup was actually more of a trial for von Boetticher. If his reports on the matter showed him the efficient intelligence operative
he had been in the early 1920s, he still found the extrovertive fighter
pilot a cross to bear. While the attaché sought to dampen the enthusiastic von Werra, who continued to feed the American press vastly
exaggerated versions of his Canadian escape, the flier clearly happened on a much more kindred soul in Peter Riedel. Riedel found
an instant resonance with his fellow airman and a common reaction
against von Boetticher's caution in handling the case. Rather than
stay under tight control in Washington, von Werra preferred the
lights of New York; the carefree life and the proffers of marriage
from smitten women there were more to his liking than the con-
straints of his nominal superior officer in the American capital.
Completely oblivious to the legal and diplomatic procedures involved, the holder of the Knight's Cross now made peremptory demands on Thomsen and von Boetticher to arrange his direct and
immediate return to Germany. As U.S. government officials began
moving to extradite von Werra to Canada, Riedel quietly advised
his colleague on his last "escape." The air attaché sent von Werra

back to New York to collect as much as $2,000 from his newfound admirers there and to arrange with them for an airline flight under a false name to El Paso, Texas. Riedel warned the brash pilot against attracting attention with any overt behavior, but to pay for a hotel room in El Paso, then simply join the throngs of tourists crossing the bridge without visas to Juarez, in Mexico. This done, von Werra had only to get to the German legation in Mexico City. Aboard a southbound train, a uniformed Mexican unexpectedly thrust his head into the pilot's private compartment to demand a passport; von Werra instead passed the official a crisp American hundred-dollar note and heard no more. On April 18, 1941, he was back in Berlin to a festive welcome, only to be killed on October 25 that year in a flying accident.[53]

Minor though these affairs of the Christmas truce and the von Werra case were as propaganda victories, they gained importance in the context of earlier German triumphs. From his vantage point in the United States, von Boetticher saw far more clearly the limits of American power in its attempts to aid embattled England than he could perceive German failures of the moment. In his postponement of Operation SEA LION—the cross-channel invasion of England—on October 12, Hitler left unsettled the problem of Britain's defeat; he had already decided that the way to a resolution with London lay in the conquest of Moscow. Still, military necessity forced him to maintain the threat of an invasion of England while he made ready for operations eastward, and to prepare for carrying it out after the expected defeat of the Soviet Union. He had further to garrison the coasts of France and Norway and provide for an increased U-boat blockade of England as long as Churchill refused to submit.[54] As it was, Hitler left in place an unsinkable base from which the Allies launched their own invasion of the German-occupied Continent nearly four years later.

The passage of the American Lend Lease Act on March 11, 1941, highly touted as the most generous measure of the period, moved von Boetticher to no reversal of his evaluations either. He reassured his home office that the industrial bottlenecks clearly evident in American industry would preclude its meeting demands for aid to China, the Netherlands Indies, Latin America, and Greece, to say nothing of continuing aid to Britain.[55] Even so basic an item as small-arms ammunition was in such short supply in late 1940 that the American General Staff wrestled with revised troop training schedules to permit at least 60 percent of requirements to be on hand. Yet in February 1941, British purchasing agents placed an order for 900 million rounds with American manufacturers.[56]

Through the massive interventionist-isolationist debate that brewed in December 1940 over the possibility of a Lend-Lease bill, von Boetticher rejected the idea that Roosevelt's famous "garden hose" would put out his neighbor's fire. Referring again to the problems discussed in his cable of December 7, he said:

> The solution of the financial difficulties is without meaning for England's prosecution of the war. What it needs over the next 90 to 120 days is masses of weapons deliveries, aircraft, and ships. These cannot be made in this time period, even if they put all the money in the world to it.[57]

He pictured General Marshall as convinced of the limitations of the American army and capable of only limited sacrifices to aid England.[58] Thomsen, while striving to muddy the American debate where he could by subsidizing isolationist elements and organizing protests,[59] was in complete agreement with his military attaché on the inevitable delay necessary before the goods would be forthcoming. The two drew similar conclusions on the long-term implications of Lend Lease for Britain that have rung strangely true with the passage of time since the war. In late February, von Boetticher, in a lengthy analysis of the effects of the bill whose passage he expected momentarily, summarized the situation. Jewish ideology prevailed to a considerable extent, and Lindbergh feared Roosevelt would use the law to drive the country into war. The legislation relieved the American government of a dependence on the faltering British finance and permitted direct American subsidy of the arms program. He dwelt on the vast expansion of presidential power that the projected measure entailed, explaining that the executive could now dictate the entire economic policy of the United States. With the conditions attaching to Lend Lease and its $7 billion outlay of goods ($1.3 billion from existing army and navy stocks), von Boetticher reflected that Roosevelt could ask in return for "whatever he considered proper in the interest of the United States" in warships, oil, territory, or money.

Thus, the English are at the mercy of the Americans and will be all the more dependent on them the more their financial situation deteriorates and their armaments industry is further destroyed by the German air attacks; and the more in consequence the [task of] supplying goods and of supplying all parts and states of the British Empire, . . . passes over fully to the United States.[60]

In his eyes, Britain had become a "vassal" state to American interest, a characterization in which von Boetticher presaged the long-term fate of England and the conclusions of even British historians about the role of Lend-Lease in the waning of the British imperium.[61] The passage of the bill at first brought no dramatic increase in supply, which still lagged far behind the combined demands of American defense establishments and the embattled British. Deliveries under Lend Lease by the end of 1941 totaled only $173 million of the projected $7 billion, and the first shipments were largely foodstuffs.[62] To all appearances, then, though he insisted still on the expected American industrial performance after mid-1941, von Boetticher was not far wrong when he called Roosevelt's promises of Lend-Lease aid "golden bullets" that could not be fired from field guns or rifles.[63] His characterization of an incipient imperial presidency reflects a theme that appeared more frequently during the American involvement in Southeast Asia more than twenty-five years later.[64]

Lend Lease could not prevent British disaster in the Balkans and the Mediterranean that spring. Reduced to harassing actions on the fringes of Europe, British arms had enjoyed some successes in 1940 in that general region, especially in keeping control of the 2,000-mile sea lifeline between Gibraltar and the naval base of Alexandria, Egypt. Marred only by the fiasco at Dakar in September 1940,[65] the British cause advanced further when the Greeks threw back an Italian invasion of their country in October, the same month that Spanish dictator Francisco Franco deftly sidestepped Hitler's attempts to involve him in German operations, especially in designs on Gibraltar, despite his moral debt to Hitler.[66] On the night of November 11–12, a brilliant British naval foray against the Italian fleet anchorage at Taranto put five Italian capital ships out of action. With Mussolini's humiliation, the British had transformed the Mediterranean balance of forces, and in December, the British

Eighth Army threw Italian forces out of Egypt and back into their Libyan colony. The following month, English and Commonwealth divisions also began a decisive campaign that utterly destroyed the Italian garrison in Ethiopia by mid-May, leaving only holdout towns that surrendered one by one until November 1941.[67]

All this brought a German response in January. German air units operating from Sicily cut the Mediterranean lifeline between Gibraltar and Alexandria, dive bombing and sinking one cruiser and so damaging the armored aircraft carrier *Illustrious* that she spent a year in the United States for repairs.[68] By February, the Eighth Army ran into far more proficient German troops of the Afrika Korps under Generalleutnant Erwin Rommel, whose tactical genius and chivalry wrung praise even from Churchill himself.[69] The prime minister's decision to aid the Greeks in renewed fighting against Italian forces and against the threatened invasion by German troops massing in the docile German satrapies of Rumania, Hungary, and Bulgaria is presented as a principled measure in the elevated prose of his account of the war,[70] but his military commanders saw disaster ahead.[71] The gesture was "morally sublime, but militarily ridiculous."[72] When in late March a military coup in Yugoslavia changed earlier tolerance for German enticements, Hitler launched Operation MARITA on April 6, a campaign that reduced Yugoslavia and Greece to occupied countries and sent British forces reeling out of the Balkans, their last foothold on the Continent. In May, another German move took the island of Crete in a spectacular but costly airborne assault, completing the German mastery of that outpost by June 2.

Von Boetticher drew continued sustenance for his own frame of reference from these events. He wrote off the Italian garrison in East Africa as it became apparent that its plight was hopeless. Through mid-April, when he noted the surrender of 40,000 Italians in the area,[73] there was none of the enthusiasm that marked his summations of news reports on German operations. The Luftwaffe's intervention in the Mediterranean had made a great impression on American military onlookers, and Hanson Baldwin had declared to von Boetticher in January that a new chapter had opened there. The attaché later approvingly reported on the argument in the American press that the Luftwaffe had reversed the usual guarantees that seapower had given to British expeditionary efforts in the past.[74] On March 26, he reported on the dubious British figures of 150,000 troops supposedly sent from Eighth Army rosters to Greece; there were in fact only 58,000, most of whom never got to their defensive positions before German forces struck.[75] Once the rapid German mop-up of the Balkans was over, von Boetticher fairly gloated over the confusion that the stroke produced in British leadership over subsequent German moves. This uncertainty spread to American leaders. Both governments, he testified, feared that Spain would now join the Axis, and that the German Luftwaffe had proved that it could spare forces for war in the Balkans and sustain the nightly raids over southern England as well. The German initiative also endangered American strategy since all appearances pointed to an imminent British collapse, and another wave of alarm arose at the possibility of a German takeover of the strategic post of Dakar from Hitler's Vichy French captives.[76] American intelligence officers, in a verifiable instance behaving as von Boetticher usually portrayed them, issued such loud and long criticisms of Churchill's political meddling in military affairs that Marshall finally ordered them to be silent on the subject.[77]

For all this, von Boetticher could not predict from his post what the Balkan diversion had done to the German schedules for Operation BARBAROSSA. The five-week delay in the opening of the attack on Russia and the inevitable equipment losses in the Balkans boded ill for the German divisions striving to take Moscow later in the year. His reports also reveal his own lack of information on German plans. When the Wehrmacht began massing in Bulgaria, he had only newspaper sources to rely on and begged Berlin for an "orientation."[78] No one informed him either that his dispatch of unit designations and strengths of British troops in Greece was a waste of time and cable traffic. In one of the improbabilities of the campaign, the British and ANZAC troops disembarking at the docks of Pireaus confronted the figure of the German military attaché in Athens, Maj. Christian Clemm von Hohenberg, who stood in full view among their ranks, counting them as they left their ships.[79]

In the first half of 1941, other indications of American resolve to preserve a British bastion became ever more numerous. The first of these, and kept so secret that no inkling of it appeared in the German attaché's reports, was the two-month-long series of staff conversations between American and British military and naval staffs that produced the so-called ABC-1 agreement. The combined American and British staffs met to determine joint methods to defeat Germany and its minions if the United States entered the war; to coordinate the use of Allied forces, and to map strategy, force structures, and command arrangements.[80] Unmistakably directed against Germany as the principal enemy, the conversations enunciated the strategy of defeating Hitler first.[81] The two parties were now in an undeniable de facto military alliance, making it ever less likely that von Boetticher's circle of confidants would bring Roosevelt around to an isolationist viewpoint. More visible cooperation arising from the staff conversations came in the form of U.S. Navy plans to protect convoys on the way to Britain. A logical extension of the Lend-Lease program since the goods were valueless if they did not reach Britain whole, the measures made incidents with German naval units unavoidable, especially after Hitler announced on March 1 that submarines would attack neutral shipping in the war zone he declared to exist around Iceland.[82] American bases extended outward from Newfoundland to Greenland by April. Von Boetticher, on his part, dubiously greeted the navy's reinterpretation of its neutral zone as including the Azores Islands and Iceland as beyond American capabilities and part of the campaign of bluff after the British disaster in the Balkans and the collapse of British control of the Mediterranean.[83] He took Roosevelt's declaration of unlimited emergency on May 27 in the same light. Von Boetticher read the declaration as another admission of American official reservations on the survival of England that were prominent since the past September. Roosevelt, he reiterated, wanted to take the British fleet after England's collapse and sail it against Japan. Once he had reduced that threat, he would return the reinforced American navy to the Atlantic, transferring the main effort there. Preliminary American strategy therefore was to seize the Canary Islands, the Azores, and Dakar to safeguard these outposts beforehand: "The speech shows in what a high degree the initiative lies with Germany and how much America is in the defensive under the uncertainty over coming German measures and the concern for a rapid decision forced by the Axis. In my reporting nothing has changed."[84]

In his misinterpretation of American strategic priorities after the ABC-1 conversations, von Boetticher still fathomed American designs on the Atlantic islands and Dakar. Three days before the un-limited emergency speech, Roosevelt had ordered the preparation of a preemptive army and Marine Corps expedition to take the Azores. Once the urgency of that operation faded with Hitler's assault on the Soviet Union in June, the same 1st Marine Brigade and army elements relieved the British garrison in Iceland in July.[85] Instead of conceding that the Americans had now managed to stymie German naval strategy in the western north Atlantic with a chain extending from Argentia through Greenland to Iceland,[86] von Boetticher returned to the continued difficulties of providing American shipping to support the force already on the island and to transport reinforcements to it if the need arose. With his eye on the consequences of the occupation of Iceland for Britain in the future, he suggested that it was merely a portent of the eventual American control of all prewar British trade routes.[87] As so often in the past, he accurately reflected the state of American readiness of the moment; American army planners had perforce rejected as unfeasible until November or later an expedition to Dakar and the Cape Verdes Islands for the same logistical reasons von Boetticher was citing to support his statements on the slim means of resupply for American forces in Iceland.[88]

Concurrent with the shift of strategic weight in the North Atlantic, von Boetticher's entree into official circles survived intact the sudden American elimination of all German consular offices, the German Library of Information in New York City, the German Tourist and Railway Agencies, and the *Transozean* news agency on June 16.[89] Thomsen's hitherto serviceable propaganda net collapsed at one blow, though he could still subsidize isolationist groups and American legislators. Von Boetticher's importance to him as a source of information and a transmitter of the German viewpoint gained accordingly. By now, though, the world's attention had shifted to the scene of Hitler's newest triumphs in eastern Europe.

A review of the attaché's reports on American reaction to Operation BARBAROSSA reveals that it was for their author another opportunity to kindle the flame of respect for German arms among his American listeners, but other themes recur here. Far removed from the German staff planning for the undertaking, von Boetticher may have known of a general intent to attack Russia, but of the scheduling of the invasion, he knew little in detail. Whispers of the impending German attack were as widespread in the United States as they were in Europe,[90] but von Boetticher scorned the rumors[91] in late April. He further reported on news accounts predicting a German assault to secure wheat and oil supply from Russia as absurd: "as if such things would not permit of an easier and less bloody solution with Russia through treaties."[92] Yet there was no hint of surprise or chagrin in his dispatch of June 22, when the German onslaught against Russia began. The circles close to him were hoping for a rapid and decisive German victory and a simultaneous collapse of the British defenses in the Middle East, he said. No real Lend-Lease help was possible for Russia in the near future, he predicted, since any shipments to Stalin robbed the British pipeline, just starting to flow with goods, and the American army as well.[93] Marshall was grousing two months later, when Lend-Lease aid had already started to Russia and arrogant Russian demands beset him, that the Air Corps had planes grounded because there were no spare parts to repair and maintain them. By October 1941, Roosevelt was prepared to send not only equipment, but "volunteer" officers to accompany shipments of aircraft to ensure that they would operate on the Russian front.[94]

The G–2 argument with General Lee in London flared again. Eleven days after Lee reported a total of 4,420 operational planes in the entire Luftwaffe, Germany flew 3,272 against the Russians, General Miles told Marshall. Since the common wisdom was that the Luftwaffe always kept a 100 percent reserve behind an active front, British estimates were woefully low. With the latter figures coming from "the German attaché here, whose information so far has proved to be absolutely reliable . . . ," Miles deduced that the Germans had on the Russian front alone in June 1941 a force greater than Lee's estimate for the whole Luftwaffe.[95] Proferred in all probability in good faith, the aircraft figures von Boetticher gave were false. Postwar revelations of Luftwaffe records show that the German Air Force operated 2,770 planes on the first day of Operation BARBAROSSA, or 61 percent of the entire Luftwaffe strength.[96] Miles's inclination to believe the higher figures was also consistent with the common sentiment of the moment that Hitler actually would crush his newest victim in a matter of six to eight weeks and the equally widespread opinion that bade Red Russia good riddance.[97] Roosevelt at this point encountered "the strongest opposition since the beginning of the war."[98] The opinion was also strong that once Hitler had dealt with Russia, he would finish Britain once and for all.[99]

While representing these advances for his mission, von Boetticher suffered yet other personal affronts. The first of these, in the weeks after BARBAROSSA began, again involved his assistant attaché for air, Peter Riedel. Finally overcoming his chief's opposition to his connection with an American, Riedel married Helen Klug on June 30, 1941, in Alexandria, Virginia. Von Boetticher in fact staged an elaborate reception for the newlyweds at his home above Georgetown and presented the couple with a large silver plate inscribed with the names of all of Riedel's embassy coworkers as a memento. The guest list included most of the German Embassy staff, several Japanese guests, and many of the Americans he usually listed as close to him, Lt. Col. Truman Smith and Maj. Albert C. Wedemeyer evident among the celebrants.[100]

Setting out on a honeymoon trip through his wife's home town of Terre Haute in Indiana and then west to Arizona, Riedel soon noticed odd traffic patterns behind his vehicle. As he passed through each state along the way, local FBI agents were following him. The resourceful Riedel noted the license plate numbers of each of the shadowing vehicles. He came to enjoy the game once he understood what was happening and actually befriended some of the agents who tracked him to a remote resort ranch in Arizona. Agents from the Colorado regional office were taking their task more seriously. On the way through the state and again on the way back, these G-men harassed the couple and entered into confrontations on the road and in hotel parking lots. Riedel took sudden turns and doubled back on his surprised pursuers. Helen kept a detailed chronology of events,[101] and Riedel cabled the list of license plates and his summary of events to von Boetticher from Tucson on July 9. The attaché immediately lodged an impassioned protest with the State Department, but American officers who tried to intervene for him met adamant rebuffs from Assistant Secretary of State Adolf Berle, who personally ordered the surveillance, as retribution for similar treatment of an American air attaché in Berlin.[102] On the way home, Riedel and his new bride parted company in St. Louis, whence Riedel intended to fly to Washington. In the airport traffic, the FBI team lost the couple, and Riedel, perceiving this, stopped to call the city's FBI office to report his whereabouts and his flight plans to a very nonplussed senior-agent-in-charge.[103] Riedel's processed 8-mm motion picture later continued to embarrass the FBI. Footage of bureau cars and agents trying to avoid showing up in the frames was later intercepted by the FBI, which was screening all the mail headed into the German Embassy.[104]

The second sobering event was the end of von Boetticher's practice of turning over actual telegrams from the Luftwaffe to Smith as of August 18, 1941. Insofar as the exchange benefited both sides so handsomely, it is difficult to surmise the reasons for the halt. Albert C. Wedemeyer, who also knew of the trade-offs, remembered that General Marshall ordered its cessation because it had become impolitic to continue it.[105] On the German side, however, a more overriding reason seems also to have contributed to the demise of the arrangement. A month after the "Digest of Telegrams" at the War Department drew to an abrupt close, the German Foreign Office sent out a circular letter to all military attachés except those in Washington, Santiago de Chile, and Rio de Janeiro warning that a reliable source had confirmed that all American attachés around the world were giving every scrap of information they collected to the British.[106] Because the last of von Boetticher's transmittals contained statistics on German losses in the east as well as those over the English homeland, the intelligence was of untold value to Britain.

Of even more value to Britain in the long run was the fact that the attack on Russia forged the first links in the wartime coalition that eventually defeated Hitler. Churchill's willingness to forget Stalin's late "indifference to our survival" and his forbearance of the Russian demands for an immediate creation of a second front in western Europe were matched by Roosevelt's extension of Lend Lease to the Soviet Union.[107] Von Boetticher viewed askance the mission of Harry Hopkins to Moscow in July. The American staff had completed an evaluation of the Russian campaign based on materials that he had supplied, and the American military did not share Hopkins's enthusiasm for Russia's survival until the following spring. Hopkins, he asserted, had "as little grasp of the Russian reserve situation as the American attaché in Moscow."[108] The United States advanced its first billion dollars (of eleven billion by 1945) to Russia on November 6, which prompted von Boetticher to repeat for the Russian case the judgments that he had made when

Lend Lease became available to Britain in March: loans of billions would change nothing, since the situation did not hinge upon money for the immediate future but upon the delivery of a ready supply of munitions to the front, where they were needed.[109] He placed a similar construction on the Churchill-Roosevelt meeting of August 9–12 at Argentia Bay off Newfoundland that resulted in the Atlantic Charter, a broad statement of purpose in opposing fascism. Despite the president's elaborate measures to screen his journey from the press, it was no secret to von Boetticher, who divined the meaning of the departure of all the military and naval chiefs from Washington on August 7.[110]

As the president and the prime minister issued their communiqué of ideals on the twelfth, von Boetticher contended that no meeting could change power relationships. The occupation of Iceland was a favor to Germany because it further tied American fleet units to the area and drew ships from the American Pacific Fleet and hence away from Japan. The posting of 8,000 men on the island was only sensible if Japan stayed quiescent and if a Russian victory were guaranteed. The same strategic considerations hobbled any further American aspirations and designs on the Atlantic islands. These realities summed up, he said, the "contradictions of the Jewish world view and that of true Americans."[111] Thus, he addressed the unspoken and unanswered question that hung over the Atlantic Conference with its statement of ideals: How soon would America enter the war?[112]

By now the German attaché had also passed another milestone in American military preparedness, one that he himself had erected. In July 1941, the point at which von Boetticher consistently predicted that the American military industrial economy would begin performing prodigies, the U.S. Army had surpassed a strength of 1,400,000 after Roosevelt called the National Guard to the colors and a Selective Service Act passed on September 16, 1940.[113] He applied a very sanguine judgment to the American army's mobilization thus far. The active regular army and the Air Corps would be fully equipped by spring 1942. Only five divisions were then ready, two of those completely equipped with new weapons. The entire army, including the National Guard, would receive modern gear by spring 1943, and special task forces were being prepared for amphibious assaults. A solemn caution followed:

In my reports I have regularly noted the development of American armaments and the armament industry, also their weaknesses. I urgently warn against overestimating the weaknesses and underestimating American efficiency and the American determination to perform. It is easy to draw incorrect conclusions from statements and criticism in the American press. In cases of doubt, I recommend that my evaluation be used as a basis.

As I have done for years, I repeat in particular my report that the American officers' corps of the Army and the Air Corps in general meets high requirements and that the influence of the tradition going back to Washington and Steuben, and thereby to Frederick the Great, supports the structure of the American armed forces. They are . . . giving the greatest attention to the problem of modern warfare.[114]

Von Boetticher was in fact being generous. The American establishment dealing with war production at that moment wrestled not only with the allocation of British orders, the demands of Lend Lease, and the equally contending demands of the army and navy, but also with its own unwieldy structure and the lack of basic strategic assumptions on which to base plans. Since the inception of the War Production Board (WPB) in August 1939 and its successor, the Office of Emergency Management, the high-level civilian agencies Bernard Baruch pressed Roosevelt for followed each other in quick order, but without ever achieving the appointment of a single civilian manager for the whole mobilization. The evolutionary history of the agencies under the executive branch before the American entry into the war is well recorded elsewhere, but it remains to be emphasized that in their proliferation they mirrored the willful confusion of the president's administrative style. Keeping the reins in his own hands, Roosevelt permitted the overlapping civilian agencies to compete with each other in setting priorities but left the actual procurement and contracting powers in the hands of the military and naval services. Initiated on January 7, 1941, the Office of Production Management (OPM) had two co-equal heads, an anomaly the president spent some awkward moments trying to explain.[115] On April 11, 1941, the purely advisory Office of Price Administration and Civilian Supply (OPACS), which was to operate only in the civilian sector, could not in practice stay out of OPM's jurisdiction, though the latter operated strictly in the realm of defense contracts. Another provision on August 28 split OPACS into an advisory Office of Price Administration and a coordinating Supply Priorities and Allocations Board. None of it was lasting, and the whole structure underwent additional hasty metamorphosis when war came to the United States.[116] Von Boetticher's analysis of these organizational changes probably appeared in a subseries of his reports entitled *Rüstung und Wirtschaft*, now lost to the record except for vestiges.[117] In addition, the General Staff itself was showing the strains of merely expanding existing peacetime staff echelons and was in evident need of reorganization, something that only came about in March 1942.[118]

The army after mid-1940 governed procurement operations by the so-called Munitions Program of June 30, 1940. This scheme called for an increasing production capability to support a graduated growth of the army through progressive stages to four million men, and the structures von Boetticher recounted in his cable of July 11, 1941, were the visible and growing result of this program. Still a defensive blueprint in keeping with the early RAINBOW 2 Plan calling only for hemispheric defense, its specifics and its problems were well known to the German attaché since they were duly publicized.[119] Marshall himself had doubts that the strength of 2,800,000 could be exceeded at the industrial capacity then in full use.[120] The passage of the Lend Lease Act and the events in the Balkans, to say nothing of the implications of the ABC-1 talks, led to totally new reappraisals of the strategy, the strength, and the matériel necessary to make war by July 1943 under the new assumptions of the RAINBOW 5 Plan: offensive operations in Europe against Nazi Germany with the probability of war on a second front in the Pacific. Under the hand of Maj. Albert C. Wedemeyer, the whole program took shape as a contingency plan through the summer, finally naming a total of 8,795,658 men and 215 divisions for the army.[121] For von Boetticher, the salient point about this Victory Program was that he was absolutely in the dark about it. His normally talkative contacts breathed not a word of the new plan to him. He had only some vague notice of it and cited it by name after its mention in the press in October and November 1941.[122] He discovered its actual content in December, when an Air Corps captain, unnamed to this day, delivered a copy of the plan to isolationist Senator Burton K. Wheeler, who in turn handed to a *Chicago Tribune* correspondent his handwritten notes summarizing the program. On December 4, the

Tribune, the *New York Daily News,* and the *Washington Times-Herald,* three isolationist papers, ran expository articles under headlines screaming of "F.D.R.'s War Plans." Though Ladislas Farago claims that von Boetticher received a copy of Wheeler's notes as well and transmitted them to Germany by courier, the attaché's analysis of the news articles, the only apparent basis for his discussion of the revelations, gives no indication that he had come into possession of either a copy of the plan or Wheeler's notes.[123] The attaché concluded that the revelation showed that "America is the wirepuller of this war," and is only playing for time. He could not predict, he said, where the offensive of 1943 would come but speculated that it would be where a suitable land front already existed such as in Russia, the Middle East, or Africa. In addition, he warned that Norway and Sweden were also likely candidates for American designs against Germany. The affair might have done the Roosevelt administration permanent damage had not the Japanese attack on Pearl Harbor three days later intervened to halt suddenly the isolationist-interventionist argument.

Von Boetticher's observance of events prior to that attack continued to emphasize the restraint exercised on American strategies by Japan's forward policy in the Pacific. The attaché reports in this period rarely considered developments in Europe without raising the specter of Japan for American military and naval authorities. Emboldened by the lightning German victory in western Europe in spring 1940, Japan moved into the northern half of the Vichy-controlled Indochina with "observers" as a prelude to a later military takeover and less successfully sought concessions on oil in the Netherlands East Indies. Undergirding the Japanese strategy of the moment was the necessity for advancing southward toward the riches of raw materials that Japan did not naturally possess, but that it desperately needed to sustain its aspirations as the center of a so-called Greater East Asia Co-Prosperity Sphere. Countervailing American behavior after mid-1940 shifted from protests against specific violations of American interest to a broader program of restricting Japanese expansion.[124] The unpreparedness of the United States left it only one path in this endeavor, that of diplomacy—diplomacy, in Herbert Feis's phrase, with a "shadowy border on which silhouettes of future American armies and navies were dimly etched."[125]

Through the summer of 1940, when General Marshall actually expected an attack on Oahu to prevent American fleet units from moving to the Atlantic to reinforce England,[126] von Boetticher apparently dropped his consideration of Japan while riveting his attention on the English drama. He barely mentioned that country in cables, with the exception of advising caution on Berlin on July 10, when he noted that the *New York Times* had relayed the content of a speech by the German military attaché in Tokyo, Col. Gerhard Matzky, who had urged the Japanese not to be left out while the European situation gave them a free hand. Although his subsequent cables on the Japanese advantages of the moment showed that he agreed with his brother officer in Tokyo, von Boetticher felt that Matzky's performance forced him into embarrassing explanations in Washington, implying that Matsky needed a muzzle.[127]

From September 1940 to December 1941, he further reflected upon each of the major developments in the Japanese-American descent to war as a positive advantage for the Axis and as further evidence for the weakness of the United States. American strategy, he still thought, was to settle the Pacific Ocean tension by using English ships there. American diplomacy, supporting this, would seek to divorce Japan and Russia and to draw the latter to the United States.[128] Japanese adherence to the Tri-Partite Pact of September 27, 1940, arrived at only after agonizing approaches and designed to scare the United States into isolation, had the opposite effect. It identified Japan as the Asian arm of the Nazi order in Europe and offered American opinion a clearly defined threat on which to focus from that direction.[129] Sterile in the long run, the pact still had a heavy effect on military and naval attitudes in the United States, completely overshadowing the announcement of the total American embargo of scrap iron of the previous day. Von Boetticher regarded it as a German victory and maintained that the wire-pullers could now see that the American General Staff was correct. He outlined the added injury that the embargo would mean for the American economy, especially in strategic raw materials, if Japan shut off its exports of silk and other rare items to the United States. As to threats of American naval measures, he said, "Miracles do not happen. For the time being the American fleet can dare to fight Japan only in cooperation with the strongest English naval forces."[130]

Beginning in January 1941, a hasty series of conferences referred to as ADB conversations, among the American, the British, and the Dutch military commands in the Pacific purported to discuss plans to ensure the preservation of the common interests of the participants, namely the security of sea communications and the defense of Singapore, the massive British naval base on the Malayan peninsula.[131] In the same month that he was reporting on Anglo-American confusion over the Balkan disaster, von Boettticher recorded that news reports of a common strategy uniting Manila, Singapore, and Batavia (Netherlands East Indies) were "foolish, their purpose unrecognizable."[132] At the same time, and in words more somber and specific, the American chief of staff and the chief of naval operations rejected the ADB report in July because it was inconsistent with the earlier unpublicized American-British conversations (ABC-1) in Washington. The elaborate military and naval commands envisaged in the ADB report contradicted the "Germany-first" principle established in ABC-1, and the American staffs questioned much of the strategy designed to hold the British fleet bastion at Singapore.[133] Churchill repeatedly stressed the strategic import of the huge base in his attempts to draw American naval strength to its defense. He nevertheless followed a contradictory policy of advertising Singapore's defense as second only to Britain's, while starving its garrison in favor of British forces in the Middle East and Africa.[134] Britain's survival in the face of a German threat of invasion made these compromises necessary, even in the realization that the English war effort depended on raw materials from the Malayan Peninsula and the East Indies. The atmosphere of complacency and illusion among the garrison was realistically remarked upon in British press at the time.[135] American contributions to the base's defense were virtually nil, its fate implied as American units began a shift to the Atlantic in early 1941. Roosevelt admitted in a letter to Harold Ickes that "it is terribly important for the control of the Atlantic for us to keep peace in the Pacific. I simply have not got enough Navy to go around—and every little episode in the Pacific means fewer ships in the Atlantic."[136]

Von Boetticher perceived this, too. In fact, Singapore became for him something of a false tocsin on which the United States rang warning notes to Japan by planting news stories of large reinforcements there. By September 1941, he was bemusedly speculating that if he added up all the reinforcements supposedly sent to the base, he would surely discover that there would not be enough room for all the men and planes in Singapore.[137] He lost no time in informing the Japanese military attaché in Washington, General Isoda, of these trends and the correct interpretation of the various statements of the Roosevelt administration. He regarded the Japanese military representatives in the city as very unsophisticated in this regard, credulously susceptible to American propaganda and weak in military-political acumen. Captain Riedel had stood by them but despaired of teaching them anything. He asked therefore that his own reliable reports be sent to the German attaché in Tokyo to help inform the Japanese High Command.[138]

Von Boetticher was nothing if not consistent with his earlier positions through the last year of his active work at the embassy. When Japan concluded a neutrality pact with the Soviet Union in Moscow on April 13, 1941, he reported that it had "the effect of a thunderclap"[139] among the military in the United States. With its rear secure from attack by Russia, Japan could pursue its southward movement with some impunity. American policy had failed to capitalize upon earlier Russo-Japanese antagonism, he concluded, and could now only wallow in the self-contradictions. Japanese tactics complemented German ones of the moment in the Balkans. Out of fear of Japan, a large fleet-building program began but was now crowding out the building space necessary for desperately needed freighters for Britain, a situation that limited the idea of an American supremacy at sea, he said. He and the chargé d'affaires were at one, he also reported, in their belief that German victories in Europe, combined with this Japanese coup, would lead, not to "more war-lust in America, but to a strong sobering," since they were not ready for a two-front war despite arms increases. As the named enemies of America, Japan and Germany would not "wait patiently while America decides their fate."[140]

This was again one-sided. If von Boetticher delineated well the effect of the pact on American uniformed officers, he should have been able to assess its similar effect on the German Foreign Office, where it was received with "surprise and annoyance." The Axis alliance partners continued to surprise each other through the rest of the year, the German turn coming next with the opening of BARBAROSSA. The alliance proved otherwise hollow in the wake of the latter development. While Hitler had professed an indifference to Japanese help against the Russians before the attack,[141] it was just over a week old when German Foreign Minister von Ribbentrop's first entreaties to Japan to consider seizing the Russian port of Vladivostok came to the Japanese capital. Japan should then advance west to "meet German troops advancing to the east halfway."[142] On July 2, Japan opted instead for further thrusts south in strength,[143] while attempting to conclude hostilities in China. Japanese forces occupied all of Indochina on July 23, which in turn brought on the final round of negotiations with the United States.

At this Japanese initiative, von Boetticher sought again to detail American weaknesses, predicting only empty threats, possibly economic measures, and asserting that Japan could do anything it pleased in the western Pacific. The incomplete armament and the Pacific threat had paralyzed American freedom of action.[144] He pictured the naval balance of power accurately, but it was the same economic measures that he touched on so lightly that drove Japan to the brink after the United States froze all Japanese assets and embargoed all exports to the international miscreant on July 25. While desperately trying to hold negotiations open to the last, Japan prepared for war.[145] In the opinion of the leading official historian of the first two years of the Pacific war, Louis Morton, the American position stiffened to the point that American military strategy and political objectives in August 1941 were out of phase. RAINBOW 5 called for commitment to Europe and a defensive stance in the Pacific, accepting even the loss of the Philippines if necessary.[146] Von Boetticher's analyses of the contradictions in American policy thus bore more than a modicum of truth.

The conflicting demands of American policy east and west were even more apparent to von Boetticher when German and American naval forces clashed in the Atlantic on September 4. Nine days later, Roosevelt ordered the U.S. Navy to shoot on sight at U-boats found in the neutrality zone and to escort convoys to Britain as far as Iceland.[147] Hitler, on his side, refused adamantly to permit German attacks on American shipping regardless of its location.[148] Von Boetticher discussed without much alarm each of the celebrated incidents in what was now an undeclared sea war, saying that it would only lead to a splitting of the naval forces on hand. The sinking of the destroyer USS *Reuben James* on October 31, with the loss of 115 men, would, he wrote, lead to the siphoning off of more fleet strength from the Pacific, increasing the freedom of action of Japan as long as it did not cut off American raw material supply or endanger American outposts such as the Philippines.[149] The serious naval incidents were the extension of the American shipments of Lend-Lease goods to England and Russia, but the German attaché interpreted the next logical step as actually deleterious for Britain. The decisive reason for the revision of the Neutrality Law of 1939 was to work American will upon England. The fact that American armed forces could now travel by transport ship to England to occupy bases that the Americans had been building in Ulster and Scotland meant that the United States could physically prevent Britain from giving up the ghost and simultaneously form a northern front against Germany.[150]

When the Japanese blow fell on Pearl Harbor on December 7, von Boetticher again looked only to narrow tactical realities of the moment and not to the larger implications of that act. As surprised as the Americans, he barely summarized the damage to navy fleet units, underestimating it at first, before pointing up the dilemma of American war policy with the destruction of the battleships of the Pacific Fleet. Within four days of the German declaration of war on the United States overtaking the German Embassy, he still spoke of the time necessary to complete an American mobilization. With ill-concealed satisfaction, he noticed that all the public announcements on Dakar, the Atlantic islands, and the heroics of the Russian front, where the German Army Group Center was opening its last, but futile, drive for Moscow even at that moment, had ceased. Only one sobering remark entered his last report from Washington and it appears inadvertent; the war would be a long one, he declared, citing Roosevelt's speech of December 9 without enthusiasm: "America must lose a short war with a rapid decision because it cannot produce the necessary weapons without some time."[151]

At eight o'clock in the morning of December 11, Thomsen, intent on delivering a copy of the German declaration of war into the hands of the secretary of state, Cordell Hull, arrived at the State-War-Navy Building. His American equivalent in Berlin, Prentiss Gilbert, had already received the notice from the German Foreign Office. In an awkward scene, Hull, knowing full well what was coming and delaying his arrival for nearly an hour, breezed by the waiting delegates, then directed them one flight up to the office of Ray Atherton, head of the department's European Division. Thomsen and Heribert von Strempel, the German Embassy's first secretary, were left cooling their heels for another half hour outside Atherton's office while the press gathered in the lobby of the building. Once the business of guaranteeing safe passage and exchange for his staff was done, Thomsen and von Strempel descended in the elevator to the ground floor. The doors opened to a barrage of flash bulbs and shouting newsmen.[152] Formal German diplomacy in the United States was at an end for the next decade and a half.

8

YET AGAIN VANQUISHED

EVEN as Hans Thomsen and Heribert von Strempel tarried at the State Department with the German declaration of war against the United States weighing heavy upon them, Olga von Boetticher made ready to retrieve her daughter. With her own foreboding, she boarded a train at Union Station for Lynchburg, Virginia. The implications of the Japanese attack sank in only slowly for her daughter, a young journalism major in her senior year at Randolph-Macon Woman's College. In an account of events written forty years later, Hildegard von Boetticher described her shock at the sudden onslaught.[1] Her thoughts at that point were on nothing so much as her responsibilities as chairman of the Christmas dance committee. Classmates flocked to her once it became clear that she was bound for wartime Germany. While she was still making out where the Hawaiian fleet anchorage was, she answered a summons from the college president, Dr. Theodore Jack. Jack solemnly informed her that the American government was actually offering to allow her to continue her last year of studies. He also told her on this occasion that, with his acquiescence, the Federal Bureau of Investigation (FBI) had had her under almost constant surveillance for some years, and even discreetly oversaw her dates with Naval Academy midshipmen. In the aftermath of telephone exchanges with her parents on the 9th, she knew she could not stay while her family was repatriated in accord with international law. The college's student weekly, *Sun Dial*, with a polite Southern gentility, took no notice of her disappearance from the ranks of the class of 1942. She and her mother got home to the R Street house in Washington late on the evening of the eleventh, where Swiss legation personnel were already discussing the packing of the household. Outside, someone had chalked a swastika on the sidewalk.

In the seven-day interim allowed the Axis emissaries in Washington to settle their private affairs, the legation staffs were under close watch and, as the time progressed, increasingly confined to their embassies. In one of his last acts, Hans Thomsen concluded with Charles Bruggmann, the Swiss ambassador, a protocol that placed all the fixed assets of the German Embassy in the hands of the Swiss legation in Washington for safekeeping.[2] The two von Boetticher women were free to take a last hasty rail trip to Buffalo, New York, to visit the elder von Boetticher daughter and her husband on December 13. Adelheid Miller continued a teaching career in medicine with her husband, David, at the University of Buffalo through the war years and into the 1970s. At the time of Pearl Harbor, von Boetticher's son, Friedrich Heinrich, was hospitalized in Towson, Maryland, and his future in the country was open to question now. In the middle of his six-month sojourn in American custody, von Boetticher directed a successful appeal to the U.S. State Department requesting that his son be allowed to stay in the United States.[3] The Miller family recalled that amid the polite interrogations of the time, American authorities more than once broached the idea that General von Boetticher would be welcome to stay, too.[4] Friedrich Heinrich von Boetticher remained in treatment until his release in December 1944, when he immediately volunteered for American military service. Late in 1945, he reached Japan in time for occupation duty in that country with the U.S. Fifth Air Force. A year later, still in uniform, he became an American citizen. He lived out his life in the United States under a slightly altered name and died in Chicago in September 1997, his story generally unknown.[5]

Through the third week in December 1941, the Axis diplomatic staffs from around the country, and some from Latin America as well, assembled under the close scrutiny of the FBI in three hastily chosen centers prepared for them. The German consular staffs mustered at the now somber splendor of the Greenbrier Hotel at White Sulphur Springs in West Virginia's Allegheny mountains. Still today one of America's premier resorts, the complex was home to families, servants, and even household pets for six months as the State Department organized the exchange of more than 1,600 persons—1,054 of them German legation personnel from posts in the United States—for American embassy staffs similarly interned abroad.

The preparations were decidedly ad hoc. The surprised hotel administration received hasty telephone inquiries from the State Department on December 18, and internees began arriving the next day. FBI agents herded the bulk of these solicitously quarantined guests through Washington's Union Station and aboard specially hired coaches of the C&O Railroad headed for the now tightly guarded facility. Hildegard von Boetticher, with no advance notice of the train's destination, was astonished to find herself speeding in the dark through Lynchburg, Virginia, which she had left seven days before, and wishing she could leap from the coach in which she was riding.

Life at the hotel was tolerable, though the internees lived under constant observation, with the grounds floodlit and patrolled at night. American press accounts, replete with gossip and scandal leaked by hotel staffers or invented outright, gleefully reproduced speculation on various factions forming among the various national elements inside the gilded cage.[6] Frau Thomsen continued as a center of attention with her purportedly vocal disdain for the accommodations at the facility.[7]

The worst aspect was the boredom. A daily routine soon established itself in the hotel. The internees relieved its predictability by the traffic in gossip and speculation about a departure date, a surge of buying whenever the word spread about a new shipment of American goods in the hotel shops, and the occasional spark of a love interest among the younger internees. Hildegard von Boetticher developed a fondness for a Bulgarian boy, but the close proximity of clucking elders confined any meetings to secluded paths and rooftops. Her energies eventually went into the development of a school for the younger German children, though the absence of textbooks and basic equipment limited the effort to bare fundamentals.[8] Her father never dwelt on any of these mundane matters in his own recollections of the internment, confining himself to bromides on the efficient American management of the whole business.[9] One of Hildegard's FBI overseers at the hotel at one point revealed to her that he was among the agents who had kept an eye on her social life at Randolph-Macon. "You went to all the best football games," he confided.[10]

Peter Riedel and his wife of five months, Helen, equally astonished at the news of the Japanese attack during a Sunday morning
visit to the National Gallery of Art on Washington's Mall, were immediately caught up in the flurry of security measures. Riedel reported immediately to the embassy, where he joined the frantic destruction of official documents. His elaborate files on American
aircraft production went into the basement furnace in the stream
consisting of most of the paper still on hand in the attaché's offices.
He tried to salvage the large book of graphic representations he
used to keep his chief abreast of developments by concealing it in a
suitcase of his own effects, but one of his colleagues reported this to
the general. The outsize charts headed for the flames, along with,
he bitterly noted, the last of his respect for von Boetticher.[11] As an
American citizen, Helen remained free to tend to the closing of their
affairs in Washington. The couple found that a squad of FBI agents
had moved into an apartment next to theirs to oversee their movements. The events of the previous July during their honeymoon
had become FBI lore, and relations with these shadows remained
amicable. When Riedel reported aboard the train to West Virginia
on December 19, Helen remained briefly behind and joined her
husband on the twenty-second. She was not the only American-
born wife of an Axis diplomat, and he realized she could have
opted to leave him and stay home at any point during these events.

From memory and the flow of newspapers he could still receive
in the hotel, Riedel continued to formulate realistic assessments on
American aircraft production. He shared his last report with Col.
Giuseppi Gaeta, the Italian air attaché, and eventually with his
Japanese opposites, when they transferred to the Greenbrier to dis-
place the Italians in March 1942. His fond hope was to raise an
alarm in Germany about burgeoning American capacities. The report he prepared became, in his account, the last divisive issue between him and von Boetticher as they reached Germany.

FBI interviewers at the Greenbrier gave Riedel special attention.
They listened politely to his professions of intent to return to the
United States one day to become an American citizen and to his ob-
servations on lax American security measures.[12] The bureau also
passed on to the State Department, the Treasury, and the Board of
Economic Warfare Riedel's complaints that income taxes in the
United States were half what he had to pay out on his $600 monthly

salary.[13] In one of these sessions, Riedel also alluded to a trunk full of his 8-mm motion picture films with aerial footage shot all over the United States, Mexico, and South America. He often fixed the camera to a small pylon on the glider's fuselage to record his maneuvers. The trunk, then at the Security Storage Company in Washington, became the object of further FBI attention.[14] Among the other, more valuable property Riedel left behind in the United States was his Kranich glider. With no provision for shipping it home, it became U.S. government property. But the agents may have been after something more in these "debriefing" sessions.

The bureau was abuzz with another issue attaching to Riedel. An employee at the Boeing Aircraft Company in Seattle, Washington, had sent to the German Embassy in his name a single copy of a confidential monthly report on production statistics. Apparently unsolicited by Riedel but intercepted in the FBI's surveillance and interception of the embassy's mail, this solitary report by itself could not add much to his inductive assessments of these matters, but it brewed up a storm of paper within the company and the FBI until three months after the departure of the Axis diplomats from the United States. H. B. Fletcher, Special [FBI] Agent in Charge at Seattle, went so far as to fabricate a dummy Army Air Corps classified report, wiped clean of fingerprints, which was left in an open area at the Boeing plant in the hope that the culprit would repeat the treasonous act.[15] Any prints then found on the report would reveal the identity of the spy; nothing came of all these exertions, and larger events soon overtook the Boeing plant and Hoover's G-men.

The bureau's activities with the Greenbrier internees meshed with the State Department's obligation under international law to arrange for the repatriation of the Axis diplomats. These transfers became the responsibility of the State Department's Special Division.[16] Most of the preparations involving the Greenbrier fell to the division's Robert L. Bannerman. Bannerman oversaw the processing of and accounting for all the stored baggage and goods, and the transport and the care and feeding of the internees, whose numbers swelled to 7,424 by the spring of 1942.[17] He also began arranging for the necessary shipping to carry all those with diplomatic status back to their native countries. By early March 1942, the American government had reached agreements with neutral powers for the use of five vessels, two of them the Swedish liners M/S *Gripsholm* and S/S

Drottningholm.[18] The contingent of German internees at the Greenbrier was scheduled for the latter's first voyage in early May 1942. On April 8, the department cabled the American legation in Bern the details of the proposed transatlantic track of *Drottningholm* from New York to Lisbon for transmission to the German government.[19]

The process was never smooth. The Japanese insisted on sending their citizens and officials through third countries, and the coordination of shipping for Americans still in Europe also required endless cable traffic with other European governments. The German Foreign Office briefly interrupted everything at this point by linking agreements and guarantees for the safe passage of its own diplomats to questions about the return of other German citizens being detained in Latin America for internment in the United States. The presence of German U-boats off American shores after January 1942 complicated matters the more. *Drottningholm* was to sail brilliantly lit from dusk to dawn. For this first voyage in her wartime role, she was painted completely white and wore the legend DIPLOMAT, the ship's name, and her national registry in bold fifteen-foot letters, accompanied by a large painted Swedish flag, all running down both the vessel's sides below the length of its superstructure. Thus attired, the ship arrived in New York from Gothenburg on May 1.

Last-minute details came together in a rush. With space aboard the liner limited, Bannerman had to curtail the amount of luggage accompanying each passenger, which left a large collection of personal goods for disposition after the war's end. Von Boetticher left behind the extensive library he had brought with him, which included many valuable first editions associated with Frederick the Great. The German naval attaché had to abandon an American refrigerator and a washing machine he had crated for transfer home. The storage company in Washington delivered the specified luggage to the city's railroad station for dispatch to the piers at Jersey City, New Jersey, on a single day's notice.[20] The internees could carry what they had with them at the Greenbrier, and a nine-car special train, the first of three, left White Sulphur Springs at 11:45 in the evening of May 6 with the first German contingent from the hotel. The remaining Axis staffs followed at one-hour intervals thereafter. Everything was timed to stage the crowd aboard the *Drottningholm* for passage by evening of the seventh. Passengers arriving at the Pennsylvania Railroad's Exchange Place station in Jersey City were hustled without baggage to buses that transported them directly to the foot of the ship's gangplank. There each person had to demonstrate that he or she carried no more than $300 in American money; any excess was confiscated for deposit in locked accounts in a New York bank for the duration of the war. Bannerman congratulated himself on excluding members of the FBI, the military and naval intelligence establishments, the Internal Revenue Service, and Customs from these proceedings. Local police moved things along. The only delay came in an improbable tableau played out when a young American woman rushed at the queue to plead tearfully with a slight blond German man to stay with her in the United States. The mortified object of this entreaty wordlessly embraced the girl, then moved to the ship's gangway.[21] At 7:50 P.M. the ship left Jersey City's Pier F with 948 German, Hungarian, Italian, and Bulgarian passengers aboard. Another 8 "supernumeraries" and 267 crew put the complement at just five spaces less than the absolute capacity of the ship. In gathering dusk, *Drottningholm*, bound for Lisbon, nosed out to open sea under U.S. Coast Guard escort.[22]

For all the haste surrounding its departure, the ship made a calm passage.[23] The thirty-seven-year-old, 11,285-ton vessel took nine days to make Lisbon, never approaching its seventeen-knot top speed. Hildegard von Boetticher reported that the first and only lifeboat drill was a disaster; many passengers who had donned life jackets in their berths below made the mistake of inflating them there and then could not fit through the hatchways to the main deck to assigned boat stations. The mood aboard became more sober as the ship approached European waters. *Drottningholm* hauled up and twice circled a large life raft adrift in the sea lanes while everyone crowded on deck straining to see signs of life. The realities of existence for the young men aboard were shortly to put many in uniform. On May 16, the ship pulled into the Tagus River estuary and a landing in Europe.

Lisbon was a calm but momentary refuge, a way station for people on a road to uncertain fates. The German diplomatic establishment in the city turned out to greet and take custody of the contingent of their countrymen from America. The military attaché in the city, Luftwaffe Maj. Gen. Karl Kettembeil, followed the arrivals with his camera and recorded the ship at quayside, von Boetticher's family, Peter Riedel and Helen, and other Washington embassy staffers.[24] Von Boetticher's daughter exchanged her remaining dollars for escudos and bought the last pair of shoes she was to see for some time. Her father intervened more than gruffly, however, when one of the German welcomers approached her with an offer of a job as an English-language radio personality in Lisbon. Years later she realized that she might have been rescued from a role as a minor Tokyo Rose or a Lord Haw Haw.[25] By the afternoon of the seventeenth, the entire party was bound for German-occupied France.

Aboard three rickety trains, the arrivals were made as uncomfortable as possible. The carriages were open to the soot thrown out of the engine. They had no toilets or accommodations for washing. The uneven roadbeds caused the cars to rock precariously at even moderate speeds, and one of the three trains actually left the rails, though without injury to the occupants. Pitching through the night, they slowed next morning outside the French seaside resort of Biarritz, just over the Spanish border. Craning at the window in her anticipation of next developments, Hildegard von Boetticher never saw her father leave his seat. As the train rolled along the open concourse, a German military band, more elegant and polished than anything in her recent memory, struck up lively marches for the occasion. Only after she and her mother had descended to the platform did von Boetticher's daughter again glimpse her father. His easily recognizable figure, which had remained in civilian attire through the period of internment, now appeared at the top of the steps of the next coach in the immaculate uniform of a Wehrmacht *General der Artillerie*.

Opposite this scene in the station, another loaded train pulled away, its windows bearing small American flags. The U.S. Embassy staff from Berlin, housed until this point in the German resort of Bad Nauheim, was headed for Lisbon and the *Drottningholm* for passage home.

The entire diplomatic entourage from Washington next boarded more well-appointed German-run trains for a leisurely transit to Frankfurt am Main, their first stop on German soil. There, on the twenty-fifth, Nazi functionaries staged an extravagant celebration of their return. A throng of brown-shirted SA men drew up ranks at the city center. Foreign Office State Secretary Ernst von Weizsäcker, who had privately confided in von Boetticher in February 1939 about the likelihood of war that year, now offered public remarks extolling resistance of the returnees to the "American way of life" and Roosevelt's fireside chats.[26]

Whatever von Boetticher's thoughts on these events, he was soon back in the daily life of a wartime capital and the routine of a command at war. The internal politics of the regime and the military staffs running operations may have only begun to sink in for the repatriated officer. Hitler personally awarded von Boetticher the Knight's Cross of the War Service Cross on May 27, 1942. Hans Thomsen accompanied his military attaché, receiving an identical award while a beaming Field Marshal Wilhelm Keitel looked on. Hitler's observations that day remain unrecorded, but they probably reflected his earlier assessments of the attaché given before some of his intimates. On February 2, 1942, he favorably contrasted the attaché's reporting with that of the foreign office professionals.[27] Dr. Henry Picker, a second individual who against orders jotted down Hitler's musings around his dinner table, heard the führer's favorable mention of von Boetticher as the attaché was still on the high seas headed for Lisbon. At lunch at the Wolfschanze, the secret OKW command headquarters in East Prussia, on May 18, 1942, he recorded Hitler's resolve to elevate the attaché and the chargé d'affaires to a major post after the war.[28] At his lieutenant general's rank since September 1, 1940, von Boetticher nevertheless advanced no further by the end of the conflict and never received the field command or key artillery assignment he might have merited in Hitler's eyes. How and why he effectively landed on the shelf after his return from the United States is bound up with his own representations in briefing his general staff contemporaries and with Hitler's by now developed hostile attitudes toward the confraternity of German staff officers.

Von Boetticher's diplomatic status changed with his return to Berlin. For the moment, this placed him in a network of familiar faces and collegial minds all headed by Col. Gen. Franz Halder, the Bavarian Catholic who had replaced Ludwig Beck as chief of staff in the shake-up of February 1938. On June 1, 1942, von Boetticher was transferred to the Führer Reserve with assignment to the Army General Staff section Oberquartiermeister IV-(or OQuIV), the intelligence function of the army.[29] His postwar claims about his repetition in

Berlin of the message on an American ability eventually to meet all demands may have the ring of truth, but his was a faint voice. Even the hint that the Americans might shift the balance against Germany was bureaucratic heresy among his peers at the time. Though it could not be voiced aloud among the leadership, the Germans had already reached a strategic impasse in the war. The breathtaking blitzkrieg in France in 1940 was a technically brilliant achievement but led to no decision in the West. Churchill's England remained defiant, and the Wehrmacht's failure to take Moscow and destroy the Soviet Union in a single campaign now posed greater implications for the Reich.[30] The conclusion of the war in Germany's favor eluded Hitler and the conflict became one in which productive energy and staying power would prevail. The Reich was at a clear disadvantage in these areas. Even as von Boetticher was delivering his assessment of the situation, Halder, without much demur, prepared to launch the already overstretched army in Operation *Blau*, with two axes of advance, one north of Moscow and the second aimed at the Volga city of Stalingrad and the oil reserves of the Caucasus region beyond.

Peter Riedel, reporting to various Luftwaffe echelons in Berlin, later faulted von Boetticher's revelations to the higher commands in Berlin. His former assistant attaché for air nursed his continued pique at his chief's apparent inability to credit him properly or publicly enough for his accurate assessment of events in the United States. Riedel parted company with von Boetticher for good on the Tuesday in early June when the general was invited to brief the assembled Air Ministry's weekly staff conference. Field Marshal Erhard Milch introduced von Boetticher while Riedel occupied a chair at the back of the room. Riedel later recorded that his erstwhile chief on that day spoke the appropriate words but never made the message about American potential very emphatic or clear.[31] Riedel, however, had not much more success in acquainting his colleagues in the Reich Air Ministry with the truth and decided instead to enlighten the directors, designers, and test pilots of Germany's various aircraft companies—all personal acquaintances of many years—of the real promise of the American mobilization, especially in aircraft.

Von Boetticher in fact remained in a supernumerary post doing make-work tasks for the duration of the war. His personnel records from 1942 to the last retained the notation that he was suited for service in diplomatic assignments, but with Germany's shrinking options in polite international discourse, the general was not dispatched to another such job overseas. He functioned as a high-level intelligence analyst first for the Army General Staff and later for the High Command. A selection of his reports, based on foreign newspapers and other sources arriving through neutral capitals, survived the war; the incomplete series in the German military archives comprises some fifty-eight individual submissions dated from November 1943 to July 1944, all directed to Field Marshal Wilhelm Keitel, chief of staff of the High Command. Many bear scribbled marginalia by Keitel and Gen. Alfred Jodl, the operations chief at the OKW level.[32] None of them shows any evidence of attention by Hitler himself.

The reports command interest because of the broad subjects they address in often prescient ways. In a German military leadership that had long since surrendered real strategic decision to Hitler, these assessments are the vestige of former Great Staff situational analysis. Though von Boetticher seems to have had great latitude in what he reported on, his choice of topics reflects the concerns of the moment for the German command. He returned repeatedly to several principal themes, all clearly driven by questions assailing the OKW: the problems and direction of Allied coalition war, the air offensives against the Reich, and the political and tactical issues involved in the anticipated "second front" as early as fall 1943. Occasional comment also appeared on new weapons technology or individual battles, but the focus was on larger matters.

As the report series progressed, Germany had already lost all strategic initiative in the war and had no hope of regaining it. The disaster at Stalingrad cost more than 300,000 field-trained soldiers by February 1943, the collapse of the North African front in May almost as many, and the failure of the German offensive at Kursk in July wrote an end to any hope of decisive result for German arms. The Russian summer offensive in 1943 tore great holes in the army's lines. At best, Germany could hope only for a negotiated peace with a recalcitrant Soviet Union[33] after the proclamation of the unconditional surrender policy of the western Allies at the Casablanca Conference of January 1943. Seriatim, the von Boetticher submissions chronicle the gathering defeat.

The threat of an invasion of western Europe weighs heavily in these analyses from early November 1943 on. Von Boetticher's initial assessments raised issues not only about the certainty of the invasion, but of its timing and location, linked initially to events on the Russian front, the establishment of a foreshortened and heavily fortified German line in Poland, Allied preparations in England, and the likelihood of a supporting amphibious attack into southern France launched from Corsica.[34] By mid-January 1944, he was casting the problem in light of the agreements involving senior Allied military commanders about invasion plans emanating from the recent Cairo and Teheran conferences. The limiting factors, in his opinion, were the range of Allied fighter aircraft that would support the operations and the absolute necessity of aerial superiority for the attackers. At this stage he could only speculate on the target beaches but named as a strong possibility areas such as the Kattegat, the narrow neck of the Danish peninsula, which would give an invading force more direct access to Berlin and circumvent most natural defensive river lines across the north German plain. He developed this possibility in enough detail to indicate that at least he took it very seriously. At the same time he (correctly) ruled out the Balkans, a major concern at the OKW at the time, as a potential theater of a western Allied offensive; the same limits to tactical air support would mitigate against this, and Tito's partisan forces in Yugoslavia were already doing enough to tie down German forces in the region.[35] The tensions of coalition war, von Boetticher predicted, in late February 1944, would lead to an early British recognition of Tito, "the tool of Russia," to counterbalance his sponsorship by Stalin. Russian successes in the east might also prompt an earlier invasion from the west to allow the western Allies to push the eventual meeting point with the advancing Russians as far east as possible.[36] On the very eve of the assault on northwestern France, on the other hand, he maintained that there would be more delay in launching the operation because the western Allies could not reach agreement with Stalin on the state of postwar Europe.[37] To this juncture, he never named Normandy as the target area, still less did he come close to pinpointing the date of the assault, but claimed two days after the Allied landings that OVERLORD had taken place because John G. Winant, U.S. Ambassador to Britain, and Averell Harriman, the U.S. envoy to Moscow, had settled the matter with Stalin.[38] That the operation depended vastly more on wind, weather, the press of troops and supply getting aboard ships in the embarkation areas, and the nearly absolute air superiority over the Normandy lodgement appears nowhere in these deliberations. After the invasion, his series of analyses on land operations in the west took a new heading: On the Battle for Europe. He continued to point to the possibility of other—main—thrusts onto the Continent in northern Germany. While compelling as a theoretical proposal, opening another front on the western beaches of Jutland was beyond the practical logistical capabilities of the western Allies and was never considered at Eisenhower's command headquarters. Von Boetticher may have fallen victim here to deliberate Allied deceptions promoting the idea that a larger invasion was still in the offing.

The effect of the Allied air war engrossed von Boetticher in these reports as well. At the outset of 1944, the combined bomber offensive had reached a definite new tempo, and he characterized, with some precision, the strategy of the Allied aerial assault for the next months. As of the end of 1943, he told Keitel, the Royal Air Force announced that it dropped 200,000 tons of bombs on the Reich and its occupied areas thus far in the war. Significant here was the fact that the American air forces were now ready to outstrip the British. The months-long effort of base construction in Britain would now be complemented by the consolidation of American forces in Italy.[39] His survey extended as well to Russian plans and noted that the Red Air Force's attempts to construct a strategic bomber arm were not greatly successful, but offers were mentioned in the press that foretold the use of Russian territory by American planes. Western Allied air power had built a 3-to-1 strength ratio over the Luftwaffe. He correctly predicted that the next basic element of Allied strategy would be to destroy the German fighter arm as a prerequisite to a resolute bombing assault on German industry. This accurately delineated the direction of the aerial offensive without separating it into the specific target sets in German transportation, oil, and aircraft production facilities as contemplated by British and American aviators. After months of blunder and the residual if wrong-headed faith in self-defending bomber streams, Allied air commanders by early 1944 had finally equipped fighters with external fuel tanks that permitted them to escort the bombers all the way into Germany and back. While fighting desperately to defend the Reich and its war capacity, the Luftwaffe was now in a running—and losing—battle for its very existence. Though the Reich's desperate measures wrung out production miracles in the face of the onslaught for another year, the German air defense constantly bled away its most irreplaceable resource—experienced pilots.

Von Boetticher's estimates of the future of American performance were based in part on news of U.S. aircraft production figures. Here he avowed that the numbers being discussed represented an increase he had already forecast in reports from Washington.[40] This oblique reference to the predictions based on Peter Riedel's three years of analytical work was a backhanded recognition of his assistant's contribution. The claims of American output, in short, were entirely credible, he acknowledged. His analysis further outlined the completion of the American-dominated Supreme Allied Headquarters in Britain and the air commanders who were part of it. The preponderance of British officers in the Mediterranean theater indicated to him that the British had successfully limited American influence in this traditional area of British interest. This repeated a theme common to his reports of mid-1941, in which he described the region as a strategic "arch" of British control.

This run of wartime assessments also permits some insight into German methods of intelligence assessment during the war. Von Boetticher's reflections on Allied activity and intentions were always influenced by the three-week lag between the publication of the material abroad and its arrival in Berlin by way of neutral capitals. At no point did his assessments take into account or integrate information developed by the Abwehr or other German intelligence sources.[41] His summations seem, rather, to have been the raw material for Abwehr files, and the flow of documents reflects instead the separate and contending nature of German command elements even late in the war. By spring 1944, the Abwehr itself was in near collapse, having been taken over by the SS Sicherheitsdienst under Ernst Kaltenbrunner. Throughout his written work, von Boetticher continued to beg for reliable information on the construction of Allied air bases, particularly those within striking range of possible invasion beaches around western Europe and the Mediterranean.

It may also occur to the reader of these reports years after the war that von Boetticher's repetitions of certain unvarnished truths about the progressively failing German war effort could not have made him popular in the German high command. While continuing to appreciate his work, his colleagues seem neither to have referred the reports directly to Hitler nor made them part of discussions in daily situation conferences. Von Boetticher often misread the direction of single events while trying to divine their strategic import on the spot, but the general thread of these OKW reports is decidedly and realistically pessimistic on the outcome of the war for Germany. His continued submission of these bits of sobering news may be taken as a form of "internal migration" for one without an alternative. He never, however, entered the ranks of those planning actual resistance to the regime.

The signal events of July 20, 1944, brushed von Boetticher only briefly. Nowhere is there an indication of his even remote participation in the ill-fated plot to eliminate Hitler and bring the war, at least in the West, to a negotiated standstill. For someone described after the war as an early opponent of Hitler, von Boetticher seems to have been overlooked as an individual likely to join the ranks of those ready to risk tyrannicide. The conspiracy was a badly kept secret, and it is likely he knew something of it and its timing. On the day the bomb exploded in the conference barracks at Rastenburg in East Prussia, he absented himself from Berlin, retreating alone to Potsdam and Sans Souci, the palace of his hero, Frederick. When Hitler survived the blast meant to destroy his rule, Nazi vengeance took an awful toll among von Boetticher's brother officers involved in the business. On August 13, von Boetticher was confronted in his office by a hysterical Frau Thiele, the wife of Maj. Gen. Fritz Thiele, one of the conspirators. She threw herself at his feet with weeping entreaties for her husband, seized by the Gestapo the previous day.[42] He could do nothing for the woman or her husband. She had sought him out in extremis because her husband's association with the former attaché extended back to the period 1929–1931, when Thiele had served as a communications liaison at the German Army artillery school, then under von Boetticher's command. Thiele, whose career thereafter had brought him to the higher levels of German Army signals and communication commands, went to his death in Berlin's Plötzensee Prison on September 4.

While all this transpired, von Boetticher's old assistant of Washington days, Peter Riedel, had enlarged upon his earlier diplomatic career.[43] Following his fruitless quest in the second half of 1942 to convince his colleagues in the German aircraft industry of the impossibility of outproducing the United States, Riedel faced a dilemma. Conditions in wartime Germany left him without prospects, and the steady death toll among his old friends of the prewar German flying establishment depressed him heavily. He had found for his American-born wife, Helen, the possibility of employment in the blueprint section of the Heinkel aircraft factory. A required physical examination for this revealed that she had contracted a lung ailment diagnosed first as tuberculosis. Her early treatments left her with one lung collapsed and in precarious health. By his own later account, Riedel accepted an accommodation arranged through his old friend Fritz Grosskopf—still working for the Abwehr—in which the German intelligence agency would pay him a salary that would also cover Helen's hospitalization expenses in Davos, Switzerland. In return, Riedel would become an Abwehr agent posted to the German Embassy in Stockholm. With a Luftwaffe captain's rank and the vague title of engineer attaché, he arrived in the Swedish capital on November 23, 1943. The chief of mission there was the same Hans Thomsen of his years in Washington. In the Swedish capital, German interests kept a window on the world, managed Swedish intelligence "assets" (and were equally "managed" themselves), and, equally important, preserved the arrangement in which high-grade iron ore continued to flow to the Reich along with supplies of crucial ball bearings for German industry. His immediate superior, a Luftwaffe colonel with no objection to Abwehr activities within the embassy, was a marked contrast to von Boetticher; indeed, most members of the legation had some shadowy secondary purpose. Within a year, Riedel's attitudes about duty to his country melted in the relative freedom and plenty of the neutral city.

By the summer of 1944, events in the war and his contacts with Allied operatives had Riedel in a changed state of mind. News of the Russian discovery of the concentration camp at Majdanek—reported in *Time* magazine on September 11—distressed him enough that he had a violent argument over these revelations with Hannah Reitsch, whom he visited during one of his monthly trips to Berlin. Two weeks later, he typed out a long, rambling letter[44] to the head of the American Office of Strategic Services, Maj. Gen. William

Donovan, whose daughter, Patricia, Riedel had known socially until her death in an auto accident in 1940. This communication he managed to get into American hands in Stockholm only after subsequent developments threatened him directly.

In early November 1944, a singular defection by a Luftwaffe pilot took place. This officer-pilot and a noncommissioned airman were flight-testing a new airborne radar in a Junkers twin-engine bomber. Making an escape, he crash-landed the Ju–88 in a field north of Stockholm. Furious Luftwaffe authorities demanded the return of both men and the secret radar equipment. The German sergeant, unaware of his pilot's plan, begged for return home. The Swedes repatriated him readily, but Riedel reports that he eventually received orders to get to the crash site and destroy or recover the radar equipment. He managed to visit the remote scene, accompanied by a Swedish officer, and confirmed that the radar set was intact, but he could do nothing more in the presence of a detachment of Swedish soldiers. One of his embassy colleagues, a Gestapo operative, was also enjoined to find the defecting pilot, then in a local hospital with a concussion, and eliminate him. Swedish security prevented this, too.

On November 16, 1944, Riedel received a telegram directing him to report immediately to Berlin. He was to receive particulars on the transfer of some German aircraft engines. Within an hour, a second cable arrived with the same message, repeated with greater urgency. By now alarmed and understanding that some of his dealings had been betrayed, he left the embassy building and placed himself under the protection of the Swedish Air Force, then applied to his host country's commission for foreigners, where he got a temporary passport.[45] Four days later, he visited the American embassy in Stockholm and had an extended discussion with a Colonel Hardison, the air attaché. He handed this officer the letter intended for General Donovan. Riedel then spent the remainder of the war and half of the year 1946 on a farm outside the Swedish capital. His letter did reach Donovan by December 1944, and a proposal floated through the American State Department to bring the German to the United States for whatever propaganda value he had. The State Department threw cold water on the plan. Despite Riedel's protestations of a political conversion, the department still had the "impression that Riedel was generally regarded as a Nazi, not only by the fervent Nazis in the Embassy, but also by those who only gave lip-service to the Nazi cause."[46] Threatened with deportation to Germany in mid-1946, Riedel quietly boarded a trawler with a British officer-friend who shared his sense of adventure and boundless horizons, and eventually arrived in Venezuela. He rejoined his wife by way of Canada only after another three years.

Von Boetticher by the end of his stint as analyst of current events had found at least one other credible professed admirer and an enhanced reputation among his peers at the OKW. German historian Percy Schramm, commissioned a major directly from the University of Tübingen faculty and assigned to keep the OKW War Diaries, had only high praise for what he considered von Boetticher's sober and balanced production. By 1944, Schramm noted, the former attaché had accepted Germany's defeat and had predicted in one of these reports that once they had gotten a foothold in France, the Americans would invade Germany itself. Field Marshal Keitel penned a disbelieving "But it will never come to such a pass!" in the margins.[47]

By late January 1945, what Keitel refused to contemplate had indeed come to pass. The Red Army stood less than 100 kilometers east of Berlin across the Oder River line and was hammering the German defenses along the Baltic coast and East Prussia. The von Boetticher family had been displaced from its three-room apartment; the general lost two successive offices to Allied bombers. Since before Christmas, foreign press deliveries to von Boetticher's office had stopped completely. He and his daughter had manned his small activity, the two of them taking trams into the threatened city from their assigned refugee quarters in a farmstead in the distant suburb of Glindow, southeast of Potsdam. The place had no indoor toilets. At the end of the month, von Boetticher sent his wife on to live with her relatives in Leipzig, where her house shortly took a direct bomb hit that reduced it to rubble.[48] On orders in mid-March, von Boetticher followed a signals detachment whose summaries of British and American radio broadcasts had supported his report series and descended upon Halle for two weeks. There the confusion of the last days of the war overtook the command; his movement orders were several times countermanded. The German High Command was split in two by early April, with the less important support functions being ordered south toward Landsberg in Bavaria.[49]

Von Boetticher drove his daughter to Leipzig, then accompanied this element alone. Leipzig, eventually occupied by American troops, lay in the Russian zone of occupation. The family would not see the man or have news of him for more than a year. His itinerary now placed him in the path of American Seventh Army units as German resistance collapsed.

The Reich's end brought degradation at the hands of the Americans. Von Boetticher surrendered himself on April 30, 1945, to troops of the American 36th Infantry Division in southern Germany and was incarcerated with other high-ranking German officers.[50] His name was already on the Allies' Central Register of War Criminals and Security Suspects, more usually called the CROWCASS List.[51] He passed from the 36th Division through the higher-level U.S. Seventh Army command chain at Augsburg with the swelling numbers of Germans seized by Allied authority. These persons were first collected at Mondorf-les-Bains, in the southeastern corner of Luxemburg. Here, von Boetticher arrived on May 23 to be reunited with his OKW superiors whom he had left some eight weeks before. Goering, Ribbentrop, Adm. Karl Doenitz, and other senior Nazis were also housed in the four-story Palace Hotel, surrounded by barbed wire and aptly code-named ASHCAN.[52] Other celebrities who had figured in the conflict of Europe were also accommodated in hotels nearby. At one point, an imperious Miklos Horthy, the former regent of Hungary, deposed and spirited out of his country for internment in Austria the previous October, had von Boetticher summoned from the wire enclosure as a dinner guest.[53] The former attaché appears almost in cameo roles in the memoirs of other observers of the time. Here, too, von Boetticher and the other prisoners met the egregious Col. Burton Andrus, the American army officer who was more Prussian than American and who controlled the detention facilities at Mondorf and, later, at Nürnberg.[54]

By midsummer, von Boetticher was transferred to Oberursel in the Taunus region of Hesse, the site of a former prison camp for Allied fliers. He was kept in a narrow cell with a detained Maj. Herbert Buechs, who had been Luftwaffe aide to Gen. Alfred Jodl. Their food was delivered on flats shoved beneath the cell door. When the increasingly lax guards failed to answer the small flag outside the cell that signaled a prisoner's need to use toilet facilities, human waste went out of the cell on newspaper sheets beneath the same door. Von Boetticher developed an increasingly severe case of phlebitis, a painful inflammation of the blood vessels, especially in the legs. One U.S. Army officer who employed von Boetticher's cell mate in interviews for the U.S. Army's historical program at this time described conditions that made him "ashamed I was an American."[55] The levels of corruption among the American jailers were such that one major commanding the Oberursel camp was court-martialed and dismissed from the army. In September 1945, another interviewer, historian Harold Deutsch of the University of Minnesota, found von Boetticher's appearance to be that of an old man overanxious to please and described him as "überschwenglich" (effusive).[56] Deutsch remembered that the keepers of the facility were members of an American paratroop unit that had been slated for return to the States, but that was diverted to this guard duty. They tended to take things out on the prisoners. When Deutsch interviewed Heinz Guderian, the panzer general quietly complained about the treatment. Deutsch later contributed to the troubles of the American major who was the center commander, from whom he had once heard, among otherwise surly observations, that the only German in the whole complex whom he could like or trust was von Boetticher.

The Oberursel detention center also lay within the area of responsibility of the Third U.S. Army. The colorful commander of that fighting element, now an occupying force, was von Boetticher's old friend, Lt. Gen. George S. Patton, Jr. Patton studiously avoided any contact with his former companion on marches across American Civil War battlefields. The two men never saw or heard from each other again.

Transferred to Nürnberg on September 24, 1945,[57] von Boetticher maintained a calculated and soft-spoken innocence before new interrogators working for the Office of the Chief Council on War Crimes. Americans are so broad-minded, he told one colonel, that they published everything in the newspapers. Germany should never have resorted to inserting Abwehr agents into the country, he proclaimed, reflecting upon his battle with the German intelligence service. His protestations of ignorance of concentration camps were transparent repetitions of what most Germans of his relative position were also pleading at the time. He cited his long acquaintance with Max Warburg to attest to his having friends among Jews.[58] At sixty-three years of age, he was, for the second time in his life, a member of a defeated German military establishment, but now a prisoner for an unforeseeable future. By his own meticulous accounting, he would spend 792 days—just over two years—in the custody of the victors.

The time was divided among boredom, petty disputes, and sometimes high-sounding resolutions addressed to senior Allied authorities. Von Boetticher sat at Nürnberg, never charged with anything, but awaiting the possibility of being called as a witness in the trials of the major war criminals. His comrades in enforced idleness uniformly detested Col. Burton Andrus. The colonel gained the reputation of a small-minded martinet for his tight administration of his various jails. Several prisoners addressed formal complaints and other plaintive statements about their treatment to higher authorities, often invoking the articles of the Geneva Convention and standing on a presumed high moral position. Given that some of these men faced the gallows for war crimes within the year, their grievances sound overly dramatic. For his part, shortly after his incarceration under Andrus's care, von Boetticher developed his own campaign against the man.

The American management of the internment facilities followed normal police procedure, especially after the suicides of some of the wanted individuals. Von Boetticher therefore was duly relieved of any instrument that could cause self-inflicted injury: nail scissors or files, shoelaces, knives of any kind. He also surrendered 3,196 Reichsmarks, 50 of this sum in silver coin; for all of these items he was given a detailed receipt. In the two years of his detention, several of his possessions disappeared during cell searches. At one point, he asked for the replacement of a Swiss travel alarm clock or compensation for it. What incensed von Boetticher more with Andrus was, however, a typewriter.

The machine had been specially ordered in Washington. A solid Royal desk model, it featured extra keys that made at one stroke letters with diacritical umlauts and the special double letter *s* common in German. No sooner had von Boetticher arrived in Mondorf than one of Andrus's captains appropriated it for the stated purpose of helping record personal data on the interned Germans. There was even a devout promise that the machine would be returned with a new ribbon when the process was finished. When von Boetticher shortly thereafter requested its return for some work of his own, he was informed that Andrus himself had moved it to his private office. Several more appeals on the matter as he moved through the succession of internment centers gave him no satisfaction. Part of the reichsmark account in his name also evaporated with time, but the typewriter remained the center of contention. The case shows von Boetticher as an experienced bureaucratic infighter who knew how to keep the telling pieces of paper that established a trail of evidence when doing battle with a military hierarchy. His tenacity in the episode offers a faint analogy to the saga of Michael Kohlhaas, the mythic German character whose single-minded pursuit of justice in the instance of two stolen horses leads to his own destruction. After von Boetticher's release in 1948, he summarized the entire sequence of events for Gen. Clarence R. Huebner, then commanding U.S. Forces, European Theater (USFET), begging the general's attention to the issue of the typewriter and including copies of all the receipts and earlier correspondence bearing on the question.[59] Nothing thereafter indicates he ever saw his Royal again—Andrus prevailed here.

On a more elevated plane, von Boetticher engaged the contemporary German catastrophe in much the same way he did the situation some twenty-seven years before. Transferred to Civilian Internment Camp No. 4 at Hersbruck in mid-November 1945, and with the use of yet another typewriter, he composed a memorandum on March 1, 1946, on the future of the German nation, especially in its relation to the United States. Alternately explaining his connections to Americans through his mother and placing himself in the role of an objective observer able to assess the German character in its confrontation with the latest disaster, he also subtly played upon the new geostrategic conditions that had already begun to separate the western Allies and their former Russian comrades-in-arms. "The goal of my life," he explained to the addressee of this essay, Robert H. Jackson, the American judge presiding over the war crimes trials,

> was and is, to work for a close cooperation and understanding between the American and the German nations. . . . During my stay in 1922 and then again from 1933 up to the outbreak of the war between

the U.S.A. and Germany, I have been working for this idea. . . . The late President Hindenburg ordered me personally in 1932 to go to America in 1933 because my ideas were his own. He considered me the only German who had a real understanding for American democracy and American ideas and history.[60]

Von Boetticher was nothing if not flexible in applying his old convictions to new conditions. Amid the repetition of the story of the mythic assignment from Hindenburg, this memorandum also reprised the same sentiments about common strategic interests between the United States and Germany that von Boetticher had addressed to Wilhelm Groener in 1919. In 1946, though, the uncomfortable truths bared under Jackson's trial proceedings had von Boetticher pleading for those Germans who had supposedly joined the Nazi Party out of ideal principle and not self-advancement. Many of those now pointing fingers at former party members, he warned Jackson, were like the scalawags of post–Civil War American history.[61] Dwelling only briefly on his own sometimes arbitrary treatment in internment, he cited Goethe's assessment of the new world to assert that America's freedom from Europe's class system and quarrels made it the hope of the future. There are Germans who can work for true understanding, "loyal to the American cause as well as to the German cause, who know America so well that they can give to the Germans every information they need and who are able to establish confidence between both, Germans and Americans."[62] The former attaché fit the description of such an individual exactly, and he ended his appeal with an even more ideal allusion to the irenic principles of the Sermon on the Mount. By odd coincidence, his words here mirrored also the same themes expressed by his former assistant attaché in his letter to William Donovan from Stockholm in September 1944. Starkly forecasting the obvious end of the war and the division and occupation of Germany, Peter Riedel also sought humane conditions for the defeated German population to produce something enduring in the future, not to plead "so much for my own sake as from the sincere desire to help bring a lasting peace between Germany and America or the Anglosaxon world."[63] For all their differences, the two argued now for an accommodation to Western culture and political principle as the redemption of the Germans. No doubt the atmosphere in the day of war crimes trials still hewed closer to the opinion of Winston Churchill holding that the Germans were always at your feet or at your throat.

Neither of the former Washington attachés could influence events according to these lights. Von Boetticher kept up a correspondence with any American who might receive his ideas. In June 1948, then living in Bielefeld, von Boetticher sent much the same message to Lt. Gen. Albert C. Wedemeyer, whose attendance at the German Kriegsakademie as a young major he had endorsed in 1936. The American officer arrived in Germany at the beginning of the crisis induced by Russian attempts to seal off the city of Berlin to the western Allies.[64] The gathering political forces of that year changed the climate of distrust to one in which Germans might become valued allies in a confrontation with the Soviet Union.

For himself and his latest message of German-American cooperation, von Boetticher could wring out little direct effect. The institution he had served for forty-five years was discredited enough that even in the face of new political conditions and a new enemy, the Allied victors in the west would not indiscriminately choose who the "good" Germans were now.

On November 6, 1946, von Boetticher arrived in Allendorf, the eleventh and last camp in his career as a prisoner. This proved fateful, for the cantonment was the earliest location of what became a fruitful German-American cooperation in collecting, assessing, and applying the historical record of the last world war. His reacquaintance with Franz Halder, the German chief of staff until 1942, placed von Boetticher among Germans who were of increasing utility to the Americans.[65]

Living and working conditions were not idyllic,[66] but as the winter progressed, von Boetticher also knew he was bound for home. Never charged with crimes or tainted with undue attachment to the Nazi cause, he spent time at Allendorf in the historical program. There he also completed the famous *"Fragebogen,"* or questionnaire, required of all ranking individuals before successfully passing the process of denazification. In von Boetticher's case, the papers and the entire case were eventually transferred to the Spruchkammer in Bielefeld in North Rhine-Westphalia.[67] While he had made his way through various stages of captivity, his wife and daughter had escaped Leipzig only days before Russian occupation authorities took over the city. Both women rode wedged onto a mattress in the back of an open truck loaded with steel barrels headed for refuge with the Prior family.[68] Annette Prior had been on the attaché's staff in Washington; the postwar grapevine allowed for invitations for the von Boettichers to head west. They had by the time of von Boetticher's release taken up residence in the Melancthonstrasse. Hence, the local German hearings authorities who passed the final judgment on all cases of German officials of the Nazi government handled the case in that locale; the proceedings in this instance were to be a mere formality.

On June 30, 1947, the former artilleryman, General Staff officer, and military diplomat left Allendorf a nominally free man. He terminated on that date his status as a prisoner of war and also formally ended an army career of exactly forty-seven years and two months. "Arbeitsfähig," (capable of work) declared the medical section of von Boetticher's release. With 80 reichsmarks in discharge pay and another 720 reichsmarks in back pay, he faced civilian life.[69] At just over sixty-five years of age, the worst seemed behind him that summer, but he had not yet seen the end of adversity.

9

"WHO KNOWS . . . ?"

WITHIN six months of his release, von Boetticher found he still had something to fear in postwar Germany. Germans under interrogation or offering attests as "friends of the court" in the laying of blame for Germany's fate raised his name more than once in these proceedings. Testimony on his performance in Washington was largely critical and continued to reflect the attitude of old Foreign Office hands who had wanted him to report from America in 1939 that the United States would intervene to stop Hitler's European diplomatic coups and mute his saber rattling.

This groundswell had already begun with the press publication of quotations from the record of various postwar interrogations. Karl Ritter, the German Foreign Office's senior economic counselor, repeated the opinion of his diplomatic service colleagues on the former German military attaché in Washington. He avowed that von Boetticher was a "dangerously stupid official" who misled Hitler about American capacities.[1] Some of the testimony gathered from these sources remained neutral or even supportive of von Boetticher. Heribert von Strempel's testimony at this time confirmed the attaché's refusal to pass propaganda material to American military authorities.[2] Six months after he breathed free again, though, another former German Foreign Office official published his memoir of the Nazi years that put more light and shadow on von Boetticher's activities in Washington.

In 1934, Erich Kordt, at the direction of higher Foreign Office authorities, reluctantly took up a position on the staff of Joachim Ribbentrop when the latter was trying to insinuate himself into a commanding position in Nazi foreign policy. The German Foreign Office establishment thought it could control Ribbentrop by keeping a close eye on him through its own man and allowing Ribbentrop's own slovenly bureaucratic habits to limit his influence or defeat him. Events of the day instead favored Ribbentrop. Unsuspecting, he kept Kordt on his staff as chief of cabinet as he ascended to the control of the entire German Foreign Office establishment in February 1938.

Erich Kordt and his brother Theo were also committed members of a resistance to Nazism centered in the diplomatic civil service.[3] He escaped the wrath of the Gestapo later during the war only because he had accepted a posting to the German legation in Nanking. American historian Harold Deutsch, in his capacity as an interrogator for the State Department, caused his transfer from Tokyo to the United States at war's end. Here he was interviewed at length in December 1945, as the Allies continued amassing evidence for the International Military Tribunals in Nürnberg. Amid wide-ranging assessments, Kordt declared that von Boetticher had committed a war crime against the German people for his underestimation of American war potential.[4] Kordt's ghost-written book, *Wahn und Wirklichkeit*, appearing in late 1947, contained, among other things, the sum of the Foreign Office faction's opinion on von Boetticher. The attaché had reinforced Hitler's generally negative predilections about the United States, said Kordt. Von Boetticher, he recalled, found also in technical areas much lacking in America. The thesis that America was not technically or morally in the position to overtake the German advantage in armaments, and that it pursued a policy of bluff was a position he held until the Japanese attack on Pearl Harbor. After the Japanese occupation of Kiska and Attu, Kordt attested, von Boetticher had handed a memorandum to the High Command in which he pressingly recommended a Japanese conquest of Alaska as an easily undertaken military operation.[5]

Kordt's recollections were problematic. At least one other German witness at the time also remembered statements attributed to von Boetticher referring to the Aleutian Islands, but these did not favor the conquest of the entire Alaska Territory by the Rising Sun. If von Boetticher did predict defeat for the American fleet in June 1942, as will be seen, even he would have considered the effort required to garrison that vast undeveloped American territory a grand waste of strategic resources. The Japanese were never so forthcoming with their German allies as to advise them of the Aleutian operations. Their seizure of Attu came one day after the disastrous Japanese defeat at Midway and represented the only part of the Japanese battle plan that succeeded.[6]

The appearance of Kordt's memoir and its publicly repeated allegations about German assessments of American potential sent a chill through von Boetticher's existence at the time. It emerged just as his case was pending before the Bielefeld Spruchkammer. He immediately mounted a determined and effective defense with Kordt's increasingly nervous publisher through the spring of 1948. By mid-February, he had in hand five copies of the book and began marshaling his counterarguments and soliciting testimony on his own behalf.[7] On February 15, he had sent to Franz Halder a detailed rebuttal of Kordt's charges, including copies of his reports from Washington. The publishing house relayed all this as well to Kordt, who begged a postponement of a meeting between himself and von Boetticher. In early March, the former attaché had also heard from Hans Thomsen, then in Hamburg. His former chief of mission in Washington backed his version of things completely and advised him to "make whatever use of my stated position that you think fit. I am ready and willing to repeat it under oath if this is necessary."[8] Another veteran of the Washington Embassy from von Boetticher's staff, Wilhelm Wolff, weighed in from his home in Wilhelmshafen. Wolff forwarded to von Boetticher a more critical assessment of Kordt based on the impressions of Kordt's colleagues in Tokyo. Wolff's source characterized Kordt as a "fanatic defender of the old professional diplomats." Kordt tended to censor anyone who fueled Hitler's biases about the weaknesses of Germany's potential enemies.[9]

More damning recollections on these matters, especially the question of Alaska, came later from another source. As he set about garnering character references from supporters, von Boetticher belatedly heard from the erstwhile naval attaché in Washington. Never as visible as his military counterpart in the embassy,[10] Robert Witthoeft-Emden clearly nursed his own recollections of events before the war. Although the two men had had amicable professional and social meetings in Berlin during the war years, Witthoeft in 1949 wrote to von Boetticher about a number of occasions when he felt his purely naval area of responsibility had been encroached upon in embassy reports sent home by the military attaché. Vague as these bureaucratic sensitivities may have been, Witthoeft did raise again the matter of von Boetticher's purported reaction to the Japanese occupation of the two Aleutian Islands in 1942. There can be no doubt that such an analysis attributed to von Boetticher circulated among higher Wehrmacht staffs in which the returned attaché equated the occupation of the islands as a death knell for the American Pacific fleet; the U.S. Navy would have to react, according to Witthoeft's recollection of von Boetticher's memorandum, if only out of reasons of prestige, and would thereby meet its entire or partial destruction. Presented with a copy of his Washington colleague's analysis, and asked for a naval estimation of it, Witthoeft remembers, he was obliged to "tear it apart." Moreover, he was again incensed that von Boetticher had seen fit to make such a pronouncement on a matter of naval operations, something outside his area of competence.[11] This exchange put definition on von Boetticher's position in June 1942. Witthoeft did not accuse him of advocating a Japanese occupation of the entire Alaska Territory, only of predicting an American naval disaster in the major fleet engagement that was the object of the whole Japanese plan at Midway.

The Kordt affair kept up a fitful life until late 1951. In the meantime, the potential effect of the allegations concerned von Boetticher enough on another front. He sought a modicum of protection by getting a head start in the whole business with the American occupation authorities. On April 29, 1948, he had mailed a copy of the Kordt book to the Historical Division, Operational History (German) Section, of Headquarters, U.S. Forces, European Theater (USFET) and weighed in with his own version of events before the matter had a chance to achieve a life and a momentum of its own within the American headquarters. He appended a copy of an affidavit that he had also solicited from Franz Halder,[12] the former German Army chief of staff who had started his association with the Historical Division as a prisoner but by now was something of a favorite son among the American historical officers within the USFET command. The Halder testament flatly contradicted each of Kordt's assertions in turn and avowed that von Boetticher had in the author's presence attempted to disabuse Hitler of his unrealistic notions about American politics and his host country's potential for mobilization during a military attaché conference in February 1939.[13] It was at this same conference that Hitler so mesmerized von Boetticher, according to Peter Riedel.

Halder's declaration seems to be the first in a series of these character references for the former attaché as well. Sardonic German wits often referred to these postwar documents as *Persil-scheine,* so named for a popular brand of soap. Such an affidavit made the bearer "clean," absolved of too close an association with the Nazi Party or indefensible events in the war. The favorable mention of von Boetticher in the OKW War Diaries as published under Percy Schramm's hand in the 1960s may have also been contrived at von Boetticher's request. Another such reference appeared in the memoir of General der Kavallerie (Lt. Gen.) Siegfried Westphal, who also made von Boetticher out as an opponent of Hitler already before 1933.[14] That von Boetticher's name never appeared among the ranks of the conspirators—no survivor of that ill-fated effort ever mentions him—still leaves the impression that these quiet affirmations of his character and political orientation served to protect his reputation and future in the postwar period. That Kordt's assertions of von Boetticher's influence on Hitler were exaggerated is today apparent. The attaché's reports were variable enough, however, to be dangerous for those in Berlin hoping to give the dictator pause by pointing up American potential. Kordt himself seemed more inclined toward peace with von Boetticher four years after the contretemps started. He wrote in late 1951 to say that he was hardly trying to impugn circles of Germans one way or the other and enclosed copies of just four of the attaché's Washington cables on which he had based his judgment of military reporting from there.[15] By this time, the international Cold War atmosphere, western Germany's gratifying economic recovery, and the existence of two contending alliances on the European landmass had overtaken the acrimony between the two.

The U.S. Army historical section that employed German officers became another focus of a burgeoning American effort that had distinct Cold War overtones. By 1948, the Germans in the program had largely been paroled to private life, but these men maintained a direct connection with historical labor that had more than passing academic interest. They contributed heavily to the formulation of U.S. Army fighting doctrine. With the Berlin crisis of 1948 and 1949 requiring a massive airlift to sustain the city and confronting a vast superiority in Russian numbers across the now fortified intra-German border known as the Iron Curtain, the American military began to incorporate the best of German defensive combat tactics against thrusts by heavy armored formations. Much of the German historical effort focusing on this was published in a series of Department of the Army pamphlets meant for extensive use in Army training schools.[16] The entire output was a testament to the generally high quality of the German military staff system. Franz Halder became the commanding spirit behind this program and continued his close advisory association with the American military presence in Europe. Von Boetticher contributed heavily to the agenda, not only with his own writing but, with his fluency in English, as an editor who checked the accuracy of translations made. In 1951, the program also engaged him to index the entire series as a means of making the German experience of the war available to American military analysts.[17]

When the German declaration of war ended the Nazi government's diplomatic representation in Washington, General von Boetticher had failed in his self-imposed mission of schooling the American people with the German viewpoint through the medium of the American military establishment. The limitations of his position made any real and lasting result impossible, though he continued to repeat his faith in the effect of his presence in his official cables. He certainly retained close relationships inside the War Department Military Intelligence Division, as Hans Thomsen repeatedly attested, but the political effect of these contacts was negligible. American officers who might have respected or admired von Boetticher personally, who privately welcomed a German resurgence in Europe, or who entertained isolationist sympathies had their opinions recorded in the attaché reports to Germany. But no one achieved Truman Smith's notoriety and reputation in the White House itself for opposing national policy. Smith remains, even with the availability of his memoirs and broad samplings of his timely reports from Germany, an enigmatic figure whose class attitudes have now become more clear and representative of the American officer corps as a whole. Even with the president's wrath hobbling his career, Smith retained George Marshall's faith and confidence. There is even room for the belief that Smith and the Military Intelligence Division used the continuing contact to the advantage of the United States and euchred whatever they could from the German attaché. In the summary lines of his wife's memoir, however, there can be no doubt of Smith's unchanging attitudes toward Franklin Roosevelt.[18]

Von Boetticher's connection with Smith serves as another measure of the events of the time. He was clearly, for the attaché, a barometer of private professional misgivings among American officers. The dissent he recorded among these men, especially in the intelligence directorate, was real. If he constructed his own interpretation of events, he also received confirmation and sustenance for his views from his contacts in the American War Department. He placed far too great a faith in the depth, extent, and effect of those sentiments, however. In merely assuming, though, that he spoke this way out of a conversion to Nazi axiom, his critics have not sought out the more long-standing predilections for an exaggerated belief in his own mission.

Von Boetticher's frame of reference in this regard also based itself on his vision of a divine inspiration among soldiers. In his postwar writing he refers continually to the German General Staff heritage from the nineteenth Century as an unobtrusive but powerful catalytic agent acting upon the German people.[19] A permissible observation in the case of the German staff combating the presumed evils of social democracy, it was far less valid when applied to American military structure. The American electorate was far closer to the British in its suspicion of standing armies and their associated expense. Yet von Boetticher consistently regarded the two institutions as equals in their abilities to transmit moral values and political truths to citizens at large. Under the elder von Moltke, he even argued, the German Staff was the strongest guarantor of peace in the face of unspecified political currents driving toward war. In identical words, he had described the American staff in its resistance to Roosevelt's apparent bent for hostilities against Germany. Based on this romantic ideal, his thinking and his allusions to the eventual vindication and predominance of a small, spiritually pure circle consisting of men such as Lindbergh and his General Staff friends became ever more unrealistic.

Despite this unreality, the continued viability of his contacts with these elements made possible von Boetticher's pursuit of relations with his host army that were in marked contrast with those of Franz von Papen, his distant predecessor. The trade of information that von Boetticher engaged in on this basis was remarkable for its occurrence amid rising tensions between the United States and Germany and for the fact that it gave the American War Department a practical means of balancing the exaggerated, faulty, and purposefully misleading British intelligence assessments conveyed to Washington at the time. Moreover, in the conscious choice of the well-established quid-pro-quo system over any resort to espionage, von Boetticher made that system an element of the life of a military attaché that has been unexplored. In and of itself, however, the reciprocal arrangements could not bridge the deep political cleft between the American and the German state systems in the early 1940s.

Von Boetticher's romantic ideal at least partially explains the obviously anti-Semitic content of his reports. Both he and Thomsen larded their cables with occasionally scathing references to Jewish influences in America. Though this sort of phraseology was frequent among German diplomats and civil servants seeking to have their reports taken seriously at the higher echelons of Nazi government, von Boetticher reserved it for those elements in American political or military life who contradicted his own predictions on future American strategy and its momentarily struggling logistical base. He tended to stick to a limited number of stock phrases when describing these Jewish influences, even when they were not Jewish, but he certainly repeated them often enough to make his later exculpatory reminiscences on the subject suspect. Hitler, he wrote in seeming incredulous disbelief in 1947, actually thought that the entire American government was controlled by Jews and formulated policy toward the United States accordingly.[20] Yet if von Boetticher was guilty of an anti-Semitism perfunctory or deep, it certainly had some limits. Across all the private jottings and formal reports of a lifetime, he never left such extended and negative abstract theorizing on the place of Jews in society or their genetic inferiority, as did some members of the American officer corps and its educational system in his own time. His anti-Semitic phrases also do much to reflect the atmosphere in the United States of the time. Von Boetticher lived in a city with an American governing establishment that still suspected the presence of Jewish officials in the Roosevelt government, snubbed Jews in its country clubs, and excluded them from higher rank in its military. The anti–New Deal rhetoric of the moment fell back on some of the same anti-Semitic sentiments that von Boetticher included in his reports.

He certainly appears better in this regard by comparison with one of the chiefs of mission in Washington, Hans Heinrich Dieckhoff. Dieckhoff remained the official ambassador even as Thomsen acted in his stead in the American capital. In Berlin, Dieckhoff filled official documents on American affairs with openly anti-Semitic cant.[21] After his internment and return to Germany, the analytical pieces von Boetticher sent to the German High Command through the end of the war contain none of the references to Jewish wire-pullers common in his Washington reports. Upon his repatriation, his daughter later remembered, von Boetticher was presented with a list of expropriated Jewish properties in Berlin, some of them sumptuous. He refused any part of such an award for his services and moved to a rather sparse walk-up flat with his wife and his daughter, only to be bombed out of it later in the war. He retained title to the family property outside Dresden until the end of the war, when the area fell under Russian occupation.

Von Boetticher's faith in the ability of his few military contacts to guarantee the behavior of the American government also fueled a vestige of the old attaché–foreign office tensions. Dieckhoff and Thomsen, who both found occasion to remark on von Boetticher's unfailing connections at the War Department, also found it necessary to argue against the validity of his assumptions and expectations on results from this source. Because of von Boetticher's expectations, there is also a basic divergence in the approach of the diplomats and the attaché. Although von Boetticher continued to believe that he would quietly prevail in the end, Thomsen never felt so sanguine about the outcome of his rear guard action and his efforts to contribute to the continuation of American neutrality. On the other hand, the chargé d'affaires never questioned the technical side of von Boetticher's work.

In the contrast between the failure of his missionary task and the accuracy of his technical reporting, a curious dualism leaves him an unsympathetic figure, but the purely military estimates in his reports were nevertheless correct to the end. At the time the Japanese attacked Pearl Harbor, the United States had mobilized a bare 15 percent of its industrial capacity for war,[22] and von Boetticher well knew of the continuing reluctance of many professional military officers to split further the American output with the western allies and later with Russia under "cash and carry" or Lend-Lease arrangements. This realization added to his interpretation of the success of his mission with his American hearers as well, but his understanding of the state of American readiness and the still untapped potential of his host country also made his predictions on the American industrial mobilization as precise as they could possibly have been at the moment. Thus, his critics have falsely charged him with demeaning American war-making potential, when in fact he never ceased to point it up. The real American mobilization came after Pearl Harbor, not before.

His unremitting emphasis on the necessary interim before the American industrial upswing would have an effect also underlay his conviction that the Wehrmacht would produce a decision in the war before the United States could enter the lists against Germany. At each successive stroke against England, in the Balkans, and in Africa, von Boetticher pronounced it as having the desired effect among perceptive American witnesses and further proving that the initiative remained with Germany. Even when Hitler turned on Stalin, the German attaché in Washington expected a speedy outcome. In his deep appreciation of real American weaknesses of the moment, von Boetticher was paradoxically enough blind to the overcommitment of German forces and the strategic weight piling up against his own country. The breathtaking tactical results of the campaign in the Low Countries and France in 1940 were strategically barren and produced no end to the war. Hitler's decision to reduce London by attacking Moscow inevitably sealed Nazi Germany's fate. Von Boetticher shared the disastrous limitations of his brother generals in perceiving the weakness of the German position, especially after the failure to reduce the Soviet Union in a single campaign that might have drawn the war at least to a standstill in late 1941.

Von Boetticher's influence on the German strategy of the war remains difficult to assess. That some of his cables came to the full attention of the OKW staff and to Hitler is evident from the observations of Maj. Gerhard Engel and Dr. Henry Picker, surreptitiously scribbling notes at Hitler's table. Von Boetticher certainly did not contribute anything to Hitler's racial interpretations of American politics, already well formulated in *Mein Kampf*,[23] but he probably added marginally to his own stature by reinforcing Hitler's attitudes and assumptions with his verbiage about Jewish wire-pullers in America. He in no way governed Hitler's adoption of war as part of his program in Europe but may indeed have influenced Hitler's timing by making clear the temporary limits of American readiness for a specific two-year period. Those who accused von Boetticher of judging the United States as permanently incapable of offsetting German initiatives read his cables only selectively. The increasingly desperate German diplomats who hoped to rein in Hitler's plans by pointing to an American colossus took out some of their disappointment on the attaché who would not cooperate in sending home ominous assessments. It is also entirely probable that Wilhelm Keitel, always attuned to Hitler's biases and inclined to give the führer only good news, passed on only those cables that fulfilled his purpose and maintained his position within the pantheon of German command. Hitler therefore received decidedly mixed messages, something his own willful perceptions contributed to in any case.

With military pensions restored a year after his release, von Boetticher joined his wife and daughter in Bielefeld. Also settling nearby after the war was his brother Adalbert. This jurist, who had occupied posts in the Nazi judiciary throughout the Hitler regime, quietly resumed a law career in the Federal Republic.[24] The general later moved to the city's quiet suburb, Schildesche.

He soon took up again a warmhearted correspondence with Douglas Southall Freeman. The content of these letters was also a philosophic return to several early themes that von Boetticher had established in his thinking as early as 1919. He turned to a pronounced religious outlook in his later life. To build a front against communism, he wrote in July 1948, there must be a "change of the whole mentality and attitude in the direction of the norms prescribed in the Sermon on the Mount."[25] Nearly a year later, he echoed the distant past when he proposed the establishment of a George Washington Society to embody the

spiritual unity of the United States and Germany—it is a high goal. Cooperation of the defeated ones with the victorious ones and a real friendship of both; that is the last word of history, that is the solution of the problems of our time in the spirit of Jesus Christ.[26]

The same idea occupied him still in 1952 in the age of international summit meetings, which served a purpose, he admitted, but he wanted again the "unselfish cooperation of a small number of military men, scientists" who will sustain "an offensive spiritual fight against the Soviet philosophy of life."[27] On Freeman's death on June 13, 1953, the correspondence transferred to Freeman's longtime associate, Mr. J. Ambler Johnston, the Richmond architect who had always chauffeured Freeman on the forays of the "Valley Campaign" that tramped the Virginia battlefields in the 1930s.

Freeman added his efforts to other causes in the von Boettichers' lives in the postwar years. Among the fonder hopes that the family held was to enjoy unhindered foreign travel to see the growing family in Buffalo, New York. Though his daughter Adelheid could travel to Germany, von Boetticher and his wife were denied their repeated visa requests until 1950.[28] Kordt's allegations still carried weight with the State Department in 1949.[29] As if to add to the bureaucratic life of the case, in summer 1950, a flurry of teletype inquiries among U.S. Army field intelligence units in Europe was still ascertaining von Boetticher's whereabouts, but for reasons unspecified.[30]

It is also probable that Freeman led one of America's premier Civil War scholars to von Boetticher around this time. In what has become a classic on this question, historian Jay Luvaas sought to trace the intellectual influences of the American war between the states on foreign military establishments before 1914. Though he acknowledges his debt to von Boetticher at the outset,[31] his exhaustive survey of German military literature on the subject found German officers more critical of American tactics than enamored of them.[32] Von Hindenburg's supposed parting instruction to von Boetticher in 1933 may be tempered with this realization.

By late 1951, Freeman was also writing endorsements for von Boetticher's newest son-in-law, who was just leaving the British Army.[33] In 1947, Hildegard had married a British officer, Capt. Horace Marsden. The couple migrated to Canada in 1951, where Marsden took a seat on the Toronto Stock Exchange. For the younger von Boetticher daughter, this return to North America was a welcome change of scene. By 1957, already the mother of three, she enrolled in the University of Waterloo at Kitchener, Ontario, to complete the undergraduate degree she had begun at Randolph-Macon Woman's College in 1938. In June 1959, Randolph-Macon belatedly awarded her the liberal arts baccalaureate she should have received seventeen years earlier.[34] She also finished master's degree work at Waterloo and joined the faculty as an instructor in the German-Slavic Department. At her death in 1988, Hildegard von Boetticher Marsden was Dean of Women at the university.[35]

With great energy, von Boetticher continued his own historical research and writing, in one case to unforeseen effect. In 1951, he penned a short memoir entitled "The Art of War," in which he again summed up his own career and the purposeful training of the German General Staff in familiar ideal terms. This essay passed through the staff of the army historical command in Europe and was included in its monographic output. In incongruous passages he harnessed the message of Jesus Christ to the General Staff education that was to "kindle the holy fire in the hearts of the officers so that they may be equal to the highest climax of life, to war, and that they may be able to overcome the weaknesses of their time."[36]

Just how out of step this declaration was in postwar Germany became apparent when the editors of the journal *Wehrkunde* included it in the issue of September 1964.[37] The publication of these sentiments raised a small furor for the Munich-based journal. Even in the Cold War atmosphere of the mid-1960s, this particular reformulation of the old Prussian warrior spirit was anathema to the new German democracy and to the Bundeswehr wrestling with a "usable past" suitable for indoctrinating members of the German forces integrated into the North Atlantic Treaty Organization at the time.[38] As one living part of the Bundeswehr's past, however, von Boetticher continued to speak before younger military audiences, especially on the feast day of Saint Barbara, the patron of artillerymen.[39]

Von Boetticher's output after 1945, whether in memoir or historical treatments, added to his vision of the storied hero. The Parsifal figure—the mythic image of a holy and decisive individual—who rises above the political and human travail of the moment and prevails against all odds was for him forever a compelling one. He clung to these notions as visible equally in the careers of Frederick the Great, Schlieffen, von Hindenburg, George Washington and several of the icons of the American Civil War. In the end, he applied them to himself and his fruitless mission in Washington. He continued to write and speak in this vein long after events destroyed the basis for this view of the world.

The magisterial figure of Schlieffen continued to occupy him in this way. Von Boetticher published an expanded fairly straightforward biography of Schlieffen in 1957 that also recalled the man's moral effect on the German military profession.[40] An expanded but still slim rendition of the 1933 edition of the biography, the later work is still cited in the continuing literature on the Prussian field marshal. His later commentary deviates not in the slightest from the earlier Groener interpretation that sought to enthrone Schlieffen's genius and lay the blame for the failure of 1914 on the younger von Moltke, who necessarily modified the great "Plan" in its execution during the opening days of World War I.[41] Von Boetticher in fact carried with him the cache of Schlieffen papers that Groener had arranged to have loaned to him by the German military archives at Potsdam in the 1930s. This long-term retention of source materials in itself led to some controversy with later students of German military history.

It gradually became clear that von Boetticher had in his home a sizeable collection not only of Schlieffen's papers, but of other official files as well. The Schlieffen items included handwritten drafts and his marginalia on General Staff studies from his active-duty years. Original archival papers from Groener and Wilhelm von Schleicher were also under his roof, as well as a copy of a lengthy Reichswehr-produced film on the battle of Tannenberg. Von Boetticher's own outlines, notes, and historical drafts were intermingled with the official paper as he labored to produce his own commentaries on events that reflected the glories of traditional German military training and thinking. Negotiations over the eventual disposition of these archives began when German military historian (and retired colonel) Hermann Teske visited von Boetticher in Bielefeld in May 1960.[42] Intermittently over the next six years, he continued an always tentative campaign aimed at housing at least the official material in the military records offices of the Bundesarchiv. Von Boetticher's reaction to Teske's efforts were inevitably gruff and negative. He repeated his position that he would not be separated from these treasures and formally wrote their final disposition into his will: they would transfer to his daughters upon his death. In part, he justified this by citing the German Foreign Office's refusal to offset the cost of returning his household goods to Germany from the United States after 1945. Teske observes that his financial well-being and a substantial pension made the recovery of the goods no special fiscal burden for von Boetticher. The general further regarded the Schlieffen items as gifts to him from Schlieffen's own daughter, Elizabeth, and Schlieffen's granddaughter. Not even the added entreaties of Eberhard Kessel,[43] another historian and a longtime friend of von Boetticher's, could reverse the aging general's mind on this. The collection reached the German military archives in time, but only by an indirect road.[44] The Schlieffen legacy governed his life in yet another way, too.

His attachment to the field marshal's name and reputation caused von Boetticher to enter into an unusual liaison late in life. A widower for a dozen years after the death of his wife, Olga, in April 1953 he wrote an almost boyish admission to Ambler Johnston in Richmond in September 1965 that he had remarried.[45] His bride was a woman who had associated closely with the von Boetticher household in Bielefeld since at least 1947, when she was a member of the wedding party attending Hildegard von Boetticher. Von Boetticher had not informed either of his two daughters, both now in North America, but on September 6, 1965, he quietly married Anna Josepha von Hahnke, known all her life as "Bela." A woman of little means and an already evident dependency on alcohol, she seemed an odd choice for a retired general to spend his declining years with. She was, however, the daughter of former Gen. Wilhelm von Hahnke, onetime chief of the Kaiser's Military Cabinet,[46] and his wife, Elizabeth, who was herself the only daughter of the great Schlieffen. Von Boetticher not only had championed the myth of the soldier who had so influenced his earlier military formation, but had now rescued from penury and shame this German hero's granddaughter. This was not merely an act of generosity, but a final endorsement of his life's career and work. It is inconceivable that he would have similarly taken under his roof any scion of a National Socialist family. His own family was stricken at this news, though, as Johnston learned from von Boetticher's elder daughter in Buffalo, just a week after he learned of the marriage.[47]

A more formal personal memoir that von Boetticher worked on until the end of his life never reached publication. Entitled "So War Es," it often showed the effects of its author's advancing age, and the continuing influence of the "Halder school" of interpretation of the fate of the German military. His last great writing project, a draft called "Der Ruf zum Licht," showed the penchant for mystical religiosity and the residual romantic idealism that increasingly characterized his outlook.

For all of his habitual industry, von Boetticher confessed to Johnston the loneliness of his older age.[48] He visited the United States three times: in 1954, as a guest of the Air Force; in 1958, when he saw his two daughters in Buffalo and Kitchener and then was Johnston's guest in Richmond; and in 1961, when he spent a day in the Library of Congress researching George Washington's military career. He refused to leave Germany even in his declining years after a heart attack in 1965. The last laboriously typed letter he sent to Johnston, a month before his death, almost plaintively raised again the question:

> Who knows that I was sent to Washington by personal order of President Hindenburg who told me that I had to give up my military ambitions because a much higher Problem had to be solved by me: the foundation of a real and deep friendship between the United States and Germany?[49]

If he sought to leave this as a lasting image of himself, he succeeded among his friends in Richmond, who relished and repeated the story of von Boetticher's mandate from von Hindenburg's hand.[50] He himself clung to this romantic and visionary notion of his service in Washington to the end. His performance, with its vastly misplaced hopes for a wide political effect, combined with a remarkable technical grasp of America's military problems in the prewar period, marks him as a proponent not of Nazi ideology but of an older system of the Imperial German Army and its vestiges under von Seeckt: a superb technical proficiency often divorced from political feasibility or reality. It was a system that Hitler emasculated, but often with the willing cooperation of its members.[51] Von Boetticher, with most of his brother officers, could not find the moral basis or energy to resist this effectively, and his idealistic portrayals of German soldierly virtue after the war obscured the fact that the German Army had become a participant in the destruction of the nation and a bystander in the evils perpetrated by the regime it served.

On September 28, 1967, Friedrich von Boetticher died in the quiet backwater of Schildesche, a suburb of the North Rhine-Westphalian city of Bielefeld. Typical of the man who had selflessly labored in the perfection of the intricacies of the great Schlieffen Plan, he had laid out in detail the specifics of his own funeral. A detail of young Bundeswehr soldiers, too young to comprehend von Boetticher's part in their own history, carried him in precise, funereal step to the waiting earth. A representative of the German Defense Ministry centered a wreath on the coffin before its descent. In attendance at the general's invitation were his former chief at the embassy in Washington, Hans Thomsen, and his wife. Peter Riedel, already ten years in the United States and a citizen of that country working for Trans World Airlines, was absent. It may have pleased the former attaché that this small event took place in a Germany allied to the United States of America.

NOTES

Preface

1. For a brief survey of the opinion for and against the man, see the section on "The Literature on von Boetticher" in the Selected Bibliography, p. 294.

Chapter 1

1. David Brinkley, *Washington Goes to War* (New York: Alfred A. Knopf, 1988), p. 37. Brinkley apparently refreshed his memory by consulting a leading account of German espionage in the period, David Kahn's *Hitler's Spies: German Military Intelligence in World War II* (New York: Macmillan, 1978), p. 77, which discusses the rocketry report in a different, more realistic context.

2. The colored description of the man nevertheless shows up in the more recent work by Joseph E. Persico, *Roosevelt's Secret War: FDR and World War II Espionage* (New York: Random House, 2001), pp. 43–44.

3. This family information is taken from interviews with General von Boetticher's two daughters, Hildegard Marsden, August 22, 1973, and Dr. Adelheid Miller, August 24, 1973. A letter from Mrs. Marsden to the author, April 23, 1973, also contained some preliminary information. The most complete account of the Boyes-Wippermann genealogy comes from the exhaustive research done by [General] von Boetticher's father, Walther. von Boetticher's grandson has retained in the family Walther's invaluable "Nachrichten über den Lemgo-Hamburger Zweig der Familie Wippermann," unpublished typescript manuscript, 1934.

4. Walther v. Boetticher, "Nachrichten über den Lemgo-Hamburger Zweig der Familie Wippermann," p. 21.

5. Von Boetticher always made much of the memory of the estate, lost after World War II. Particularly dear to him was the statue of *Fortuna* executed by Balthazar Permoser (1651–1752), who also created statuary and the reliefs in the frieze on the world-famous Zwinger Museum in Dresden. In 1958, an engraved reproduction of *Fortuna* graced von Boetticher's Christmas cards to his friends. Copy in J. Ambler Johnston Papers, Virginia Historical Society Archives, Battle Abbey, Richmond, Viginia., Box 1, folder 2.

6. In the summer of 1912, his performance in a French examination at the War Academy requiring an interpreter's ability won him a prize of 800 Marks, which he used to travel to the Loire valley, Orleans, and Paris. Friedrich v. Boetticher, "So War Es," [unpublished typescript memoir, n.d., but ca. 1964], p. 38. Copy in author's files. Original work is in the von Boetticher papers, N323, Bundesarchiv/Militärarchiv (BA/MA), Freiburg im Breisgau (Germany).

7. v. Boetticher papers, handwritten journals and daily diaries, N323, BA/MA. Von Boetticher kept these handwritten notes on his daily activities every day of his life from 1904 until shortly before his death in 1967. The diary booklets are supplemented by dozens of other notebooks in which he penciled poetry, long quotations, and notes on subjects that concerned him. His handwriting is difficult.

8. The date of von Boetticher's entry into service is fixed in the German Army's Official "Personal-Nachweis, von Boetticher, Friedrich," TAGO Film Project A3365 German Army Officers' 201 [Personnel] Files, RG 242 Captured German Records, National Archives and Records Administration, College Park, Maryland; Summary Army Personnel File [copy in author's possession] and in the predictably laudatory obituary, "General der Artillerie v. Boetticher," *Artillerie Rundschau* 6 (December 1967): 155.

9. Officially, ensign as a rank, but the term also connoted the status of a volunteer who had not entered the service through one of the recognized cadet schools. This circumstance usually required extraordinary recommendations by a regimental commander and high character affidavits. See: John Wheeler-Bennett, *The Nemesis of Power: The German Army in Politics, 1918–1945*, Compass ed. (New York: Viking Press, 1967), p. 10n.

10. On these divisions, and on the ragged German adaptation of military technology generally in these years, see Eric Dorn Brose, *The Kaiser's Army: The Politics of Military Technology in Germany during the Machine Age, 1870–1918* (Oxford: Oxford University Press, 2001), pp. 26–42.

11. v. Boetticher, "So War Es," p. 31. He noted that at this same time the complete electrification of the barracks, the telephone, and the typewriter arrived simultaneously in German military life at the regimental level. Although he could see immediately the application of carbon paper in making file copies of orders and reports, he remarks that there was virtually no one who could type acceptably well enough to make immediate use of this development. Two things everyone should learn to do, he once told his younger daughter, are to type and to fly an airplane. Marsden Interview.

12. Martin Kitchen, *The German Officer Corps, 1890–1914* (Oxford: Clarendon Press, 1968), pp. 152–154. The army's attempt to control soldiers' activities and even to censor incoming and outgoing mail caused continued tension and scandal.

13. v. Boetticher, "So War Es," p. 28.

14. "Olga v. Boetticher, geb. Freiin v. Wirsing" in Dokumenten-Mappe-Familenpapiere, [file consists of a six-segment bound folder; each has records of Olga v. Wirsing, the last containing information on her burial and the black-bordered death notice]; Chief of the GenStb, Az21 G. Z. (K), Nr. 628/36, Berlin, 12 June 1936, to the Generalleutnant und Militaerattache, through the 3 Abt. Att.Gr. This file from the Chief of Staff was signed by Ludwig Beck and transmits proofs of the Aryan origins of both v. Boetticher and his wife, an obvious sign of political realities under the Nazi regime. Both documents in v. Boetticher papers, N323, BA/MA, Freiburg im Breisgau.

15. v. Boetticher, "So War Es," p. 29.

16. Hildegard von Boetticher, the youngest of the children, to whom we owe the preservation of much of the family record, saw her mother as a sometime tragic figure and the marriage as something of a trial. She assiduously collected her mother's papers and left them to a women's society in Germany at her death in 1988. Marsden Interview.

17. Martin van Creveld, *The Training of Officers: From Military Professionalism to Irrelevance* (New York: The Free Press, 1990), p. 27. Twenty-nine years of age, von Boetticher was at the exact statistical mean of men admitted in the years just before World War I.

18. Gordon A. Craig, *The Politics of the Prussian Army, 1640–1945*, Galaxy ed. (New York: Oxford University Press, 1964), p. 287; Larry H. Addington, *The Blitzkrieg Era and the German General Staff, 1865–1914* (New Brunswick, N.J.: Rutgers University Press, 1971), p. 12. Addington convincingly shows how the German staff always sought to defeat its enemies within striking range of the German borders, preferably in what was known as a *Kesselschlacht*, a "cauldron," or encirclement, battle that would annihilate the enemy army. Cannae was a decisive encirclement battle in which the Carthaginian general Hannibal defeated a Roman

army in 216 B.C. Classes at the Kriegsakademie studied Hannibal's decisive maneuver battle as among the purest forms of victory for German arms, always threatened on two fronts and driven by necessity to defeat one enemy quickly in order to turn and face the other.

19. Van Creveld, *The Training of Officers*, pp. 27–28.

20. Friedrich von Boetticher, "The Art of War; A Military Testament," unpublished typescript, Bielefeld, May 1951, p. 3. The association was a close and continuing one until Groener's death in 1939. Von Boetticher counted Groener among the greatest professional influences in his life. His memoir, "So War Es," is dedicated "to the memory of Wilhelm Groener, the man of selflessness and truth."

21. Morris Janowitz, *The Professional Soldier: A Social and Political Portrait*, Free Press paperback ed. (New York: The Free Press, 1964), p. 145. Janowitz describes in the American military system a means of "tapping" junior officers for the right staff positions. Company grade officers [lieutenants and captains] actively seek such patronage and the notice of their seniors. See also Kenneth A. Jolemore, "The Mentor: More Than a Teacher, More Than a Coach," *Military Review* 46 (July 1986): 4–17.

22. Gerhard Ritter, *The Sword and the Scepter: The Problem of Militarism in Germany*, vol. 2, *The European Powers and the Wilhelmian Empire, 1890–1914* (Coral Gables, Fla.: University of Miami Press, 1970), p. 264. Ritter gives an account of the military-diplomatic wrangle over the German declaration of war in the last days of July 1914 and the transmission of the mobilization order by the jittery Chief of General Staff, Helmuth von Moltke.

23. v. Boetticher, "So War Es," p. 50.

24. For an excellent summary of the popular mood in Berlin at the time, see Modris Eksteins, *Rites of Spring: The Great War and the Birth of the Modern Age* (Boston: Houghton Mifflin, 1989), pp. 55–94.

25. Germany, Reichsarchiv, *Der Weltkrieg, 1914–1918: Das deutsche Feldeisenbahnwesen*, vol. 1, *Die Eisenbahnen zu Kriegsbeginn* (Berlin: E.S. Mittler & Sohn, 1928), p. 49. This is the German official history of the field railways, the single completed book of a planned multivolume series that was to chronicle the role of German military rail services in the war. It covers activity through the end of November 1914 in the west and to the end of February 1915 in the east. Von Boetticher's position, responsible for "general military matters" on Groener's staff, is shown in an organization chart on page 220 (Anl. 5).

26. v. Boetticher, "So War Es," pp. 62–64. Actually assigned to the army group under General Max von Gallwitz, he acquitted himself so well in handling rail elements during the maneuver battles in Masuria that von Gallwitz himself handed von Boetticher his first major military decoration, the Iron Cross, First Class. Von Boetticher's memoirs at this juncture also show the heavy influence of the Hindenburg myth so deliberately cultivated after the war. His summary personnel file shows his assignment to the Gallwitz HQ in February 1915.

27. Samuel L. A. Marshall, *World War I* (New York: American Heritage Publishing, 1971), p. 191.

28. v. Boetticher, "So War Es," p. 70. Groener called the two men to Budapest even as the campaign against the Serbs began. The von Boetticher Personnel File also provides skeletal information on this assignment.

29. Map and legend: "Balkanstraße: Fahrt Deutschland-Bulgarien-Konstantinopel," in "Akten des Hauptmann v. Boettichers aus der Tätigkeit des bevoll. Generalstabsoffizier in Sofia, 16.11.15-19.6.18," [folder] Erinnerungen aus dem Kriege 1914/1918, v. Boetticher papers N323, BA/MA. There were seven subordinate harbor commanders, each with detachments of two to six German military managers running things. Eight months after von Boetticher's arrival as second in command, the Sofia central office had twenty-nine officers, and the whole net had a strength of sixty-seven assigned.

30. Ltr., v. Eulitz, Königliche Sächsischer Militär-Bevollmächtigter to v. Boetticher, February 4, 1918 [Briefbuch 9293] in folder, Erinnerungen aus dem Kriege 1914/1918. v. Boetticher papers, N323, BA/MA.

31. Von Boetticher Summary Personnel File, p. 5; "General v. Boetticher," *Artillerie Runchschau* obituary.

32. U.S. American Expeditionary Force, G-2, General Staff, *Histories of Two Hundred and Fifty-One Divisions of the German Army Which Participated in the World War (1914–1918)* (Washington, D.C.: Government Printing Office, 1920), pp. 737–738. American opinion of the 241st Infantry Division was low by the end of the war. Its heavy losses in prisoners, especially on July 18, 1918, resulted in its "fourth class" rating by American Expeditionary Forces intelligence officers.

33. Walther Hubatsch, *Germany and the Central Powers in the World War, 1914–1918*, ed. Oswald Backus (Lawrence: University of Kansas Press, 1963), p. 69.

34. The General Staff, Intelligence Section (G2A1) American Expeditionary Forces, *The German and American Combined Daily Order of Battle, 25 September 1918–11 November 1918, Including the Meuse-Argonne Offensive* (Chaumont, France: American Expeditionary Forces, 1919), pp. 21–22.

35. "General von Boetticher," *Artillerie Rundschau* obituary. He received the last save one of the decorations presented. The Crown Prince of Saxony personally placed the order around von Boetticher's neck. Of all his military decorations, his younger daughter remembered, he was proudest of this one. Marsden Interview, August 22, 1973. See cover portrait: the *Orden* is the Maltese Cross device with swords worn at the throat.

36. Harry Rudin, *Armistice, 1918* (New Haven, Conn.: Yale University Press, 1944), pp. 54–55; Hubatsch, *Germany and the Central Powers in the World War*, pp. 112–113; see also Helmut Häussler, *General William Groener and the Imperial German Army* (Madison: State Historical Society of Wisconsin for the Department of History, University of Wisconsin, 1962), p. 115.

37. Wheeler-Bennett, *Nemesis*, p. 16. See also Walter Goerlitz, *History of the German General Staff, 1657–1945*, trans. Brian Battershaw (New York: Frederick A. Praeger, 1952), p. 199.

38. Dorothea Groener-Geyer, *General Groener: Soldat und Staatsmann* (Frankfurt am Main: Societäts Verlag, 1955), p. 351.

39. Gerald Feldman, *Army, Industry, and Labor in Germany, 1914–1918* (Princeton, N.J.: Princeton University Press, 1966), pp. 182–192. See also: Wilhelm Groener, *Lebenserinnerungen: Jugend, Generalstab, Weltkrieg*, hersg. von Friedrich Frhr. Hiller von Gaertringen (Osnabrück: Biblio Verlag, 1972), p. 521.

40. Ibid,. pp. 396–399.

41. Häussler, *General William Groener*, pp. 95, 117–118; Richard C. Watt, *The Kings Depart: The Tragedy of Germany: Versailles and German Revolution* (New York: Simon and Schuster, 1968), pp. 176–177.

42. J. Benoist-Mechin, *History of the German Army Since the Armistice*, vol. 1, *From the Imperial Army to the Reichswehr* (Zürich: Scientia A.G., 1939), pp. 30–31.

43. Lamar Cecil, *Wilhelm II*, 2 vols., *Emperor and Exile, 1900–1941* (Chapel Hill: University of North Carolina Press, 1996), 2:292–293. Bizarre alternatives for the fate of the Kaiser included a plan to have him wounded or even risk his death at the front to generate a groundswell of sympathy for the last representative of the doomed German monarchy.

44. Gordon A. Craig, "Reichswehr and National Socialism: The Policy of Wilhelm Groener," *Political Science Quarterly* 63 (June 1948): 199. See also idem, *Politics of the Prussian Army*, p. 347.

45. F. L. Carsten, *The Reichswehr and Politics, 1918–1933*, California paperback ed. (Berkeley: University of California Press, 1973), p. 58.

46. Arthur Rosenberg, *Imperial Germany: The Birth of the German Republic, 1871–1918*, Beacon paperback (Boston: Beacon Press, 1964), pp. 161–162.

47. For a discussion on this key issue, which placed the civilian politician in the odd position of signing a military armistice, see Klaus Epstein, *Matthias Erzberger and the Dilemma of German Democracy* (Princeton, N.J.: Princeton University Press, 1959), p. 274.

48. Ibid., pp. 275–276; Rudin, *Armistice, 1918*, pp. 306–319. In June 1940, Adolf Hitler would have this same rail car drawn to the identical spot in the forest of Compiégne in June 1940 and add insult to injury by forcing the defeated French to sign an armistice that marked the beginning of four years of German occupation.

49. Ibid., p. 381. In a thirty-six-day period, the German command was pledged to (1) evacuate the west bank of the Rhine and a neutral zone on the east bank; (2) allow for three occupation bridgeheads around Mainz, Coblenz, and Cologne; and (3) leave intact all major factories, rail stocks, and other facilities in the specified areas. See also Louis Snyder, *Documents of German History* (New Brunswick, N.J.: Rutgers University Press, 1958), pp. 368–369.

50. Ibid., pp. 427–428. Other details dealt with the return of river barges and lighters where these were seized for German use in the war.

51. v. Boetticher, "So War Es," p. 95.

52. Edmund Marhefka, *Der Waffenstillstand*, vol. 3, *Die deutsche Waffenstillstands kommission* (Berlin: Deutsche Verlagsgesellschaft für Politik und Geschichte, 1928), p. xv. A list of the transportation subcommittee members is on page 415.

53. Samuel Shartle, *Spa, Versailles, Munich, an Account of the Armistice Commission* (Philadelphia: Dorrance & Co., 1941), p. 43. When the Germans were eating humble pie, claims Shartle, the Americans and the British were sympathetic; there was a feeling of "don't kick the other fellow when he is down, but when he gets up and gives evidence of hostility, the situation changes."

54. Matthias Erzberger, *Erlebnisse im Weltkrieg* (Stuttgart: Deutsche Verlagsanstalt, 1920), p. 159.

55. Marhefka, ed., *Die deutsche Waffenstillstandskommission*, pp. 140–141.

56. Shartle, *Spa, Versailles, Munich*, p. 55. A year after the armistice went into effect, the Germans by their own count had delivered all but 39 of the locomotives and 3,975 cars. See Marhefka, ed., *Die deutsche Waffenstillstandskommission*, p. 333.

57. Klaus Epstein, *Matthias Erzberger and the Dilemma of German Democracy*, pp. 290–291.

58. Ibid., p. 290n.

59. The two separate WAKO branches continued in being from November 12, 1918, through July 7, 1919. See "Die deutsche Waffenstillstands-Kommission, Bericht über ihre Tätigkeit vom Abschluss des Waffenstillstandes bis zum Inkrafttreten des Friedens, dem deutschen Reichstag vorgelegt in Januar 1920," in Marhefka, ed., *Die deutsche Waffenstillstandskommission*, p. 411. The dates of activity for the commission are given on page 418. After the peace was signed on June 28, 1919, the Spa delegation retreated to an *Abwicklungsstelle der WAKO, Spa, Berlin* [Transition Office of the WAKO, Spa, in Berlin]. A second, larger branch office then opened in Düsseldorf on July 8, 1919, to continue dealing with Allied demands and German compliance with the armistice terms. The transport subcommittee was thereafter taken over entirely into the rump General Staff, a development over which von Boetticher expressed his satisfaction to Erzberger. Ltr., Maj. v. Boetticher to Erzberger, Berlin, July 2, 1919, Erzberger papers, NL97/50, Bundesarchiv.

60. Epstein, *Erzberger*, p. 351n. From Versailles three weeks before the peace was signed, von Boetticher relayed an eight-page memorandum to Erzberger assessing the political-economic dislocations in England, France, and the United States that betrayed uncertainties, disagreements, and nervousness among the Allies about the peace document to be signed and the timing of it. Though written in moderate tones, the assessment proved unduly optimistic about the effect world opinion might have in favor of the Germans. Memorandum, Maj. v. Boetticher for Hochzuverehrender Herr Reichsminister, Versailles, June 7, 1919, NL 97/49I, Erzberger papers, Bundesarchiv.

61. Epstein, *Erzberger*, pp. 386, 389n. In a repetition of an event typical of the German legal system of the time, the two men convicted and imprisoned for the murder, Heinrich Schulz

and Heinrich Tillessen, were pardoned and released after the Nazi regime's arrival in power. See "Reich Pardons Assassins," *New York Times,* April 11, 1933, p. 14. The Organization Consul, a monarchist group that still venerated the departed Kaiser and was responsible for Erzberger's death and that of Walther Rathenau, had strong ties to the remnant German Navy. Tillessen's brother commanded the naval cadet school at Mürwick. See F. L. Carsten, *The Reichswehr and Politics, 1918–1933* (Berkeley: University of California, 1973), p. 134.

62. Groener Papers, Microcopy M-137, roll 2, Stück 213 [no frame numbers], U.S. National Archives and Records Administration. German originals are in Nachlass Groener, Wilhelm, BA/MA N46/130, Wichtige Tagesfragen, p. 108.

63. Von Boetticher memorandum, "Thoughts on the Approaching Peace Negotiations." Groener noted "Sehr gut!" on his copy, with the additional reminder: "Discussed with Graf Brockdorff Rantzau in Berlin on 4/4." Nachlaß Groener, NA46/130; see also Groener, *Lebenserinnerungen,* p. 484.

64. "Thoughts on the Approaching Peace Negotiation," pp. 1–2.

65. Ibid., p. 3.

66. Ibid., p. 11.

67. v. Boetticher, "So War Es," pp. 133–134. The two discussed the power-political balances affecting Germany in frequent informal talks. Ebert, according to this memoir, supplied von Boetticher with a key to the garden entrance of the presidential house so that the officer could come and go at will.

68. Edward Hallett Carr, *German-Soviet Relations between the Two World Wars, 1919–1939,* Albert Shaw Lectures in Diplomatic History, 1951 (Baltimore: Johns Hopkins University Press, 1951), pp. 4–5, 13.

69. The remnant of the wartime Supreme Command was dissolved on September 19, and the staff that had operated from the eastern German fortress at Kolberg was incorporated into the new Reichswehr Ministry. Groener retired from the army on the same day. See Carsten, *The Reichswehr and Politics,* p. 58.

70. v. Boetticher, "Deutschlands nächste politische Aufgaben," March 23, 1920, Nachlass Seeckt, N247/203, BA/MA, pp. 2–7.

71. Ibid., pp. 5–6. "Most respectfully submitted" to von Seeckt, the memorandum also contained thoughts on the character of the new German Army under these conditions. Germany needed a "politically intact, sharply disciplined army with leaders who understand the new period and the suffering of the people" (p. 6).

72. U.S. Department of State, *The Treaty of Versailles and After: Annotations of the Text of the Treaty,* Dept. of State Publication 2724, Conference Series 92 (Washington, D.C.: Government Printing Office, 1947), p. 319. Specified also in Article 160 were the existence of no more than seven divisions of infantry and two of cavalry, with two corps headquarters, all in view of the internal disorder in the defeated country. The Allies saw the remnant of the German Army as a police force.

73. Goerlitz, *History of the German General Staff,* p. 211. See also R. G. L. Waite, *Vanguard of Nazism: The Free Corps Movement in Post-War Germany, 1918–1926* (New York: W. W. Norton, 1952), pp. 182–184.

74. Groener, *Lebenserinnerungen,* p. 513. Groener also reflects here on the business of ridding the army of "the dregs attached to it in the war and in the time of revolution, if a firm and clear-sighted hand guides the effort."

75. Harold J. Gordon, *The Reichswehr and the German Republic, 1919–1926* (Princeton, N.J.: Princeton University Press, 1957), p. 66. It was not impossible for a proven field commander to stay on, and some General Staff officers also found themselves unemployed. Ernst Roehm, for instance, was a Bavarian General Staff officer whose temperament and thirst for action led him to South America in search of adventure. He returned to become chief of staff of the Nazi *Sturmabteilung* (SA), the brown shirts that became Hitler's street battalions. Von Boetticher was also in another favored class among German officers since he had begun his service in the field artillery, which had a higher proportion of its members represented in the new army. See Goerlitz, *History of the German General Staff,* p. 228.

Chapter 2

1. Arnold Wolfers, *Britain and France between Two Wars: Conflicting Strategies of Peace Since Versailles* (New York: Harcourt Brace and Co., 1940), pp. 11–20.

2. On this development generally, see James S. Corum, *The Roots of Blitzkrieg: Hans von Seeckt and German Military Reform* (Lawrence: University Press of Kansas, 1992), pp. 25–50. Corum assesses v. Seeckt's resurrection of the German military establishment especially as a rigorously select professional confraternity given to principles of maneuver warfare. Still standard accounts of von Seeckt's reorganization and redirection of the German armed forces of the time are in Walter Goerlitz's *History of the German General Staff, 1657–1945* (New York: Praeger, 1952), pp. 222–228; John W. Wheeler-Bennett's *The Nemesis of Power: The German Army in Politics, 1918–1945,*Compass Books ed. (New York: Viking Press, 1967), pp. 95–102; Francis L. Carsten, *The Reichswehr and Politics, 1918–1933*, California Paperback ed. (Berkeley: University of California Press, 1973), pp. 53–57; and Harold J. Gordon, Jr., *The Reichswehr and the German Republic, 1919–1926* (Princeton: Princeton, N.J., University Press, 1957), pp. 223–228.

3. Paul Schneider, *Die Organization des Heeres* (Berlin: E.S. Mittler Verlag, 1931), pp. 43–45. See also Harold J. Gordon, Jr., *The Reichswehr and the German Republic*, p. 179.

4. Edward L. Homze, *Arming the Luftwaffe: The Reich Air Ministry and the German Air Industry, 1919–1939* (Lincoln: University of Nebraska Press, 1976), p. 6.

5. Heinz Höhne, *Canaris*, trans. J. Maxwell Brownjohn (Garden City, N.J.: Doubleday & Co., 1979), pp. 154–155. See also Manfred Kehrig, *Die Wiedereinrichtung des deutschen militärischen Attachédienstes nach dem ersten Weltkrieg, 1919–1933* (Boppard am Rhein: Harald Boldt Verlag, 1966), p. 59.

6. U.S. Department of State, *The Treaty of Versailles and After* (Washington, D.C.: Government Printing Office, 1947); see articles 159–179. These articles comprised the so-called Military Clauses of the Treaty.

7. Alfred Vagts, *The Military Attaché* (Princeton, N.J.: Princeton University Press, 1967), p. 49; Kehrig, *Wiedereinrichtung*, pp. 106–116. Much of this detail on von Boetticher's early post–World War I career stems from this source, the only comprehensive treatment of the German struggle to reconstitute an official system of reporting on foreign armies.

8. Kehrig, *Wiedereinrichtung*, p. 127. Kehrig notes that the officers detailed abroad in this fashion stayed on the annually published rank lists with the exception of those sent to the Soviet Union. These disappeared without a trace in Germany and surfaced again after a tour with German formations in Kazan (armor training) and Lipetsk (aviation) and other centers of the German military resurgence in Russia.

9. Helm Speidel, "Reichswehr und Rote Armee," *Vierteljahrshefte für Zeitgeschichte* 1 (January 1953): 11.

10. On the Russian political factors leading to accommodation with the Germans, see Robert Conquest, *Harvest of Sorrow: Soviet Collectivization and the Terror-Famine* (New York: Oxford University Press, 1986), pp. 50–53. Conquest quotes Lenin's remark of March 15, 1921, at the time of the Tenth Party Congress and the retreat to the New Economic Policy: "We are barely holding on."

11. Waldemar Erfurth, *Die Geschichte des deutschen Generalstabes von 1918 bis 1945*, Studien und Dokumente zur Geschichte des Zweiten Weltkrieges, herausgegeben vom Arbeitskreis für Wehrforschung in Stuttgart, vol. 1 (Göttingen: Musterschmidt Verlag, 1957), p. 98. The first informal meetings of the "special group" were in the home of then-Maj. Kurt von Schleicher, a friend of von Boetticher's and another protégée of Groener's. Von Seeckt placed the activity under Abteilung 1 of the evolving army command in late 1920 and used staff officers who had served with him during World War I to continue the discussions.

12. John Erickson, *The Soviet High Command: A Military-Political History, 1918–1941* (New York: St. Martin's Press, 1962), p. 148.

13. Speidel, "Reichswehr und Rote Armee," p. 19.

14. Ibid., p. 33.

15. Gordon, *The Reichswehr and the German Republic*, p. 179. Gordon has the *Sondergruppe* originating only in 1921.

16. "Service Chronology [Dienstlaufbahn]," in Personalnachweis von Boetticher, Friedrich [1st version], under date of 4 July to 9 July 1920: "Teilnahme an der Konferenz in Spa," A3365 German Army Officers' 201 Files, Period 1900–1945, RG242, Captured German Records TAGO Film Project, Reel/Box 61. See also v. Boetticher Summary Personnel file, which also put von Boetticher at the conference two days before von Seeckt's appearance there. The "201" reference here is to the U.S. Army's file designator number for personnel records in the War Department's *Decimal File System: A Subjective Decimal Classification with a Complete Alphabetical Index for Use of the War Department and the United States Army*, 1943 ed. and subsequent revisions (Washington, D.C.: Government Printing Office, 1943). Captured personnel records were also referred to with this shorthand.

17. Otto Gessler, *Reichswehr Politik in der Weimarer Zeit* (Stuttgart: Deutsche Verlags Anstalt, 1958), pp. 158–159. See also *Das Kabinett Fehrenbach, 25 Juni bis 4 Mai 1921*, ed. by Peter Wulf, "Akten der Reichskanzlei, Weimarer Republik," herausgegeben für die Historische Kommission bei der Beyerischen Akademie der Wissenschaft (Boppard am Rhein: Harald Boldt Verlag, 1972). Records of the various sessions of the conference between July 8 and July 14 at the Villa des Sorbiers and the Hôtel d'Annette et Lubin. Von Boetticher's name does not appear among the conferees listed at the tables but he was probably among the staffs supporting the main attendees.

18. Edward Hallett Carr, *International Relations between the Two World Wars, 1919–1939* (New York: Harper and Row, Torchbook ed., 1966), p. 54; Gustav Stolper et al., *The German Economy, 1870 to the Present* (London: Weidenfeld and Nicolson, 1967), pp. 82–84.

19. Frank W. Walters, *A History of the League of Nations*, 3 vols. (London: Oxford University Press, 1960), I:105–106. Lithuania had adopted a decided tilt toward Russia during the latter's war with Poland in 1920, allowing passage to Russian troops in their advance and then mounting resistance to counterattacking Poles when the war went against the Russians. The Lithuanian government had moved to Vilna at the initial retreat of the Poles, then was ousted from the city by victorious Polish columns.

20. Gaines Post, Jr., *The Civil-Military Fabric of Weimar Foreign Policy* (Princeton, N.J.: Princeton University Press, 1973), pp. 108–110. In his memoir, von Boetticher contrasts the involvement of the German Foreign Office in this case with what came later; Friedrich v. Boetticher, "So War Es," unpublished typescript memoir, n.d., but ca. 1964.

21. Denis Mack Smith, *Mussolini* (New York: Alfred A. Knopf, 1982), pp. 96–99.

22. v. Boetticher, "So War Es," pp. 183–185. "Such a war should not come too soon," v. Boetticher quotes Mussolini as saying. An entente with Germany could only come after evidence of political stability in that unquiet country.

23. Ibid., p. 188.

24. Ibid., p. 191. Five years later he was amused to read in a Berlin daily that although the Italians had been sending military officers to Berlin on similar missions since 1923, the German Army never saw fit to return the visits.

25. Col. Edward Davis, USA, "Military Attaché," typescript manuscript [1933], pp. 449–450. U.S. Army Military History Institute, Carlisle Barracks, Pennsylvania. Davis had served with Allenby in Jerusalem in 1917, had wide experience in Greece and Macedonia before the American entry into World War I, and was on a confidential mission in the Netherlands just before his assignment to Berlin. "Von Boetticher and I tried to work together for the repair of general relationships between the two countries," reports Davis. Compiling these memoirs in 1933, he refers to von Boetticher as "Fritz," now a "lieutenant general on duty as German Military Attaché in Washington, an ideal man for such a position" (p. 449).

26. Col. R. S. Thomas, Assistant Secretary, Army War College Historical Section, "A Compilation of Correspondence on the Representation of the American Army in the Reichsarchiv, 1920–1940," File No. 2444, Thomas Files, U.S. Army Military History Institute, Carlisle Bar-

racks, Pennsylvania. With the disappearance of the Great Staff in late 1919, its historical offices were transferred to the Reichsarchiv. As the German Army was resurrected after March 1935, the military archives and the research and writing activities returned to the new Staff as the *Forschungsanstalt für Kriegs- und Heeresgeschichte,* responsible directly to the German Chief of the Army Staff. The British official history program also traded information with the Germans, but never received the volume the Americans did. On the origins of the arrangement from the American side, see Charles B. Burdick, "Foreign Military Records of World War I in the National Archives," *Prologue: The Journal of the National Archives* 7 (Winter 1975): 212–220. The first two officers dispatched to the job, Lt. Col. Walter Krueger and Col. Lewis Stone Sorley, left only vestiges of information on the relationship. See Ltr., Krueger to the President of the Reichsarchiv, Ritter Merz von Quirnheim, June 29, 1922, "Miscellaneous Orders," Box 1, Krueger Papers, U.S. Military Academy Archives; Lewis Stone Sorley, "Some Recollections," pp. 118–129 [segment: "Duty in Germany"], Lewis Stone Sorley Papers, U.S. Military History Institute, Carlisle Barracks, Pennsylvania.

27. Detlev J. K. Peukert, *The Weimar Republic: The Crisis of Classical Modernity,* trans. by Richard Deveson (New York: Hill and Wang, 1979), chapter 9, "Americanism versus *Kulturkritik,"* passim.

28. Heath Twichell, *Allen: The Biography of an Army Officer, 1859–1930* (New Brunswick, N.J.: Rutgers University Press, 1974), pp. 239–240.

29. Marsden Interview.

30. Kehrig, *Wiedereinrichtung,* p. 87; Letter, Gen. d. Art. a. D. Horst von Mellenthin to author, October 15, 1973.

31. Truman Smith, *Berlin Alert: The Memoirs and Reports of Truman Smith,* ed. and with an introduction by Robert Hessen (Stanford, Conn.: Hoover Institution for War, Peace, and Revolution, 1984), p. 60. This passage is also quoted in William Shirer's *The Rise and Fall of the Third Reich* (New York: Simon and Schuster, 1960), pp. 46n–47n. Smith repeated a ten-point programmatic description of the growing Nazi Party and its goals but was uncertain at this point about its ability to build strength north of the Danube.

32. A description of this incident was first related to the author in a telephone conversation with Smith's widow, Katherine A. H. Smith, November 23, 1973. Hesse turned into a prolific, but notably right-wing, author.

33. Interview, Col. Manfred Kehrig with author, June 18, 1988. Warburg's acquaintance with von Boetticher stemmed from the Warburg family's commercial dealings with the Wippermann family in Hamburg dating back through the last century. By this time, the Warburg family was also well established in the United States.

34. Von Boetticher to unnamed colonel, December 5, 1923, correspondence file at the Army War College, 1923–1924, "G–4 Notes on Communications Zone," February 26, 1924. U.S. Army Military History Institute.

35. On the enormity of German fiscal problems generally at this time, see Gerald Feldman, *The Great Disorder: Politics, Economics, and Society in the German Inflation, 1919–1924* (New York: Oxford, 1993). A brief summary of the dislocations that began with heedless German deficit monetary policy in 1914 designed to finance the war also appears in Eric E. Rowley, *Hyperinflation in Germany: Perceptions of a Process* (Aldershot, England: Scolar Press, 1994), pp. 1–9.

36. V. Boetticher, "So War Es," p. 192. Von Boetticher admits that by 1924 he had had a falling out with the officer known as the "Sphinx" among his peers. The sometimes colored memoirs do not offer any detail on this.

37. Gordon, *The Reichswehr and the German Republic,* pp. 297–299.

38. See his "Deutschlands nächste politische Aufgaben," March 24, 1920, in item 203, N247 Von Seeckt Nachlass, BA/MA, Freiburg im Breisgau. The Seeckt papers contain several of von Boetticher's circulated staff papers. See also Michael Geyer, *Aufrüstung oder Sicherheit: Die Reichswehr in der Krise der Machtpolitik, 1924–1936* (Wiesbaden: Franz Steiner Verlag, 1980), p. 35.

39. Friedrich von Berthelsdorfer [pseud.], "Die Grossmächte und die Weltkrise," *Die Grenzboten: Zeitschrift für Politik, Literatur, und Kunst,* 79 (December 20, 1920): 283–286. The author's name on the article was almost the same used on his passport in 1924 in the clandestine visit to the Italian head of state.

40. Friedrich v. Boetticher, "Deutsche Not," *Wissen und Wehr, Zweimonatshefte* 2(5 [Sept.-Okt] 1921): 245–254.

41. He was particularly adept at comparing French claims from 1919 to 1922 with those of Louis XIV's Court of Reunion, long-term French support of anti-Hapsburg influences, French encouragement of Polish high-handedness in the plebiscite areas in his own time, and their stretching of the meaning of the Saarland "police" functions so as to station a full regiment of French infantry, two additional rifle battalions, one regiment of cavalry, and a half regiment of artillery in the area, a total of 7,765 men. See v. Boetticher, *Frankreich . . .* (Leipzig: Verlag von K. F. Kohler, 1922), pp. 88–91.

42. Wolfers, *Britain and France between Two Wars,* p. 14. "This was an age-old French credo," remarks the author. France's total security would not be complete unless it militarily controlled the entire left bank of the Rhine and the bridges across it.

43. Jere C. King, *Generals & Politicians: Conflict between France's High Command, Parliament, and Government, 1914–1918* (Berkeley: University of California Press, 1951), p. 12. The American president Wilson vigorously opposed these French plans as an affront to the principle of self-determination.

44. v. Boetticher, *Frankreich . . . ,* p. 75. "Half the world entered the struggle," he wrote, "young noble nations, among them such as the Americans, who believed they fought for a high human ideal and had no inkling at the time that France used them to realize its predominance in Europe and the border on the Rhine, the centuries-old goals of conquest."

45. Some of these themes were also developed in von Boetticher's "Frankreichs Vordringen zum Rhein," *Wissen und Wehr* 3, no.1 (1922): 47–65.

46. Friedrich von Boetticher, *Friedrich der Grosse als Lehrer . . .* (Berlin: E. S. Mittler & Sohn, 1925), p. 21. Von Boetticher was an avid private collector of Frederician memorabilia.

47. Ibid. p. 35. See also v. Boetticher, "Friderizianisches Führertum vor 170 Jahren," *Wissen und Wehr,* 9 (April 1928): 193–206.

48. Jeffrey Herf, *Reactionary Modernism: Technology, Culture, and Politics in Weimar and the Third Reich,* paperback ed. (New York: Cambridge University Press, 1986), pp. 5–9. Already evident in the late Wilhelmian Reich's confrontation with an implacably encroaching technology in twentieth-century existence, the attempts to reconcile the actual world with ideal philosophies clinging to a romanticized past are explored in Herf's imaginative work. National socialism as a *völkisch* ideology had also to define itself in a modern world and adapt to the technical requirements of governing a nation and expanding a modern armed force while retaining racist and decidedly antimodern romantic notions.

49. Ibid., p. 23. See also Hans Kohn, *The Mind of Germany, The Education of a Nation,* Torchbook ed. (New York: Harper and Row, 1965), pp. 14–16. Kohn reviews the effect of romantic myth on the German soul, which regarded as hypocritical all the western liberal ideals in the post–World War I atmosphere. Another work in which this element is treated in more controversial ways is Peter Viereck's *Metapolitics; the Roots of the Nazi Mind* (New York: Capricorn Books, 1965).

50. Friedrich von Boetticher, *Graf Alfred von Schlieffen, Sein Werden und Wirken* (Berlin: Schlieffen Verlag, 1933), p. 10ff. A much-expanded version, *Schlieffen* (Göttingen: Musterschmidt Verlag), appeared in 1957.

51. Von Boetticher based this work on original research into von Schlieffen's Nachlass in the Reichsarchiv, opened to him by Wilhelm Groener, by then Reichswehrminister, and into the private Schlieffen family papers through Groener's acquaintance with the Schlieffen family. See *Schlieffen,* p. 5, "Vorwort."

52. Wilhelm Groener, *Das Testament des Grafen Schlieffens; Operative Studien über den Weltkrieg* (Berlin: E.S. Mittler & Sohn, 1929), p. 7. Another noteworthy effort with a similar

approach is that of Hugo von Freytag-Loringhoven, *Generalfeldmarschall Graf von Schlieffen; Sein Leben und die Verwertung seines geistigen Erbes im Weltkrieg* (Leipzig: Historia Verlag Paul Schraepler, 1920), one of the earliest published professional critiques of Field Marshal Helmuth von Moltke's execution of the strategic German right-wing sweep through Belgium and the Netherlands that opened World War I.

53. In Schlieffen's words (but also ascribed to the Danish astronomer Tycho Brahe): "Viel leisten, wenig hervortreten, mehr sein als scheinen," the unofficial motto of the German General Staff officer. This maxim was still being reverently quoted in the literary campaign in German military publications at the end of the Weimar epoch. See Hindenburg's autographed dedication in Gen. Friedrich v. Cochenhausen, ed., *Von Scharnhorst zu Schlieffenm 1806–1906* (Berlin: E.S. Mittler Verlag, 1933).

54. See, for example, Jehuda L. Wallach, *Das Dogma der Vernichtungsschlacht: Die Lehren von Clausewitz und Schlieffen und ihre Wirkungen in zwei Weltkriegen* (Frankfurt am Main: Bernard & Greaefe Verlag für Wehrwesen, 1967), p. 57.

55. Dennis Showalter, "From Deterrence to Doomsday Machine: The German Way of War, 1890–1914," *The Journal of Military History* 64 (July 2000): 679–710. Showalter surveys the literature on the phenomenon of German planning through the close of the Wilhelmine Reich.

56. On these developments, see Christoph M. Kimmich, *Germany and the League of Nations* (Chicago: University of Chicago Press, 1976), pp. 76–79.

57. League of Nations, Documents for the Preparatory Commission for the Disarmament Conference Entrusted with the Preparation for the Conference for the Reduction and Limitation of Armaments, Series I [typescript] (Geneva, 1925), pp. 45–48. See also Frank P. Walters, *A History of the League of Nations*, 2 vols. (London: Oxford University Press, 1952), 1:365.

58. Raymond J. Sontag, *A Broken World, 1919–1939* (New York: Harper and Row, 1971), pp. 134–138.

59. League of Nations, Preparatory Commission for the Disarmament Conference, Verbatim Report, 3d Meeting (Public), Tues., May 18, 1926, at 4 p.m., Chairman: M. Jonkheer Loudon [typescript] (Geneva, 1926), pp. 8–9.

60. Graf Johann Bernstorff, *The Memoirs of Count Bernstorff* (New York: Random House, 1936), pp. 342–343. Since the French would never disarm, no matter what we say or do, he asserts here, the Germans would follow the old diplomatic trick of putting your opponent in the wrong and yourself in the right. League Secretary Walters noted that Bernstorff had a difficult task but "performed it with dignity and a certain stiff courtesy, through which, however, the bitterness of a Germany deprived of her beloved army was allowed to appear." See Walters, *A History of the League of Nations*, 1:365.

61. See John Wheeler-Bennett, *Information on the Reduction of Armaments* (London: George Allen & Unwin, 1925), pp. 61–62. Requin was a practiced veteran of French military representation at League disarmament talks. He was a member of the Temporary Mixed Commission discussing these matters in 1920. In 1922, he submitted a draft that sought the recognition of a French alliance system in Europe as part of a League system of security.

62. On the political, financial, and international pressures on French military policy in the interwar period, see Irving M. Gibson, "Maginot and Liddel Hart: The Doctrine of Defense," in *Makers of Modern Strategy*, ed. Edward M. Earle (New York: Atheneum, 1970), pp. 367–370.

63. The "Verbatim Record" has this paraphrase of von Boetticher's remarks: "Colonel von BOETTICHER (Germany) (translation) regretted that the definition of the word "criterion" had not been given at the beginning of the discussions when a vote was taken on the question of material in service. He had looked up the definition of this word in Larousse and found that it meant something which enabled one to appreciate or judge of a thing, and this appeared to have exactly the same signification as the English word "standard." As regards the other point, the question at issue is not whether trained reserves constitute a practical criterion, but whether they formed a standard of comparison.

League of Nations, Preparatory Commission for the Disarmament Conference, Minutes, June 1926, Sub-Commission A, Record of Proceedings of the EIGHTH Meeting, June 26, 1926, 9:30 A.M., pp. 11–12.

64. League of Nations, Preparatory Commission for the Disarmament Conference, Sub-Commission A, Military Subcommission, Minutes, August 27, 1926 [bound typescript] (Geneva, 1926), pp. 1–2.

65. John W. Wheeler-Bennett, *Disarmament and Security Since Locarno, 1925–1931, Being the Political and Technical Background of the General Disarmament Conference, 1932*, reprint of the 1932 ed. (New York: Howard Fertig, 1973), pp. 54–57.

66. Von Boetticher to Col. Joachim v. Stülpnagel, 17th Infantry Regt., Braunschweig, August 12, 1926, Nachlass Stülpnagel, Briefwechsel des Gen. d. Inf. Joachim v. Stülpnagel as Kdr. Inf Rgt 17, 1.3.26–1.2.27, N5/21, BA/MA [Freiburg im Breisgau].

67. Ibid. He was "badly situated," he reported, and could not think of letting his wife come to Geneva. News of his "old Dresden artillerymen" gladdened him. Geyer's *Abrüstubng oder Sicherheit*, p. 85n, presents von Boetticher's correspondence with Foreign Ministry Secretary von Bülow from Geneva as one influence on Reichswehr attitudes on domestic politics affecting the League process.

68. Friedrich v. Boetticher [unsigned article], "Militärpolitische Übersicht: Die Genfer Verhandlungen über Sicherheit und Abrüstung," *Wissen und Wehr* 8 (1928): 251–254.

69. Reichswehr Ministerium, *Rangliste des Deutschen Reichsheeres, Nach dem Stande vom 1 Mai 1927* (Berlin: E.S. Mittler & Sohn, 1927), p. 8; von Boetticher "201" file.

70. Kehrig, *Wiedereinrichtung*, p. 94.

71. Otto Gessler, *Reichswehr Politik in der Weimarer Zeit* (Stuttgart: Deutsche Verlags-Anstalt, 1958), p. 233.

72. Wheeler-Bennett, *Disarmament and Security*, p. 361. Wheeler-Bennett noted (in 1931) that the adoption of the draft for the status quo was a "reaffirmation of the doctrine of one law for the victor and another for the vanquished." He predicted that without some satisfaction to its claims, Germany must leave the conference and may leave the League "an action which would be both deplorable and disastrous to that institution since in all probability she would not leave alone."

73. John W. Wheeler-Bennett, *The Pipe Dream of Peace* (New York: William Morrow & Co., 1935), p. 6.

74. J. Ambler Johnston, Echoes of 1861—1961 (privately printed, 1970), p. 53.

75. Von Mellenthin to author, October 15, 1973.

76. Von Boetticher letter, May 9, 1951, response to questionnaire [May 7, 1951] from Hermann Mau, General Secretary, Deutsches Institut für die Geschichte der nationalsozialistischen Zeit, Munich, seeking personal recollections on the influence of Nazism on the Reichswehr before the Nazi takeover of power. Von Boetticher Papers, N323, BA/MA, Freiburg im Breisgau. In one event of the time, however, von Boetticher's friend Wilhelm Groener fell victim to the machinations of Wilhelm Schleicher. See Gordon Craig, "Reichswehr and National Socialism: The Policy of Wilhelm Groener, 1928–1932," pp. 194–229; and Theodor Eschenburg, "The Role of Personality in the Crisis of the Weimar Republic," in *Republic to Reich: The Making of the Nazi Revolution* (New York: Vintage Books, 1972), pp. 16–29.

77. U.S. Department of State, *Foreign Relations of the United States, 1932*, 4 vols. (Washington, D.C.: 1940), vol. 1, *General*, pp. 489, 527–28. Hereafter cited as *FRUS* with appropriate publication data. See also Editor's note with summary of events in this new phase of talks at Geneva in U.S. Department of State, *Documents on German Foreign Policy, 1918–1954*, Series C, 5 vols. (Washington, D.C.: Government Printing Office, 1959–1966), vol. 1 (1957) *The Third Reich: First Phase*, pp. 18–19. This series is hereafter referred to as *DGFP* with appropriate series and volume data.

78. Kehrig, *Wiedereinrichtung*, pp. 146–147. Kehrig's account shows that the Foreign Office was not especially reticent on the idea. State Secretary Bernhard von Bülow agreed after several meetings with representatives of the Reichswehr's Personnel Office.

79. Testimony of Ritter von Leeb, International Military Tribunal, *Trials of War Criminals before the Nuremberg Military Tribunal under Control Council Law No. 10, October 1946 to April*

1949, vol. 10, case 12, U.S. vs v. Leeb (Washington, D.C.: Government Printing Office, 1951), p. 170. See also International Military Tribunal, *Trials of the Major War Criminals before the International Military Tribunal, Nuremberg, 14 November 1945–1 October 1946*, 42 vols. (Nuremberg: International Military Tribunal, 1948), 16:606, 614–618, for the testimony of German Foreign Minister Konstantin von Neurath on the subject.

80. Reichswehr Minister to the Foreign Office, January 5, 1933 (Secret) Subj: Appointment of Attachés, Captured German Records, RG242, Micro-copy T-120, 3611/9786, E687262–264. The original list read:

Washington—Generalmajor von Boetticher
London—Oberst Geyr von Schweppenburg
Paris—Generalmajor Kühlenthal
Rome—Oberst Fischer
Warsaw—Generalmajor Schindler
Prague—Oberst von Falkenhorst
Moscow—Oberstleutnant Hartmann

Schleicher also begged the Foreign Office to send apologies to the governments of Argentina, Mexico, Spain, and Turkey for not sending attachés immediately, pleading financial problems that prevented Germany from sending men to every country that at that moment posted attachés to Berlin.

81. Generaloberst Franz Halder, "Selection and Training of German Officers for Military Attaché Duty," MS P-097, U.S. Army, Europe, Foreign Military Studies Series [typescript], 1951, pp. 7–10. Halder maintained that there never was a formal program to prepare attachés for their work after World War I (p. 2). Although this is technically true, the men in the group sent out in 1933 had magnificent references for their official dealings with foreigners. Von Boetticher's old T–3 section and the *Völkerbund Abteilung* had many alumni among the attachés now appointed. Kühlenthal, Fischer, Schindler, and von Boetticher had all headed the T–3 Section in the 1920s; Schindler had also been with von Boetticher in Geneva.

82. General der Panzertruppen [Lt. Gen.] Leo Geyr von Schweppenburg, *The Critical Years* (London: Allan Wingate, 1952), p. 9. Geyr suggests that the ambitions of von Schleicher were common knowledge among the Foreign Office professionals and gave grounds for von Hoesch's suspicions. "I cannot say the Embassy helped make me feel at home . . . ," says Geyr of his early days in London, but he overcame his misgivings and had a good working relationship with the ambassador.

83. Leopold von Hoesch to State Secretary, Foreign Office [Bernhard von Bülow], January 3, 1933, T-120, 3611/9786, E687293. RG 242 Captured German Records Microfilmed at Alexandria, Virginia. National Archives and Records Administration.

84. Halder, "Selection and Training of German Officers for Military Attaché Duty," p. 11. Halder maintains that the men were "the very flower of the officers' corps and were considered as such abroad."

85. Von Bülow, handwritten note on Draft Instruction of January 5, 1933. A further marginal note indicates that the notifications that von Schleicher had requested in his note of the same date went out from the Foreign Office on the following day, January 6. T-120, 3611/9786, E687265.

86. Prittwitz u. Gaffron to Foreign Office, March 3, 1933, T-120, 2741/5863, E428922.

87. For summary comments on the difficulties of the old German attaché system, see Vagts, *The Military Attaché*, pp. 15–28; and Gordon A. Craig, *The Politics of the Prussian Army, 1640–1945* (New York: Oxford University Press, 1966), pp. 266–273. Of the voluminous literature on the subject, two of the still most useful texts are Gerhard Ritter, *Die deutschen Militär-Attachés und das Auswärtige Amt: Aus den verbrannten Akten des Grossen Generalstabs* (Heidelberg: C. Winter, 1959); and Heinrich Otto Meisner, *Militärattachés und Militärbevollmächtigte in*

Preussen und im Deutschen Reich: ein Beitrag zur Geschichte der Militärdiplomatie (Berlin: Rütten & Loening [1957]).

88. Kehrig, *Wiedereinrichtung*, pp. 146–147. Kehrig provides a good summary of the discussion and the leading points at issue.

89. Service Instructions for Military and Naval Attachés and Their Aides Attached to German Embassies and Legations, T-120, 3611/9786, E687298-303, Captured German Records, RG 242, NARA. The 1935 revision of the original instruction is in Kehrig, *Wiedereinrichtung*, pp. 207–210.

90. Von Boetticher's elder daughter recalled her father's attitude toward the victor of Tannenberg and later Reich President as "filial." Interview, Dr. Adelheid [von Boetticher] Miller with author, Buffalo, N.Y., August 24, 1973. (Dr. David K. Miller participated with his wife in this interview.) This devotion is paradoxical for the fact that von Boetticher's benefactor Groener had suffered betrayal on several separate occasions at von Hindenburg's hand. In the discussions leading to the armistice in World War I, Hindenburg contrived to allow the odium for the acceptance of that document to fall on a number of people other than himself; one of these was Groener. Nor would Hindenburg defend Groener before the military court of honor that finally vindicated the latter in 1922. In 1932, Hindenburg's lack of support during the crisis that followed Groener's ban on Hitler's S.A. contributed to Groener's forced resignation. Despite Hindenburg's treatment of him during the collapse of the German Empire in the last days of World War I, Groener believed that "in the interest of the New Army, the myth of von Hindenburg should be preserved. It was necessary that one great German figure should emerge from the war free from all the blame that was attached to the General Staff. That figure had to be Hindenburg." See John W. Wheeler-Bennett, *The Wooden Titan; Hindenburg in Twenty Years of German History* (New York: Oxford University Press, 1936), p. 221. Groener's attitude was so consistent with von Boetticher's ideas on combating the French attempt to saddle the German national self-consciousness with the entire burden of guilt for the war that the two can only be seen as the closest of intellectual collaborators.

91. Friedrich von Boetticher, "Impressions and Experiences of the Military and Air Attaché in Washington during the Years 1933–1941," MS B-484, U.S. Army, Europe, Foreign Military Studies Series, April 27, 1947, p. 8; J. Ambler Johnston, *Echoes of 1861–1961*, pp. 53–54; Douglas Southall Freeman, *The South to Posterity* (New York: Charles Scribner's Sons, 1939), pp. 166–167. As Freeman repeats the story, Hindenburg called after von Boetticher as he left the president's office, "`That is the war for us to study.'" In his "So War Es," pp. 294–295, von Boetticher's later-life memoir, he is indefinite as to the date of the event. It occurs here in the context of von Hindenburg's earlier request that von Boetticher prepare a radio address to be given on February 28, 1933, the 100th anniversary of Alfred von Schlieffen's birth. He claims that the British ambassador was kept waiting in the anteroom while the two discussed the American Civil War.

92. Von Boetticher Personnel Record; Halder, "Selection and Training of German Officers for Military Attaché Duty," p. 11; see also General der Artillerie Anton Frhr. von Bechtolsheim, "The German Attaché System," MS P-097a, U.S. Army, Europe, Foreign Military Studies Series, February 1952, p. 5. Both Halder and von Bechtolsheim assert that Foreign Office preparation of the attachés consisted of rapid, perfunctory introductions and no real information. Von Boetticher family lore added one poignant anecdote to the series of events. Even as von Boetticher prepared to leave Germany, his younger daughter recalled in 1973, the realities of Nazi ideology touched his life when he purchased some needed furniture at one of Berlin's larger department stores, a Jewish concern. His name appeared the following day in the local editions of the *Völkischer Beobachter* as one who "hat bei Juden gekauft." [patronized a Jewish store] His reaction was to return to the same store for other items. Marsden Interview, August 22, 1973. A review of the Berlin edition of the *Beobachter* for the period January to April 1933, however, turned up no mention of this.

Chapter 3

1. Selig Adler, "The War Guilt Question and American Disillusionment, 1918–1928," *Journal of Modern History*, 23 (March 1951): 4–28, passim. See also Dixon Wecter, *The Age of the Great Depression, 1929–1941* (Chicago: Quadrangle Books, 1971), pp. 300–302; and David M. Kennedy, *Freedom from Fear: The American People in Depression and War, 1929–1945*, The Oxford History of the United States (New York: Oxford University Press, 1999), pp. 381–425. Early criticism of Hitler and Nazi Germany hardly overcame the indifference of Americans to events in Europe, and the influx of Jewish immigrants from Germany even fueled a wave of anti-Semitism in America.

2. v. Prittwitz u. Gaffron to the Foreign Ministry, Cable No. 108, March 16, 1933, *DGFP*, C, 1. pp. 173-175. Editorials, especially in the *New York Times*, uniformly condemned the new German regime. See for example: "Hooligan S. A. Men," *New York Times*, March 10, 1933, p. 11. In late March, the leading German-language newspaper in America, the *New Yorker Staatszeitung*, emphatically denounced the Nazi persecution of Jews in a signed editorial by the paper's publisher, Benjamin F. Ridder: "Blind Fanaticism," *New Yorker Staatszeitung*, March 23, 1933, p. 6, col. 1.

3. v. Prittwitz to Foreign Minister, March 11, 1933, *DGFP*, C, I, pp. 147–148. He could not do otherwise, he told his old friend Konstantin von Neurath, "without betraying myself." In a measured analysis a year later, he retained some hope for a German-American understanding. See *Deutschland und die Vereinigten Staaten seit dem Weltkrieg*, Heft 7, Vorträge des Carnegie-Lehrstuhls für Aussenpolitik und Geschichte in Berlin (Berlin: Verlag B. G. Teubner, 1934).

4. v. Prittwitz to Luther, Cable No. 182, April 5, 1933, T-120, 5141/K1226, K318546.

5. "Foreign Service: Comings and Goings," *Time* 21 (April 24, 1933): 12.

6. "Germany Appoints Military Attachés," *New York Times*, January 11, 1933, p. 13. Datelined Berlin on January 10, the article listed the reasons for the appointments as the recent Five-Power Declaration and noted (incorrectly) some of the highlights of von Boetticher's career to that point. The article resulted from a Reichswehr Ministry press release.

7. v. Boetticher to *Reichswehrministerium*, April 16, 1933, T-120, 2741/5863, E428932. This three-page summary of the trip, his reception in New York, and other details was his first report from America.

8. Kiep to Foreign Office, Cable No. 60, April 11, 1933, T-120, 274115863., E428927. Kiep's exchange was with Gerhard Köpke of Abteilung II of the Foreign Office, responsible for military matters. Köpke also got the Berlin office of the *Stahlhelm* to intercede with the New York affiliate in the interest of toning down the reception committee.

9. Friedrich v. Boetticher "So War Es," [unpublished typescript memoir, n.d., but ca. 1964] pp. 313–314.

10. The now-standard work in English on Hitler's foreign policy is Gerhard L. Weinberg's *The Foreign Policy of Hitler's Germany*, paperback revised ed. (Atlantic Highlands, N.J.: Humanities Press, 1994), 2 vols. The essay "The World through Hitler's Eyes" offers a solid introduction to the subject and surveys the state of opinion on it in Ibid., vol. 1, *A Diplomatic Revolution in Europe, 1933–1936*, pp. 1–24. Also among the best explications of the various positions taken in a still developing literature on Nazi foreign policy is the segment (chapter 12) on the subject in Ian Kershaw's *The Nazi Dictatorship: Problems and Perspectives of Interpretation*, 3rd ed. (London: Edward Arnold, 1993), pp. 108–130. Kershaw makes clear that the two varying interpretations are not mutually exclusive. The most rigid timetable of the "intentionalists" would have to bow to local conditions and take advantage of presented opportunities on the world stage as emphasized by "structuralist" views. Wolfgang Michalka's *Nationalsozialistische Aussenpolitik* (Darmstadt: Wissenschaftliche Buchgesellschaft, 1978) contains a representative selection of articles on varying interpretations on the subject. For the only written declaration of Hitler's avowed principles governing future German relations with its neighbors, see

Hitler's Zweites Buch: Ein Dokument aus dem Jahr 1928, with introduction and commentary by Gerhard L. Weinberg (Stuttgart: Deutsche Verlags-Anstalt, 1960), p. 160. This eight-point analysis emphasizes the hopelessness of Germany's disarmed position in the face of the League system and the eternal enmity of France. Hitler did not here set down a long-range "program," but a set of Euro-centric observations on strategic realities at the same time von Boetticher was at Geneva in the midst of disarmament talks. See also Zachary Shore, *What Hitler Knew: The Battle for Information in Nazi Foreign Policy* (Oxford: Oxford University Press, 2003), pp. 14–15.

11. On the difficulties of achieving political and administrative control of the traditional German civil service, see Martin Broszat, *The Hitler State: The Foundation and Development of the Internal Structure of the Third Reich* (New York: Longman, 1981), pp. 241–261. Additional detail on the process of civil service reform is in Jane Caplan, *Government without Administration: State and Civil Service in Weimar and Nazi Germany* (Oxford: Clarendon Press, 1988), pp. 169–183.

12. Robert Gellately, *Backing Hitler: Consent and Coercion in Nazi Germany* (Oxford: Oxford University Press, 2001), p. 256. Gellately argues convincingly that the mass of Germans accepted Nazi depredations against their political enemies and that the regime did nothing to conceal its program, but in fact trumpeted its successes in the print and broadcast media.

13. John Lukacs, *The Hitler of History* (New York: Vintage Books, 1997), pp. 128–175.

14. On the discussion of "continuity versus change" in German foreign policy from 1871 to 1945, see Klaus Hildebrand, *The Foreign Policy of the Third Reich* (Berkeley: University of California Press, 1973), pp. 1–11. The theme is also elaborated upon in Joseph W. Bendersky's *A History of Nazi Germany* (Chicago: Nelson-Hall Publishers, 1985), pp. 191–192.

15. Klaus Hildebrand, *Das vergangene Reich: Deutsche Außenpolitik von Bismarck bis Hitler, 1871–1945* (Stuttgart: Deutsche Verlags-Anstalt, 1995), p. 572.

16. Norman Rich, *Hitler's War Aims,* vol. 2, *The Establishment of the New Order* (New York: W. W. Norton, 1974), p. 417.

17. Telephone conversation, Joseph Waggaman, Waggaman-Brawner Realty Company, Washington, with the author, January 23, 1973. Mr. Waggaman remembered von Boetticher as a "fine gentleman" with whom he had annual dealings when the lease on the house came up for renewal. Rents were normally paid from embassy accounts with the Riggs National Bank in the city. The house was also large enough to accommodate von Boetticher's considerable library, which included his many scarce editions by Frederick the Great and on military history generally. He had insisted that he be allowed to move the collection to America. Marsden Interview, August 22, 1973.

18. The literal translation of this rank is colonel-general, the equivalent of a four-star general in the American and British military establishments.

19. Paul Beauvais, *Attachés Militaires, Attachés Navals, et Attachés de l'Air* (Paris: Editions A. Padrone, 1937), p. 128.

20. v. Boetticher to Reichswehrministerium [RWM], April 21, 1933, T-120, 2741/5863, E428935. He did not comment further on the short ceremony in which he handed over his credentials to Franklin Roosevelt on the same day as this report.

21. v. Boetticher to RWM, Rpt. 8, June 13, 1933, ibid., E428975.

22. Douglas MacArthur, *Reminiscences* (New York: McGraw-Hill Book Co., 1964), p. 97. Despite von Boetticher's later claims of close ties with the American chief of staff, MacArthur makes no mention of the German officer in his memoirs.

23. D. Clayton James, *The Years of MacArthur, 1880–1941,* 3 vols. (Boston: Houghton Mifflin, 1970) I:373–374. James cites von Blomberg's plaintive memoir of the episode as evidence of MacArthur's anti-German bias: ". . . He did not like us Germans. . . . To have known why would have been enlightening since the general was such an outstanding figure. He was aggressively Anglo-American and therefore, of course, unsympathetic to our national traits." Blomberg, "Erinnerungen bis 1933," p. 3, cited in ibid., p. 677.

24. v. Boetticher to RWM, April 21, 1933, T-120, 2741/5863, E428936.

25. v. Boetticher to RWM, August 5, 1933, ibid., E429012.

26. War Department Biography, November 28, 1929, in General Officers' Biography File, U.S. Army Center of Military History, Washington, D.C.

27. Fred H. Botticher to author, July 30, 1973.

28. G–2 Records, Synoptic Index, "Attaché, Military, German in Washington," Part I, p. 5. RG 165, War Department Military Intelligence Division Records. This file is an extensive record of Boetticher's activities in the United States. Each official contact with the War Department or any field installation is recorded and the permission noted. The attaché often entered routine requests for permission to visit American installations around the country for himself and other visiting German technicians. The exchanges themselves were destroyed, leaving only this office record showing the dates of receipt of each request, the date permission was granted, and sometimes cryptic entries denoting German activities.

29. v. Boetticher to RWM, May 30, 1933, T-120, 2741/5863, E428964.

30. Mabey provided von Boetticher with a copy of his own speech with a warm, if routine, cover letter, all of which the recipient sent home with the evaluation that: "in reality the speech was—still much more than appears in the actual text—a recognition not only of an understanding with Germany, but also of a trust for the new German leadership and the formation of things in Germany." v. Boetticher to RWM, June 28, 1933, T-120, 2741/5863, E428985.

31. Ibid., E428987–88.

32. v. Boetticher to RWM, Truppenamt, Rpt. 12/1933, July 27, 1933, ibid., E4529001–02.

33. v. Boetticher to RWM, Truppenamt, Anl., 2 Rpt. 13/1933, August 3, 1933, ibid., E429010.

34. v. Boetticher to RWM, Truppenamt, Rpt. 14/1933, August 30, 1933, ibid., E429016. Dawes's contribution to the American war effort in France had been significant. As a brigadier general, he had headed the Allied Purchasing Commission during the last war and negotiated all American supply contracts with the French, a considerable undertaking, since the great majority of the provender and most of the heavy military equipment came from French sources. His international reputation, stemming from the German reparations plan that bore his name, made him a celebrity worth mentioning in this context for von Boetticher.

35. v. Boetticher to RWM, June 28, 1933, ibid., E428986–88.

36. T. Bentley Mott, *Twenty Years as a Military Attaché* (New York: Oxford University Press, 1937), pp. 111–112. The traditional, rigid "Prussian" discipline of West Point had to be unlearned in World War I, insisted Mott. American soldiers required the reasons back of any military order, as with the French. "If we are to draw inspiration from any foreign source, it should not be from the Germans or the English, but from the French."

37. Forrest C. Pogue, *Ordeal and Hope*, vol. II (1966) of *George C. Marshall* (New York: The Viking Press, 1963–1987), pp. 106, 238. General Marshall had frequent wartime conferences on strategic and personnel matters with General Pershing, under whom he had served as AEF chief of staff in World War I. See also Sumner Welles, *Seven Decisions That Changed the World* (New York: Harper and Bros., 1951), p. 34.

38. Russell F. Weigley, *The American Way of War: A History of United States Military Strategy and Policy* (New York: MacMillan, 1973), pp. 210–211.

39. v. Boetticher to RWM, Truppenamt, Rpt. 11, July 11, 1933, T-120, 2741/5863, E429006.

40. Von Boetticher's pique with the French "campaign" already rose in May 1934 when the U.S. Congress declared May 20 General Lafayette Memorial Day. The French attaché presented one of Lafayette's sabres at an exhibition in New York for the occasion. Already at this juncture the German attaché saw von Steuben's traditional image threatened: "The views are changing on which of the cosoldiers of Washington should be placed in the foreground." v. Boetticher to RWM, Truppenamt, May 25, 1934, "The 100th Anniversary of the Death of Lafayette," T-77, OKW1106/906, 565516.

41. v. Boetticher to RWM, Truppenamt, Anl. 2, Rpt. 32/1934, September 26, 1934, "The Struggle for the Soul of the American Army," T-77, OKW1106/906, 5658736.

42. Ibid., 5659738.

43. v. Boetticher to RWM, Truppenamt, Anl. 10, Rpt. 13/1935, March 25, 1935, T-120, 2741/5863, E429425ff. Included as a summation of unofficial opinion among American officers was von Boetticher's recounting of his discovery on his desk of a Frederician *Thaler* of some value with this accompanying note from an unidentified American officer: "This old Thaler will always remind us of 16 March."

44. Ibid.

45. Telephone interview, March 12, 1975, Genevieve Bastide with the author. Bastide was one of Lombard's secretaries between December 1939 and the French collapse in 1940.

46. "Autobiography," an incomplete memoir transcribed from tape recordings [1962], p. 67, Ralph E. Truman Papers, Harry S Truman Library, Independence, Missouri.

47. Mrs. Ralph E. (Olive) Truman to author, March 30, 1974.

48. v. Boetticher to RWM, Truppenamt, Anl. 1, Rpt. 33/1934, October 4, 1934, T-120, 2741/5863, E429195. Still, he cautioned against publicizing his honors in the German press.

49. "Parade Climaxes Division Review: 35th Passes in Review at Two O'Clock—General von Boetticher Chief Reviewing Officer," Emporia *Gazette* (September 27, 1935), pp. 1, 2. His photograph, accompanying the article, shows him in the uniform of the old Reichswehr, without the Nazi cap and tunic devices that had become standard a year earlier.

50. v. Boetticher to RWM, Truppenamt, Anl. 7, Rpt. 17/1934, June 7, 1934, "Trips of the Military Attaché," T-77, OKW1106/904, 5656639. See also Anl. 1, Rpt. 20/1934, July 17, 1934, "Report of the Trips of General von Boetticher to the Middle and Far West," T-120, 2741/5863, E429163ff.

51. v. Boetticher to RWM, Anl. 1, Rpt. 20/1934, July 17, 1934, ibid., E429168.

52. Ibid.

53. Weinberg, *The Foreign Policy of Hitler's Germany*, vol. 1, *A Diplomatic Revolution in Europe, 1933–1936*, p. 159ff. See also Karl Dietrich Bracher et al., *Die nationalsozialistische Machtergreifung*, 2d ed. (Köln: Westdeutscher Verlag, 1962), pp. 766–784.

54. Arnold Toynbee, ed., *Survey of International Affairs, 1933* (London: Oxford University Press, 1934), p. 226ff.

55. Unsigned memorandum, "The Crisis of the Disarmament Conference, April 28–May 13, 1933," May 15, 1933, *DGFP*, C, I, p. 493. Hitler had confirmed the validity of the interpretation by ordering military training for 250,000 reservists in the SA. Bracher, et al., *Die nationalsozialistische Machtergreifung*, p. 797.

56. Department of State, *FRUS 1933* (Washington, D.C.: 1934), I:143–145.

57. George A. Gordon, Chargé d'Affaires, American Embassy, to German Secretary of State, No. 2421, May 20, 1933, ibid., pp. 159–164. See also Adolf Hitler, *Speeches of Adolf Hitler*, ed. by Norman Baynes, 2 vols. (London: Oxford University Press, 1942), II:1041–1058.

58. Davis to Secretary of State, May 19, 1933, ibid., pp. 154–158. The proposal was actually a rewording of one Herbert Hoover presented in 1932 with General MacArthur's concurrence. See James, *Years of MacArthur*, I:378–81.

59. Minutes of a conference of ministers on September 12, 1933, *DGFP*, C, I, p. 797.

60. Brig. Gen. George V. Strong, WD Biography File, U.S. Army Center of Military History.

61. v. Boetticher to RWM, Truppenamt, Anl. 1, Rpt. 16/1933, September 12, 1933, T-120, 2741/5863, E429029.

62. v. Boetticher to RWM, Truppenamt, Anl. 6, Rpt. 18, October 10, 1933, "Interview of October 3, 1933, Subj: Disarmament," ibid., E429052–54.

63. Cordell Hull, *The Memoirs of Cordell Hull*, 2 vols. (New York: Macmillan, 1948) I:239–241.

64. Toynbee, *Survey 1933*, p. 296ff.

65. Minutes of Conference of Nazi Cabinet Ministers, October 14, 1933, *DGFP*, C, I, pp. 922–926.

66. v. Boetticher to RWM, Truppenamt, Anl. 1, Rpt. 19/1933, October 18, 1933, "Confidential Report on the German Step of October 14, 1933 and the First Military-Political Result in the United States," T-120, 2741/5863, E429064–66. Von Boetticher begged his readers to keep the content of his report confidential in order to protect his sources and keep them willing to provide him with such information in the future.

67. v. Boetticher to RWM, Truppenamt, Anl. 2, Rpt. 22/1933, November 22, 1933, "Disarmament Questions," ibid., E429089.

68. Betts Interview, January 23, 1974; Marsden Interview, August 22, 1973. He also hired flutists from the National Symphony in Washington to play Frederick's compositions that interspersed his own short presentations on the Prussian monarch. See reports of his field lectures at Fort Benning during automatic weapons training there in Anl. 4, Rpt. 22/1933, November 22, 1933, T-120, 2741/5863, E42902–95.

69. Marsden Interview, August 22, 1973; Miller Interview, August 24, 1973. The von Boetticher and Scammell family relations were very close. One of Hildegard Marsden's earliest memories of America was of a severe tonsilitis attack she suffered while a weekend guest at the Scammell house. Scammell also accompanied the German attaché on cross-country trips.

70. Among its organizers, the foundation counted one of the more renowned military commentators of the time in Hoffman Nickerson and the secretary of the Carnegie Endowment for International Peace, James Brown Scott. The organization managed to get the patronage of some of the leaders of World War I fame, among them Peyton March and Hunter Liggett, but a more moving spirit was Col. Arthur Conger, whose quasi-official visits in 1919 to the German High Command and later to Matthias Erzberger raised German hopes unduly at the time. The foundation, without an official organ in the first four years of its existence, published intermittent articles in *Army Ordnance* before establishing the quarterly *Journal of the American Military History Foundation* in 1937 as a worthwhile scholarly serial. After several revisions in name, the foundation survives today as the Society for Military History, which publishes the respected *Journal of Military History* under the auspices of the George C. Marshall Foundation and the Virginia Military Institute, Lexington, Virginia.

71. Scammell to J. Fred Rippy, April 26, 1935, American Military Institute files, Industrial College of the Armed Forces Library, Washington, D.C. Charles A. Beard had suggested the general theme for the session to Scammell at a meeting at Scammell's house in early April. Von Boetticher, present at the meeting, met the prominent and controversial isolationist historian for the first time here.

72. Kerner to Scammell, November 20, 1935, AMI Files. Desperate in October, Scammell tried to recruit the new chief of staff, Gen. Malin Craig, as one of the participants, only to be turned down. Memo for Gen. Craig, October 18, 1935, Subj: Address on Force and Policy; Ltr., Craig to Scammell, October 22, 1935, AMI Files. Scammell finally took on the job himself and spoke before the convention.

73. Generalleutnant Friedrich von Boetticher, "The Struggle against Overwhelming Odds," *Review of Military Literature* 15 (December 1935): 5–26.

74. Ibid., pp. 15, 26. See also Scammell to Alan French, October 22, 1935, AMI Files, in which Scammell, attempting to induce French to sit in as discussion leader, cites the title of von Boetticher's paper as "Washington and Frederick the Great: Two Fighters against Overwhelming Odds."

75. William E. Dodd, Jr., and Martha Dodd, *Ambassador Dodd's Diary, 1933–1938* (New York: Harcourt Brace and Co., 1941), p. 202. Their meeting, during one of von Boetticher's visits home for consultations, took place in the home of the American attaché in Berlin, Col. Jacob Wuest, whose acquaintance with von Boetticher also survived the war.

76. Von Boetticher's original letter to Freeman is not among the Freeman Papers, but Freeman's response includes an enthusiastic offer for a guided tour of the Richmond battlefields.

DSF to v. Boetticher, April 5, 1935, Douglas Southall Freeman Papers, container 27, folder 46, Library of Congress Manuscript Division.

77. v. Boetticher to RWM, Truppenamt, Anl. 6, Rpt. 19/1933, May 6, 1933. Von Boetticher attended in full uniform and heard Freeman acknowledge his presence in connection with allusions to two Prussian officers, Heros von Borcke and Justus Scheibert, who served the Southern cause under Confederate Gen. Jeb Stuart.

78. Archibald G. Robertson, "Memorandum of 1st Manassas Rerun" [16–17 October 1937], J. Ambler Johnston Papers, Miscellaneous File, Battle Abbey [Virginia Historical Society Archives], Richmond, Virginia. Johnston was an architect by profession, but an enthusiastic student of the Civil War. He frequently chauffeured Freeman during the battlefield visits.

79. DSF to v. Boetticher, November 21, 1935, Freeman Papers, container 26, folder 46. The warm nature of the friendship was also attested to in the author's interview with J. Ambler Johnston, June 23, 1973, at his home in Richmond, Virginia.

80. v. Boetticher to RWM, Truppenamt, Anl. 1, Rpt. 33, 1933, October 2, 1935, T-120, 2741/5863, E429334. This was included in a summary of extensive travel from July through September of the year. "This does not," he emphasized, "have to do with one-time impressions nor with the repetition of views of rare individuals who want to demonstrate their own importance or one-sided attitudes."

81. DSF to v. Boetticher, June 20, 1937. Reviewing the world situation of the moment, Freeman sought the answer to the relationship of German policy to world peace but remarked that "General von Boetticher would not serve a government that was not righteous." Freeman Papers, container 34, folder 46.

82. v. Boetticher to Generalstab, Waffenamt, Anl. 3, Rpt. 14/1933, September 14, 1933, T-120, 2741/5863, E429031–32. Von Boetticher's caution apparently carried the necessary weight, for the issue was not mentioned again in his reporting. The standard German infantry weapon for the war was a bolt-action rifle, the *Karabiner 98*. See WD Technical Manual, *Handbook on the German Armed Forces*, TM-E 30-451, March 15, 1941, p. VII-2.

83. v. Boetticher to v. Reichenau, September 10, 1934, T-77, OKW1106/904, 5658683.

Chapter 4

1. William L. Langer and Everett Gleason, *The Challenge to Isolation: The World Crisis of 1937–1940 and American Foreign Policy*, 2 vols., Torchbook ed. (New York: Harper and Row, 1964), I:15.

2. See Table 1: Strength of the United States Army 1919–1941, in Mark Skinner Watson, *The Chief of Staff: Pre-war Plans and Preparations*, U.S. Army in World War II (Washington, D.C.: Office of the Chief of Military History, 1960), p. 16.

3. *Report of the Chief of Staff, 1934* (Washington, D.C.: 1934), p. 22. MacArthur arrived at these figures by subtracting from total army forces those troops in garrisons overseas.

4. Walter Millis et al., *Arms and the State: Civil-Military Elements in National Policy* (New York: The Twentieth Century Fund, 1958),. p. 21.

5. v. Boetticher to Reichswehrministerium, Truppenamt, May 12, 1933, [no subject], T-120, 2741/5863, E42849. See also Rpt. 8/1933, June 13, 1933, ibid., E42897376. Both reports were based on long conversations with MacArthur in the chief of staff's office.

6. John A. Salmond, *The Civilian Conservation Corps, 1933–1942: A New Deal Case Study* (Durham, N.C.: Duke University Press, 1967), pp. 26–45.

7. v. Boetticher to Reichswehrministerium, May 12, 1933, [no subject], T-120, 2741/5863, E428956.

8. v. Boetticher to Reichswehrministerium, Rpt. 8/1933, June 13, 1933, [no subject], T-120, 2741/5863, E428982–84.

9. *Annual Report of the Chief of Staff, 1933* (Washington, D.C.: Government Prinnting Office, 1933), p. 311. See also D. Clayton James, *The Years of MacArthur*, 3 vols. (Boston: Houghton Mifflin, 1970), I:421.

10. v. Boetticher to RWM, Anl. 4, Rpt. 22/1933, November 22, 1933, "Report on Trips in the United States," T-120, 2741/5863, E429095. This report summarized movements from Fort Hoyle outside Baltimore; the Infantry School at Fort Benning, outside Columbus, Georgia; and other military posts. At Fort Benning, he was invited to attend a class that included analysis of the Battle of Tannenburg, gratifying to him. He carefully records the instances in which German-Americans sought him out during his appearances.

11. James, *Years of MacArthur*, I:426. MacArthur's leading biographer remarks that the general was probably as opposed as ever to using the army for work-relief programs, but that as an expedient the CCC had gained fine publicity for the army.

12. Maurice Matloff, ed., *American Military History* (Washington, D.C.: Office of the Chief of Military History, 1969), p. 412.

13. Russel F. Weigley, *History of the United States Army* (New York: Macmillan and Co., 1967), pp. 397, 402.

14. Jim Dan Hill, *The Minute Man in Peace and War* (Harrisburg, Pa.: Stackpole, 1964), p. 348; see also *The Army Almanac: A Book of Facts Concerning the United States Army*, 2d ed. (Harrisburg, Pa.: Stackpole, 1959), p. 124.

15. Martha Derthick, *The National Guard in Politics* (Cambridge, Mass.: Harvard University Press, 1965), p. 51. The armories built with public works money hosted local sporting events, floral shows, and the like to wide public approval.

16. The new law officially changed the designation of what was formerly called the National Militia, under a Militia Bureau, to the National Guard of the United States under a National Guard Bureau. Before this legislation, the president was constrained to petition the various state governors to activate reserve units and place them in federal service; he could now call such units up on his own authority. The act further gave federal status to enlisted men thus called into federal service. Formerly only officers were granted this status and the emoluments that went with federal service. Among other changes was the revised arrangement whereby guard officers were also to be detailed to General Staff duty and thereby contribute to their own experience and to the process of national-level war planning. *Army Almanac*, p. 119.

17. v. Boetticher to Reichswehrministerium, May 12, 1933, [no subject], T-120, 2741/5863, E428956.

18. Detail on the western tour and the evaluation of the guard's military performance and its political status is from von Boettichers Anl. 1, Rpt. 20/1934, July 17, 1934, "Report on the Trip of General von Boetticher to the Middle and Far West in the Period 9 June to 10 July 1934," T-120, 2741/5863, E429163180. Von Boetticher's relations with the 40th Division were further cemented by his friendship with Maj. Gen. Dan Barrows, the divisional commander and a professor of history at the University of California. See also Anl. 3, Rpt. 15/1934, May 24, 1934, "Talk of Professor Barrows on the Armament Question," T-77, OKW1106/904, 5658606–07 on the subject of a "pro-German" speech Barrows gave at an assembly of the Carnegie Endowment for International Peace in Washington on May 24, 1934.

19. v. Boetticher to RWM, Anl. 2, Rpt. 21/1934, July 31, 1934, "Visit to the National Guard of Pennsylvania," T-77, OKW1106/904, 5658674, and v. Boetticher to RWM, Anl. 5, Rpt. 8/1935, February 20, 1935, "Impressions on Travel and Experiences of the Military Attaché," T-77, OKW1106/904, 565889–96.

20. Constance M. Green, Harry C. Thompson, and Peter C. Roots, *The Ordnance Department: Planning Munitions for War*, (Washington, D.C.: Office of the Chief of Military History, 1955), p. 169.

21. Ibid., p. 31.

22. Harry Woodring [Secretary of War] to House Sub-Committee on Appropriations and to Senate Committee on Military Affairs, May 28, 1940, Cater Files, folder 21, Center of Military History.

23. John Killigrew, "The Impact of the Great Depression on the Army," (Ph.D. diss., Indiana University, 1960), p. IV-3.

24. Elias Huzar, *The Purse and the Sword: Control of the Army by Congress through Military Appropriations, 1933–1950* (Ithaca, N.Y.: Cornell University Press, 1950), p. 136.

25. v. Boetticher to RWM, Rpt. 9/1933, June 28, 1933, [no subject], T-120, 2741/5863, E428989.

26. James, *Years of MacArthur*, I:429–430; For Ickes's remarks on these "little peanut Army posts," see his *Secret Diaries of Harold Ickes*, 3 vols. (New York: Simon and Schuster, 1953), I:71.

27. v. Boetticher to RWM, Anl. 2, Rpt. 16/1934, May 31, 1934, "Motorization and Mechanization in the American Army," T-77, OKW1106/904, 5658626. Here he provides great detail on the age of American trucks and military prime movers.

28. v. Boetticher to RWM, Anl. 3, Rpt. 5/1935, January 30, 1935, "Reports on the U.S. Army and the Issue of the Annual Report of the Chief of Staff for 1934," T-120, 2741/5863, E429211.

29. Weigley, *History of the United States Army*, p. 411.

30. The literature on this development is vast and continues to grow unabated in the post-Cold War era. Critical assessment of the evolution of American airpower in this period is in Michael S. Sherry, *The Rise of American Air Power: The Creation of Armageddon* (New Haven, Conn.: Yale University Press, 1987), pp. 47–69. See also Walter Millis, *Arms and Men: A Study in American Military History* (New York: G.P. Putnam's Sons, 1956), pp. 269–72; and Russell F. Weigley, *The American Way of War: A History of United States Military Strategy and Policy* (New York: Macmillan, 1973), pp. 223–241. The official history of the interwar air forces still shows the effect of the "strategic" airpower arguments of the 1930s. See William A. Goss, "The Origins of the Army Air Forces," in Wesley F. Craven and James Lea Cate, eds., *The U.S. Army Air Forces in World War II*, 7 vols. (Chicago: University of Chicago Press, 1948–1957), vol. 6, *Men and Planes*, p. 327. A thoughtful treatment of the airpower theorists from Douhet to the nuclear age is David MacIsaac's "Voices from the Central Blue: The Air Power Theorists," in *Makers of Modern Strategy: From Machiavelli to the Nuclear Age*, ed. by Peter Paret with the collaboration of Gordon A. Craig and Felix Gilbert, Princeton, N.J.: Princeton University Press, 1986), pp. 624–627. For a general history of the evolution of various national examples of military and naval aviation, see also James L. Stokesbury, *A Short History of Air Power* (New York: William Morrow and Company, 1986).

31. German note of July 10, 1934, [Embassy Note II M 1434], State Dept. Decimal Files No. 701.6211/908, Box 3665, RG 59, NARA.

32. v. Boetticher to RWM, Rpt. 14, August 30, 1933, [no subject, mainly travel reports], T-120, 2741/5863, E429015.

33. Ibid. See also WD, G-2 Records, Synoptic Index, "Attaché, Military, German in Washington," RG 165, p. 24, and passim. The American G-2 Foreign Liaison Office record of requests from the German attaché for these visits contains hundreds of names and the notation that letters of introduction had been supplied through von Boetticher to these technicians. The G-2 list also appears to be incomplete.

34. Oral History Transcript of Interview, Lt. Gen. Ira C. Eaker with Hugh Ahmann [Air Force Oral Historian], February 10–12, 1975, pp. 323–324, Air Force File K239.0512-829. Copy in Library, Center for Air Force History, Bolling AFB, Washington, D.C. "I not only flew him on one or two occasions over Chancellorsville . . . [Eaker relates], but I went with him by automobile on two or three trips. He was here many years and all of us liked him very much. . . . He was very well educated, spoke English perfectly, and was especially interested in American history, all facets of it."

35. Wesley F. Craven, "The Army Air Arm between the Two World Wars, 1919–1939," in Craven and Cate, *The U.S. Army Air Forces in World War II*, vol. 1, *Plans and Early Operations*,

pp. 17–30.

36. Von Boetticher was apparently not privy to the results of the Drum Board's deliberations. In October 1933, he was still commenting on the secrecy surrounding the plans for the development of the Air Corps. Von Boetticher to RWM, Anl. 2, Rpt. 20/1933, October 25, 1933, "Allotment of Funds for Army and Military Aviation: Future Questions for Aviation. Cooperation of Commercial and Military Aviation," T-120, 2741/5863, E429073.

37. Von Boetticher's analysis of the General Staff memorandum is in Anl. 2, Rpt. 8/1934, March 23, 1934, "Fundamental Position of the Secretary of War Dern to the Question of the Enlargement and Organization of the Air Force of the American Army," T-77, OKW1106/904, 5658519–526. The entire content of MacArthur's argument appeared again in the *Chief of Staff's Annual Report* for 1934, included in the *Report of the Secretary of War to the President, 1934* (Washington, D.C.: 1934), pp. 48–51. MacArthur alluded to the element of oceanic isolation that protected the United states. This alone eliminated the need for separate air ministries such as those in European countries that had common borders with potential enemies. War there could be expected to begin with sudden, crippling air attacks.

38. v. Boetticher to RWM, Anl. 3, Rpt. 5/1934, February 16, 1934, "Takeover of the Air Mails by the Air Corps," T-120, 2741/5863, E429114–115.

39. For Lindbergh's role and his consultative interest in early American aviation development and air mail policy as well, see Walter S. Ross, *The Last Hero: Charles A. Lindbergh* (New York: Manor Books, 1974), pp. 254–260; A. Scott Berg, *Lindbergh* (New York: G. P. Putnam's Sons, 1998), pp. 291–296.

40. v. Boetticher to RWM, Anl. 1, Rpt. 7/1934, March 16, 1934, "Takeover of the Air Mails by the Air Corps of the American Army," T-120, 2741/5863, E429128–129. In his usual thorough style, von Boetticher gave detailed information about the routes across the country, adding that new night and foul weather navigation instruments were being installed in the aircraft in early March.

41. Arthur M. Schlesinger, *The Age of Roosevelt,* 3 vols. (Boston: Houghton Mifflin, 1958), vol. 2, *The Coming of the New Deal,* p. 455.

42. *Final Report of the War Department Special Committee on the Army Air Corps, July 18, 1934* (Washington, D.C.: Government Printing Office, 1934), p. 1. The membership of the Baker Board, as it was known, is listed here. Dern offered Lindbergh a seat on the committee, but the flier declined to participate. Berg, *Lindbergh,* p. 294.

43. Ibid., p. 61.

44. Craven, "The Army Air Arm between the Two World Wars," p. 32.

45. *Final Report,* pp. 66–67.

46. v. Boetticher to RWM, Anl. 1, Rpt. 21/1934, July 28, 1934, "Report on the Special Committee for the Air Corps," T-77, OKW1106/904, 5658867. Von Boetticher only took notice of the existence of a parallel commission under the chairmanship of Clark Howell, head of the Federal Aviation Commission. Though the Air Corps expected more from the Howell Commission, viewing it as more favorable to Air Corps interests than the Baker Board, the Howell Commission issued no recommendations after the Air Corps announced its intention to live with the Baker Board's resolution giving it a measure of autonomy.

47. v. Boetticher to RWM, Anl. 4, Rpt. 38/1934, November 7, 1934, "Measures for the Expansion of the Air Forces of the American Army," T-120, 2741/5863, E429199–204. He commented further on the additional Air Corps representation on the army General Staff, revisions in the promotion policies for airmen, flight and hazard pay for officers, new training requirements, and the flight programs introduced among the cadets at the U.S. Military Academy and among older career officers in order to reduce tensions between the ground services and the air arm.

48. v. Boetticher to RWM, Anl. 1, Rpt. 8/1935 February 18, 1935, "The New Organization of the Air Force of the American Army," T-77, OKW1106/904, 5658899.

49. v. Boetticher to RWM and RLM [Reichsluftfahrtministerium-Reich Air Ministry], Anl. 1, Rpt. 27/1937, July 25, 1937, "The American Army in the Fiscal Year 1937," [German film, no frame numbers].

50. Irving B. Holley, *Buying Aircraft: Materiel Procurement for the Army Air Forces*, (Washington, D.C.: Office of the Chief of Military History, 1964), pp. 61–62.

51. Bernard L. Boylan, "The Search for a Long-Range Escort Plane, 1919–1945," *Military Affairs* 30 (Summer 1966): 58.

52. v. Boetticher to RWM, Anl. 2, Rpt. 20/1933, October 25, 1933, "Allotment of Funds for Army and Military Aviation . . . ," T-120, 2741/5863, E429073–74. Von Boetticher clearly valued Foulois highly: ". . . one of the last fliers who actually trained with the Wrights. Still today wherever he goes he flies his own plane and had no aide. . . . Humor, far-sightedness, a spiritual drive characterize this general." Von Boetticher also counted Foulois among those "personally close to me."

53. v. Boetticher to RWM, Anl. 1, Rpt. 27/1937, July 25, 1937, "The American Army in the Fiscal Year 1937," [German film, no frame numbers].

54. *Final Report*, pp. 64–65.

55. Lloyd Morris and Kendall Smith, *Ceiling Unlimited: The Story of American Aviation from Kitty Hawk to Supersonics* (New York: Macmillan, 1953), p. 288. Nurtured at first with domestic airmail franchises that accounted for two-thirds of its revenues until 1933, Pan Am developed a passenger business that eventually covered the globe. In expanding into South America, it had direct subsidies and planning support from not only the postmaster general and the State Department but also from the War Department.

56. v. Boetticher to RWM, with copies to RLM, Anl. 7, Rpt. 18/1933, October 9, 1933, "Aviation Policy of the United States," T-120, 2741/5863, E429056.

57. v. Boetticher to RWM, Anl. 4, Rpt. 19/1933, October 18, 1933, [American Aviation Policies]; and Anl. 1, Rpt. 20/1933, October 27, 1933, "Air Policy of the USA," [completion of Reports 18/1933, Anl. 7, and 19/1933, Anl. 4], T-120, 2741/5863, E429067, E429071. In the later report he also pointed to American zeal in cultivating American aircraft sales to China amid strong competition from German and English companies. The Chinese market from 1926 to 1934 absorbed nearly 7,000 American aircraft, or about 13 percent of a considerable American export, contributing to the overall health of the American industry. See Holley *Buying Aircraft*, p. 19. As keen as American efforts were to subsidize the sale of American war planes to nations such as China, the American government contrived at the same time with its English counterpart to prevent their sale to Germany, even for "police" purposes, believing such sales detrimental to the still proceeding Disarmament Conference at Geneva. See The Secretary of State to the British Ambassador, October 27, 1933, *Foreign Relations of the United States, 1933*, vol. II, pp. 490–491.

58. v. Boetticher to RWM, Anl. 7, Rpt. 18/1933, October 9, 1933, "Air Policy of the US," T-120, 2741/5863, E429057. Here were details of Lindbergh's flight in October over Greenland and Iceland, to the Shetlands, Sweden, Finland, and the Soviet Union, where American approaches to the regime in the same month bore early fruit in the official reception given the American flier. In some anticipation of the imminent recognition of the Soviet Union by the United States, von Boetticher told the staff of the German air ministry, "You can expect that . . . an 'air-political [*luftpolitisch*]' cooperation is in the offing," and predicted commercial air relations within two years, something impossible without normalization of relations between two nations estranged since 1917.

59. v. Boetticher to RWM and RLM, Anl. 3, Rpt. 22/1933, November 22, 1933, "Building Floating Platforms for Air Travel Across the Atlantic," T-120, 2741/5863, E429090. As his source, von Boetticher cited Eugene L. Vidal, another of his intimate contacts. Vidal, an early aviation pioneer, was director of the Bureau of Air Commerce and a dominant voice in American aviation affairs. Von Boetticher regarded him highly and used his expertise as a basis for many of his reports on aviation subjects.

60. *Report of the Federal Aviation Commission, 1935* (Washington, D.C., 1935), pp. 82–85.

61. v. Boetticher to RWM and RLM, Anl. 4, Rpt. 7/1935, February 14, 1935, "The Report of the Federal Aviation Commission," T-77, OKW1106/904, 5658886.

62. Kathleen Williams, "Development of the South Pacific Air Route," Army Air Forces Historical Study No. 45, February 1946, pp. 4–5. In 1935, Pan American covered the 8,000 miles from San Francisco to Manila via a central Pacific route touching at Honolulu, Midway, Wake Island, and Guam. With increased tensions in the area by 1940, alternate routes swung due south of Hawaii and then to New Zealand and Australia via Canton Island, the Fijis, and Noumea (New Caledonia).

63. Grayson Kirk, "Wings over the Pacific," *Foreign Affairs* 20 (January 1942): 301–302.

64. Marvin A. Kreidberg and Merton G. Henry, *History of Military Mobilization in the United States, 1775–1945*, DA Pamphlet 20-212 (Washington, D.C.: Office of the Chief of Military History, 1955), pp. 380–381.

65. Millis, *Arms and Men*, p. 272.

66. v. Boetticher to Reichswehrministerium, Anl. 1, Rpt. 24/1933, December 13, 1933, "The Armament Policy of the United States," T-120, 2741/5863, E429100–101.

67. Ibid., E429107.

68. Jean Moenk, A History of Large Scale Maneuvers in the United States, 1935–1964, unpublished manuscript (Ft. Monroe, Virginia: U.S. Army Command, 1969), p. 19.

69. v. Boetticher to Reichswehrministerium, Anl. 5, Rpt. 30/1933, September 9, 1935, "The Troop Maneuvers at Pine Camp from 20 to 27 August 1935," T-120, 2741/5863, E429296.

70. The four-army organization built upon the existing Army Corps area as follows:

First Army (North Atlantic): First, Second, and Third Corps Areas
Second Army (Great Lakes and Canadian border): Fifth and Sixth Corps Areas
Third Army (Gulf of Mexico and Mexican border): Fourth and Eighth Corps Areas
Fourth Army (Pacific Coast): Seventh and Ninth Corps Areas

The four armies were to be subordinate to the General Headquarters command by the chief of staff, who would leave his post in Washington to take over field command. See *Report of the Secretary of War, 1933* (Washington D.C.: Government Printing Office, 1933), pp. 12–13; and Kreidberg and Henry, *History of Military Mobilization,* p. 427.

71. v. Boetticher to Reichswehrministerium, Anl. 5, Rpt. 30/1935, September 9, 1935, "The Troop Maneuvers at Pine Camp from 20 to 27 August 1935," T-120, 2741/5863, E429300.

72. Ibid., E429300–301.

73. v. Boetticher to Reichswehrministerium, Anl. 1, Rpt. 33/1935, October 2, 1935, "Travel Impressions in the United States," T-120, 2741/5863, E429339.

74. Morris Janowitz, *The Professional Soldier: A Social and Political Portrait* (New York: The Free Press, 1960), pp. 236–241.

75. Douglas MacArthur, *Reminiscences* (New York: McGraw Hill Book Co., 1964) p. 90. MacArthur was roundly hooted during his address before the commencement exercises at the University of Pittsburgh in 1932, and he retained his suspicion of communist influence in the Bonus March of that year. See also Roger Daniels, *Bonus March Incident: An Episode of the Great Depression*, Contributions in American History, No. 14, Stanley I. Kutler, ed. (Westport, Conn.: Greenwood Publishing, 1971), pp. 108–109, 173–175.

76. Memorandum, G. V. H. Moseley to Ass't. Sec'y of War, [Frederick H. Payne] October 9, 1930, Box 5 (letters 1916–1945), Moseley Papers, Manuscript Div., Library of Congress. Moseley, in contrast to MacArthur, fêted von Boetticher when the latter visited the Corps Area that Moseley commanded in July 1933, insisting on having the German attaché as a house guest when he visited the IV Corps Area at Atlanta. Moseley, whose virulent anti-Semitism certainly outdid any in von Boetticher's reports, became increasingly suspect as a Nazi sympathizer after his retirement in 1938. Von Boetticher probably came to regret his association with him when, after the collapse of Nazi Germany, a U.S. Justice Department investigating

team expressed a strong interest in their relations and the extent of any possible espionage. See Oetje John Rogge, *The Official German Report, Nazi Penetration, 1924–1942, Pan-Arabism 1939–Today* (New York: Thomas Yoseloff, 1961), p. 284. Von Boetticher is quoted as having told the interrogation team that "whenever my visits carried me into the South, I always stopped at Atlanta, Georgia, and visited General Moseley, who was a good friend of mine."For Moseley's invitation to von Boetticher, see Synoptic Index, WD G-2, Attaché, German, Military in Washington, p. 5, citing Moseley's letter to Chf, Foreign Liaison Section, July 24, 1933.

77. v. Boetticher to Reichswehrministerium, Anl. 1, Rpt. 20/1934, July 17, 1934, "Report on the Trip of General von Boetticher to the Middle and Far West," T-120, 2741/5863, E429165–177.

78. His unnamed informants reflected the experience of the aftermath of the Bonus March. A piqued MacArthur demanded of each of the Corps Area commanders a list of the communists who had attached themselves to the marchers as they set out for Washington. This proved to be impossible, for no "red" leadership was evident. Maj. Gen. Malin Craig, IX Corp Area commander (San Francisco), reported that the marchers he had seen were, in fact, "vehemently anti-communist." See James, *Years of MacArthur*, I:390–391.

79. v. Boetticher to RKM [Reichskriegsministerium—Reich War Ministry], Anl. 7, Rpt. 25/1935, June 25, 1935, "Pacifism, Anti-Military Propaganda, and Communism in the U.S. and the Army," T-120, 2741/5863, E429278–79. He remarked that it especially had no appeal for negroes, who were spiritually primitive, very religious, and not ready for inclusion in American political life. This report received more than the usual attention in the German Foreign Office, being distributed to various desks in turn, and landing on State Secretary von Bülow's desk on July 11, 1935.

80. On the intellectual roots and the evolution of American neutrality and "isolationism" in this period, see Justus D. Doenecke, *The Battle against Intervention, 1939–1941*, The Anvil Series, ed. by Henry Trefousse, (Malabar, Florida: Krieger Press, 1997).

81. Cordell Hull, *The Memoirs of Cordell Hull*, 2 vols. (New York: Macmillan Co., 1948. I:338.

82. Robert A. Divine, *Roosevelt and World War II* (Baltimore: Johns Hopkins University Press, 1969), p. 7; see also Roosevelt's "Chautauqua Address," August 14, 1936, U.S. Department of State, *Peace and War* (Washington, D.C.: Government Printing Office, 1943), pp. 323–329.

83. v. Boetticher to RKM, Anl. 7, Rpt. 19/1936, May 26, 1936, "Arms Commerce and Arms Manufacturing, May 1936," T-78, H27/47, roll 657, frame 328, lists the American firms that were required to register as producers of materials that would be subject to export restrictions in the event of foreign wars.

84. v. Boetticher to RKM, Anl. 2, Rpt. 31/1935, September 14, 1935, "The Position of the U.S. in the Italo-Abyssinian War," T-120, 2741/5863, E429313.

85. v. Boetticher to RKM, Anl. 1, Rpt. 33/1935, October 2, 1935, "Travel Impressions in the U.S.," T-120, 2741/5863, E429335.

86. Divine, *Roosevelt and World War II*, pp. 11–13.

87. Allen Guttmann, *American Neutrality and the Spanish Civil War* (Boston: D.C. Heath and Co., 1963), p. 9. For Hull's statement, see *Peace and War*, pp. 292–293, and Hull, *Memoirs*, I:435.

88. v. Boetticher to RKM, Anl. 8, Rpt. 35/1935, October 19, 1935, "Position of the U.S. in the Italo-Ethiopian Conflict," T-120, 2741/5863, E429369. This details the dispatch of Maj. Norman E. Fiske to Rome on October 16. v. Boetticher to RKM, Anl. 1, Rpt. 38/1935 November 18, 1935, "Position of the United States in the Conflict between Italy and Abyssinia," T-120, 2741/5863, E429389 gives the vita of Capt. John Meade, who went to Addis Ababa in November. See James Dugan and Laurence Lafore, *Days of Emperor and Clown: the Italo-Ethiopian War, 1935–1936* (Garden City, N.Y.: Doubleday and Co., 1973), pp. 143–144.

89. v. Boetticher to RKM, Anl. 4, Rpt. 6/1936, February 26, 1936, "The Neutrality Policy of the United States (2d Report)," T-120, 2741/5863, E429423–26.

90. George F. Kennan, *American Diplomacy, 1900–1950* (New York: Mentor Books, 1951), p. 49.

91. Elting E. Morison, *Turmoil and Tradition, A Study of the Life and Times of Henry L. Stimson* (Boston: Houghton Mifflin and Co., 1960), pp. 401–402. American nonrecognition of the Japanese act remained a passive policy and did nothing to produce a reversal of it.

92. Herbert Feis, *The Road to War; The Coming of the War between the United States and Japan* (Princeton, N.J.: Princeton University Press, 1950), p. 3; Hull, *Memoirs*, I: 281–282.

93. Fred Greene, "The Military View of American National Policy, 1904–1940," *American Historical Review* 66 (January 1961): 374–375.

94. v. Boetticher to RKM, Anl. 4, Rpt. 37/1935, November 1, 1935, "The Position of the United States on the Conflict between Italy and Abyssinia (7th Report)," T-120, 2741/5863, E429383. In his first report on the developing Ethiopian crisis, he also alluded to the fact that American officers saw American neutrality in the case as being retribution for the lack of British support for American policy during the tension following the Manchurian annexation by Japan in 1931. See Anl. 2, Rpt. 31/1935, "The Position of the U.S. in the Italian Abyssinian War," September 14, 1935, *ibid.*, E429313.

95. Memorandum by the Undersecretary of State (William Phillips) of a Conversation with the Soviet Commissar for Foreign Affairs (Litvinov) in U.S. Dept. of State., *FRUS, 1933*, 5 vols. (Washington, D.C.: Government Printing Office, 1949), vol. 3, *The Far East*, pp. 463–465. See also Adam Ulam, *Expansion and Co-existence; The History of Soviet Foreign Policy* (New York: Frederick A. Praeger, 1968), p. 214.

96. v. Boetticher to RWM, Anl. 3, Rpt. 20/1933, October 25, 1933, "The Military Situation in the Far East," T-120, 2741/5863, E429081.

97. v. Boetticher to RKM, Anl. 8, Rpt. 8/1934, March 28, 1934, "Further Evaluations of Japanese Intentions: The Military Situation in the Pacific Ocean," T-120, 2741/5863, E429135.

98. v. Boetticher to RKM, Rpt. 10/1933, July 7, 1933, "Evaluation of the American General Staff of the Japanese Army," T-120, 2741/5863, E428994. Von Boetticher in fact repeated here the clichés of the 1930s regarding the Japanese and their military: they are copyists, their troops are belabored with such inhuman conditions and outdated doctrine and weapons, still believing in the violent bayonet charge against modern firepower. Burnett, according to von Boetticher, felt that Japan "in a war with a power that had absorbed the lessons of World War I [would] have to learn some severe lessons and basically revise . . . tactics."

99. Louis Morton, *Strategy and Command, The First Two Years* (Washington, D.C.: Office of the Chief of Military History, 1962), p. 37. See also the author's "National Policy and Military Strategy," *The Virginia Quarterly Review* 36 (Winter 1960), passim.

100. A detailed account of the evolution of strategic thinking for the western Pacific and U.S. Army and Navy tensions over the defense of the Philippines appears in Edward S. Miller's *War Plan Orange: The U.S. Strategy to Defeat Japan, 1897–1945* (Annapolis, Md.: Naval Institute Press, 1991), pp. 53–64. See also Ronald H. Spector, *Eagle against the Sun: The American War with Japan* (New York: The Free Press, 1985), pp. 54–71.

101. v. Boetticher to RKM, Anl. 1, Rpt. 32/1935, September 23, 1935, "Speech of General MacArthur," T-120, 2741/5863, E429317–20.

102. v. Boetticher to RKM, Anl. 2, Rpt. 26/1934, August 23, 1934, "Report on the Flight of Ten Bombers from the U.S. to Alaska," T-120, 2741/5863, E429191. The flight leader was Lt. Col. (later Gen.) Henry H. "Hap" Arnold, chief of Army Air Forces in World War II.

103. Kurt v. Tippelskirch to v. Boetticher, 24 December 1936, Schriftwechsel, O Qu IV - Mil. Att. Washington, 24.12.36–2.10.42, RH2/2942, Bundesarchiv/Militärarchiv, Freiburg im Breisgau. Von Tippelskirch told von Boetticher in his letter that he intended to keep the attaché informed on German intentions from his side and begged the attaché to keep him similarly informed. The personal correspondence with v. Tippelskirch continued through two changes

of command at the Attachéabteilung, and after v. Tippelskirch had turned the post over to Col. Horst von Mellenthin in late 1939.

Chapter 5

1. Herbert Feis, *The Road to Pearl Harbor* (Princeton, N.J.: Princeton University Press, 1950), p. 16; Robert A. Divine, *Roosevelt and World War II* (Baltimore: Johns Hopkins University Press, 1969) pp. 16–18.

2. Allan R. Millett and Peter Maslowski, *For the Common Defense: A Military History of the United States of America* (New York: The Free Press, 1984), p. 386.

3. Walter Warlimont, *Inside Hitler's Headquarters, 1939–1945* (New York: Frederick A. Praeger, 1964) pp. 6–7.

4. Gen. d. Art. Horst v. Mellenthin (a.D.), The Attaché Branch of the Army General Staff, Foreign Military Study MS #P-041j, HQ, USAREUR, Historical Division, 1952, pp. 20–21.

5. The earlier reports from April 1933 to April 1936 also suffered damage and partial loss. The few surviving reports for those years all show scorched edges in their microfilmed images, and some have a third of the page or more burned off. It is likely that von Boetticher's missing material for this period perished in this way. See Robert Wolfe, ed., *Captured German and Related Records: A National Archives Conference,* Papers and Proceedings of the Conference on Captured German and Related Records, November 12–13, 1968, Washington, D.C. (Athens, Ohio: Ohio University Press, 1974), p. xvi; and Gerhard L. Weinberg, "Copies of German World War I Records in the National Archives," typescript manuscript, n.d.; see also Thomas E. Skidmore, "Survey of Unpublished Sources on the Central Government and Politics of the German Empire, 1871–1918," *American Historical Review* 65 (July 1960): 850, which mentions the fate of post-Wilhelmine records as well.

6. Luther to Foreign Ministry, Cable No. 53, March 9, 1936, *DGFP*, C, V, p. 66. (See Chapter 2, note 77 for explanation of *DGFP*.)

7. v. Boetticher to RKM, Anl. 2, Rpt. 12/1936, April 7, 1936, "Military-Political Influence of Public Opinion in the United States from 7 March to 7 April 1936," T-120, 2741/5863, E429447–48.

8. J. Sontag, *A Broken World, 1919-1939* (New York: Harper and Row, 1971), p. 292.

9. Naval Message No. 9707, Naval Air Station, Anacostia to NAS, Lakehurst, 0245 hours, 7 May 1937, Bureau of Aeronautics (U.S. Navy) Records, NARA.

10. U.S. Dept. of Commerce, Bureau of Air Commerce, Report No. 11, "The Hindenburg Accident: A Comparative Digest of the Investigation and Findings, with the American and Translated German Reports Included," by Ralph W. Knight, Chief, Air Transport Section [bound typescript], Washington, D.C., August 1938, pp. 1–2.

11. See the highly speculative and even specious interpretation by Michael Mooney, *Hindenburg* (New York: Dodd, 1972). More cautious is A. A. Hoehling's *Who Destroyed the Hindenburg?* (New York: Popular Library, 1962), which mentions v. Boetticher as an interested source.

12. Hoehling, *Who Destroyed the Hindenburg?* p. 207. Von Boetticher responded this way to a query from Hoehling in 1961.

13. Telephone Interview, Vice Adm. Charles E. Rosendahl, with the author, December 20, 1973.

14. Warren F. Kimball, "Dieckhoff and America: A German's View of German-American Relations, 1937–1941," MA thesis, Georgetown University, Washington, D.C., 1965, pp. 2–3. Dieckhoff's reputation was based on his service in the Foreign Office as an expert on American affairs. American Ambassador William E. Dodd thought highly of him, though his favor was not reciprocated.

15. Ibid., pp. 10–11.

16. Dieckhoff to Foreign Ministry, Cable No. 144, June 2, 1937, *DGFP*, D, III, p. 304. On May 26, two Republican Spanish bombs killed 31 German sailors aboard the ship in an unprovoked air attack in the harbor at Ibiza (Balearic Islands). On May 31, five German vessels cannonaded the Spanish town of Almería with 200 rounds. Von Boetticher brought the story to his audience in great detail, apparently convincing it of the necessity for retaliation against the "Red" forces. See also Hugh Thomas, *The Spanish Civil War* (New York: Harper and Row, 1961), pp. 440–441.

17. As *Generalleutnant* (Major General) after October 1, 1933, he held the equivalent rank of a Corps Area commander in the U.S. Army. v. Boetticher "201" file; Interview, Gen. Albert Cody Wedemeyer with the author, June 14, 1974.

18. Ltr., Col. Charles Burnett to Smith, Oct. 4, 1936, reproduced in Smith, "Facts of Life," unpublished memoir in Yale University manuscript collection [1964], p. 71. The letter is reproduced without the reference to von Boetticher in Robert Hessen, *Berlin Alert: The Memoirs and Reports of Truman Smith* (Stanford, Cal.: Hoover Institution Press, 1984), p.27.

19. Ibid.

20. v. Boetticher to RKM, Anl. 8, Rpt. 28/1935, July 9, l935, "Change of the American Military Attaché in Germany," T-120, 2741/5863, E429290.

21. Gen. Albert C. Wedemeyer, *Wedemeyer Reports* (New York: Henry Holt, 1958), pp. 33, 37.

22. Bruce Bidwell, History of the Military Intelligence Department of the Army General Staff, Part III, Washington, 1959–1961, pp. XXX-15–XXX-17. Copy in the Center of Military History. The liaison between the U.S. Army's Historical Division and the German Army's Military Historical Branch (which received German military records back from the Reichsarchiv to begin its own existence in 1937) continued under the cordial relations maintained between the two staffs. An American officer was on station in the Reichsarchiv until April 1, 1938, and records were sent upon request to the American military historians until 1940. Col. R. S. Thomas, "A Compilation," [Data concerning establishment in the German Office of Military Records (Reichsarchiv)] May 3, 1944, Thomas Files, folder 2444, U.S. Army Military History Institute, Carlisle Barracks, Pennsylvania.

23. Joseph W. Bendersky, *The "Jewish Threat": Anti-Semitic Politics of the U.S. Army* (New York: Basic Books, 2000), pp. 75–166. passim. In his pioneering research in this too-little discussed aspect of American military intellectual life, the author examines the roots of officers' suspicion of Bolshevik influences and their purported Jewish origins. Chief among the officers holding these views were especially those of the military intelligence community.

24. Ibid. pp. 259–265. The racial attitudes of the time became the stock of War College lectures, cloaked with the authority of academic degrees.

25. Marsden Interview, August 22, 1973; Miller Interview, August 24, 1973. The couple entered into a professional and teaching career at the University of Buffalo (New York), lasting until their retirement in 1974.

26. Adalbert v. Boetticher, born in 1889, was a *Landgerichtsrat* in Zwickau when he became Party Member No. 422138 on February 1, 1931. Ltr., Dr. David Marwell, Director, Berlin Document Center, to author, January, 24, 1991, copies of Nazi Party cards enclosed. *Personalverzeihnis des höheren Justizdienstes: Ein alphabetisches Verzeichnis der planmäßigen Beamten des höheren Justizdienstes mit Angaben über ihre Dienstlaufbahn*, bearbeitet im Büro des Reichjustizministeriums (Berlin: Carl Heymanns Verlag, 1938), p. 22. See also Konrad Jarausch, *The Unfree Professions: German Lawyers, Teachers, and Engineers, 1900–1950* (New York: Oxford University Press, 1990), pp. 100–103. Jarausch sees those joining from 1930 to 1933 as the opportunists.

27. Von Boetticher wrote to Freeman on May 20, 1936 of his trip. On July 6, he sent his friend a postcard to note his return to the United States. The card bears a dockside photo of father and son in Hamburg, the younger man still in uniform. Freeman Papers, Correspondence 1936, Box 27, folder 46, Library of Congress, Manuscript Division.

28. F. H. Boetticher to author, July 30, 1973. The younger von Boetticher had been diagnosed with schizophrenia in his adolescence and hence was susceptible to this sanction under Nazi law. His condition was much later, in the United States, judged to be manic depression.

29. Ibid.; Miller Interview, August 24, 1973; Wedemeyer Interview, June 14, 1974.

30. Nikolaus Ritter, *Deckname Dr. Rantzau; Die Aufzeichnungen des Nikolaus Ritters, Offizier im Geheimen Nachrichtendienst* (Hamburg: Hoffmann and Campe, 1972), p. 59. Ritter notes that he could not understand Canaris's reasoning here, having come to like and admire von Boetticher earlier. Ladislas Farago also recounts Ritter's story in embellished and sometimes inaccurate detail in *The Game of the Foxes* (New York: Bantam Books, 1973), pp. 47–62.

31. Foreign Logistical Organisations and Methods, A Report for the Secretary of the Army, October 15, 1947, p. 30.

32. Adolf Hitler, *Hitler's Secret Book*, introduction by Telford Taylor (New York: Grove Press, 1961), p. 91. Hitler here discusses the overwhelming productivity and competitiveness of the American automobile industry alone.

33. Hans L. Trefousse, *Germany and American Neutrality, 1939–1941* (New York: Octagon Books, 1969), p. 13.

34. Bernard M. Baruch, *The Public Years* (New York: Holt Rinehart and Winston, 1960), p. 264.

35. Lt. Col. Marvin A. Kreidberg and 1st Lt. Merton G. Henry, *History of Military Mobilization in the United States, 1775–1945*, DA Pamphlet No. 20-212 (Washington, D.C.: Office, Chief of Military History, 1955), pp. 507–515; Harry Yoshpe, "Study of Experience in Industrial Mobilization in World War II; Plans for Industrial Mobilization, 1920–1939," typescript manuscript, Army Industrial College, Department of Research, November 1945, p. 9.

36. Baruch, *The Public Years*, p. 263. During an acceptance speech for an award at the annual American Ordnance Association dinner on October 2, 1935, Baruch had lavishly castigated the presumption in Hitler's so-called Peace Speech of May 21, 1935. "Hitler and peace!" he said, "the very terms are antithetical! He is the greatest menace to world safety." Bernard Baruch, "The Art of Victory," *Army Ordnance* 16 (November–December 1935): 140–142. Von Boetticher brought his protest to the War Department on December 30, 1935, only to have the chief of ordnance reply that the journal was entirely civilian controlled and that he did not dictate its policy on publication. WD, G-2, Synoptic Index, Attaché Military, German in Washington, Part I.

37. Yoshpe, "Study of Experience in Industrial Mobilization in World War II," pp. 10–11; R. Elberton Smith, *The Army and Economic Mobilization* (Washington, D.C., 1959), pp. 39–40.

38. Report of the Assistant Secretary of War [Harry H. Woodring], 1936, in *Report of the Secretary of War to the President 1936* (Washington, D.C.: Government Printing Office 1936), p. 21.

39. Robert H. Connery, *The Navy and Industrial Mobilization in World War II* (Princeton, N.J.: Princeton University Press, 1951), pp. 44-45. See also Robert H. Ferrell, "The Merchants of Death, Then and Now," *Journal of International Affairs* 26 (1972): 30.

40. Conflicting army-navy claims on production from specified factories began in 1935 when the navy submitted its list of 40,000 requisite items from 18,000 separate bidders. The army's list, with some 12,000 producers, named many of the same suppliers. The necessity for closer planning became obvious. See Harold J. Tobin and Percy Bidwell, *Mobilizing Civilian America* (New York: Council on Foreign Relations, 1940), p. 61.

41. Smith, *The Army and Economic Mobilization*, p. 41.

42. W. Glenn Campbell, ed., *Economics of Mobilization and War* (Homewood, Ill.: Richard D. Irwin, 1952), pp. 11–12; Roderick L. Vawter, *Industrial Mobilization, the Relevant History*, rev. ed. (Washington, D.C.: National Defense University Press, 1983), p. 6.

43. Col. John A. Wagner, QMC, "Strategic Raw Materials," *Quartermaster Review* 15 (January-February 1936): 44; v. Boetticher to RKM, Anl. 1, Rpt. 15/1936, April 25, 1936, "War Raw Materials," [German film].

44. Wagner, "Strategic Raw Materials," p. 43.

45. v. Boetticher to RKM, Anl. 1, Rpt. 27/1937, July 25, 1937, "The American Army in the Fiscal Year 1937," [German film].

46. v. Boetticher to the RKM, Anl. 3, Rpt.34/1937, October 13, 1937 [German film], and Anl. 1, Rpt. 42/1938, December 9, 1938, "Military Economic Problems and the Pan American Policy of the United States," [German film].

47. Stetson Conn and Byron Fairchild, *The Framework of Hemispheric Defense* (Washington, D.C., 1960), p. 7. See also William L. Langer and S. Everett Gleason, *The Challenge to Isolation;* Torchbook ed., *The World Crisis of 1937–1940 and American Foreign Policy,* 2 vols., (New York: Harper and Row, 1964), p. 132. The authors maintain that the economic support was to flow from the United States to Latin America instead of the reverse, as von Boetticher insisted, in order to assuage the damage to Latin American economies caused by the trade dislocations after events in Europe in 1938.

48. Declaration of Lima by the Eighth International Conference of American States, December 24, 1938, U.S. Dept. of State, *Peace and War; United States Foreign Policy, 1931–1941,* Dept. of State Publication No. 1933, Washington: Government Printing Office, 1943. pp. 439–440.

49. v. Boetticher to RKM, Anl. 2, Rpt.40/1938, November 21, 1938, "Military Economic Questions," [German film].

50. Smith, *The Army and Economic Mobilization,* p. 63; Yoshpe, "Study of Experience," pp. 28–32.

51. v. Boetticher to OKH, Attachéabteilung, Anl. 1, Rpt. 28/1938, August 15, 1938, "American Industrial Mobilization," [with enclosed booklet listing all American Ordnance Districts]; Anl. 1, Rpt. 24/1938, July 15, 1938, "Industrial Mobilization in the United States"; Anl. 1, Rpt. 30/1938, September 7, 1938, "American Rearmament Measures." All in German film.

52. Russell F. Weigley, *History of the United States Army* (New York: Macmillan, 1967) pp. 415–416; Harry H. Woodring, "Supply Preparedness," *Army Ordnance* 17 (March–April 1937): 264.

53. "Annual Report of the Chief of Staff for the Fiscal Year 1936, Ended June 30, 1936," in *Report of the Secretary of War to the President, 1936* (Washington, D.C.: Government Printing Office, 1936), p. 31.

54. Mark Skinner Watson, *The Chief of Staff; Prewar Plans and Preparations* (Washington, D.C.: Government Printing Office, 1950), p. 154. The latter figure rose to 1,162,000 in 1940.

55. Elias Huzar, *The Purse and the Sword; Control of the Army by Congress through Military Appropriations, 1933–1950* (Ithaca, N.Y.: Cornell University Press, 1950) p. 145; See also Weigley, *History of the United States Army,* p. 417.

56. v. Boetticher to OKH, Attachéabteilung, Anl. 2, Rpt. 11/1938, April 12, 1938, "The Debate in the House and Senate on the Budget of the Army for FY 1939," [German film]; Huzar, *Purse and Sword,* p. 139.

57. v. Boetticher to OKH, Attachéabteilung, Anl. 2, Rpt. 19/1938, May 31, 1938, "Industrial Mobilization in the United States." [German film].

58. v. Boetticher to OKH, Attachéabteilung, Anl. 1, Rpt. 26/1938, June 23, 1938, "The Budget and the Combat Readiness of the American Armed Forces," [German film].

59. v. Boetticher to OKH, Attachéabteilung, Anl. 2, Rpt. 43/1938, December 16, 1938, "Industrial Mobilization, Production Affairs, and Standardization in the American Army," [German film].

60. Dieckhoff to Foreign Office, Cable No. 264, October 7, 1937, *DGFP,* D, I, pp. 633–634.

61. Dieckhoff to Foreign Office, Cable No. 1560, December 7, 1937, *DGFP,* D, I, p. 653.

62. Dieckhoff to State Secretary Weizsäcker, March 22, 1938, *DGFP,* D, I, p. 697; see also Manfred Jonas, "Prophet without Honor; Hans Heinrich Dieckhoff's Reporting from Washington," *Mid-America; An Historical Review* 47 (July 1965): 227.

63. v. Boetticher to OKH, Attachéabteilung, Anl. 1, Rpt. 30/1938, September 7, 1938, "American Rearmament Measures," [German film]. Von Boetticher estimated that it would take five months for any deliveries to Europe to start.

64. Walter Johnson, *The Battle against Isolation* (Chicago: University of Chicago Press, 1944), p. 29; Langer and Gleason, *The Challenge to Isolation*, p. 36.

65. Karl Dietrich Bracher, *The German Dictatorship; The Origins, Structure, and Effects of National Socialism* (New York: Frederick A. Praeger, 1970), pp. 366–367; Cordell Hull, *The Memoirs of Cordell Hull*, 2 vols. (New York: Macmillan Co., 1948), I: 599. Dieckhoff continued to analyze American affairs and contribute to policy from Berlin.

66. Bella Fromm, *Blood and Banquets; A Berlin Social Diary* (New York: Carol Publishing Group, 1990), p. 271. Fromm, a society columnist for the Ullstein *Vossische Zeitung* until her departure from Germany in late 1938, was heir to a wine fortune and a perceptive wit. Her genuine friendship with Thomsen—and her observations on the man in May 1938—tend to offset more critical assessments of his outlook. On this occasion, he mentioned the hostile atmosphere vis-à-vis Germans in the United States.

67. The last set of these instructions governing all German attachés abroad was issued in Berlin in September 1935. See Manfred Kehrig, *Die Wiedereinrichtung des deutschen militärischen Attachédienstes nach dem ersten Weltkrieg (1919–1933)* (Boppard am Rhein: H. Boldt, 1966), pp. 207–210.

68. Thomsen's nervousness and his expectation of further American retaliation are evident in his urgent pleas to have the German embassy's archives removed to Berlin, because they could not be destroyed quickly. See Chargé d'Affaires to Foreign Office, Cable No. 364, November 30, 1938, *DGFP*, D, IV, pp. 648–649. Manfred Jonas remarks, however, that in contrast to Dieckhoff, Thomsen was "less perceptive and less willing to shatter the illusions of his superiors." See his "Prophet without Honor," p. 232.

69. v. Boetticher to OKH, Attacheabteilung, Anl. 1, Rpt. 35/1938, October 20, 1938, "American Armament Plans," [German film].

70. v. Boetticher to Tippelskirch [handwritten letter], 22 November 1938, Schriftwechsel, O Qu IV, Mil. Att. Washington, 24.12.36–2.10.42, BA/MA, Freiburg im Breisgau.

71. v. Boetticher to RKM, Truppenamt, Anl. 2, Rpt. 34/1935, October 9, 1935, "Malin Craig, New Chief of Staff," T-120, 2741/5863, E429346. Von Boetticher had first met Craig at Fort Reilly, Kansas, in 1922, and a genuine if correct sort of warmth grew between them after Craig's accession to the office of chief of staff. In this same report, sent just after Craig reached that office, v. Boetticher cited Craig's remark on the attaché's being the first foreigner to visit him in his new office. He reportedly told von Boetticher to visit and consult with him often. Ibid., E429348.

72. Ibid., E429346.

73. v. Boetticher to OKH, Attachéabteilung, Anl. 1, Rpt. 30/1938, September 7, 1938, "American Armament Plans," [German film].

74. DSF to Dean Mildred Thompson, Vassar College, June 6, 1938; v. Boetticher to DSF, June 11, 1938, and DSF to v. Boetticher, September 27, 1938, all in Box 34, folder 46, Freeman Papers, [1938] Library of Congress, Manuscript Div. In the event, the younger von Boetticher daughter chose to attend Randolph-Macon Woman's College at Lynchburg, Virginia, convenient to the Freeman home in Richmond.

75. Annual Yearbooks, 1938–1942, Randolph Macon Woman's College, Lynchburg, Virginia.

76. These men were of low-enough rank that they did not appear in the monthly issues of the U.S. State Department's *Diplomatic List*, even in the late 1930s and early 1940s. An Annette Prior was v. Boetticher's secretary, the successor to Dorothea Zuckerielli. Little is available, unfortunately, to document the activities of the women in the Embassy.

77. German note of July 10, 1934, Embassy Note II M 1434, File 701.6211/908, State Dept. Decimal Files, Box 3665, RG59, National Archives and Records Administration, College Park, Maryland.

78. An excellent English-language summary of Riedel's early career is in "Peter Riedel: Last Survivor of the Rhoen," *Soaring* 29 (January 1966): 8–10. Additional corroborating information is in "Questionnaire, Peter Riedel," Directory of Aeronautical Engineering of the Institute of the Aeronautical Sciences, January 13, 1939, file copy in Peter Riedel Archival Files, Library and Archives Division, National Air & Space Museum, Washington, D.C.; see also Werner Schwipps, *Kleine Geschichte der deutschen Luftfahrt* (Berlin: Haude & Spenersche Verlagsbuchhandlung, 1968), p. 95, appendix.

79. This account is also based on two complementary sources. The first is Riedel's own untitled typescript memoir of 351 leaves completed in the mid-1940s. From this material and extensive interviews, Riedel's longtime friend Martin Simons, an Australian pilot and glider constructor himself, produced *German Air Attaché: The Thrilling Story of the German Ace Pilot and Wartime Diplomat Peter Riedel* (Shrewsbury, UK: Airlife Publishing, 1997). The unpublished version of Riedel's remembrances was made available to the author through the kindness and cooperation of Dr. Von Hardesty, curator on the staff of the National Air and Space Museum, Washington. Both versions of the story were used to construct a coherent account of Riedel's activities in the United States after 1938. Where appropriate, the unpublished version is cited as "Riedel Memoir," with appropriate page references. The two editions complement each other heavily but are not identical. A photostatic copy of the raw memoir is in the author's files; the second, original one remains with the Air and Space Museum.

80. Simons, *German Air Attaché*, p. 11. He reported that he shied away after a Goebbels speech that remarked on those opportunists signing up after January 1933 hoping to benefit from the association with the party. This revelation is not in the draft (unpublished) version of the memoirs.

81. NSDAP Zentralkartei [Central Registry, or Data Base], Berlin Documentation Center [BDC] Microfilm, Record Group 242, Foreign Records Seized Collection, A3340-MFKL-M-143 [M-143 is the microfilm roll number], frame 0160, National Archives and Records Administration; the later party card is reproduced in frame 158. In the BDC materials, there is also a correspondence file on Riedel among letters usually written by members or former members about their standing in the party. Two pieces of correspondence concern Riedel. The first is on party stationery from the Staff of the Deputy of the Fuehrer (Rudolf Hess) at the Braunes Haus in Munich, dated July, 4 1940. It is addressed to and states that a political evaluation of Riedel is required from the authorities of the Gau Leadership of Munich-Oberbayern. The letter carries the notation that "R. is to be taken over into the Engineer Corps as a 'Fl.-Stabsingenieur.'" In the reply to this request, the Gau Personnel Office Leader (signature illegible) regrets that he cannot comply because during Riedel's service in Munich, he could learn nothing about him. Partei-Korrespondenz, A3340-PK-O174, frame 2432, BDC Microfilm, NARA RG 242; response is on frame 2434. This document shows that the party headquarters in Munich still considered Riedel an active member in July 1940 and was considering a new assignment for him.

82. Riedel's character formation is a case study in psychological tension. His father died when the future pilot was twelve years old; his mother took her own life shortly thereafter. He also lost his sister Beate in a freak and avoidable motor accident, caused by another German glider pilot, Günter Groenhoff.

83. Riedel later gave his impressions of the flights in his "Formation Flying with Vultures," in Werner von Langsdoff, *Flieger und was Sie Erlebten* (Gutersloh: Verlag C. Bertelsmann, 1939), pp. 354–359. The vultures—flying in dense throngs along the Andean foothills—marked by their upward flight the presence of thermals for the glider team.

84. R. E. G. Davies, *Lufthansa: An Airline and Its Aircraft* (New York: Orion Books, 1991), pp. 20, 24, 26, which contain maps of the service lines and charts of the services offered.

85. Ibid., p. 22.

86. Riedel Memoir, pp. 3–4. Carl August Freiherr von Gablenz, one of the moving spirits behind the Lufthansa expansion and a Junkers company veteran, wondered why Riedel would abandon a successful company to join an obscure American venture.

87. Davies, *Lufthansa*, pp. 28–29.

88. Ltr., Schweyer to Riedel, December 2, 1937. The letter contains details of the shipment by freighter of a Kranich glider to Riedel with all its necessary equipment and a supply of sales literature. Riedel Estate Files. At least one South American gliding club in the 1990s traces its origins to the 1934 Georgii expedition. See the history of the (Brazilian) Clube Paulista de Planadores at www.grunaubaby.nl/Brazil%20Baby.htm.

89. New Member, under "News from Clubs and Members," *Soaring* 28 (July 1937): 12.

90. "Two Weeks of Soaring," *Soaring* 29 (August 1937): 2–3.

91. Report, Spruill Braden [American Embassy, Bogota] to State Department, Subj: Conversation with Dr. von Bauer of Scadta, March 30, 1939, State Decimal File No. 181.796 SCA 2/408, State Dept. Decimal Files, 1930–39, RG 59 Box 5667. Braden carried on a series of interviews with von Bauer to investigate the extent of Nazi penetration of the company and of the varying control of SCADTA's stock by Pan American. With Riedel already gone a year, von Bauer on this occasion told Braden that Riedel was "the world's best expert on gliding." Two months later, von Bauer seemed resigned to Riedel's departure and observed that he had been "a fairly good pilot, but that his exuberance as a glider pilot had robbed him of much of his commercial value." The latter remark is reported by Braden in Decimal File No. 821.796 SCA 2/416, ibid. Von Bauer got not one replacement for Riedel, but three, all of them unsatisfactory: one an inebriate, one of bad temper, the last a pitiful pilot. They were all Nazis, too, remarked von Bauer, and he got rid of them.

92. Simons, *German Air Attaché*, p. 22. Von Boetticher's name figured in the conversation repeatedly. The attaché did not have to know of Riedel's connections, his interviewers told him, and they would make sums of unaccountable money available for his own use.

93. G. S. Graber, *The History of the SS* (New York: Charter Books, 1978), pp. 186–188. Heydrich's rise in the ranks of the SS is detailed in Heinz Höhne's *The Order of the Death's Head: The Story of Hitler's SS* (New York: Ballantine Books, 1969), pp. 192–197.

94. "We Are Going Ahead," *Soaring* 2 (August 1938): 2–5. This article is a day-by-day chronology of the events, in which many distance, altitude, and duration records fell. In the point total for the contest, Riedel stood first with 1,486, well above the 1,271 of the second-place contender. Standings are shown in ibid., p. 8.

95. Simons, *German Air Attaché*, p. 38.

96. Ibid. For v. Boetticher, every problem was equally serious; trivial and important matters were all the same, Riedel testified to Simons nearly fifty years later. In the "Riedel Memoir," pp. 34–35, the criticism applies to the German official mentality generally, and only obliquely to von Boetticher as an instance of it.

97. RCA Radiogram, August 11, 1938, Reitsch to Peter Riedel, Deutsche Botschaft, Washington, D.C. "Hocherfreut," she signed off. The Habicht was her glider, crated and shipped aboard the liner. Riedel Estate Files.

98. Interview, Ray Klug with author, June 18, 2000. Her younger brother attested to Helen Klug's outspoken and free spirit. Interview, Dr. Regis Boyle with author and Dr. Von Hardesty, August 16, 2000. Regis Boyle and Helen Klug taught together at the Immaculata School in Washington. They remained in friendly contact until at least 1995, when the Riedels stayed in her home in Washington during a visit.

99. Watson, *Chief of Staff; Prewar Plans and Preparations*, p. 136.

100. Wayne S. Cole, *Charles A. Lindbergh and the Battle against American Intervention in World War II* (New York: Harcourt Brace Jovanovich, 1974), p. 54; on the tendentious relationship between Joseph Kennedy and Franklin Roosevelt, see Michael R. Beschloss, *Kennedy and Roosevelt: The Uneasy Alliance* (New York: W. W. Norton, 1980).

101. John M. Blum, *From the Morgenthau Diaries*, 3 vols. (Boston: Houghton Mifflin, 1965), II:48–49; Watson, *Chief of Staff; Pre War Plans and Preparations*, pp. 136–43. See also: John McVickar Haight, *American Aid to France, 1938–1940* (New York: Atheneum, 1970), pp. 55–68. The president's fixation on aircraft as one more effective and visible form of aid to the Euro-

pean democracies after the Munich Conference also resulted from information on the state of French aircraft he got from the American ambassador in Paris, William Bullitt. Bullitt, also privy to Lindbergh's assessments, relayed French requests for 1,000 planes after Munich. See Kenneth S. Davis, *The Hero: Charles A. Lindbergh and the American Dream* (Garden City, N.Y.: Doubleday & Co. 1959), p. 384.

102. Eaker Interview, p. 247.

103. Samuel I. Rosenman, comp., *The Public Papers and Addresses of Franklin Delano Roosevelt*, 13 vols. (New York: Macmillan, 1938–1950), vol. 8 (1950), pp. 70–74.

104. "The Armament Program, An Editorial," *Army Ordnance* 19 (March-April 1939): 293.

105. Keith D. McFarland, *Harry H. Woodring, A Political Biography of FDR's Controversial Secretary of War* (Lawrence: University Press of Kansas, 1975), pp. 185, 194.

106. Keith D. McFarland, "Woodring vs. Johnson: FDR and the Great War Department Feud," *Army* 26 (March 1976): 40. An open secret in the War Department, the feud had come to von Boetticher's attention, too; he mentioned Johnson's ambition and his energy in this context in his Anl. 2, Rpt. No. 43/1938, December 16, 1938, "Industrial Mobilization, Production Affairs, and Standardization in the American Army,"[German film].

107. v. Boetticher, Witthoeft, Thomsen for the Supreme Command of the Wehrmacht, Military Attaché Sections, Cable No. 8, January 22, 1939, *DGFP*, D, IV, p. 672.

108. v. Boetticher to OKH, Attachéabteilung, Anl. 1, Rpt.2/1939, January 13, 1939, "American Armament (2d Report [for 1939])," [German film].

109. Hanson W. Baldwin, "Our New Long Shadow," *Foreign Affairs* 17 (April 1939): 465–476. Baldwin, military correspondent for the New York *Times*, predicted that the new naval and air strength was "part of a revised and hardened foreign policy. To carry out that policy the United States will become one of the most strongly armed nations in the world and will cast its shadow across distant seas." Despite von Boetticher's objections to this assertion, he later came to respect Baldwin.

110. Kreidberg and Henry, *History of Military Mobilization*, p. 491.

111. v. Boetticher to OKH, Attachéabteilung, Anl. 1, Rpt. 15/1939, April 18, 1939, "The American Rearmament: Propaganda and Fact," [German film].

112. Ibid.

113. Ibid., See also Report of the Assistant Secretary of War for 1939, in *Report of the Secretary of War to the President, 1939* (Washington, D.C.: Government Printing Office, 1939), p. 19.

114. See, as an example, the address of the chief of ordnance, Maj. Gen. Charles M. Wesson, "Fundamentals of Preparedness, Some Facts and Figures of the New Ordnance Programs," *Army Ordnance* 19 (May–June 1939): 329–336.

115. Gordon A. Craig, "The German Foreign Office," in Gordon A. Craig and Felix Gilbert, eds., *The Diplomats*, 2 vols. (New York: Atheneum, 1967) 2: 435–436.

116. Rosenman, comp., *The Public Papers and Addresses of Franklin Delano Roosevelt*, 8:11.

117. Memorandum by the Director of the Protocol Department [Baron v. Dörnberg], January 4, 1939, *DGFP*, D, IV, p. 667.

118. Thomsen to Undersecretary Ernst Woermann, October 21, 1939, *DGFP*, D, VIII, p. 330.

119. Susan Canedy, *America's Nazis: A Democratic Dilemma, A History of the American Bund* (Menlo Park, Calif.: Markgraf Publications Group, 1990), pp. 194–196.

120. Martin Blumnenson, ed., *The Patton Papers, 1885–1940* (New York: Houghton Mifflin, 1972), p. 970.

121. Mrs. Ruth Ellen [Patton] Totten to author, March 16, 1973.

122. Friedrich v. Boetticher, "So War Es," [unpublished typescript memoir, n.d., but ca. 1964], pp. 364–365. When he protested the political cost to Germany of such a patently untrue "revelation," says von Boetticher, Hitler summarily turned away from him and spoke not another word to him during the luncheon. Von Boetticher would attempt to put other meaning and content into his confrontation with Hitler immediately after the war.

123. Riedel Memoir, p. 53.

124. Ibid., p. 54. Riedel was of the erroneous opinion that von Boetticher's career was in jeopardy because of his reputed stance, but was rescued by the intervention of Werner von Fritsch, commander in chief of the German Army until his own dismissal a year before the attaché meeting of 1939. Von Boetticher was nominated to the Washington post *before* Hitler's arrival in power and never faced a politically motivated recall.

125. "So War Es," pp. 358–372.

126. Ibid., pp. 366–367. He estimates that old hands within the ministry did not want to form a front against Hitler openly and sought indirectly to construct reasons for the dictator to fear his foreseeable military adventures.

127. Martin Broszat, *The Hitler State: The Foundation and Development of the Internal Structure of the Third Reich* (New York: Longman, 1981), p. 250.

128. Klaus-Jürgen Müller, *The Army, Politics, and Society in Germany, 1933–1945: Studies in the Army's Relation to Nazism* (Manchester: Manchester University Press, 1987), pp. 36–40.

129. Gerhard L. Weinberg, "Munich after 50 Years," in *The Origins of the Second World War*, ed. by Patrick Finney (London: Arnold, 1997), p. 406. This text first appeared in *Foreign Affairs* 67 (1988):165–178. Brauchitsch was, at the moment, trying to divorce his wife and marry a younger woman, an enterprise in which Hitler supported him. Blomberg, a widower, had contributed to his own demise by unwittingly marrying a young War Ministry secretary who had been a prostitute; Hitler had been a witness at his wedding.

130. See Williamson Murray, "Net Assessment in Nazi Germany in the 1930s," in Finney (ed.) *The Origins of the Second World War*, pp. 316–333.

131. Simons, *German Air Attaché*, p. 50; Riedel Memoir, pp. 53–58.

132. The War Department underwrote much of the expense of maintaining Riedel's glider at this time, though the courtesy was also extended to other air attachés in Washington at the time. See War Department Bulletin No. 9, Washington, July 21, 1939, which circulates these authorizations, embodied in P.L. 102, 76th Congress, "an act to authorize the Secretary of War to provide for the sale of aviation supplies and services to aircraft operated by foreign military and air attachés accredited to the United States."

133. Riedel Memoir, p. 66. In Kansas and Missouri, Riedel toured the Stearman, Beech, and Cessna factories. These were not at the time turning out even the trainer aircraft necessary to an expansion of American aviation might.

134. Yoshpe, "Study of Experience in Industrial Mobilization in World War II," p. 63; Millis, *Arms and the State; Civil-Military Elements in National Policy* (New York: G.P. Putnam's Sons, 1956) p. 54.

135. Millis, *Arms and the State*, pp. 53–54.

136. Watson, *Chief of Staff; Pre War Plans and Preparations*, pp. 87–91.

137. v. Boetticher to OKH, Attachéabteilung, Anl. 1, Rpt. 30/1938, September 7, 1938, "American Rearmament Measures," [German film]. See also Stanley W. Dziuban, *Military Relations between the United States and Canada* (Washington, D.C.: Office of the Chief of Military History, 1959), pp. 3–4, for comment on Roosevelt's speech of August 18, 1939, at Kingston, Ontario, in which he promised that the United States would not stand idle if Canada were threatened by an overseas empire.

138. v. Boetticher to OKH, Attachéabteilung, Anl. 1, Rpt. 30/1938, September 7, 1938, "American Rearmament Measures," [German film].

139. Personal detail here is taken from Smith's "Facts of Life," pp. 113–114.

140. Franklin L. Ford, "Three Observers in Berlin; Rumbold, Dodd, and François-Poncet," in Craig and Gilbert, *The Diplomats*, 2:448.

141. Smith, "Facts of Life," p. 102.

142. Truman Smith, *Berlin Alert: The Memoirs and Reports of Truman Smith*, ed. and with introduction by Robert Hessen (Stanford: Hoover Institution Press, 1984), pp. xvi, 86–92; see also Truman Smith, Air Intelligence Activities, typescript, 1956, original in Yale University Li-

brary Manuscript Collection. A balanced general account of these visits and their effect is in A. Scott Berg, *Lindbergh* (New York: G.P. Putnam's Sons, 1998) pp. 354–360.

143. Davis, *The Hero*, pp. 380–382.

144. Farago, *The Game of the Foxes*, p. 608; Berg, *Lindbergh*, p. 378.

145. Trefousse, *Germany and American Neutrality, 1939–1941*, p. 23.

146. Farago, *Game of the Foxes*, p. 608.

147. v. Boetticher to Attaché Group, Army and Air, Cable No. 276, August 25, 1939, *DGFP*, D, VII, p. 275.

148. Thomsen to Foreign Ministry, Cable No. 282, August 28, 1939, *DGFP*, D, VII, p. 376.

149. Memorandum by Secretary of the Navy Charles Edison, September 2, 1939, *FDR, His Personal Letters*, 3 vols., edited by Elliott Roosevelt (New York: Duell Sloan and Pearce, 1950) 2:915. See also: James MacGregor Burns, *Roosevelt, The Lion and the Fox* (New York: Harcourt, Brace and Co., 1956), p. 394.

Chapter 6

1. "Fireside Chat," September 3, 1939, Samuel I. Rosenman, compiler, *The Public Papers and Addresses of Franklin Delano Roosevelt*, 13 vols. (New York: The Macmillan Co., 1938–1950).

2. Basil Rauch, *Roosevelt from Munich to Pearl Harbor* (New York: Creative Age Press, 1950), p. 137.

3. William L. Langer and S. Everett Gleason, *The Challenge to Isolation; The World Crisis of 1937–1940 and American Foreign Policy*, Torchbook ed., 2 vols. (New York: Harper and Row, 1964), pp. 211–212. It also became immediately evident who would benefit from these patrols when American naval vessels relayed the locations and courses of German vessels to British warships.

4. Klaus Hildebrand, *The Third Reich*, trans. P. S. Falla (London: George Allen & Unwin, 1984), p.49.

5. John Lukacs, *The Hitler of History* (New York: Vintage Books, 1998), p. 148.

6. Thomsen to Foreign Office, Cable No. 282, August 28, 1939, *DGFP*, D, VII, pp. 376-378. Thomsen also anticipated a possible break in relations once a war started in Europe. (See Chapter 2, note 77 for explanation of DGFP.)

7. Dieckhoff Memorandum, September 7, 1939, *DGFP*, D, VIII, pp. 21–22.

8. Hans L. Trefousse, *Germany and American Neutrality, 1939–1941* (New York: Octagon, 1969), p. 27; Klaus Hildebrand, *Deutsche Aussenpolitik, 1933–1945, Kalkül oder Dogma* (Stuttgart: Verlag W. Kohlhammer, 1973), p. 96.

9. Johanna M. Meskill, *Hitler and Japan: The Hollow Alliance* (New York: Atherton Press, 1966), pp. 10–18; Paul W. Schroeder, *The Axis Alliance and Japanese American Relations, 1941* (Ithaca, N.Y.: Cornell University Press, 1958), p. 14. Japanese surprise at the Nazi-Soviet Pact, coming just as Japan fought pitched battles with the Red Army on the Manchurian border, left Japan indifferent to German advances of the moment.

10. Cordell Hull, 2 vols. (New York: Macmillan, 1948), *The Memoirs*, I:717.

11. See the discussion of Hitler's perception of Japan's role in his own plans in Eberhard Jäckel, *Hitler in History* (Hanover, N.H.: Brandeis University Press, 1984), pp. 66–87.

12. Thomsen to Foreign Office, Cable No. 585, October 30, 1939, *DGFP*, D, VIII, p. 359. He divided the country into two counterbalancing viewpoints, one of which saw the war in moral terms and prayed for the destruction of "Hitlerism," the other regarding it as purely a European affair. Both schools housed an antipathy for Nazism and a determination to see no American troops involved.

13. Saul Friedländer, *Prelude to Downfall: Hitler and the United States, 1939-1941* (New York: Alfred A. Knopf, 1967), p. 43.

14. Thomsen to Foreign Office, Cable No. 684, November 20, 1939, *DGFP*, D, VIII, pp. 432–434. The latter recommendation was consistent with his earlier enunciated principle of never giving the appearance of direct intervention in American politics. See his Cable No. 416, September 24, 1939, in ibid., p. 127.

15. See especially Sr. Mary Hugh Gottsacker, O.S.F., "German-American Relations, 1939–1941, and the Influence of Hans Thomsen" (Ph.D. diss., Georgetown University, 1968), pp. 179–221, passim.

16. His wife and daughter had traveled to Germany in midsummer 1939. As they left European waters bound for the United States on their return in late August, the ship's captain received orders to return to Hamburg. The vessel, with many emigré Jews on the passenger list, retraced its course to the mouth of the Elbe, and the mood among the distraught Jewish passengers on board became suicidal. Marsden Interview, August 22, 1973.

17. D. S. Freeman, Diary for 1939, Entry for September 19, 1939, Freeman Papers, Box 1 (Diaries 1907–1946), Manuscript Div., Library of Congress. Other entries of the period indicate Freeman's sympathy for the Allies but a resolve to stay out of war. He lamented the death of "a British and French social order that were in their own way beautiful. What can we do about it? Why should we rush into a burning building that may be doomed? Thank God for the Atlantic Ocean," ibid., entry of September 5, 1939.

18. Betts Interview, January 13, 1974.

19. The Military Attaché to OKW Ausland, Urgent Cable No. 427, September 27, 1939, *DGFP*, D, VIII, p. 158.

20. Ibid., p. 159.

21. Sumner Welles, *The Time for Decision* (New York: Harper, 1944), p. 149.

22. v. Boetticher to Luftwaffe Operations Staff, Cable No. 693, November 1, 1939, T-120, B21/594, B005282.

23. Interrogation of Heribert von Strempel by Rebecca Wellington and Lt. Enno Hobbing, November 18, 1945, at Oberursel, Records of the Department of State Special Interrogation [Poole] Mission to Germany, 1945–1946, Microcopy 679, Roll 3, frame 00542–00545, National Archives and Records Administration. The effort was also informally known as the Poole Mission, after its head, DeWitt C. Poole, who had been the editor of *Public Opinion Quarterly.*

24. v. Boetticher to OKW Ausland, Army and Air Attaché Groups, Cable No. 323, September 9, 1939, T-77, 1029/1029, 6502296.

25. Peyton to ACofS, G-2, WD, November 21, 1939, Subj: Foreign Liaison Report, RG 165, Box 1300 (G-2 Regional Files), folder IG 5920–5930 (Germany), National Archives and Records Agency, College Park, Maryland. He further explained that no other country was getting anything either, so he did not feel discriminated against.

26. Peyton to ACofS, G-2, WD, February 20, 1940, RG 165, Box 1300, Regional Files (Germany), folder IG 5920-5930. National Archives and Records Administration, College Park, Maryland.

27. Ltr., Welles to Marshall, April 22, 1940, RG 165, Records of the G-2, Attaché, Military, German in Washington, file 2321-B-27; and Ltr., [Brig. Gen. Sherman] Miles to Ass't Sec'y of State Breckinridge Long, May 21, 1940, in ibid.

28. Ltr., Col. John A. Crane, [Chief, Foreign Liaison Section, G-2], to Peyton, June 11, 1940, in ibid.

29. See Msg., Peyton to G-2, WD, September 20, 1940, RG 165, G-2 Msg. files, Box 114, Acc. No. A-47-J08, National Archives and Records Administration, College Park, Maryland.

30. Wedemeyer Interview, June 14, 1974.

31. Marsden Interview, August 22, 1973.

32. Police report and Embassy Complaint to State Dept. Div. of Protocol, November 14, 1939, State Dept. Dec. file 701.6211/1110, Box 3666, RG59, State Department Decimal Files, National Archives and Records Administration. By December 12, 1939, Assistant Attorney General O. John Rogge of the Department of Justice received the case from the State Depart-

ment and closed the matter. Shulte enjoyed a certain publicity in the 1950s for pastoral work among Eskimo populations and became the "flying priest of the Arctic."

33. Hope Ridings Miller, *Embassy Row: The Life and Times of Diplomatic Washington* (New York: Holt, Rinehart and Winston, 1969), p. 237. As Hitler overran one country after another in Europe, the staffs of the Washington embassies of those conquered nations remained stranded in the American capital. Their plight engendered much sympathy in the local press. Miller was editor of the society page of the Washington *Post*.

34. Executive Order No. 8244, September 8, 1939, in WD Bulletin No. 18, September 12, 1939, *General Orders, Bulletins, and Numbered Circulars, War Department, 1920-1939* (Washington, D.C., 1940).

35. *Report of the Secretary of War to the President, 1939* (Washington, D.C., 1939), Table B [follows p. 56]; *Report of the Secretary of War to the President, 1940* (Washington, D.C., 1940), Table B [faces p. 31].

36. Mark Skinner Watson, *The Chief of Staff: Prewar Plans and Preparations* (Washington, D.C.: Office of the Chief of Military History, 1950), pp. 158–159. The "triangular" division consisted of three infantry regiments with scaled-down divisional support units and was far more flexible and mobile than the older "square" divisions of four regiments that had fought on the static battlefields of World War I. Because of the 17,000-man increase, the army could also begin forming new corps level headquarters, the echelon that would control as many as three divisions in battle.

37. Constance M. Green, Harry C. Thompson, and Peter C. Roots, *The Ordnance Department: Planning Munitions for War* (Washington, D.C.: 1955) pp. 185–186.

38. Lt. Col. Marvin A. Kreidberg and 1st Lt. Merton G. Henry, *History of Military Mobilization in the United States Army, 1775–1945*, DA Pamphlet No. 20-212 (Washington, D.C.: Office, Chief of Military History, 1955), p. 548.

39. Biennial Report of the Chief of Staff, July 1, 1941, in *Report of the Secretary of War to the President, 1941* (Washington, D.C., Government Printng Office 1941), pp. 47-48.

40. v. Boetticher to OKW Ausland and Attachégruppen Heer und Luft, Cable No. 453, October 1, 1939, T-120, B21/594, B00491-92.

41. Harry M. Yoshpe, "Bernard M. Baruch: Civilian Godfather of the Military M-Day Plan," *Military Affairs* 29 (Spring 1965): 11.

42. v. Boetticher to OKH Ausland and Attachégruppen, Heer und Luft, Cable No. 381, September 18, 1939, T-120, B21/594, B004935-36.

43. Ibid., B004937.

44. v. Boetticher to OKW Ausland and Attachégruppen, Heer und Luft, Cable No. 528, October 17, 1939, T-120, B21/594, B004943-44.

45. v. Boetticher to OKW Ausland and Attachégruppen, Heer und Luft, Cable No. 609, November 3, 1939, T-120, B21/594, B004948.

46. v. Boetticher to OKW Ausland and Attachégruppen, Heer und Luft, Cable No. 719, December 1, 1939, T-120, B21/594, B004955-56.

47. Ibid.

48. Langer and Gleason, *Challenge to Isolation*, p. 290.

49. John McVickar Haight, *American Aid to France, 1938–1940* (New York: Atheneum, 1970), p. 155.

50. Maurice Matloff and Edwin M. Snell, *Strategic Planning for Coalition Warfare, 1941–1943* (Washington, D.C.: Office of the Chief of Military History: 1953), pp. 7–8.

51. Brig. Gen. Henry J. Reilly, "Background for Lightning War," *Infantry Journal* 47 (January–February 1940): 2–11, passim. As a captain, Reilly had won fame and laurels as the commander of "Reilly's Battery," which figured heavily in the relief of the besieged legations in Peking during the Boxer Rebellion.

52. Forrest C. Pogue, *Ordeal and Hope*, vol. II (1966) of *George C. Marshall*, 4 vols (New York: The Viking Press, 1963–1987), p. 121.

53. v. Boetticher to OKW Ausland, Cable No. 453, October 1, 1939, T-120, B21/594, B004939–40.

54. v. Boetticher to OKW Ausland, Cable No. 609, November 3, 1939, T-120, B21/594, B004946.

55. Herbert Feis, *The Road to Pearl Harbor* (Princeton, N.J.: Princeton University Press, 1950), p. 41.

56. "Oshima Arrives," New York Times, November 10, 1939, p. 8. See also Carl Boyd, *Hitler's Japanese Confidant: General Oshima Hiroshi and MAGIC Intelligence, 1941–1945* (Lawrence: University Press of Kansas, 1993), p. xi. Oshima had been military attaché in Berlin from 1934 until 1938, when he became ambassador. He returned to Berlin as ambassador again in February 1941. As Boyd's book makes clear, Oshima's wartime observations from his post were intercepted and read by American code breakers, providing one of the best sources of American intelligence on the German prosecution of the war.

57. Boetticher to OKW Ausland, Attache Groups, Army and Air, Cable No. 688, November 21, 1939, T-120, B21/594, B004953. By juxtaposition with another event, this conference became memorable for von Boetticher's son, who recalled the dinner as a dour affair with an assembly of uncommunicative Japanese, all armed with briefcases. Immediately afterward, father and son drove to Walter Reed Army Medical Center in Washington, where von Boetticher's mentor on Japanese affairs, Col. Charles Burnett, lay dying of cancer. In their last moments together, in the recollection of the attaché's son, there was a poignant silence. When Burnett died on November 27, the younger von Boetticher heard his mother lament the passage of their "last true friend in America." Friedrich Heinrich Botticher to author, July 30, 1973.

58. Gerhard L. Weinberg, "Hitler's Image of the United States," *American Historical Review* 64 (July 1964): 1012.

59. Hanson Baldwin to the author, August 7, 1973; Riedel Telephone Interview, September 19, 1976.

60. *Kriegstagebuch des Oberkommandos der Wehrmacht (Wehrmachtführungsstab), vol. 1, 1 August 1940–31 December 1941*, compiled and commented upon by Hans-Adolf Jacobsen (Frankfurt am Main: Bernard & Graefe Verlag für Wehrwesen, 1965), pp. 107E–108E. The assessment in the OKW study is attributed not to von Boetticher directly, but to then-Maj. Walter Warlimont.

61. Andreas Hillgruber, *Hitlers Strategie; Politik und Kriegführung 1940–1941,* (Frankfurt am Main: Bernard & Graefe Verlag für Wehrwesen, 1965), p. 375. Hitler continued to follow the reports from Washington closely from October 1 through early December 1939, Hillgruber maintains, and characterized the attaché's output as "colored" (gefärbt). Ibid., pp. 195–196. He also judges the attaché reports as pessimistic because they and the OKW study made Hitler realize that time was against him.

62. Gerhard Engel, *Heeresadjutant bei Hitler, 1938–1943; Aufzeichnungen des Majors Engel,* Hildegard von Kotze, ed. (Stuttgart: Deutsche Verlags-Anstalt, 1974), p. 47. Note taking on Hitler's random remarks was supposedly forbidden, but the führer's comments on von Boetticher's work show up here and in another, more extensive work by Dr. Henry Picker, who also recorded these rambling discourses. At least until von Boetticher's return to Germany in 1942, Hitler expressed approval for the attaché's work.

63. Memorandum, Ambassador Dieckhoff, Berlin, September 7, 1939, *DGFP,* D, VIII, pp. 21–22.

64. Hillgruber, *Hitlers Strategie,* pp. 196–199.

65. H. Duncan Hall, *North American Supply* (London: HMSO and Longmans Green & Co., 1955), p. 41.

66. John Morton Blum, *From the Morgenthau Diaries,* 2 vols. (Boston: Houghton Mifflin, 1959), II:116–117.

67. v. Boetticher to OKW Ausland, Attache Groups, Army and Air, Cable No. 366, March 15, 1940, T-120, B21/594, B005432-33. A "Vertrauensmann" of Thomsen's also confirmed Woodring's resistance to the president's wishes. See his Cable No. 400, March 20, 1940, ibid., B005442. The "leading military writer in the country, Hanson Baldwin," was independently writing articles that presented the true relationship of power, wrote the attaché, something he clarified for the Japanese attaché, who did not seem to understand the implausibility of the British claim.

68. Keith D. MacFarland, *Harry H. Woodring, A political Biography of FDR's Controversial Secretary of War* (Lawrence: University Press of Kansas, 1975), pp. 203–204.

69. v. Boetticher to OKW Ausland, Attaché Groups, Army and Air, Cable No. 469, March 29, 1940, T-120, B21/594, B005457.

70. v. Boetticher to OKW Ausland, Air and Army General Staffs, through the Attaché Sections, Cable No. 538, April 3, 1940, *DGFP*, D, IX, p. 73.

71. U.S. Minister in Denmark (Atherton) to Sec'y of State, April 9, 1940, and Chargé in Germany (Kirk) to Sec'y of State, April 9, 1940, *FRUS*, 1940, I:144–145. (See Chapter 2, note 77 for explanation of FRUS.)

72. Earl Ziemke, *The German Northern Theater of Operations, 1940-1945*, DA Pamphlet No. 20-271 (Washington, D.C.: Government Printing Office, 1959), pp. 40–59, 63–112.

73. v. Boetticher to Army Chief of Staff, Cable No. 594, April 9, 1940 (Citissime), T-77, 1029/1029, 6502429-30.

74. Memorandum, Col. Horst von Mellenthin, OKH Attachéabteilung, GenStdH No. 1194/40, May 3, 1940, T-77, 902/902, 6502434.

75. Bruce Catton, *War Lords of Washington* (New York: Harcourt, Brace & Co., 1948), p. 21. See also Langer and Gleason, *The Challenge to Isolation*, p. 469, which sees the campaign as "one of the most terrific shocks . . . ever experienced" by the American people.

76. v. Boetticher to OKW Ausland, Chiefs of Staff, Army and Luftwaffe, Cable No. 922, May 11, 1940, *DGFP*, D, IX, p. 329.

77. v. Boetticher to OKW Ausland, Attaché Groups, Cable No. 949, May 16, 1940, *DGFP*, D, IX, p. 352.

78. v. Boetticher to OKW Ausland, Attache Groups, Cable No. 950, May 16, 1940, as quoted in Friedländer, *Prelude to Downfall*, p. 93. Discovered by Friedländer in the Bonn Foreign Office Archives, this cable is missing from the microfilm record of serial B21.

79. v. Boetticher to Chiefs of Staff, Army and Luftwaffe, Cable No. 999, May 23, 1940, T-120, 19/4, 12111.

80. v. Boetticher to Halder, March 28, 1940, T-120, B21/594, B005449-53. The language employed also reflects the rivalry between the old army regulars and the newer OKW echelons in the German Wehrmacht. Halder's response of May 6 was merely soothing and concluded with his "aufrichtigsten Dank für Ihre erfolgreiche Arbeit und für Ihre vorzügliche Berichterstattung als Militärattaché." Halder to v. Boetticher, May 6, 1940, ibid., frame B005454.

81. Thomsen later cited von Boetticher's Cable No. 681 of April 18 on the subject.

82. Thomsen to Foreign Office, Cable No. 988, May 22, 1940, *DGFP*, D, IX, pp. 41–5l.

83. Ladislas Farago, *The Game of the Foxes* (New York: Bantam Books, 1973) pp. 47–52. Canaris gave Ernst von Weizsäcker no satisfaction, claiming that the agent, known only as Bergmann, was unknown to the Abwehr.

84. v. Boetticher to OKW Ausland, Attaché Groups, Army and Air, Cable No. 999, May 23, 1940, T-120, 19/4, 12112. The inclusion of Freemasons in this context, when there was no Masonic influence on American government circles, is attributable only to von Boetticher's open attempts to appeal to mentalities in the OKW staff around Hitler and to Hitler himself. The phrase is a strictly National Socialist construction.

85. Walter S. Ross, *The Last Hero; Charles A. Lindbergh* (New York: Manor Books, 1974), pp. 295–296. Ross estimates that more people listened to Lindbergh's first speech of September 15, 1939, than to Roosevelt's fireside chat of September 3. Lindbergh especially embarrassed

Roosevelt because Roosevelt could not give guarantees that the flier was entirely wrong about the cost of a coming war.

86. v. Boetticher to OKW Ausland, Attaché Groups, Army and Air, Cable No. 999, May 23, 1940, T-120, 19/4, 12113.

87. Ibid.

88. Thomsen to Foreign Office, Cable No. 616, April 10, 1940, *DGFP*, D, IX, p. 80.

89. State Sec'y to Embassy in the United States, Cable No. 403, April 19, 1940, ibid., p. 208.

90. Thomsen to State Sec'y v. Weizsäcker [personal letter] April 24, 1940, ibid., pp. 231–232. Thomsen's characterization of von Boetticher's view of his own position once war had broken out is consistent with Peter Riedel's recollection that after September 1, 1939, von Boetticher tended to act as Thomsen's equal in the daily situation conferences Thomsen ran in the embassy. Riedel telephone interview with author, September 19, 1976.

91. Harold Ickes, *Secret Diaries of Harold Ickes*, 3 vols. (New York: Simon and Schuster, 1953), III:188, entry for May 19, 1940.

92. Watson, *Chief of Staff*, pp. 169–171.

93. v. Boetticher to OKW Ausland, Attaché Groups and Air Ministry, "American Armament Plans," Cable No. 1047, June 1, 1940, T-120, 19/4, 12166–69.

94. v. Boetticher to OKW Ausland, Attaché Groups and Air Ministry, Cable No. 1057, June 1, 1940, ibid., 12172. The field guns never got aboard ships before France collapsed. On June 5, the total number of planes that had reached the Allies was only 600. See Ickes, Secret Diaries, III:199–200, entry of Wednesday, June 5, 1940. On the consignment of the rifles, see Hall, *North American Supply*, p. 57.

95. v. Boetticher to OKH Attachégruppe, RLM, Cable 1121, June 9, 1940, T-120, 19/4, 12251.

96. v. Boetticher to OKH Attachégruppe, RLM, Cable No. 1162, June 13, 1940, ibid., 12268.

97. Blum, *Morgenthau Diaries*, II:164.

98. Robert E. Sherwood, *Roosevelt and Hopkins: An Intimate History* (New York: Harper and Bros., 1948), pp. 143, 147–149.

99. MacFarland, *Harry H. Woodring*, pp. 229–230. See also Elting E. Morrison, *Turmoil and Tradition, a Study of the Life and Times of Henry L. Stimson* (Boston: Houghton Mifflin, 1960), pp. 480–482. Woodring was also followed five weeks later by the obstreperous Louis Johnson, who went out of office still protesting that Roosevelt had promised him Woodring's post. Johnson's successor was Robert P. Patterson, a jurist.

100. v. Boetticher to OKW Ausland, OKH Attaché Group, Chief of the General Staff, Air Ministry, Chief of the Air Staff, Cable No. 1649, August 6, 1940, "The Background of Lindbergh's Emergence in Public and the Campaign against Him," *DGFP*, D, X, p. 413. Adler was no doubt doubly troublesome in von Boetticher's eyes; he was the general manager of the New York Times Corporation, whose "pernicious influence" he had charted in 1934.

101. Charles A. Lindbergh, *The Wartime Journals of Charles A. Lindbergh* (New York: Harcourt, Brace and Jovanovach, 1970), p. 352.

102. v. Boetticher to Chiefs of Army and Air Staffs, OKW Ausland, Cable No. 1146, June 11, 1940, T-120, 19/4, 12259.

103. Truman Smith, "Facts of Life," typed manuscript, Yale University manuscript collection, [1964], pp. 118–119. A copy of this document is in the author's files. Smith vaguely remembers that it was Bernard Baruch who eventually prevailed upon Roosevelt at Marshall's request to call off the dogs.

Chapter 7

1. Overheated suspicions of foreign influences produced isolated incidents in which people broke into private homes to demand salutes to the American flag from suspected Nazis and Communists. Harold Ickes, *Secret Diaries of Harold Ickes*, 3 vols. (New York: Simon and

Schuster, 1953), 2:21, entry of June 15, 1940. On this phenomenon generally see Geoffrey Perrett, *Days of Sadness; Years of Triumph, The American People, 1939–1945* (New York: Coward, McCann, Geohagen, 1973), pp. 87–103, *passim*; David M. Kennedy, *Freedom from Fear: The American People in Depression and War, 1929–1945*, The Oxford History of the United States (New York: Oxford University Press, 1999), pp. 460.

2. Walter Johnson, *The Battle against Isolation* (Chicago: University of Chicago Press, 1944), p. 104; Gerald E. Wheeler, *Admiral William V. Pratt, U. S. Navy; A Sailor's Life* (Washington, D.C.: Government Printing Office, 1974), pp. 392–393. Pratt, a former chief of naval operations, carried on his own campaign for aid to England in the columns of his *Newsweek* magazine articles.

3. Ltr., Charles A. Lindbergh, Jr., to author, March 21, 1973.

4. Friedrich v. Boetticher. "So War Es," [unpublished typescript memoir, n.d., but ca. 1964] pp. 355–356. Von Boetticher places the meeting on October 28, 1938, during a conference of the Institute of Aeronautical Sciences in Philadelphia. The younger Wright brother told him that he and his brother had German aviation pioneer Otto Lillienthal to thank for paving their way. Having overheard this as he approached, a smiling Lindbergh agreed with this remark, says von Boetticher.

5. v. Boetticher to OKW Ausland, OKH Attachéabteilung, and RLM Attachégruppe, Cable No. 1195, June 15, 1940, T-120, 19/4, 12291.

6. v. Boetticher to OKW Foreign Department, Chiefs of Army and Luftwaffe General Staffs, Cable No. 1493, July 20, 1940, *DGFP*, D, X, p. 254. (See Chapter 2, note 77 for explanation of *DGFP*.)

7. Slightly differently expressed, this rationale figured strongly in the handbills and arguments circulated by White's Committee. See Walter Johnson, *The Battle against Isolation* (Chicago: University of Chicago Press, 1944), p. 107.

8. Rosenman (comp.), Radio Address, July 19, 1940, *Public Papers and Addresses of F.D.R.*, IX:293–303. See especially p. 302 for the thinly veiled language that von Boetticher took to represent Roosevelt's unremitting attitude on the German threat.

9. v. Boetticher to OKW Foreign Section, OKH Attaché Section, Cable No. 1493, July 20, 1940, *DGFP*, D, X, p. 255.

10. Charles A. Lindbergh, *The Wartime Journals of Charles A. Lindberg*, (New York: Harcourt, Brace, Jovanovitch, 1970) pp. 374–375, shows the occasion to have been anything but a display of smooth cooperation among his isolationist comrades despite von Boetticher's portrayal of them as the united groundswell against Roosevelt.

11. v. Boetticher to OKW Foreign Dept., OKH Attaché Section, Cable No. 1649, August 6, 1940, *DGFP*, D, X, pp. 413–415. See also J. J. Pershing, "Keep the War from the Americas; We Must Help Britain at Once," *Vital Speeches* 6 (August 15, 1940): 646.

12. Walter Ross, *The Last Hero: Charles A. Lindbergh* (New York: Manor Books, 1974), pp. 292–293.

13. v. Boetticher to OKW Foreign Dep't., OKH Attaché Section, Cable No. 2231, October 16, 1940, *DGFP*, D, XI, pp. 307–309 and footnote.

14. Leonard Doob, "Goebbels' Principles of Propaganda," *Public Opinion Quarterly* 14 (Fall 1950): 425.

15. Memorandum, June 27, 1941, enclosure to Ltr., J. Edgar Hoover to Brig. Gen. Sherman Miles [G-2] of the same date, MI 2801-1054/48, MID Records, RG 165, National Archives and Records Administration.

16. MID Records, WDGS, Record Group 165, File 183-316/147B, National Archives, Washington, D.C. Copy in author's files.

17. Memorandum, G-2 [Miles] to Provost Marshal, April 29, 1941. Synoptic Index, Attaché, Military, German in Washington, file 10606-S3/104, NARA. The original of the Miles memo was destroyed, and only an extract remains in the "synoptic index" kept on von Boetticher in the WD G-2.

18. Walter L. Langer and S. Everett Gleason, *The Undeclared War, 1940–1941* (New York: Harper, 1953), p. 483.

19. WD MID "A History of the Military Intelligence Division, December 1941–2 Sept 1945," [n.d.] typescript copy in U.S. Army Center of Military History, p. 3.

20. Smith continued to have trouble with administration attempts to harass him for an alleged public remark that FDR was as dead from the waist up as he was from the waist down. Later exonerated of making this rumored insult, the characterization nevertheless accurately summed up Smith's viewpoint on the president.

21. Brig. Gen. Raymond E. Lee, *The London Journals of General Raymond E. Lee,* ed. James Leutze (Boston: Little, Brown and Co., 1972), pp. xiii–xv. In the only instance when von Boetticher and Lee met, according to this diary, the German officer undertook to educate Lee on what was propaganda coming out of Berlin and what was not. Any announcements emanating from the Oberkommando der Wehrmacht were trustworthy; the rest was "all written by those propaganda fellows, and you must pay no attention to it." Entry of June 4, 1940, p. 5. On Lee's access to British intelligence offices, see General Sir Edmund Ironside, *Time Unguarded, The Ironside Diaries, 1937–1940* (New York: David McKay, 1962), pp. 10–11.

22. Laurence Lafore, *The End of Glory; An Interpretation of the Origins of World War II* (New York: Lippincott, 1970), p. 167.

23. Scanlon to G-2, December 18, 1940, Subj: Effective Strength of the German Air Force, WD MID Records, RG 165, File No. 2082-812, part 3, NARA.

24. Miles to Milattaché, London, March 12, 1941, Cable No. 1421, WD MID Records, file 2082-812/77 part 3; Chart, attachment to Memorandum, Brig. Gen. Sherman Miles to CofSA Gen. George C. Marshall, January 8, 1941, Subj: Present Strength of the German Air Force. In this chart Miles presented in tabular form the comparisons of estimates on German air strength that G-2 was receiving from the attachés in Berlin and those in London. Other reports supporting the Berlin estimates (and von Boetticher's figures) were arriving also from attachés in Vichy and in Berne, Switzerland.

25. At least one German officer was surprised to hear of the arrangement. Gen. d. Artillerie Horst von Mellenthin (a. D.), then a colonel and head of the German Army's Attachéabteilung, said in obvious understatement: "Er war eigentlich nicht ganz nach den regulations [he was really not entirely according to regulations]. Ltr., Gen. v. Mellenthin to author, October 15, 1973.

26. Cajus Bekker, *The Luftwaffe War Diaries* (Garden City, N.Y.: Doubleday & Co., 1968), p. 149. See also Hanson W. Baldwin, *The Crucial Years, 1939–1941; The World at War* (New York: Harper and Row, 1976), p. 145, and Winston S. Churchill, *The Second World War,* 5 vols. (Boston: Houghton Mifflin, 1949), vol. 2: *Their Finest Hour,* p. 339.

27. H. Duncan Hall, *North American Supply* (London: HMSO and Longmans Green and Co., 1955) p. 205.

28. F. W. Winterbotham, *The Ultra Secret* (New York: Harper & Row, 1974), pp. 49–51.

29. Hanson W. Baldwin, *Battles Lost and Won* (New York: Harper and Row, 1966), p. 54.

30. v. Boetticher to OKW Ausland, Chief, Luftwaffeführungsstab, Cable No. 1852, August 31, 1940, T-120, 35/20, 22779.

31. Thomsen to Foreign Office, Cable No. 1875, September 3, 1940, *DGFP,* D, IX, p. 12. Among v. Boetticher's friends, Douglas Freeman confided to his diary: "It's the only time in my life when I have wished I were in Congress. If I were I'd move his impeachment before night." Freeman Diary, Entry Tuesday, September 3, 1940, Box 1, Freeman papers, Library of Congress Manuscript Div.

32. v. Boetticher to OKW Ausland, OKH Attachéabteilung, Chiefs of Army and Luftwaffe, Cable No. 1874, September 3, 1940, T-120, 35/20, 22801.

33. U.S. Bureau of the Budget, War Records Section, *The United States at War* (Washington, D.C.: Government Printing Office, 1946), p. 19.

34. Hall, *North American Supply,* p. 209.

35. Andreas Hillgruber, *Hitlers Strategie; Politik und Kriegführung 1940–1941* (Frankfurt am Main: Bernard & Graefe Verlag für Wehrwesen, 1965), p. 197. Hillgruber notes the effect on Hitler of von Boetticher's characterization of plummeting British morale under the "blitz" in September 1940. He also depicts the reports from Washington as moving from the pessimism of late 1939 to an optimism rising to euphoria by mid-1940.

36. Ibid., p. 376, note 126.

37. Churchill, *Their Finest Hour*, p. 560. Britain had lost over 4 million tons of shipping since the start of the war, well below the level at which it could sustain itself.

38. Richard M. Leighton and Robert W. Coakley, *Global Logistics and Strategy, 1940–1943* (Washington, D.C.: Government Printing Office, 1955), p. 58; Edward R. Stettinius, Jr., *Lend Lease, Weapon for Victory* (New York: Macmillan & Co., 1944), p. 135.

39. Hall, *North American Supply*, p. 258; Thomsen to Foreign Office, Cable No. 2594, November 29, 1940, T-120, 84/81, 62163.

40. On June 17, 1940, Strong had sent Marshall a memorandum recommending against any further dispatch of matériel to the Allies, owing to their imminent defeat. Mark Skinner Watson, *The Chief of Staff: Prewar Plans and Preparations* (Washington, D.C.: Government Printing Office, 1955), p. 114; See also Thomas Parrish, *The ULTRA Americans: The U.S. Role in Breaking the Nazi Codes* (New York: Stein and Day, 1986), p. 60.

41. Ibid.

42. v. Boetticher to OKW Ausland, OKH Attacheabteilung, Cable No. [missing], August 18, 1940, T-77, 1029/1029, 6502473.

43. Quoted in Churchill, *Their Finest Hour*, p. 338.

44. v. Boetticher to OKW Ausland, OKH Attachéabteilung, Chiefs of Staff, Army and Luftwaffe, Cable No. 2039, September 24, 1940, T-120, 35/20, 22892. It was a patent attempt to convince Americans that Britain could fight indefinitely, he wrote, but Hanson Baldwin had also contradicted the Strong remark in print and the General Staff still valued the word of the German attaché over that of its own War Plans Division chief.

45. Vortragsnotiz, [OKW Briefing Notice], December 9, 1940, Summary of v. Boetticher Report of December 4, 1940, T-77, 1029/1029, 650554. Chaney, an Air Corps officer, headed what at this stage was the Special Observer (SPOBS) Mission and became the first commander of the formally established European Theater of Operations once the United States entered the war.

46. Bradley F. Smith, *The Ultra-Magic Deals and the Most Secret Special Relationship, 1940–1946* (Novato, Calif.: Presidio, 1992), pp. 43–46; see also David Alvarez, *Secret Messages: Codebreaking and American Diplomacy, 1930–1945* (Lawrence: University Press of Kansas, 2000), p. 76.

47. v. Boetticher to Wehrmachtführungsstab, Cable No. 2818, December 25, 1940, T-77, 1029/1029, 6502571; Telephone Interview, Mrs. Truman Smith with author, November 23, 1973. An additional cable on the subject shows Thomsen to be the deep cynic here. "The Americans have been moved by the proposal and now reject the propaganda that the Germans had done away with Christmas, the latter an emotionally primitive gesture, to which the Americans are receptive." Thomsen to Foreign Office, Cable No. 2819, December 25, 1940, ibid., 6502572.

48. The account of von Werra's exploits are in Kendal Burt and James Leasor's *The One That Got Away* (New York: Ballantine Books, 1956). As one of the war's human escape sagas, his story inspired a motion picture. Today, various sites on the Internet continue to celebrate this story, but none has added much more detail to the sole original version. A more recent study of the family in a doctoral dissertation by a Swiss student, Wilfried Meichtry, reveals that the adventuresome and irrepressible von Werra was given up for adoption by destitute parents in 1915. When his adoptive parents also abandoned him and his older sister in 1932, the eighteen-year-old Franz stowed away aboard a steamer bound for New Orleans. His visit in 1941 was therefore his second to American soil. See Meichtry, "Zwischen Ancien Regime und Moderne: die Walliser Adelsfamilie von Werra," Abstract in *Berner Historische Mitteilungen*, published by the Historical Institute of the University of Bern, 1999, pp. 16–17.

49. v. Boetticher to OKW Ausland, Cable No. 198, January 23, 1941, T-77, 1029/1029, 6502683. Amid other matters von Boetticher answered here a query as to whether one Maj. Helmut Wiek was in a Canadian POW camp. He noted only that "hundreds" of German pilots were arriving in camps in Canada and he could not predict Wiek's whereabouts.

50. Burt and Leasor, *The One That Got Away*, pp. 198–201.

51. v. Boetticher to OKW Ausland, Cable No. 314, February 4, 1941, T-77, 1029/1029, 6502685. According to the cable, the "best American sources" suggested this course of action to him.

52. Burt and Leasor, *The One That Got Away*, p. 204.

53. Martin Simons, *German Air Attaché: The Thrilling Story of the Germain Ace Pilot and Wartime Diplomat Peter Riedel* (Shrewsbury, UK: Airlife Publishing, 1997), *pp.* 95–97.

54. Peter Fleming, *Operation Sea Lion* (New York: Simon and Schuster, 1957), pp. 302–303; Norman Rich, *Hitler's War Aims*, 2 vols. (New York: W.W. Norton, 1974), 2:162–163.

55. v. Boetticher to OKW Ausland, OKW Attachéabteilung, RLM Attachégruppe, Cable No. 2662, December 7, 1940, *DGFP*, D, XI, pp. 814–816.

56. Watson, *Chief of Staff*, pp. 312–315.

57. v. Boetticher to OKW Ausland, OKH Attachéabteilung, Cable No. 2767, December 19, 1940, T-77, 1029/1029, 6502658.

58. v. Boetticher to OKW Ausland, OKH Attachéabteilung, Cable No. 466, February 22, 1941, T-77, 1029/1029, 6502743. See also Forrest C. Pogue, *Ordeal and Hope*, vol. II (1966) of *George C. Marshall*, 4 vols. (New York: Viking Press, 1963–1987) p. 70; Watson, *Chief of Staff*, p. 315.

59. Thomsen to Foreign Office, Cable No. 354, February 7, 1941, *DGFP*, D, XII, pp. 60–62. Here Thomsen cataloged his latest orchestrations of efforts among groups sympathetic to isolationism or to Germany. Among them was a "Mother's Crusade to Defeat H.R. 1776," the latter being the designation of the bill on the House of Representatives calendar.

60. v. Boetticher to OKW Foreign Dept., OKW Attaché Section, Chief of General Staff; RLM Attaché Group, Cable No. 505, February 25, 1941, *DGFP*, D, XII, pp. 162–163.

61. Corelli Barnett, *The Collapse of British Power* (New York: William Morrow & Co., 1972), pp. 591–592."Lend-Lease," says the author, "gradually consummated the process Churchill had begun of transforming England into a satellite warrior-state dependent for its existence on the flow of supplies across the Atlantic."

62. Watson, *Chief of Staff*, p. 322; Hall, *North American Supply*, p. 294; Stettinius, *Lend Lease*, p. 96.

63. v. Boetticher to OKW Ausland, OKH Attachéabteilung, Cable No. 924, April 5, 1941, T-77, 1030/1030, 6502936.

64. See Arthur Schlesinger, *The Imperial Presidency* (Boston: Houghton Mifflin, 1973), p. ix. The gradual accretion of power by the presidency past the bounds of balance laid out in the Constitution has centered around the conduct of foreign policy, argues Schlesinger, especially on the decision to go to war. The author defends Roosevelt's actions by citing the notion of emergency powers. See pp. 100–126, passim.

65. Here the British futilely attempted to wrest this strategic West African port, only 1,870 miles from the Brazilian port of Natal, from Vichy French control. Von Boetticher reported on the surprise the raid produced in the American General Staff, but noted that the American State Department "wirepullers" were involved. v. Boetticher to OKH Attachéabteilung, Cable No. 2045, September 25, 1940, T-120, 35/20, 204895–96.

66. Charles Burdick, *German Military Strategy and Spain in World War II* (Syracuse, N.Y.: Syracuse University Press, 1968), pp. 50–52. German planning to seize Gibraltar continued into 1944, but the undertaking of 1940, Operation FELIX, never got beyond the staff study stage and amounted therefore to "so much waste paper." See also: Gen. d. Fliegertruppen Werner Kreipe, "The Battle of Britain," in *The Fatal Decisions, ed.* Seymour Freidin and William Richardson, (New York: Berkeley Publishers, 1958), p. 32.

67. Winston S. Churchill, *The Second World War*, 6 vols. (Boston: Houghton Mifflin, 1948–1953), vol. 3, *The Grand Alliance*, p. 92.

68. David Thomas, *Nazi Victory; Crete 1941* (New York: Stein and Day, 1973), p. 48. American authorities, especially Averell Harriman and Harry Hopkins, made possible the repair work in American yards. See Averell Harriman and Elie Abel, *Special Envoy to Churchill and Stalin, 1941–1946* (New York: Random House, 1975), p. 57.

69. Churchill, *The Grand Alliance*, p. 200.

70. Ibid., pp. 94–100, passim. See also George E. Blau et al., *The German Campaigns in the Balkans (Spring 1941)*, DA Pamphlet No. 20-260 (Washington, D.C.: Dept. of the Army, November 1953), pp. 10–15.

71. Thomas, *Nazi Victory*, pp. 58–59. Adm. of the Fleet Andrew Cunningham immediately made plans to evacuate the same troops he was transporting to Greece and became the more embroiled in a controversy over guarantees to ensure the withdrawal of Commonwealth troops (the Australian 6th Division and a single New Zealand Division) in equal proportion to British troops.

72. Baldwin, *Battles Lost and Won*, p. 62.

73. v. Boetticher to OKW Ausland, Cable No. 1041, April 17, 1941, T-77, 1030/1030, 6502964. See also Cable No. 1211, April 30, 1941, ibid., 6503036. He indignantly reported on British propaganda to the effect that the Italian defeat would release 300,000 Commonwealth troops to fight further north; no such strength became available.

74. v. Boetticher to OKW Ausland, Cable No. 126, January 16, 1941, T-77, 1029/1029, 650624.

75. v. Boetticher to OKW Ausland, OKH Attachéabteilung, Cable No. 816, March 26, 1941, T-77, 1029/1029, 6502841. On March 24, 1941, von Boetticher had received instructions from home to play up the exaggerated British figures since "the more bragging the English have done here, the more effective will be their defeat." Memo by Hans Kramarz (Head of Pol. Div. IM), March 24, 1941, *DGFP*, D, XI, p. 349.

76. v. Boetticher to OKW Ausland, OKH Attachéabteilung, Cable No. 1192, 1941, T-77, 1030/1030, 6503029-31.

77. Pogue, *Ordeal and Hope*, p. 129. One officer declared before Stimson that it was the "most disastrous inference by a political leader in military strategy since the Civil War."

78. v. Boetticher to OKW Ausland, OKH Attachéabteilung, Cable No. 712, March 17, 1941, T-77, 1029/1029, 6502813.

79. I. S. O. Playfair et al., *The Mediterranean and the Middle East*, 2 vols. in 8 parts (London: Her Majesty's Stationery Office, 1954–1987), 2, part 2:79.

80. "United States-British Staff Conversations, Report," March 27, 1941, in 79th Cong., lst Sess., Hearings before the Joint Committee on the Investigation of the Pearl Harbor Attack, part 15 (Washington, 1946), pp. 1487–1488 [hereafter Pearl Harbor Attack Hearings]; Maurice Matloff and Edwin M. Snell, *Strategic Planning for Coalition Warfare, 1941–1942* (Washington, D.C.: Government Printing Office, 1953), pp. 34–62.

81. Pearl Harbor Attack Hearings, part 15, p. 1491.

82. Samuel E. Morison, *History of U.S. Naval Operations in World War II*, 15 vols. (Boston: Little, Brown and Co., 1950–1965), vol. 1: *The Battle of the Atlantic* (1950), p. 57.

83. v. Boetticher to OKW Ausland, OKH Attachéabteilung, Cable No. 1203, April 29, 1941, T-77, 1030/1030, 6503033. On April 18, 1941, Adm. Ernest J. King, following Roosevelt's announcement of April 10, extended the new definition of the Western Hemisphere to the area west of 260° W. longitude. Morison, *The Battle of the Atlantic*, p. 61.

84. v. Boetticher to OKW Ausland, OKH Attachéabteilung, Cable No. 1550, May 28, 1941, T-77, 1030/1030, 6502117.

85. Morison, *The Battle of the Atlantic*, pp. 66-67.

86. Holger Herwig, "Prelude to Weltblitzkrieg; German Naval Policy toward the United States, 1939–1941," *Journal of Modern History* 33 (December 1971): 664.

87. v. Boetticher to OKW Ausland, OKH Attachéabteilung, Cable No. 2139, July 9, 1941, T-77, 1030/1030, 6503261, and Cable No. 2144, July 9, 1941, ibid., 6503257.

88. Stetson Conn and Byron Fairchild, *The Framework of Hemispheric Defense* (Washington, 1960), p. 120. The War Plans Division opted instead for the development of bases in the threatened bulge of Brazil where Axis forces might be expected to land in an invasion launched from Dakar. Von Boetticher knew of these plans and predicted that the shipping shortages would "make difficult if not impossible" operations against Dakar and the Portuguese possessions. v. Boetticher to OKW Ausland, OKH Attachéabteilung, Cable No. 1800, June 14, 1941, T-77, 1030/1030, 6503177.

89. The Secretary of State to the German Chargé, June 16, 1941, *FRUS, 1941,* 5 vols. (Washington, D.C.: Government Printing Office, 1959), vol. 2, *Europe,* p. 629. (see Chapter 2, note 77 for eexplanation of *FRUS.*) Sumner Welles, acting for Hull, cited as a reason for the removal of the German agencies their "improper and unwarranted activities."

90. From August 1940 on, the State Department was receiving word of the BARBAROSSA plan. See Cordell Hull, *The Memoirs of Cordell Hull,* 2 vols. (New York: Macmillan, 1948), 2: 967–968. Hull had Sumner Welles inform the Soviet ambassador in Washington, Oumansky, who, in his suspicion, immediately told Thomsen what he had learned from American sources. See also Adolf Berle, *Navigating the Rapids, 1918–1971* (New York: Harcourt Brace Jovanovich, 1973), p. 518; and Naval Attaché of German Embassy in the Soviet Union to the OKM, April 24, 1941, *Nazi-Soviet Relations, 1939–1941* (Washington, D.C.: Government Printing Office, 1948), p. 330.

91. v. Boetticher to OKW Ausland, OKH Attachéabteilung, Cable No. 534, March 1, 1941, T-77, 1029/1029, 6502762. The rumors, he later said, were "Klatsch from the diplomatic-military poison kitchens of Washington." Cable No. 862, March 14, 1941, ibid., 6502808.

92. v. Boetticher to OKW Ausland, OKH Attachéabteilung, Cable No. 1211, April 30, 1941, T-77, 1030/1030, 6503036.

93. v. Boetticher to OKW Ausland, OKH Attachéabteilung, Cable No. 1903, June 22, 1941, *Ibid.,* 6503216. Thomsen, in reaching the same conclusion on Lend Lease, reasoned that such aid was only for democracies, and a sudden "alliance-type" relation with the Soviet Union was neither ideologically nor practically possible. Thomsen to Foreign Office, Cable No. 1894, June 22, 1941, *DGFP,* D, XII, p. 1082.

94. Watson, *Chief of Staff,* p. 329–330.

95. Memorandum, Brig. Gen. Sherman Miles to Marshall, June 28, 1941, WD MID Records, RG 165, file 2082-813, pt 3, NARA, Washington, D.C.

96. W. H. Tantum IV and E. J. Hoffschmidt, *The Rise and Fall of the German Air Force, 1939–1945* (Old Greenwich, Conn.: WE, 1969), p. 165. Argument persists on the total figure, and statistics vary depending upon the inclusion of sundry types of reconnaissance, transport, and liaison aircraft. Bekker, *The Luftwaffe War Diaries,* Appendix 10, p. 373, gives the lowest figure, 1,945.

97. James M. Burns, *Roosevelt, The Soldier of Freedom, 1940–1945* (New York: Harcourt Brace Jovanovich, 1970), p. 111; Langer and Gleason, *The Undeclared War,* pp. 542–543; Stimson foresaw a Russo-German war of no more than three months' duration. Ibid., p. 537. "America," he wrote in the next weeks, "seems to have lost her way." Bundy and Stimson, *On Active Service,* p. 371.

98. Saul Friedländer, *Prelude to Downfall, Hitler and the United States, 1931–1941* (New York: Alfred A. Knopf, 1967), p. 255.

99. Langer and Gleason, *The Undeclared War,* p. xiii. See also T. R. Fehrenbach, *F.D.R.'s Undeclared War* (New York: David McKay, 1967), pp. 242–244.

100. Helen [Klug] Riedel, "Reception Guests, July 3, 1941," typescript, Riedel Estate Files.

101. Helen's Diary from June 28 through July 23, 1941, typescript, Riedel Estate Files. An account of the episode is also in Simons, *German Air Attaché,* pp. 104–112; Riedel Memoir, pp. 196–213. (See Chapter 5, note 79.)

102. Memorandum for Brig. Gen. Sherman Miles, July 9, 1941, in Synoptic Index, Attaché, Military, German in Washington, part II, p. 63; Riedel telephone interview, September 19, 1976. Berle does not mention the episode in his *Navigating the Rapids*.

103. Riedel Memoir, pp. 196–213; Simons, *German Air Attaché*, pp. 104–112; FBI records obtained through a Freedom of Information Act request by Dr. Von Hardesty, National Air and Space Museum, confirm the sequence of these events in the minutest detail. See [Unsigned] Summary Report to Director, "German Activities (Peter Riedel)" July 2, 1941, p. 36, in FOIA File 340074, May 10, 1991. This file contains numerous reports, pp. 35–130, from McKee and other local field agents marking the movements of the Riedels across the American midwest. Reports and directives flew back and forth from FBI headquarters for months, one of these including the original German wording of Riedel's telegram to von Boetticher and the translated response to this. Much of the activity seems like waste motion, but the descriptions of it are always couched in terms designed to mollify higher authority.

104. Special Agent S. K. McKee to Director, Federal Bureau of Investigation, Re: Lieutenant Peter Riedel, September 10, 1941. Dr. Von Hardesty FOIA files, Item 132.

105. Wedemeyer Interview, June 14, 1974.

106. Runderlass to all Military Attachés, except Washington, Rio, Santiago, Tokyo, Nr. Pl. I-M 2799, September 22, 1941, T-78, 656/656, 0188.

107. Winston S. Churchill, *The Grand Alliance*, p. 452.

108. v. Boetticher to OKW Ausland, OKH Attachéabteilung Cable No. 2585, August 4, 1941, T-77, 1030/1030, 6503376. See also Robert Sherwood, *Roosevelt and Hopkins; An Intimate History* (New York: Harper and Row, 1948), pp. 323-348. passim. Sherwood states too that Hopkins had little understanding of the front but based his evaluation of Russian chances on Stalin's priority demands for raw materials, something that indicated a strong faith in a longer war than Hitler had planned for the Soviets.

109. v. Boetticher to OKW Ausland, OKH Attachéabteilung, Cable No. 3893, November 9, 1941, T-77, 1030/1030, 6503727.

110. v. Boetticher to OKW Ausland, OKH Attachéabteilung, Cable No. 2634, August 7, 1941, T-77, 1030/1030, 6503377. The Japanese attaché sent the same information to Tokyo on the same day and may have gotten it from his colleague. See Joseph P. Lash, *Roosevelt and Churchill: 1939–1941; The Friendship That Saved the West* (New York: W. W. Norton, 1976), p. 393.

111. v. Boetticher to OKW Ausland, Cable No. 2752, August 14, 1941, T-77, 1030/1030, 6503396-97.

112. Lash, *Roosevelt and Churchill*, p. 391; Harriman and Abel, *Special Envoy*, p. 76; Sherwood, *Roosevelt and Hopkins*, p. 351; Friedländer, *Prelude to Downfall*, pp. 266–267.

113. *Secretary of War Report, 1941*, Table A [follows p. 104]. By actual count, there were 1,442,182 officers and men, exclusive of Philippine Scouts, that organization counting another 11,944.

114. v. Boetticher to OKW Ausland, OKH Attachéabteilung, Cable No. 2194, July 11, 1941, *DGFP*, D, XIII, p. 126.

115. *The United States at War*, p. 54; Lt. Col. Marvin A. Kreidberg and 1st Lt. Merton G. Henry, *History of Military Mobilization in the United States Army, 1775–1945*, DA Pamphlet No. 20–212 (Washington, D.C.: Office, Chief of Military History, 1955), pp. 684–685.

116. Kreidberg and Henry, *History of Military Mobilization*, pp. 685–686; Walter Millis, *Arms and the State; Civil-Military Elements in National Policy* (New York: The Twentieth Century Fund, 1958), pp. 55–59.

117. He mentioned William Knudsen and Sidney Hilman frequently in cable traffic, but the "Rüstung . . ." series went home by diplomatic pouch since these reports always had innumerable attachments consisting of clipped articles from American newspapers and trade journals. These dispatches were increasingly delayed as German shipments moved from Washington to South American air termini to await infrequent air mail flights from Rio over Dakar and Rome to Berlin. On this, see Ltr., OKH GenStb, Attachéabteilung I/Pr to Aus.

Amt, Kurierrferat, June 6, 1941, T-77, 1030/1030, 6503128, and Attaché in Rio to OKH Attachéabteilung, May 29, 1941, Ibid., 6503130, which reports to the Berlin office that PANAGRA airline left German freight behind, claiming there was no room for it on flights.

118. James E. Hewes, *From Root to MacNamara: Army Organization and Administration, 1900–1963* (Washington, D.C.: Center of Military History, 1975), p. 63; Pogue, *Ordeal and Hope*, p. 9.

119. R. Elberton Smith, *The Army and Economic Mobilization*, (Washington, D.C.: Government Printing Office, 1959) pp. 130–133; Kreidberg and Henry, *History of Military Mobilization*, pp. 660–666.

120. Watson, *Chief of Staff*, p. 337.

121. Ibid., pp. 344–345; Langer and Gleason, *The Undeclared War*, pp. 735–741.

122. v. Boetticher to OKH Ausland, OKH Attachéabteilung, Cable No. 4050, November 18, 1941, T-77, 1030/1030, 6503763.

123. Ladislas Farago, *The Game of the Foxes* (New York: Bantam Books, 1973) pp. 614–615. The statements Farago attributes to von Boetticher here are in fact from Thomsen's cable of the same day, No. 4250, December 4, 1941, *DGFP*, D, XIII, pp. 950–951. Another principal in the story, Capt. Tracy B. Kittredge (USNR), then a member of the same naval intelligence establishment as was Farago at the time, several years later remarked that the news of the leak was cabled to Berlin and other Axis capitals. See his "A Military Danger: The Revelation of Secret Strategic Plans," U.S. Naval Institute *Proceedings* 81(July 1955): 734.

124. John L. Snell, *Illusion and Necessity: The Diplomacy of Global War, 1939–1945* (Boston: Houghton Mifflin, 1963), p. 78.

125. Herbert Feis, *The Road to Pearl Harbor* (Princeton, N.J.: Princeton University Press, 1950) p. 60.

126. Pogue, *Ordeal and Hope*, pp. 168–169.

127. v. Boetticher to OKW Ausland, OKH Attachéabteilung, Cable No. 1406, July 10, 1940, T-120, 19/4, 12413-15.

128. v. Boetticher to OKW Ausland, OKH Attachéabteilung, Cable No. 2036, September 24, 1940, T-78, 656/656, 0884.

129. John Huizenga, "Yosuke Matsuoka and the Japanese-German Alliance," in Gordon A. Craig and Felix Gilbert, *The Diplomats, 1919–1939*, 2 vols. (New York: Atheneum, 1967), 2:631; Paul W. Schroeder, *The Axis Alliance and Japanese-American Relations* (Ithaca, NY: Cornell University Press, 1958), p. 166.

130. v. Boetticher to OKW Ausland, OKH Attachéabteilung, Chiefs of Gen. Staff, Army, & Luftwaffe, and Luftwaffe Operations Staff, Cable No. 2079, September 28, 1940, T-78, 656/656, 0880-81. He further surmised from his own research that Japan had a year's supply of scrap.

131. "American-Dutch-British conversations, Singapore, April, 1941, Report," in *Pearl Harbor Attack Hearings*, part 15, p. 1558.

132. v. Boetticher to OKW Ausland [Abschrift] Cable No. 919, April 5, 1941, T-77, 1030/1030, 6502932.

133. Memorandum, CNO, CofSA to Special Observers, London, July 3, 1941, Subj: "Comment on Report of the A.D.B. Conversations," in *Pearl Harbor Attack Hearings*, part 15, p. 1677.

134. Raymond Callahan, "The Illusion of Security: Singapore, 1919–42," *Journal of Contemporary History* 9 (April 1974): 85–86. When the Russo-German war began, the Soviet Union also took priority over Singapore as a recipient of British supply. On this controversy, see also Basil H. Liddell Hart, *History of the Second World War* (New York: Putnam and Sons, 1970), pp. 230–232.

135. Christopher Thorne, *Allies of a Kind; the United States, Britain, and the War Against Japan, 1941–1945* (New York: Oxford University Press, 1978), pp. 54–56.

136. FDR to Ickes, July 1, 1941, in Ickes, *Secret Diaries*, 2:567.

137. von Boetticher to OKW Ausland, OKH Attachéabteilung, Cable No. [missing], September 9, 1941, T-77, 1030/1030, 653473.

138. von Boetticher to OKW Ausland, OKH Attachéabteilung, Cable No. 919, April 5, 1941, T-77, 1030/1030, 6502932. In September, with the tension of Japanese-American relations always rising, he told Berlin that the Japanese had "no clear idea of the relationships of power. They are not industrious enough and . . . not well educated. . . . Thus they fall on every deceptive report. . . ." Cable No. 3197, September 15, 1941, T-78, 656/656, 0395-96.

139. v.Boetticher to OKW Ausland, OKH Attachéabteilung, Cable No. 1017, April 14, 1941, T-77, 1030/1030, 6502945.

140. v.Boetticher to OKW Ausland, OKH Attachéabteilung, Cable No. 1033, April 15, 1941, *Ibid.*, 6502968-72.

141. Huizenga, "Matsuoka and the Japanese-German Alliance," p. 639.

142. Foreign Minister to the Embassy in Japan, Cable No. 942, July 1, 1941, *DGFP*, D, XIII, p. 62. Von Ribbentrop made this suggestion based on his assertion that the Wehrmacht had already broken the back of the Red Army.

143. Feis, *The Road to Pearl Harbor*, p. 227; Louis Morton, *Strategy and Command; The First Two Years* (Washington, D.C: Office of the Chief of Military History, 1972), pp. 93–94.

144. v. Boetticher to OKW Ausland, Chief of Army and Luftwaffe General Staff, Cable No. 2435, July 25, 1941, *DGFP*, D, XIII, pp. 216–217.

145. Snell, *Illusion and Necessity*, p. 82.

146. Louis Morton, *Strategy and Command: The First Two Years* (Washington, D.C.: Government Printing Office, 1962), p. 96–97.

147. Morison, *The Battle of the Atlantic*, pp. 79ff.

148. Karl Doenitz, *Memoirs, Ten Years and Twenty Days*, trans. R.H. Stevens, in collaboration with David Woodward (Cleveland: World Publishing Co., 1959), p. 150; Friedländer, *Prelude to Downfall*, pp. 292–293.

149. v. Boetticher to OKW Ausland, Cable No. 3786, November 1, 1941, T-77, 1030/1030, 6503699.

150. v. Boetticher to OKW Ausland, OKH Attachéabteilung, Cable No. 3964, November 14, 1941, T-77, 1030/1030, 6503741.

151. v. Boetticher to OKW Ausland, OKH Attachéabteilung, Cable No. 434, December 10, 1941, *Ibid.*, 6503838.

152. Bertram D. Hulen, "Hull Very Frigid to Visiting Envoys," *New York Times*, December 12, 1941:3. Thomsen had already communicated the purpose of his visit by telephoning Hull at his home earlier that morning. The verbatim copy of the German note, handed to the chargé d'affaires in Berlin, is carried in the U.S. Department of State *Bulletin*, December 13, 1941. The text of the declaration and the department's press release may also be viewed on the Web site of The Avalon Project at Yale Law School, www.yale.edu/lawweb/avalon/wwii/gerdec41.htm.

Chapter 8

1. Hildegard Marsden, "Waiting for Letters," typescript [copy in author's files], pp. 4–6. Marsden Interview, August 22, 1973; Miller Interview, August 24, 1973.

2. The essence of this protocol was repeated by Bruggmann on May 23, 1945, when he turned all of the material of the defeated Reich over to the U.S. government. See "Protocol" in Foreign Interest Section, Representation Branch, Division of Protective Services, Office of Consular Affairs, "History of the Former German Embassy and Other German Diplomatic Property while under the Control of the Department of State, 1945–1950," typescript, Washington, 1951, pp. 67–70. RG 59 Special War Problems Division. [Copy in author's files.]

3. Ltr, Friedrich v. Boetticher to State Department, February 4, 1942, State Dept. Decimal files 701.9411/1539 1/2, quoted in Arnold M. Krammer, "In Splendid Isolation: Enemy Diplomats in World War II," *Prologue* 17 (Spring 1985): 39.

4. Miller Interview, August 24, 1973. The author's specific inquiry to the FBI under the Freedom of Information Act resulted in no corroboration of this.

5. Ltr., Fred H. Botticher to author, July 30, 1973; Death Certificate, Cook County, Illinois, Fred H. Botticher, September 27, 1997.

6. "Interned Enemy Envoys Plot and Fight in 'Grand Hotel,'" *Washington Times-Herald*, April 30, 1942, in file, "Newspaper Articles about Greenbrier Hotel in Times-Herald," Special War Problems Subject File, 1939—1954, RG59, Box 112.

7. Krammer, "In Splendid Isolation," pp. 34–35.

8. Marsden, "Waiting for Letters," p. 15.

9. Friedrich v. Boetticher, "So War Es," [unpublished typescript memoir, n.d., but ca. 1964], p. 391. A spare paragraph skims over all the events of the six months of inactivity at the Greenbrier.

10. Marsden Interview, August 22, 1973.

11. Martin Simons, *German Air Attaché: The Thrilling Story of the German Ace Pilot and Wartime Diplomat Peter Riedel* (Shrewsbury, UK: Airlife Publishing, 1997), p. 119.

12. Memorandum, February 12, 1942, Hardesty FOIA File 340074, p. 194.

13. Reports to each of the government agencies named are in Hardesty FOIA File 340074, pp. 207–210.

14. Harry M. Kimball, Memorandum for Mr. Ladd, Re: Peter Riedel, Assistant Military Attaché for Air, German Embassy, March 26, 1942, in ibid., p. 221. "The thought has occurred that it might be desirable to obtain these films from the Security Storage Company for examination," concludes Kimball.

15. Hardesty FOIA File 340074, pp. 222–234. See Fletcher letter to Director [J. Edgar Hoover], July 6, 1942, Attention: Technical Laboratory, RE: Peter Riedel, Espionage-G, Hardesty FOIA File, p. 234. Suspicion fell on an employee with the German surname Hoffman. The wealth of self-justificatory detail from field agents and the continual, direct intervention from Hoover himself is evident in these exchanges.

16. On the evolution of the division and its responsibilities after its establishment on September 1, 1939, see Graham H. Stuart, "Special War Problems Division," *Department of State Bulletin* 11 (July 2, 1944): 6–8. Stuart summarized the work of the division, renamed in 1944, in this and four additional articles with the same title. It existed at first to handle the rescue and repatriation of American citizens caught in the European war zone, coordinate humanitarian activity with the International Red Cross, and guarantee the transmission of funds for these purposes. As the war progressed, the division also assumed the work of locating and repatriating both Allied and Axis prisoners of war. See also United States, National Archives and Records Service, *Federal Records of World War II*, volume 1, *Civilian Agencies*, Entry 1161, "Special War Problems Division," pp. 730–731.

17. Robert L. Bannerman to Mr. Fitch, Subj: General Report on Diplomatic Exchange, July 30, 1942, NARA RG 59, State Department, Special War Problems Div., Subj File 1939–1954, Box 112, "SS Drottingholm, Apr. 26, 42, Axis Removal from the United States," folder 3/5, p. 1. The collection of German, Japanese, and Italian "undesirables" all over Latin America and their transport to the United States enlarged the problem proportionally. The State Department records enumerated the various ships involved, their dates of arrival in American ports, and their various complements of foreign personnel.

18. Ibid., p. 2. The other vessels were of Portuguese registry.

19. Dept. of State to American Legation, Bern, Cable 887, April 8, 1942. Subj. Files 1939–1954, "Exchange Vessels: SS Drottningholm and MS Gripsholm," Box 72, RG 59 Dept. State, Special War Problems.

20. Robert L. Bannerman to Security Storage Company, "S.S. Drottningholm, Apr 26, '42, Axis Removal from United States," Box 112, folder 2/5, RG 59, State Department Special War Prob. Subj Files 1939–1954.

21. Marsden, "Waiting for Letters," p. 21.

22. R. L. Bannerman to Mr. Fitch, Subj: "Departure of the SS Drottningholm from Jersey City with 948 German, Italian, Hungarian, and Bulgarian Ex-officials on the Diplomatic Exchange," Box 72, "Exchange Vessels SS Drottningholm and SS Gripsholm," RG 59, State Department, Special War Problems Division, Subj. Files, 1939–1954.

23. Once a proud addition to the Scottish Allen Line, *Drottningholm* started life as the *Virginian* in late December 1904. One of two liners that featured then-radical turbine engines driving three screws, it always had problems with its drive-gear mechanisms and propellers, which made for a noisy passage. The ship also proved susceptible to heavy seas. Passengers ruefully called her "Rollingholm." Her physical appointments were above average for upper-class patrons. Her history may be seen on the Web site "The Great Ocean Liners" at www.greatoceanliners.net/virginian.html. Hildegard von Boetticher describes the creaking of her decking even in light seas. See Marsden, "Waiting for Letters," p. 21.

24. The run of photos from that occasion survived in the Riedel family materials and remains today in the Riedel Estate Files, Smithsonian's Air and Space Museum, Library and Archives Division collection.

25. Marsden, "Waiting for Letters," p. 25.

26. Paul Seabury, *The Wilhelmstrasse: A Study of German Diplomats under the Nazi Regime* (Berkeley: University of California Press, 1954), p. 120.

27. Jochman, Werner, ed., *Adolf Hitler: Monologe im Führer Hauptquartier, 1941–1944: Die Aufzeichnungen Heinrich Heims* (Hamburg: Albrecht Knaus Verlag, 1980), p. 254. Heims was adjutant to Martin Bormann; an early Nazi Party member, he was welcomed into Hitler's coterie and recorded much of the early "table talk." When he was dispatched to other Party duties, he was replaced by Dr. Henry Picker.

28. Henry Picker, *Hitlers Tischgespräche im Führerhauptquartier, 1941–1942* (Stuttgart: Seewald Verlag, 1963), pp. 352–353. Picker remarks that Hitler read only what he wanted to see in von Boetticher's reports. Von Boetticher after his return contributed to a clearer picture of American potential at the OKW level, but without real effect.

29. "Auszug!" Pers. Akte 63, [transfer notice effective June 1, 1942] signed Keitel, in Personal Nachweis, Boetticher, Friedrich von, A3365 German Officers' 201 Files, Period 1900–1945, Reel 61, TAGO Film Project, RG 242 Captured German Records.

30. Evidence exists that Hitler himself thought the war could not be won on terms he originally thought. See John Lukacs, *The Hitler of History* (New York: Vintage Books, 1998), p. 157, which cites the testimony of Col. Gen. Alfred Jodl at Nürnberg after the war.

31. Riedel Memoir, pp. 280–283. (See Chapter 5, note 79.)

32. The collection appears as "Berichte des Gen. d. Art. v. Boetticher 30.11.43–15.7.44 am Chef, OKW," OKW/87, 340 leaves, RW4, v. 868 K-1, BA/MA, Freiburg im Breisgau. Copy in author's files. Subsequent citations of this material are from this source; pagination cited is first that given in the original individual reports, with the bracketed numbers reflecting serial pagination applied to the whole report series by the archivists at the BA/MA. It is probable that other similar reports also circulated to the General Staff throughout 1942 and at the OKW level earlier in 1943. At least one additional one, on the Allied invasion of southern France in August 1944, was published in translation on a French Web site by Col. Manfred Kehrig, a close postwar friend of von Boetticher's.

33. On the possibilities of this outcome at the time von Boetticher's reports were circulating, see Vojtech Mastny, "Stalin and the Prospects for a Separate Peace in World War II," *American Historical Review* 77 (1972): 1365.

34. Friedrich v. Boetticher, "Die Zweite Front," 30.11.43 [second report, first report on 5.11.43], in RW4, v. 868 K-1, pp. 3–4 [336–337]. Despite the likelihood of von Boetticher's estimates here, the invasion of southern France, when it came off in August 1944, was launched primarily from the Italian port of Naples, with some assaulting elements coming from the North African harbor of Oran.

35. Friedrich v. Boetticher, "Die Zweite Front, Dritter Bericht: Invasionsoperationen," 12.1.44 [January 12, 1944], in RW4, v. 868 K-1, p. 2. In assembling this summary, von Boetticher also considered operations at the head of the Adriatic and a thrust north to Munich. He also noted that the Americans had amassed considerable railroad equipment in England and could use Continental rail nets effectively.

36. Friedrich v. Boetticher, "Das Zurückweichen des Britischen Reiches und der Vereinigten Staaten vor Sowjet-Rußland und die Invasion," 25.2.1944 [February 25, 1944], in RW4, v. 868 K-1, pp. 2–3 [238–239]. This implied prediction of the success of an invasion and the defeat of Germany at this stage of things did not seem to provoke a reaction at the higher levels of the OKW.

37. Friedrich v. Boetticher, "Zur Invasion," 8.6.1944 [June 8, 1944], in ibid., p. 2 [p. 65].

38. Ibid. He emphasized the wording of the Eisenhower communiqué that alluded to a "Common Plan of the United Nations for the Liberation of Europe with our Great Ally the Soviet Union."

39. Friedrich v. Boetticher, "On the Air War, Situation Beginning of 1944," 3.1.1944 [January 3, 1944], ibid., p. 1 [309].

40. Ibid., p. 6 [314].

41. Transmittal Letter, F[ührer] H[aupt] Qú[artier] to Generalstab des Heeres, to Abt. Fremde Heere West, 20 Jan. 1944, p. 236, transmitting copies of six of von Boetticher's reports to the army intelligence staff for western Europe; Letter, F. H. Qu. to Fremde Heere West, 1 Apr. 1944, p. 177; and Letter, F. H. Qu. to General Staff of the Army, Fremde Heere Ost, 14 Apr. 1944, p. 162. All of these cover letters request the return of the material to OKW. All files in RW4, v. 868 K-1.

42. Marsden Interview, August 22, 1973. On Thiele's fate after the failure of the plot (and for one of the best accounts of the plot generally), see Peter Hoffmann, *The History of the German Resistance, 1933–1945* (Cambridge, Mass.: MIT Press, 1977), p. 515. Thiele had attempted to put off his pursuers by denouncing his predecessor, another member of the conspiracy, which availed him nothing. See also Erich Zimmermann and Hans-Adolf Jacobsen, comp., *Germans against Hitler, July 20, 1944* (Bonn: Berto Verlag, 1960), p. 183, for the Death Register Number, the date of the appeal of the Peoples' Court sentence against Thiele, and the same date's abrupt denial of any mercy.

43. The following account of Peter Riedel's wartime service and subsequent adventures is from Simons, *German Air Attaché*, pp. 164ff.

44. This letter is reproduced in its entirety in Simons, *German Air Attaché*, pp. 185–195.

45. The Swedish government was caring for more than 40,000 foreign refugees by mid-1944. Riedel joined the ranks of some 5,000 Germans (including Austrians and Sudeten Germans) who had fled the Nazi government. See Memorandum No. 3644, Herschel V. Johnson [U.S. Ambassador to Sweden] for Secretary of State, July 4, 1944, Subj: The Political Refugee Situation in Sweden. RG 84 Department of State Records, General Records, 1940–1944, Entry 3195, Box 119, File 1944. National Archives and Records Administration, College Park, Maryland.

46. James Clement Dunn, Assistant Secretary [of State] to Dear Bill [Maj. Gen. William J. Donovan], Director, Office of Strategic Services, February 27, 1945, RG 59, General Records of the Department of State, 1940–1944, Decimal File 103.918/12-2444, Central Decimal File, Box 145, 103.918/12-144 to 103.91802/298. National Archives and Records Administration, College Park, Maryland. The department was unwilling, Dunn went on, to assume the responsibility for bringing Riedel to the United States or to an active theater of operations. An earlier letter in the same file from Joseph Grew to Francis Biddle on February 9 shows that the idea was actively reviewed at the Justice Department as well.

47. *Kriegstagebuch der Oberkommando der Wehrmacht*, comp. and ed. by Percy Schramm, 5 vols. (Frankfurt am Main: Bernhard Graefe Verlag, 1960-1965), 5:1805; see also Schramm, *Hitler als militärischer Führer*, 2d rev. ed. (Frankfurt am Main: Atheneum Verlag, 1965), p. 185, which repeats the same passage that assesses von Boetticher in the OKW War Diaries.

48. Marsden, "Waiting for Letters," pp. 125–132. Though his rank entitled him to an official car, von Boetticher never used it to commute. He sat with his daughter in air-raid shelters as the city crumbled under air attack.

49. 36th Infantry Division, G-2 Periodic Report No. 417, May 2, 1945, in G-2 Journal, File 335-2.2, National Archives and Records Administration, College Park, Maryland.

50. Ibid.

51. Card Index File for J[udge] A[dvocate] G[eneral] (Army) Wanted War Criminals List. "On Crowcass Detention List No. 1," (10-45) 13, RG 153 National Archives and Records Administration, College Park, Maryland.

52. Robert Conot, *Justice at Nuremberg* (New York: Harper and Row, 1983), p. 31. For a detailed report on the hotel, its accommodations, and the general tenor of its "guests," see also Burton C. Andrus, *I Was the Nuremberg Jailer*, with Desmond Zwar (New York: Tower Publications, 1969), pp. 17–29.

53. Miklos Horthy, *Memoirs* (London: Hutchinson [1956], p. 247. Horthy was interned in a smaller hotel across the street from the Palace Hotel. Von Boetticher's ability to answer the invitation seems to indicate that he was not regarded as important as many of the bigger fish in the place.

54. Conot, *Justice at Nuremberg*, p. 31.

55. Maj. Kenneth Hechler, "The Other Side of the Hill; The 1945 Background on Interrogation of German Commanders," United States Army, Historical Division, Washington, D.C., July 30, 1945, typescript MS, pp. 150–151, U.S. Army Military History Institute, Carlisle Barracks, Pennsylvania. Hechler later became a U.S. representative from West Virginia's 4th District, 1959–77. At this point, he was a historical officer working with the Schuster Commission, named for George Schuster of Hunter College in New York, an entity gathering material and interviews on German commanders for the War Department Historical Section, then still under the Army's G-2.

56. Interview, author with Harold C. Deutsch, April 12, 1973, National War College, Washington, D.C.

57. Von Boetticher recorded the dates of his stay and his new locations at every transfer during his captivity in a file labeled "Gefangenschaft," von Boetticher papers, N323, BA/MA, Freiburg on Breisgau.

58. Testimony of FRIEDRICH von BOETTICHER taken at Nurnberg, Germany, on 12 October 1945, 1430–1545, by Col. Howard A. Brundage, JAGD, OUSCC, p. 5. RG 238, U.S. Counsel for the Prosecution of Axis Criminality, Interrogations, Summaries of Interrogations, and Related Records, Box 1, Abegg–Boetticher. National Archives and Records Agency, College Park, Maryland. The transcript of this interview makes it seem completely routine. The interrogator hardly seemed prepared to pursue any detail or catch any contradictions in von Boetticher's account of himself, and the general seems to be in control of the interview by its end.

59. v. Boetticher to General Clarence R. Huebner, HQ, USFET, Heidelberg, 12th July 1948, File "Beschwerden über in der Gefangenschaft abhanden gekommenes Eigentum," in v. Boetticher papers, N323, BA/MA, Freiburg im Breisgau.

60. v. Boetticher to Mr. Justice Robert H. Jackson, Nürnberg, Palace of Justice, Confidential, 1st March 1946, p. 2, v. Boetticher Papers, N323, BA/MA Freiburg im Breisgau.

61. Ibid., p. 4. He may here have been indirectly alluding to the case of his own brother, who had joined the Nazis in February 1931, but who also managed to continue a career in the German judiciary after the war.

62. Ibid., p. 5.

63. Simons, *German Air Attaché*, p. 187. Riedel reserves disdain, however, for German General Staff officers and counsels their elimination. He had observed their "geistiger Hochmut" [spiritual arrogance] and their "lack of courage toward superiors and an inability to report unpleasant truths" (p. 193).

64. v. Boetticher to Wedemeyer, June 29, 1948, Correspondence, v. Boetticher papers, N323, Freiburg im Breisgau. Repeating the theme of cooperation between the United States and Germans of goodwill, he now remarked: "Many times it has been stated, rightly or wrongly, that during the Nazi time German generals failed to make suggestions before it was too late. I do not want to evade a similar responsibility now." Wedemeyer had spent the end of the war as theater commander in China and became heavily involved in the acrimonious politics surrounding the American postwar failure in the civil war there. At the time of this visit to Germany, he was chief of the Plans and Operations Division of the War Department General Staff.

65. Ltr., Col. D. T. Beeler, Acting Chief, Operational (German) Branch, To Whom It May Concern, 26 June 1947, HQ, European Command, Office of the Chief Historian, APO 757, testifies to von Boetticher's role since November 1946 in compiling "an accurate history of German counter-operations for the War Department." v. Boetticher Papers, N323, BA/MA, Freiburg im Breisgau.

66. Memorandum, Arnold Lissance to Walter H. Rapp [Appendix B], 7 May 1947, Subj: War Notebooks of Gen. F. Halder, in *The Halder Diaries: The Private War Journals of Colonel General Franz Halder*, introduction by Trevor N. Dupuy (Boulder, Colo.: Westview Press, 1976), pp. 1592–1593. The enclosure, known as Steinlager Allendorf, was near the University of Marburg. Conditions there were primitive.

67. Ltr., Victor Parker (USWD Civilian), 301 Military Intelligence Company, 2nd Detachment, APO 175, US Army, To Whom It May Concern, Subj: Denazification trial for von Boetticher, Friedrich, 18 June 1947, File Schreiben zur Entnazifizierung, v. Boetticher Papers, N323, BA/MA, Freiburg im Breisgau. His new address put him in the British area of occupation.

68. Marsden, "Waiting for Letters," pp. 148–149. In the harrowing trek, the women kept their ears open for radio broadcasts that daily named the persons swept up in the Allied prisoner haul. There was no mention of the general.

69. Certificate of Discharge, [Control Form D.2] certified by John Y. Bohn, 1st Lt. FA, 30 June 1947, copy in v. Boetticher Papers, N323, BA/MA, Freiburg im Breisgau.

Chapter 9

1. Gordon Craig, *From Bismarck to Adenauer; Aspects of German Statecraft* (New York: Harper and Brothers, 1968), p. 94 n. See also a summary of these charges in Kathleen McLaughlin, "U.S. War Potential Deceived Hitler," *New York Times*, November 8, 1947, p. 7.

2. Interrogation of Heribert von Strempel by Rebecca Wellington and Lt. Enno Hobbing, 18 November 1945, at Oberursel, Poole Mission Files.

3. For a summary of Erich Kordt's career, see Harold C. Deutsch, *The Conspiracy against Hitler in the Twilight War* (Minneapolis: University of Minnesota Press, 1968), pp. 18–20. Kordt belonged to a generation of dangerous career diplomats who, in Heinrich Himmler's words, were "young enough to want, but old enough to think."

4. Result of an Interrogation of Dr. Erich Kordt, 15–16 December 1945 at Washington, D.C., Records of the Department of State Special Interrogation Mission to Germany, 1945–1946, Microcopy 679, Roll 2, frame 0424 (page 23 of original document).

5. Erich Kordt, *Wahn und Wirklichkeit*, with Karl-Heinz Abshagen (Stuttgart: Union deutsche Verlagsgesellschaft, 1948), p. 142. Abshagen was also the first biographer of Wilhelm Canaris, the Abwehr chief who was executed in April 1945. Kordt's assertion attributing to the attaché the possibility of a Japanese conquest of Alaska cannot be corroborated.

6. H. P. Willmott, *The Barrier and the Javelin: Japanese and Allied Pacific Strategies, February to June 1942* (Annapolis: Naval Institute Press, 1983), pp. 90–91. In the complex Japanese strategy of the moment, the seizure of the islands was to serve as a lure to draw the American fleet into a decisive engagement in the Pacific Ocean north of Midway. Its second purpose was as a counter to the American base at Dutch Harbor, which remotely threatened the major Japa-

nese base at Paramushiro, located in the northern Kuriles immediately south of the (Soviet) Kamchatka peninsula.

7. This material he carefully preserved in "Nach der Gefangenschaft," Bd. II/Erich Kordt/Angriffe gegen Boetticher/Koestring. v. Boetticher Akten, N323, BA/MA, Freiburg im Breisgau. The documents cited next are from this file.

8. Hans Thomsen to v. Boetticher, March 7, 1946, ibid.

9. Wolff to v. Boetticher, no date, enclosing letter and report of Wolfgang Uhmann to Wolff, April 24, 1948, ibid.

10. Witthoeft's reports from Washington were never microfilmed or published after the war, as were von Boetticher's in the joint project on captured German records pursued by the U.S. National Archives and the American Historical Association.

11. Witthoeft to v. Boetticher, March 13, 1949, file "Schriftwechsel Witthoeft" in von Boetticher papers, N323, BA/MA, Freiburg im Breisgau. Witthoeft had briefly held command of all German naval elements in the Black Sea during the war before the wholesale retirement of senior German admirals with Grand Adm. Erich Raeder in 1943.

12. v. Boetticher to Historical Division, Operational History Section (German), HQ, US-FET, April 29, 1948, "Nach der Gefangenschaft Akten, N323, BA/MA, Frieburg im Breisgau.

13. Erklärung, Franz Halder, Neustadt, 20 February 1948, Kreis Marburg/Lahn. v. Boetticher Papers N323, Freiburg im Breisgau. Copy in author's files. Halder had this document officially attested to by Capt. Merle F. Finley, 7734 EUCOM Historical Detachment, then located in Neustadt.

14. Siegfried Westphal, *Erinnerungen* (Mainz: Von Hase und Kohler Verlag, 1975), p. 383. Twenty years von Boetticher's junior, Westphal had risen to become chief of staff at the Oberbefehlshaber West command (Rundstedt) during the war.

15. Kordt to v. Boetticher, Oct. 11, 1951, v. Boetticher Papers, N323, BA/MA, Freiburg im Breisgau.

16. On the evolution of this series, see Kevin Soutor, "To Stem the Red Tide: The German Report Series and Its Effect on American Defense Doctrine, 1948–1954," *The Journal of Military History* 57 (October 1993): 653–688.

17. Col. William S. Nye, Chief Historian, USAREUR, "Preface," *Guide to Foreign Military Studies, 1945–1954: Catalog and Index*, Headquarters, United States Army, Europe [Karlsruhe], 1954, pp. iii–iv.

18. Katherine Alling Hollister Smith, "My Life," II, April 1939–1945, unpublished manuscript. [1974], pp. 124–125. At Roosevelt's death in April 1945, Katherine Smith reports on the excitement of learning the news from Constantine Brown, reporter for the Washington *Star:* "The evil man was dead."

Writing this in the year 1974 I know how right we were to hate him so bitterly. There is no ill foreign or domestic that cannot be traced back directly to his policies. Our decline, our degeneracy stems from that man and his power mad, greedy wife.

19. v. Boetticher, "Impressions and Experiences of the Military and Air Attaché at the German Embassy in Washington during the Years 1933–1941," [April 1947] p. 22.

20. Ibid., p. 4.

21. See: Memo [Dieckhoff], November 2, 1940, *DGFP*, D, X, No. 279, pp. 457–458. (See Chapter 2, note 77 for explanation of *DGFP*.) Dieckhoff also published a tract that hewed to standard Nazi propaganda on Roosevelt's submission to Jewish influences in pushing for war: *Zur Vorgeschichte des Roosevelt-Krieges* (Berlin: Junker und Dünnhaupt, 1943). Both are alluded to in Warren F. Kimball, "Dieckhoff and America: A German's View of German/American Relations, 1937–1941," *The Historian* 27 (February 1965), p. 48. Though he feared the practical international consequences of German government-sponsored anti-Semitism, he shared in the common biases of his profession and class.

22. U.S. Bureau of the Budget, War Records Section. *The United States at War: Development and Administration of the War Program by the Federal Government*, Washington, D.C.: Government Printing Office, 1946, p. 103.

23. Adolf Hitler, *Mein Kampf* (München: Zentralverlag der NSDAP, 1938), p. 723.

24. The all too regular occurrence in which practitioners of Nazi jurisprudence received appointments to new posts in the postwar Germany is examined in Ingo Müller, *Hitler's Justice: The Courts of the Third Reich* (Cambridge, Mass.: Harvard University Press, 1991), pp. 261ff. Von Boetticher outlived his younger brother, who lived not far from him in Bielefeld and died in the city on August 22, 1959.

25. v. Boetticher to DSF, July 18, 1948, Box 94, folder 46, Freeman Papers, Manuscript Division, Library of Congress.

26. v. Boetticher to DSF, May 1, 1949, Box 99, folder 46, loc. cit.

27. v. Boetticher to DSF, November 20, 1952, Box 113, folder 93, loc. cit.

28. Don A. Gribble, Chief, Visa Section, American Consulate, Bremen, Germany, to Mrs. Friedrich von Boetticher, June 18, 1948, v. Boetticher Papers, General Correspondence, N323, BA/MA, Freiburg im Breisgau.

29. Ltr., v. Boetticher to Douglas Southall Freeman, June 12, 1949, DSF Papers, Box 99, folder 46, Manuscript Division, Library of Congress. Of the four reasons adduced for disallowing the visa, three had to do with von Boetticher's German Army service; the last alluded to a German book that had criticized his work. The following year von Boetticher wrote to Freeman that his wife's travel to the United States had been approved June 20, 1950. Ltr., v. Boetticher to DSF, June 21, 1950, Box 103, folder 46, loc. cit.

30. TWX [teletype msg.] CIC Region IX Wurzburg to HQ 66th CIC HQ USAREUR, 291300Z June 1950, replying to circular inquiry on v. Boetticher's current location. The exchange gives the distinct impression that the CIC had no inkling that von Boetticher at this juncture was still working for the USAREUR Historical Division, right under their noses. Documentation in file Boetticher, Friedrich, XE008222, [personal name files] Box 23A, Army Investigative Records Repository [IRR] Files, RG 319, National Archives and Records Administration, College Park, Maryland. These CIC inquiries closed out a file on von Boetticher that had been opened by the army on April 15, 1933, the date of his arrival in New York enroute to Washington to take up his office as the attaché in the United States.

31. Jay Luvaas, *The Military Legacy of the Civil War: The European Inheritance* (Chicago: University of Chicago Press, 1959), p. viii.

32. Ibid., p. 130. "They found the war instructive in matters of materiel and technology; it even offered useful examples in coast defense and joint army-navy operations. But insofar as the tactics of the three arms was concerned, the Germans placed their trust in their own experiences."

33. Exchange of letters, DSF–Hildegard v. Boetticher Marsden, December 1951, DSF Papers, Box 108, folder 69, loc. cit.

34. Photo feature article [unsigned]. *Randolph-Macon Woman's College Alumnae Bulletin*, 53 November 1959: 37. Mrs. Marsden is shown receiving the degree from college president William F. Quillian, Jr. The unusual circumstances of the time are briefly explained.

35. Later biographical information on Mrs. Marsden derives from the Canadian Federation of University Women's Web site, www.wlu.ca/~wwwlib/cfuw/bio.html. A scholarship fund in her name was established in 1988, and a co-operative day nursery also bearing her name serves faculty and attendees of the University of Waterloo today.

36. Gen. d. Art. Friedrich v. Boetticher, "The Art of War," typescript, Bielefeld, May 25, 1951, copy in author's files. He apparently meant this as a contribution to the knowledge of his professional military friends. Freeman also received a copy with a special dedication. Another version, "Military Leadership and General Staff Principles and Spirit" (1965), found its way to Johnston in late 1965. Christmas Card with encl., v. Boetticher to JAJ, December 15, 1965, J. Ambler Johnston Papers, Virginia Historical Society Archives, Battle Abbey, Rich-

mond, Virginia.

37. Friedrich v. Boetticher, "Feldherrntum und Generalstab," *Wehrkunde*, XIII (September 1964): 453–459. Von Boetticher sent the English-language versions to his old Richmond friends as well, and an English-language version is in the archives of the Virginia Historical Society, file Mss7:3 UB210.B66338.1.

38. Donald Abenheim, *Reforging the Iron Cross: The Search for Tradition in the West German Armed Forces* (Princeton, N.J.: Princeton University Press, 1989), p. 4.

39. The saint usually appears bearing a crenellated tower, much like a large chess piece, a symbol of the one in which her pagan father supposedly imprisoned her to keep her away from any suitors. When he learned she had become a Christian, he caused her execution. Shortly thereafter, lightning struck him dead. Her association with artillery stems from her first role as the guardian against sudden or unwelcome events or surprises, such as the one that had visited her father. Early artillery pieces, with a penchant for exploding in the midst of their users, were often as dangerous to the cannoneers as to their targets.

40. Friedrich v. Boetticher, *Schlieffen* (Göttingen: Musterschmidt Verlag, 1957).

41. Antulio J. Echevarria, II, "An Infamous Legacy: Schlieffen's Military Theories Revisited," *Army History, The Professional Bulletin of Army History* (Summer-Fall 2001): 4.

42. Hermann Teske, *Wenn Gegenwart Geschichte wird . . .* (Neckargemünd: Kurt Vowinckel Verlag, 1974), pp. 91–95.

43. Kessel is the principal biographer of the elder von Moltke.

44. Yet other family literary possessions found a home in other institutions. In the early 1950s, von Boetticher yielded up all of his father's genealogical and local Saxon historical volumes to the Herder Institute in Marburg, where they continued to the turn of the twentieth century to form a central part of the institute's holdings. See "Die Boetticher-Sammlung," *Die Sondersammlungen der Bibliothek*, p. 1, University of Marburg website: www.uni–marburg.de/ herder-institut/bibliothek/sondersammlungen.html.

45. v. Boetticher to JAJ, September 13, 1965, Johnston Papers, Box 1, Folder 9, Battle Abbey, Richmond, Virginia.

46. For an assessment of von Hahnke's importance in German military developments, see Erich Dorn Brose, *The Kaiser's Army: The Politics of Military Technology in Germany during the Machine Age* (Oxford: Oxford University Press, 2001), pp. 117–118.

47. Adelheid Miller to JAJ, September 19, 1965, in ibid. It is also clear that Johnston had met Bela von Hahnke during one of his own earlier visits to von Boetticher in Bielefeld. Interview, author with Col. Manfred Kehrig, June 18, 1989.

48. v. Boetticher to JAJ, November 26, 1960, Johnston papers, Box 1, folder 4, loc. cit.

49. v. Boetticher to JAJ, August 26, 1967, Johnston Papers, Box 2, folder 11, loc. cit.

50. See Douglas Southall Freeman, *The South to Posterity: An Introduction to the Writings of Confederate History* (New York: C. Scribner's Sons, 1939), pp. 166–167. Johnston happily recounted the rumor that German Field Marshal Erwin Rommel had come to Virginia in the 1930s to visualize the terrain of American Civil War battlefields. When he entertained von Boetticher on three occasions in Richmond after the war, he invited his local circle of the Civil War Roundtable, some of whom swore to the truth of the "myth." Von Boetticher set this straight, and Johnston is certain that the German they remembered was none other than von Boetticher himself. See his *Echoes of 1861–1961*, privately printed by the author, 1970, p. 56.

51. For one assessment of this process, see Helmut Graml, "Die Wehrmacht im Dritten Reich," *Vierteljahrshefte für Zeitgeschichte* 45 (July 1997): 365–384. On the continuing Nazi emasculation of the German officer corps under the press of the war, see also Magregor Knox, "1 October 1942: Adolf Hitler, Wehrmacht Officer Policy, and Social Revolution," *The Historical Journal*, 43 (September 2000): 801–825.

SELECTED BIBLIOGRAPHY

The basic raw material for this study is from the records of the German Foreign Ministry, the German Army (Heer) High Command, and the German Supreme Command (Wehrmacht) now preserved in the microfilmed Captured German Records at the U.S. National Archives and Records Administration in Washington, D.C. Special mention is necessary of the guides to this material. Among these the most indispensable are George O. Kent's *A Catalog of Files and Microfilms of the German Foreign Ministry Archives*, 4 vols. (Stanford, Conn.: Hoover Institute, 1966), and the National Archives's own *Guides to the German Records Microfilmed at Alexandria, Virginia*. Of the latter, the following were the most pertinent for research on the German military attaché in Washington: *Records of Headquarters, German Army High Comnand* (Numbers 12, 29, and 30), and Records of Headquarters, *German Armed Forces High Command* (Numbers 7, 17, 18, and 19). Also of value in uncovering material on von Boetticher's work at Geneva from 1926 to 1929 was Hans Aufricht's *Guide to League of Nations Publications; A Bibliographical Survey of the Work of the League, 1920–1947* (New York: AMS Press, 1966). The published *Documents on German Foreign Policy*, Series C and D, were useful not only for their selection of English translations of German documents, but also for their inclusion of lists of original German Foreign Office serial files and descriptions of their contents. The microfilmed record of these original files has retained the German serial designations to show the provenance of the material. Following the German serial designation and separated from it by a shil (/) is the American National Archives microfilm roll number. The documentary citations throughout this study thus include both American and British microfilm information and the cross-referenced German serial designations. The following list repeats this information to facilitate the replication of research.

Unpublished Documentary Materials

National Archives and Records Administration

Card Index File for Judge Advocate General, U.S. Army, Wanted War Criminals List, "Crowcass List No. 1" RG 153.

Files of the Foreign Office Branch II FM—Military Attaché, Washington, January 1933–April 1936, Microcopy T-120, Serial 5863.

Files of Foreign Office Section POL XIII, United States—Military Affairs, May 1927–February 1935, Microcopy T-120, Serial K1848.

Files of the State Secretary, U. S. A. in the Foreign Office, 1933–1941, Microcopy T-120, Serials 19, 35, 64, 84, 589, 593, 987, 1527, 1543, 1857, B21, M342.

General Records of the Department of State, Central Decimal File, RG 59.

OKH, General Staff of the Army Files, Records of the Attaché Section, Oberquartiermeister IV Files. Messages to Attachés abroad, Microcopy T-78, Serial H27.

OKW File "Military Attaché Washington 1. 4. 34.–20. 3. 35," Microcopy T-77, Serial 904 (Overlaps with T-120, Serial 5863).

OKW File "Wehrwirtschaft" series, Microcopy T-77, Serials 979, 980.

OKW Files, Military and Naval Attachés from 1 January 1933–December 1938, Microcopy T-77, Serial 874.

OKW Files, Records of Military Attaché Conferences, 1934, Microcopy T- 77, Serial 902.

OKW Section for Wehrmacht Propaganda Files, Microcopy T-77, Serials 1029, 1030.

Personalnachweis von Boetticher, Friedrich, A3365 German Army Officers' 201 Files, Period 1900–1945 Captured German Records, TAGO Film Project, Reel 61.

Records of the Department of State, General Records, 1940–1944, RG 84.

Records of the U.S. Department of State Interrogation Mission (Dewitt C. Poole Mission), 1945–1946. Microcopy M679, 3 rolls, Interrogation records of Friedrich von Boetticher, Hans Borchers, Ulrich v. Gienanth, Erich Kordt, Friedrich v. Prittwitz u. Gaffron, Heribert von Strempel, and Hans Thomsen.

Records of the War Department General Staff, G-2 Military Intelligence Division) Foreign Liaison Branch, "Attache, Military, German in Washington" (Synoptic Index and Associated files). Record Group 165. These materials also contain the Federal Bureau of Investigation sources cited in this study.

Specially produced microfilm of General von Boetticher's Cables from January 1936 to September 1939, Army files H27/48, Courtesy of the Bundesarchiv-Militärarchiv, Freiburg im Breisgau. 1973. 277 frames. Documentation refers to this collection as "BA/MA German film."

Testimony of Friedrich von Boetticher, taken at Nürnberg, Germany, on 12 October 1945, 1430–1545, by Col. Howard A. Brundage, JAGD, OUSCG, typescript.

U.S. Army, Records of the Investigative Records Repository, Dossier, Boetticher Friedrich, XEOO8222; Auswertestelle Oberursel, [personal name files] Box 23A, Army Investigative Records Repository [IRR] Files, RG 319, National Archives and Records Administration, College Park, Maryland.

U.S. Army Military History Institute, Carlisle Barracks, Pennsylvania

"A Compilation of Correspondence on the Representation of the American Army in the Reichsarchiv, 1920–1940," File No. 2444, [Col. R. S.] Thomas Files.

Davis, Col. Edward, USA, "Military Attaché," typescript manuscript, (1933), 603 leaves.

Sorley, Col. Lewis. "Some Recollections," [1957], 156 leaves, Lewis Stone Sorley Papers.

Other

J. Ambler Johnston Papers, Battle Abbey, Richmond, Virginia

Peter Riedel Estate Files, courtesy of Mr. Paul Hanak, Fort Worth, Texas. File material and photographs from Riedel's career. This material has been deposited under Riedel's name at the Library and Archives Collection, National Air and Space Museum, Washington, D.C.

Peter Riedel file, CR-385000-01, Archives File, Library and Archives Division, National Air and Space Museum, Washington, D.C.

Records of the American Military Institute, Correspondence, Planning Papers for Joint American Historical Association—American Military Institute Joint Session at the AHA

Convention, December 1935, at Chattanooga, Tenn. AMI Files, Industrial College of the Armed Forces Library, Washington, D.C.
Walter Krueger Papers, U.S. Military Academy Archives.

Bundesarchiv/Militärarchiv

Nachlass, Friedrich v. Boetticher, N-323, Bundesarchiv-Militärarchiv, Freiburg im Breisgau. Individual files found in this material are cited as appropriate in notes.
Nachlass Groener, Wilhelm, N46/76, "Kriegsgeschichte, Briefe und Material, 1905–1929" [finished drafts of two papers circulated by v. Boetticher].
Nachlass [Hans v.] Seeckt, N247/203, Heft 1, 1920 [typewritten drafts of three papers written and circulated by v. Boetticher in 1920].
Nachlässe [Wilhelm] v. Schleicher, N42/33, Bd. I, 1924–30, Budesarchiv/Militärarchiv, Freiburg im Breisgau.

Freedom of Information Act (FOIA) Files

Federal Bureau of Investigation [Clarence M. Kelley, Director], April 14, 1976, releasing FBI correspondence files in MID 2801-1054, in War Department Military Intelligence Division files in the National Archives and Records Administration.
Federal Bureau of Investigation file 269834 on Friedrich von Boetticher, created for Dr. Alfred M. Beck, March 14, 1988 [author's files].
Federal Bureau of Investigation file 340074 on Peter Ernst Riedel, created for Dr. Von Hardesty, May 10, 1991 [copy in author's files].

The Literature on von Boetticher

Opinion on Friedrich von Boetticher the man and the attaché differs widely in the memoir and historical literature on the diplomacy and intelligence operations of the period. Older German Foreign Office hands, especially those connected with the resistance to Nazism, would agree with the recollection of von Boetticher as a "dangerously stupid official" found in the statement of former Ambassador Dr. Karl Ritter, economic specialist on assignment to the German Foreign Office, *New York Times*, November 7, 1947, quoted in Gordon A. Craig, *From Bismarck to Adenauer; Aspects of German Statecraft*, Torchbook ed. (New York: Harper and Row, 1965), p. 94. This sentiment found echo in numerous references to von Boetticher in postwar research on German policy, intelligence, and espionage, most notably in Gerhard L. Weinberg's "Hitler's Image of the United States," *American Historical Review* 69 (July 1964): 1006–1021, and Joachim Remak's "Hitlers Amerikapolitik," *Aussenpolitik* 6 (November 1955): 711. Yet another student of German-American relations in 1940 and 1941 has devoted a whole chapter to "General von Boetticher's America" in which he employed the general's eminently quotable cables to allow the man to at once reveal and condemn himself. (See James Compton, *The Swastika and the Eagle; Hitler, the United States, and the Origins of World War II* [London: The Bodley Head, 1968], chapter 7, passim). Ladislas Farago, an American publicist, himself a veteran of the American naval intelligence service of World War II, dismissed the German attaché as an "amiable extrovert with easy drawing room manners," but really a "pompous ass" who consorted with a disgruntled isolationist clique in the prewar American army. See his *The Game of the Foxes* (New York: Bantam Books, 1973), p. 607. Andreas Hillgruber, a German historian of Hitler's strategic ideas, isolates what he calls a strong optimism in von Boetticher's later "colored" reporting from America but does not seek its cause in his *Hitlers Strategie; Politik und Kriegführung, 1940–1941* (Frankfurt am Main: Bernhard und Graefe Verlag für Wehrwesen, 1965), p. 196. Von Boetticher also found his defenders and admirers fewer in number. Chief among them are military professionals, German and American. One veteran German staff officer of World War II, Siegfried Westphal, recalled in 1975 that von Boetticher "was a declared opponent of Hitler long before 1933" in his *Erinnerungen* (Mainz: Von Hase und Kohler Verlag, 1975), p. 383. Percy Schramm, the Göttingen University historian who kept the *Oberkommando der Wehrmacht* (High Command) War Diaries during the war, had only the highest praise for the former attaché in a volume entitled *Hitler als militärischer Führer*, 2d. rev. ed. (Frankfurt am Main: Atheneum Verlag, 1965), p. 185. So, incidentally, did the chief of staff of the *Oberkommando der Wehrmacht*, Field Marshal Wilhelm Keitel, who rates von Boetticher as a "scharfsinniger Kopf" in an official military evaluation (von Boetticher Summary Personnel File; copy in author's possession). Almost every American who knew von Boetticher favored him as a gentleman and as a man of high culture and military competence. In a variety of interviews and exchanges of correspondence that developed detail not uncritical of von Boetticher, most of his American contemporaries viewed him, as did Hanson Baldwin, "with respect." This evaluation was contained in a letter from Baldwin (former military correspondent of the *New York Times*) to the author, August 7, 1973; General George S. Patton, Jr.'s daughter, Ruth Ellen Totten, also wrote to the author in a similar vein on March 16, 1973. And last, the best interpreter of military attachés as a genre and no defender of things military, Alfred Vagts has also noted that Hitler lavishly praised von Boetticher's reports, but misinterpreted them. (See Vagts, *The Military Attaché* [Princeton, N.J.: Princeton University Press, 1967], p. 60.) Alone among those commenting on von Boetticher's often fractious cables, Vagts voices this generalization but does not elaborate on how or why Hitler misread the reports or in what detail he actually read them at all. So disparate a summary of opinion on the man awakens the suspicion that his story is more complex than thus far revealed.

Published Documentary Material

Annual Reports of the Secretary of War to the President, 1933–1941, Washington, D.C.: Government Printing Office, 1933–1941.

Das Kabinett Fehrenbach, 25 Juni bis 4 Mai 1921, edited by Peter Wulf, "Akten der Reichskanzlei, Weimarer Republik," herausgegeben für die historische Kommission bey der Beyerischen Akademie der Wissenschaft. Boppard am Rhein: Harald Boldt Verlag, 1972.

Hitler, Adolf. *Hitler's Secret Conversations, 1941–1944*. New York: Farrar Strauss and Young, 1953.

———. *The Speeches of Adolf Hitler, April 1922–August 1939*, translated and edited by Norman H. Baynes. London: Oxford University Press, 1942.

International Military Tribunal, *Nazi Conspiracy and Aggression*, 10 vols. Washington, D.C.: Government Printing Office, 1946.

———. *Trials of the Major War Criminals before the International Military Tribunal*, 42 vols. Nürnberg: IMT, 1947.

Kotze, Hildegard, ed. *Heeresadjutant bei Hitler, 1938–1943; Aufzeichnungen des Majors Engel*. Stuttgart: Deutsche Verlags-Anstalt, 1974.

Kriegstagebuch des Oberkommandos der Wehrmacht. [Wehrmachtführungsstab], edited by Helmuth Greiner and Percy Schramm, 5 vols. Frankfurt am Main: Bernard & Graefe Verlag für Wehrwissen, 1960–1965.

League of Nations. *Documents of the Preparatory Commission for the Disarmament Conference Entrusted with Preparation for the Conference for the Reduction and Limitation of Armaments*. Geneva: League of Nations, 1925–1931.

Lindbergh, Charles A. *The Radio Addresses of Charles A. Lindbergh, 1939–1940*. New York: Scribner's Commentator, 1940.

Marhefka, Edmund, ed. *Der Waffenstillstand; Das Dokumentationmaterial der Waffenstillstand-verhandlungen*, 3 vols. Berlin: Verlagsgesellschaft für Politik und Geschichte, 1928.

Picker, Henry. *Hitlers Tischgespräche im Führerhauptquartier, 1941–1942*, edited by Andreas Hillgruber and Percy Schramm. Stuttgart: Seewald Verlag, 1963.

Robertson, Esmonde. *Hitler's Prewar Policy and Military Plans, 1933–1939*. London: Longmans, 1963.

Rosenman, Samuel I., ed. *The Public Papers and Addresses of Franklin D. Roosevelt*, 13 vols, New York: Harper and Bros., 1950.

Trevor-Roper, H. R. *Blitzkrieg to Defeat; Hitler's War Directives, 1939–1945*, Holt Paperback ed. New York: Holt Rinehart and Winston, 1971.

U. S. Dept. of State, *Documents on German Foreign Policy, 1918–1945*, Series C, 5 vols. Washington, D.C.: Government Printing Office, 1957–1966.

———. *Documents on German Foreign Policy, 1918–1945*, Series D, 13 vols. Washington, D.C.: Government Printing Office, 1949–1964.

———. *Foreign Relations of the United States*. Washington, D.C.: Government Printing Office, 19—. Pertinent volumes for period 1933–1941.

———. *Peace and War; United States Foreign Policy, 1931–1941*, Dept. of State Publication No. 1933. Washington D.C.: Government Printing Office, 1943.

Personal Interviews

Mrs. Genevieve Bastide (telephone), March 6, 1975

Brig. Gen. Thomas J. Betts, USA, Ret'd., January 13, 1974

Prof. Harold C. Deutsch, April 12, 1973

Transcript, Air Force Oral History Interview, Lt. Gen. Ira C. Eaker with Mr. Hugh Ahmann, Washington, D.C., April 9, 1975, Air Force Archival File K239.0512-829

Mr. J. Ambler Johnston, June 23, 1973

Col. David Kramer, USAF, December 20, 1988

Mr. and Mrs. Horace Marsden, August 22, 1973 (Mrs. Marsden was the younger daughter of General von Boetticher)

Mr. and Mrs. David K. Miller, August 24, 1973 (Mrs. Miller was the older daughter of General von Boetticher)

Mr. Peter Riedel (telephone), September 19, 1976

Vice Adm. Charles E. Rosendahl, USN, Ret'd. (telephone), December 23, 1973

Mrs. Truman (Katherine A. H.) Smith, November 23, 1973

Brig. Gen. Paul W. Thompson, USA, Retd, December 27, 1974

Mr. Joseph Waggaman, January 23, 1973

Gen. Albert C. Wedemeyer, USA, Ret'd, June 14, 1974

Correspondence

Mr. Hanson Baldwin, August 7, 1973

Mr. Fred H. Boetticher, July 30, 1973

Col. Malin Craig, Jr., May 28, 1976

Mr. Arthur J. Ericsson, September 18, 1973

Mr. J. Ambler Johnston, 1973

Charles A. Lindbergh, March 21, 1973

Oberstleutnant Dr. Manfred Kehrig, February 22, 1973

Mrs. Hildegard Marsden (correspondence with author, 1973–1987)

Mr. and Mrs. David K. Miller, 1973

Mrs. Truman (Katherine A. H.) Smith, 1973

Mrs. Ruth Ellen (Patton) Totten, March 16, 1973
Mrs. Ralph (Olive) Truman, March 25, 1974
Gen. d. Artillerie (a. D.) Horst v. Mellenthin, October 15, 1973

Manuscripts

American Forces in Germany, Asst. Chief of Staff, G-2, (comp.). American Representation in Occupied Germany, directed by Col. Irvin L. Hunt, USA, typescript, 2 vols. [1923]

Bechtolsheim, General der Artillerie Anton Freiherr von. The German Attaché System, USAREUR Monograph #P-097a, 1952.

Boetticher, General der Artillerie Friedrich von. Military Attaché to Washington, 1933–1941, USAREUR Monograph #B-484, 1947.

———. The Art of War—A Military Testament, USAREUR Monograph #P-100, 1951.

———. General der Infanterie Kurt von Tippelskirch, and Generaloberst Franz Halder. U. S. Preparedness, German Estimate (1939), USAREUR Monograph #B-09, 1947.

Claussen, M. P. Distribution of Air Material to the Allies, 1939–1941: Controls, Procedures and Policies, USAF Historical Study No. 106, 1944.

Davis, Lt. Col. Edward. Military Attaché, typescript manuscript [1933], 525 leaves, U.S. Army Military History Institute, Carlisle Barracks, Pennsylvania.

Foreign Logistical Organizations and Methods, A Report for the Secretary of War, 15 October, 1947.

Halder, Generaloberst Franz et al. Selection and Training of German Officers for Military Attaché Duty, USAREUR Monograph #P-097, 1951.

Hechler, Maj. Kenneth W. The Other Side of the Hill; The 1945 Background on Interrogation of German Commanders, typescript manuscript, U.S. Army Historical Division, 30 July 1949. U.S. Army Military History Institute, Carlisle Barracks, Pennsylvania.

Marsden, Hildegard [von Boetticher]. Waiting for Letters, typescript, [ca. 1982].

Mellenthin, General der Artillerie Horst von. The Attaché Branch of the Army General Staff, USAREUR Monograph #P-041j, 1948.

Riedel, Peter. [Untitled] Memoir, n.d. [ca. 1946–] typescript, 351 leaves. (See also the citation under Simons, Martin Memoirs and Diaries.)

Smith, Col. Truman. Air Intelligence Activities; Office of the Military Attaché, American Embassy, Berlin, Germany, August 1935–April 1939, unpublished typescript, 163 leaves, 1956.

———. The Facts of Life, unpublished typescript, 1964.

Smith, Mrs. Truman (Katherine A. H.). My Life, unpublished typescript, [1974], 2 parts.

Tippelskirch, General der Infanterie Kurt von. Army High Command; Intelligence on Foreign Armies and the Foreign Intelligence Service, 1938–1945, USAREUR Monograph #P-041h, 1953.

Tippelskirch, General der Infanterie Kurt von, General der Infanterie Gerhard Matzky, and Oberst Lothar Metz. Organization and Working Methods of the Intelligence Division, 1948, USAREUR Monograph #P-041i.

U.S. Department of Commerce, U.S. Bureau of Air Commerce, Safety and Planning Division, The Hindenburg Accident; A Comparative Digest of the Investigations and Findings, with American and Translated German Reports Included, Report No. 11 by Ralph W. Knight, Chief, Air Transport Section, bound typescript manuscript, August 1938.

Weathers, Bynum E. Acquisition of Air Bases in Latin America, June 1931–June 1941, USAF Historical Study No. 63, USAF Hist. Div., Research Studies Institute, Maxwell Air Force Base, Alabama.

Williams, K. Development of South Pacific Air Route, USAF Historical Study No. 45, 1946.

Published Works

Memoirs and Diaries

Acheson, Dean G. *Present at the Creation; My Years in the State Department.* New York: W. W. Norton & Co., 1969.

Andrus, Col. Burton C. *I Was the Nuremburg Jailer,* with Desmond Zwar. New York: Tower Publications, 1969.

Berle, Adolf Augustus. *Navigating the Rapids, 1918–1971; From the Papers of Adolf A. Berle.* Edited by Beatrice Bishop Berle and Travis Beale Jacobs, Introduction by Max Ascoli. New York: Harcourt Brace and Jovanovich, 1973.

Bernstorff, Graf Johann H. *The Memoirs of Count Bernstorff.* New York: Random House, 1936.

Blumenson, Martin, ed. *The Patton Papers, 1885–1940,* Boston: Houghton Mifflin, 1972.

Brose, Erich Dorn. *The Kaiser's Army: The Politics of Military Technology in Germany during the Machine Age.* Oxford: Oxford University Press, 2001.

Broszat, Martin. *The Hitler State: The Foundation and Development of the Internal Structures of the Third Reich.* New York: Longman, 1981.

D'Abernon, Viscount Edgar. *An Ambassador of Peace.* Garden City, N.Y.: Doubleday, Doran & Co., 1931.

Dilks, David, ed. *The Diaries of Sir Alexander Cadogan, 1938–1945.* New York: Putnam, 1972.

Dodd, William E. *Ambassador Dodd's Diary, 1933–193.,* New York: Harcourt, Brace. 1941.

Doenitz, Karl. *Memoirs; Ten Years and Twenty Days.* Translated by R. H. Stevens, in collaboration with David Woodward. Cleveland: World Publishing Co., 1959.

François-Poncet, Andre. *The Fateful Years.* New York: Harcourt, 1949.

Fromm, Bella. *Blood and Banquets: A Berlin Social Diary,* reprint of 1942 edition. New York: Carol Publishing Group, 1990.

Gessler, Otto. *Reichswehr Politik in der Weimarer Zeit.* Stuttgart: Deutsche Verlags-Anstalt, 1958.

Geyr von Schweppenburg, General der Panzertruppen Leo. *The Critical Years.* London: Allan Wingate, 1952.

Groener, Wilhelm. *Lebenserinnerungen: Jugend, Generalstab, Weltkrieg,* hersg. von Friedrich Frhr. Hiller von Gaertringen. Osnabrück: Biblio Verlag, 1972.

Harriman, Averell, and Elie Abel. *Special Envoy to Churchill and Stalin, 1941–1946.* New York: Random House, 1975.

Harvey, Oliver. *Diplomatic Diaries of Oliver Harvey, 1937–1940.* London: Colins, 1970.

Hassell, Ulrich. *The Von Hassell Diaries,* with Introduction by Allen W. Dulles. New York: Doubleday, 1947.

Hitler, Adolf. *Hitlers Zweites Buch: Ein Dokument aus dem Jahr 1928,* eingeleitet und kommentiert von Gerhard L. Weinberg. Stuttgart: Deutsche Verlags-Anstalt, 1961.

———. *Mein Kampf.* München: Zentralverlag der NSDAP, 1938.

Horthy, Miklos. *Memoirs.* London: Hutchinson, [1956].

Hull, Cordell. *The Memoirs of Cordell Hull,* 2 vols. New York: Macmillan, 1948.

Ironside, General Sir Edmund. *Time Unguarded; The Ironside Diaries, 1937–1940.* Edited by Col. Roderick Mcleod and Denis Kelly. New York: David McKay, 1962.

Kennan, George F. *Memoirs, 1925–1950,* Boston: Little, Brown and Co., 1967.

———. *Memoirs 1950–1963,* Boston: Little, Brown and Co., 1972.

Kitchen, Martin. *The German Officer Corps, 1890–1914.* Oxford: Clarendon Press, 1968.

Knatchbull-Hugessen, Hugh Montgomery. *Diplomat in Peace and War.* London: J. Murray, 1949.

Kordt, Erich. *Nicht aus den Akten.* Stuttgart: Union deutsche Verlagsgesellschaft, 1950.

———. *Wahn und Wirklichkeit.* Stuttgart: Union deutsche Verlagsgesellschaft, 1948.

Lee, Raymond E. *The London Journal of General Raymond E. Lee, 1940–1941.* Edited by James Leutze, Boston: Little, Brown and Co., 1972.

Lindbergh, Anne Morrow. *The Flower and the Nettle: Diaries and Letters of Anne Morrow Lindbergh, 1936–1939.* New York: Harcourt Brace Jovanovich, 1976.
———. *War Within and Without: Diaries and Letters of Anne Morrow Lindbergh, 1939–1944.* New York: Harcourt Brace Jovanovich, 1980.
Lindbergh, Charles A. *The Wartime Journals of Charles A. Lindbergh.* New York: Harcourt Brace Jovanovich, 1970.
Luther, Hans. *Politiker ohne Partei, Erinnerungen.* Stuttgart: Deutsche Verlagsanstalt, 1960.
MacArthur, Douglas. *Reminiscences.* New York: McGraw Hill, 1964.
Mott, Thomas Bentley. *Twenty Years as a Military Attaché.* New York: Oxford University Press, 1937.
Müller, Klaus-Jürgen. *The Army, Politics, and Society in Germany, 1933–1945: Studies in the Army's Relations to Nazism.* Manchester: Manchester University Press, 1987.
Papen, Franz von. *Memoirs.* London: Andre Deutsch, 1952.
Prittwitz u. Gaffron, Friedrich. *Zwischen Petersburg und Washington.* Munich: Isar Verlag, 1952.
Rabe von Pappenheim, Friedrich Carl. *Erinnerungen des Soldaten und Diplomaten, 1914–1955.* Osnabrück: Biblo Verlag, 1987.
Ritter, Nikolaus. *Deckname Dr. Rantzau, Die Aufzeichnungen des Nikolaus Ritter, Offizier im Geheimen Nachrichtendienst.* Hamburg: Hoffmann und Campe, 1972.
Schweinitz, General Hans Lothar von. *Denkwürdigkeiten des Botschafters General v. Schweinitz,* 2 vols. Berlin: Verlag von Reimar Hobbing, 1927.
Shartle, Col. Samuel Grant. *Spa, Versailles, Munich; An Account of the Armistice Commission,* with a foreword by Lt. Gen. Robert Lee Bullard. Philadelphia: Dorrance, 1941.
Shirer, William L. *Berlin Diary.* New York: Popular Library, 1961.
Simons, Martin. *German Air Attaché: The Thrilling Story of the German Ace Pilot and Wartime Diplomat Peter Riedel.* Shrewsbury, UK: Airlife Publishing Ltd., 1997.
Smith, Truman. *Berlin Alert: Memoirs and Reports of Truman Smith,* edited by Robert Hessen. Stanford, Calif.: Stanford University Press, 1984.
Stevenson, William. *A Man Called Intrepid; The Secret War.* New York: Harcourt Brace Jovanovich, 1976.
Wedemeyer, Gen. Albert C. *Wedemeyer Reports.* New York: Henry Holt Co., 1958.
Weizsäcker, Ernst von. *Memoirs of Ernst von Weizsäcker.* Chicago: Henry Regnery, 1951.
Welles, Sumner. *The Time for Decision.* New York: Harper and Row, 1944.
Westphal, General Siegfried. *Erinnerungen.* Mainz: Von Hase u. Koehler Verlag, 1975.
Wilson, Hugh. *Diplomat between Wars.* New York: Longmans Green, 1941.

Official Works

American Battle Monuments Commission, *35th Division Summary of Operations in the World War.* Washington, D.C.: U.S. Government Printing Office, 1944.
Conn, Stetson, and Byron Fairchild. *The Framework of Hemispheric Defense.* Washington, D.C.: Government Printing Office, 1960.
General Staff, Intelligence Section. *The German and American Combined Daily Order of Battle, 25 September 1918–11 November 1918, Including The Meuse-Argonne Offensive.* Chaumont, (France): Base Printing Plant, 29th Engrs, 1919.
Hewes, James Evans Jr., *From Root to MacNamara: Army Organization and Administration, 1900–1963.* Washington, D.C.: Center of Military History, 1975.
Holley, Irving Brinton. *Buying Aircraft: Matériel Procurement for the Army Air Forces,* Washington, D.C.: Government Printing Office, 1964.
Kreidberg, Lt. Col. Marvin A., and 1st Lt. Merton G. Henry. *History of Military Mobilization in the United States Army, 1775–1945,* DA Pamphlet No. 20-212. Washington, D.C.: Office, Chief of Military History, 1955.

Leighton, Richard M., and Robert W. Coakley. *Global Logistics and Strategy, 1940–1943.* Washington, D.C.: Government Printing Office, 1955.

Matloff, Maurice and Edwin M. Snell. *Strategic Planning for Coalition Warfare, 1941–1942.* Washington, D.C.: Government Printing Office, 1953.

Morton, Louis. *Strategy and Command: The First Two Years.* Washington, D.C.: Government Printing Office, 1962.

Murray, Williamson. *Strategy for Defeat: The Luftwaffe, 1933–1945.* Maxwell AFB, Alabama: Airpower Research Institute, 1983.

Ney, Virgil. *Evolution of the United States Army Field Manual; Valley Forge to Vietnam,* Combat Operations Research Group (CORG) Memorandum, CORG-M-244, January 1966.

Nye, Col. William S. Chief Historian, USAREUR. *Guide to Foreign Military Studies, 1945–1954: Catalog and Index,* Headquarters, United States Army, Europe [Karlsruhe], 1954.

Playfair, I. S. O. et al. *The Mediterranean and the Middle East,* 2 vols. in 8 parts. London: Her Majesty's Stationery Office, 1954–1987.

Ryan, Garry D., and Timothy K. Nenninger, eds. *Soldiers and Civilians: The U.S. Army and the American People.* Washington, D.C.: National Archives and Records Administration, 1987.

Smith, R. Elberton. *The Army and Economic Mobilization.* Washington, D.C.: Government Printing Office, 1959.

U.S. Bureau of the Budget, War Records Section. *The United States at War: Development and Administration of the War Program by the Federal Government.* Washington, D.C.: Government Printing Office, 1946.

Watson, Mark Skinner. *The Chief of Staff: Prewar Plans and Preparations.* Washington, D.C.: Government Printing Office, 1950.

Ziemke, Earl. *The German Northern Theater of Operations, 1940–1945,* DA Pamphlet No. 20-271. Washington, D.C.: Government Printing Office, 1959.

Commercially Published Works

Abenheim, Donald. *Reforging the Iron Cross, The Search for Tradition in the West German Armed Forces.* Princeton, N.J.: Princeton University Press, 1989.

Adler, Selig. *The Uncertain Giant, 1921–1941: American Foreign Policy between the Wars.* New York: Macmillan, 1965.

Baldwin, Hanson W. *Battles Lost and Won; Great Campaigns of World War II.* New York: Harper and Row, 1966.

Barclay, Brigadier Cyril N. *Armistice 1918.* South Brunswick, N.Y.: A. S. Barnes and Co., 1968.

Barnett, Corelli. *The Collapse of British Power.* New York: William Morrow & Co., 1972.

Barnett, Vincent M., ed. *American Assembly; The Representation of the United States Abroad,* rev. ed. New York: F. A. Praeger, 1965.

Baur, H. *Deutsche Eisenbahner im Weltkrieg, 1914–1918.* Stuttgart: Chr. Belser, A. G., Verlagsbuchhandlung, 1927.

Beauvais, Armand Paul. *Attachés militaire, attachés navals, et attachés d l'Air.* Paris: Les Presses Modernes, 1937.

Bekker, Cajus. *The Luftwaffe War Diaries.* Garden City, N.Y.: Doubleday and Co., 1968.

Bendersky, Joseph W. *A History of the Third Reich.* Chicago: Nelson-Hall, 1985.

——. *The "Jewish Threat": Anti-Semitic Politics of the U.S. Army.* New York: Basic Books, 2000.

Berg, A. Scott. *Lindbergh.* New York: G. P. Putnam's Sons, 1998.

Beschloss, Michael R. *Kennedy and Roosevelt: The Uneasy Alliance.* New York: W. W. Norton & Co., 1980.

Bidwell, Bruce W. *History of the Military Intelligence Division, Department of the Army, 1775–1941.* Frederick, Md.: University Publications of America, 1986.

Blum, John Morton. *From the Morgenthau Diaries*, 2 vols. Boston: Houghton Mifflin, 1959.

Boetticher, Friedrich von. *Frankreich; Der Kampf um den Rhein und die Weltherrschaft*. Leipzig: Verlag K. F. Koehler, 1922.

———. *Friedrich der Grosse, als Lehrer von Lebensweisheit und Führertum für unsere Zeit*. Berlin: E. S. Mittler & Sohn, 1925.

———. *Graf Alfred von Schlieffen; Sein Werden und Wirken, Rede am 28 February 1933, dem Tage der hundertsten Wiederkehr des Geburtstages des Generalfeldmarschalls Graf Schlieffen*. Berlin: Schlieffen-Verlag, 1933.

———. *Schlieffen*. Göttingen: Musterschmidt Verlag [1957].

Boyd, Carl. *Hitler's Japanese Confidant: General Oshima Hiroshi and MAGIC Intelligence*. Lawrence: University Press of Kansas, 1993.

Bracher, Karl-Dietrich. *The German Dictatorship*. New York: Praeger, 1970.

———. *Die nationalsozialistische Machtergreifung; Studien zur Errichtung des totalitären Herrschaftsystems in Deutschland, 1933–1934*. Frankfurt a. M.: Ullstein, 1974.

Bramsted, Ernest Kohn. *Germany*. Englewood Cliffs, N.J.:Prentice-Hall, 1972.

———. *Goebbels and National Socialist Propaganda, 1923–1945*. East Lansing: Mich.: State University Press, 1965.

Brinkley, David. *Washington Goes to War*. New York: Alfred A. Knopf, 1988.

Broszat, Martin. *The Hitler State: The Foundation and Development of the Internal Structure of the Third Reich*. New York: Longman, 1981.

Brown, Jerold E. *Where Eagles Land; Planning and Development of U.S. Army Airfields, 1910–1941*, Contributions in Military Studies No. 94. New York: Greenwood Press, 1990.

Bullock, Alan. *Hitler, A Study in Tyranny*, rev. ed. New York: Harper & Row, 1964.

Burdick, Charles B. *Germany's Military Strategy and Spain in World War II*. Syracuse, N.Y.: Syracuse University Press, 1968.

Burleigh, Michael. *The Third Reich, A New History*. New York: Hill and Wang, 2000.

Burns, James M. *Roosevelt, The Lion and the Fox*. New York: Harcourt, Brace and Co., 1956.

———. *Roosevelt, The Soldier of Freedom, 1940–1945*. New York: Harcourt Brace Jovanovich, 1970.

Burt, Kendall, and James Leasor. *The One That Got Away*. New York: Ballantine Books, 1956.

Busk, Sir Douglas L. *The Craft of Diplomacy; How to Run a Diplomatic Service*. New York: F. A. Praeger, 1967.

Campbell, Wesley Glenn, ed. *Economics of Mobilization and War*. Homewood, Ill.: Richard D. Irwin, 1952.

Canedy, Susan. *America's Nazis: A Democratic Dilemma*. Menlo Park, Calif.: Markgraf Publications Group, 1990.

Caplan, Jane. *Government without Administration: State and Civil Service in Weimar and Nazi Germany*. Oxford: Clarendon Press, 1988.

Carr, Edward H. *German-Soviet Relations between the Two World Wars, 1919–1939*, Albert Shaw Lectures on Diplomatic History, 1951. Baltimore: Johns Hopkins University Press, 1951.

———. *International Relations between the Two World Wars, 1919–1939*. New York: Harper Torchbooks, 1966.

———. *The Twenty Years' Crisis*. New York: Harper and Row, 1964.

Carsten, F. L. *The Reichswehr and Politics, 1918–1933*. Oxford: Clarendon Press, 1966.

Catton, Bruce. *War Lords of Washington*. New York: Harcourt Brace and Co., 1948.

Cecil, Lamar. *Wilhelm II*, vol. 2, *Emperor and Exile, 1900–1941*. Chapel Hill: University of North Carolina Press, 1996.

Chadwin, Mark L. *The Hawks of World War II*, Chapel Hill: University of North Carolina Press, 1968. 310 pp.

Chapman Guy. *The Dreyfus Case; A Reassessment*. New York: Reynal and Co., 1955.

Churchill, Winston. *The Second World War*, 6 vols. Boston: Houghton Mifflin, 1948–1953.

Cole, Wayne S. *America First; The Battle against Intervention, 1940–1941*. Madison: University of Wisconsin Press, 1953.

————. *Charles A. Lindbergh and the Battle against Intervention in World War II.* New York: Harcourt Brace Jovanovich, 1974.

————. *An Interpretive History of American Foreign Relations,* rev. ed. Homewood, Ill.: The Dorsey Press, 1974.

————. *Senator Gerald C. Nye and American Foreign Relations.* Indianapolis: University of Minnesota Press, 1962.

Compton, James V. *The Swastika and the Eagle: Hitler, the United States, and the Origins of the Second World War.* London: The Bodley Head, 1968.

Connery, Robert. *The Navy and Industrial Mobilization in World War II.* Princeton, N.J.: Princeton University Press, 1951.

Conot, Robert. *Justice at Nuremburg.* New York: Harper and Row, 1983.

Conquest, Robert. *Harvest of Sorrow: Soviet Collectivization and the Terror-Famine.* New York: Oxford University Press, 1986.

Craig, Gordon A. *From Bismarck to Adenauer; Aspects of German Statecraft.* New York: Harper Torchbooks, 1965.

————. *The Politics of the Prussian Army, 1640–1945.* New York: Oxford University Press, 1966.

Craig, Gordon A., and Felix Gilbert. *The Diplomats, 1919–1939,* 2 vols. New York: Atheneum, 1967.

Daniels, Roger V. *Bonus March Incident; An Episode of the Great Depression,* Contributions in American History No. 14, gen. ed. Stanley I. Kutler. Westport, Conn.: Greenwood Publishing, 1971.

Davies, R. E. G. *Lufthansa: An Airline and Its Aircraft.* New York: Orion Books,1991.

Davis, Kenneth S. *The Hero: Charles A. Lindbergh and the American Dream,* Garden City, N.Y.: Doubleday & Co., 1959.

DeConde, Alexander. *A History of American Foreign Policy.* New York: Charles Scribners Sons, 1963.

Demeter, Karl. *The German Officer-Corps in Society and State, 1650–1945.* New York: Frederick A. Praeger, 1965.

Deutsch, Harold C. *The Conspiracy against Hitler in the Twilight War.* Minneapolis: University of Minnesota Press, 1968.

Diamond, Sander T. *The Nazi Movement in the United States, 1924–1941.* Ithaca, N.Y.: Cornell University Press, 1974.

Divine, Robert A. *The Illusion of Neutrality.* Chicago: University of Chicago Press, 1962.

————. *Roosevelt and World War II.* Baltimore: Johns Hopkins University Press, 1969.

Doenecke, Justus D. *The Battle against Intervention, 1939–1941.* The Anvil Series, edited by Henry Trefousse, Malabar, Fla.: Krieger Press, 1997.

Dorpalen, Andreas. *Hindenburg and the Weimar Republic.* Princeton, N.J.: Princeton University Press, 1964.

————. *The World of General Haushofer; Geopolitics in Action.* New York: Farrar & Rinehart, 1942.

Dupuy, Trevor N. *A Genius for War: The German Army and General Staff, 1807–1945.* Fairfax, Va.: HERO Books, 1984.

Earle, Edward Mead. *Makers of Modern Strategy; Military Thought from Machiavelli to Hitler.* New York: Atheneum, 1970.

Epstein, Fritz. *Germany and the United States: Basic Patterns of Issues and Conflicts.* Lawrence, Kans.: University of Kansas Press, 1959.

Erfurth, Waldemar. *Die Geschichte des deutschen Generalstabes von 1918 bis 1945,* Studien und Dokumente zur Geschichte des Zweiten Weltkrieges, herausgegeben vom Arbeitskreis für Wehrforschung in Stuttgart, vol. 1. Göttingen: Musterschmidt Verlag, 1957.

Erickson, John. *The Soviet High Command: A Military-Political History, 1918–1941.* New York: St. Martin's Press, 1962.

Epstein, Klaus. *Matthias Erzberger and the Dilemma of German Democracy.* New York: Howard Fertig, 1971.

Farago, Ladislas. *The Game of the Foxes.* New York: Bantam Books, 1973.

Feis, Herbert. *Churchill, Roosevelt and Stalin; The War They Waged and the Peace They Sought, A Diplomatic History of World War II.* Princeton, N.J.: Princeton University Press, 1957.

———. *The Road to Pearl Harbor.* Princeton, N.J.: Princeton University Press, 1950.

Feldman, Gerald D. *Army, Industry, and Labor in Germany, 1914–1918.* Princeton, N.J.: Princeton University Press, 1966.

———. *The Great Disorder: Politics, Economics, and Society in the German Inflation, 1919–1924.* New York: Oxford University Press, 1993.

Feller, A. H. and Manley O. Hudson, eds. *A Collection of the Diplomatic and Consular Laws and Regulations of Various Countries,* 2 vols. Washington, D.C.: Carnegie Endowment for International Peace, 1933.

Fest, Joachim C. *The Face of the Third Reich.* New York: Ace Books, 1970.

———. *Hitler,* translated. by Richard and Clara Winston. New York: Harcourt Brace Jovanovich, 1974.

Finney, Patrick, ed. *The Origins of the Second World War,* New York: Arnold, 1997.

Fleming, Peter. *Operation Sea Lion.* New York: Simon and Schuster, 1957.

Foster, John W. *The Practice of Diplomacy, as Illustrated in the Foreign Relations of the United States.* New York: Houghton, Mifflin, 1906.

Freeman, Douglas Southall. *The South to Posterity; an Introduction to the Writings of Confederate History.* New York: C. Scribner's Sons, 1939.

Freidin, Seymour, and William Richardson, eds. *The Fatal Decisions.* New York: Berkeley Publishing, 1958.

Friedländer, Saul. *Prelude to Downfall, Hitler and the United States, 1939–1941.* New York: Alfred A. Knopf, 1967.

Frye, Alton. *Nazi Germany and the American Hemisphere, 1933–1941.* New Haven, Conn.: Yale University Press, 1967.

Gathorne-Hardy, G. M. *A Short History of International Affairs, 1920–1934.* London: Oxford University Press, 1934.

Gellately, Robert. *Backing Hitler: Consent and Coercion in Nazi Germany.* Oxford: Oxford University Press, 2001.

Gerster, Jürg. *Der Militärattaché; seine Völker- und landesrechtliche Stellung mit besonderer Berücksichtigung der Schweizer Verhältnisse.* Zürich: Juris-Verlag, 1959.

Geyer, Michael. *Aufrüstung oder Sicherheit: Die Reichswehr in der Krise der Machtpolitik, 1924–1936.* Wiesbaden: Franz Steiner Verlag GMBH, 1980.

Goerlitz, Walter. *History of the German General Staff, 1657–1945,* translated by Brian Battershaw. New York: Frederick A. Praeger, 1952.

Golovin, Nikolai N. *The Problem of the Pacific in the Twentieth Century.* New York: Charles Scribner's Sons, 1922.

Gordon, Harold J. Jr., *The Reichswehr and the German Republic, 1919–1926.* Princeton, N.J.: Princeton University Press, 1957.

Graber, G. S. *The History of the SS.* New York: Charter Books, 1978.

Grathwol, Robert P. *Stresemann and the DNVP: Reconciliation or Revenge in German Foreign Policy, 1924–1928.* Lawrence: Regents Press of Kansas, 1980.

Greenfield, Kent Roberts. *American Strategy in World War II, A Reconsideration.* Baltimore: The Johns Hopkins University Press, 1963.

Greiner, Christian. "'Operational History (German) Section' und 'Naval Historical Team.' Deutsches militärstrategisches Denken im Dienst der amerikansichen Streitkräfte von 1946 bis 1950," in Militärgeschichtliches Forschungsamt. *Militärgeschichte: Probleme-Thesen-Wege.* Stuttgart: Deutsche Verlags-Anstalt, 1982: 409–435.

Griffith, Robert K. Jr., *Men Wanted for the U.S. Army: America's Experience with an All-Volunteer Army between the World Wars.* Contributions in Military History No. 27. Westport, Conn.: Greenwood Press, 1982.

Groener-Geyer, Dorothea. *General Groener; Soldat und Staatsmann*. Frankfurt am Main: Societäts-Verlag, 1955.

Guttman, Allen, ed. *American Neutrality and the Spanish Civil War*. Boston: D.C. Heath and Co., 1963.

Haeussler, Helmut. *General Wilhelm Groener and the Imperial German Army*. Madison: State Historical Society of Wisconsin for the Department of History, University of Wisconsin, 1962.

Hagan, Kenneth J., and William R. Roberts. *Against All Enemies: Interpretations of American Military History from Colonial Times to the Present*. Westport, Conn.: Greenwood Press, 1986.

Hagood, Maj. Gen. Johnson. *We Can Defend America*. Garden City, N.Y.: Doubleday Doran & Co., 1937.

Haight, John McVickar. *American Aid to France, 1938–1940* . New York: Atheneum, 1970.

Hall, H. Duncan. *North American Supply*. London: HMSO and Longmans Green and Co., 1955.

Hammond, Paul Y. *Organizing for Defense; The American Military Establishment in the Twentieth Century*. Princeton, N.J.: Princeton University Press, 1961.

Heinrichs, Waldo. *Threshold of War; Franklin D. Roosevelt and American Entry into World War II*. New York: Oxford University Press, 1988.

Hildebrand, Klaus. *The Foreign Policy of the Third Reich*, translated by Anthony Fothergill, Berkeley: University of California Press, 1973.

———. *The Third Reich*, translated by P. S. Falla. London: George Allen & Unwin, 1984.

———. *Das vergangene Reich: deutsche Außenpolitik von Bismarck bis Hitler, 1871–1945*. Stuttgart: Deutsche Verlags-Antalt, 1995.

Hillgruber, Andreas. *Hitlers Strategie; Politik und Kriegführung 1940–1941*. Frankfurt am Main: Bernard & Graefe Verlag für Wehrwesen, 1965.

Hinsley, F. H. *Hitler's Strategy*. Cambridge: University Press, 1951.

Hodgson, Godfrey. *The Colonel: The Life and Wars of Henry Stimson, 1867–1950*. New York: Alfred A. Knopf, 1990.

Hoehling, A. A. *Who Destroyed the Hindenburg?* New York: Popular Library, 1962.

Hoffmann, Peter, *The History of the German Resistance, 1933–1945*. Cambridge, Mass.: The MIT Press, 1977.

Höhne, Heinz. *The Order of the Death's Head: The Story of Hitler's SS*. New York: Ballantine Books, 1969.

Hough, Richard, and Denis Richards. *The Battle of Britain; The Greatest Air Battle of World War II*. New York: W. W. Norton and Co., 1989.

Hubatsch, Walther. *Germany and the Central Powers in the World War, 1914–1918*, edited by Oswald P. Backus, introduction by Henry Cord Meyer, University of Kansas publications, Social Science Studies. Lawrence: University of Kansas Press, 1963.

Huzar, Elias. *The Purse and the Sword; Control of the Army by Congress through Military Appropriations, 1933–1950*. Ithaca, N.Y.: Cornell University Press, 1950.

Jacobsen, Hans Adolf. *Nationalsozialistische Aussenpolitik, 1933–1938*. Frankfurt am Main: A. Metzner 1968.

Jäckel, Eberhard. *Hitler in History*. Hanover, N.J.: Brandeis University Press, 1984.

James, D. Clayton. *The Years of MacArthur*, 3 vols. Boston: Houghton, Mifflin Co., 1970.

Janowitz, Morris. *The Professional Soldier; A Social and Political Portrait*. New York: The Free Press, 1960.

Jarman, T. L. *The Rise and Fall of Nazi Germany*. New York: Signet Books, 1961.

Johnson, Walter. *The Battle against Isolation*. Chicago: University of Chicago Press, 1944.

Johnston J. Ambler. *Echoes of 1861–1961*. Richmond, Va., privately printed, 1971.

Jordan, W. M. *Great Britain, France, and the German Problem, 1918–1939: A Study of Anglo-French Relations in the Making of and Maintenance of the Versailles Settlement*. London: Oxford University Press, 1943.

Kabisch, General Ernst. *Die Führer des Reichsheeres 1921 und 1931*. Stuttgart: Dieck & Co., 1931.

Kahn, David. *Hitler's Spies; German Military Intelligence in World War II*. New York: Macmillan Publishing, 1978.

Kehrig, Manfred. *Die Wiedereinrichtung des deutschen militärischen Attachédienstes nach demersten Weltkrieg (1919–1933)*. Boppard am Rhein: H. Boldt, 1966.

Kennan, George F. *American Diplomacy*. New York: Mentor Books, 1951.

Kennedy, David M. *Freedom from Fear: The American People in Depression and War, 1929–1945*. The Oxford History of the United States, New York: Oxford University Press, 1999.

Kershaw, Ian. *Hitler, 1889–1936: Hubris*. New York: W. W. Norton, 1998.

———. *Hitler, 1936–1945: Nemesis*. New York: W. W. Norton, 2000.

———. *The "Hitler Myth": Image and Reality in the Third Reich*. New York: Oxford University Press, 1987.

———. *The Nazi Dictatorship: Problems and Perspectives of Interpretation*, 3d ed. New York: Edward Arnold, 1993.

Kimball, Warren F. *The Most Unsordid Act: Lend-Lease, 1939–1941*. Baltimore: Johns Hopkins University Press, 1969.

Kimmich, Christoph M. *Germany and the League of Nations*. Chicago: University of Chicago Press, 1976.

King, Jere C. *Generals & Politicians: Conflict between France's High Command, Parliament, and Government, 1914–1918*. Berkeley: University of California Press, 1951.

Koch, Hansjoachim W. *Volksgerichtshof: Politsche Justiz im 3. Reich*. Müncen: Universitas, 1988.

Kochan, Lionel. *The Struggle for Germany, 1914–1945*. New York: Harper and Row, 1967.

Koskoff, David E. *Joseph P. Kennedy*. Englewood Cliffs, N.J.: Prentice-Hall, 1974.

Lafore, Laurence. *The End of Glory; An Interpretation of the Origins of World War II*. New York: Lippincott, 1970.

Langer, William L. and S. Everett Gleason. *The Challenge to Isolation; The World Crisis of 1937–1940 and American Foreign Policy*, 2 vols., Torchbook Edition. New York: Harper and Row, 1964.

Langsdorff, Werner von. *Flieger und was sie erlebten*. Gütersloh: Verlag C. Bertelsmann, 1939.

Laqueur, Walter. *A World of Secrets; The Uses and Limits of Intelligence*. New York: Basic Books, 1985.

Lash, Joseph P. *Roosevelt and Churchill, 1939–1941; The Partnership That Saved the West*. New York: W. W. Norton, 1976.

Lerche, Charles O. and Abdul A. Said. *Concepts of International Politics*, 2d ed. Englewood Cliffs, N.J.: Prentice-Hall, 1970.

Leverkuehn, Paul. *German Military Intelligence*. New York: Praeger, 1954.

Lukacs, John *The Hitler of History*. New York: Vintage Books, 1998.

Luvaas, Jay. *The Military Legacy of the Civil War: The European Inheritance*. Chicago: University of Chicago Press, 1959.

Mack Smith, Denis. *Mussolini*. New York: Alfred A. Knopf, 1982.

Mann, Golo. *The History of Germany Since 1789*. New York: Frederick A. Praeger, 1968.

Mattingly, Garrett. *Renaissance Diplomacy*. Boston: Houghton Mifflin,1955.

May, Ernest R. *Knowing One's Enemies; Intelligence Assessment before the Two World Wars*. Princeton, N.J.: Princeton University Press, 1984.

McFarland, Keith D. *Harry H. Woodring, A Political Biography of FDR's Controversial Secretary of War*. Lawrence: University Press of Kansas, 1975.

Megargee, Geoffrey P. *Inside Hitler's High Command*. Lawrence: University Press of Kansas, 2000.

Meisner, Heinrich Otto. *Militärattachés und Militärbevollmächtigte in Preussen und im deutschen Reich; Ein Beitrag zur Geschichte der Militärdiplomatie*, Neue Beiträge Zur Geschichtswissenschaft No. 2. Berlin: Rütten & Loening, 1957.

Meskill, Johanna Menzel. *Hitler and Japan; The Hollow Alliance.* New York: Atherton Press. 1966.

Michalka, Wolfgang. *Nationsozialistische Aussenpolitik,* vol. 297. *Wege der Forschung,* Darmstadt: Wissenschaftliche Buchgesellschaft, 1978.

Miller, Hope Ridings. *Embassy Row; The Life and Times of Diplomatic Washington.* New York: Holt, Rinehart and Winston, 1969.

Millett, Allan R., and Williamson Murray, eds. *Military Effectiveness,* vol. 2, *The Interwar Period.* Series on Defense and Foreign Policy, Boston: Allen & Unwin, 1988.

Millis, Walter. *Arms and Men; A Study in American Military History.* New York: G. P. Putnam's Sons, 1956.

———. *Arms and the State; Civil-Military Elements in National Policy.* New York: The Twentieth Century Fund, 1958.

Milward, Alan S. *The German Economy at War.* New York: Oxford University Press, 1965.

Mooney, Michael Macdonald. *The Hindenburg.* New York: Dodd, 1977.

Moore, John Bassett. *A Digest of International Law, as Embodied in Diplomatic Discussions, Treaties and Other International Agreements, International Awards, the Decisions of Municipal Courts and the Writings of Jurists, . . . ,* 56th Cong. 2d Sess., HR Doc. No. 551, 8 vols., "the eighth being indexical." Washington, D.C.: Government Printing Office, 1906.

Morison, Elting E. *Men, Machines and Modern Times.* Cambridge: The Massachusetts Institute of Technology Press, 1966.

———. *Turmoil and Tradition; A Study of the Life and Times of Henry L. Stimson.* Boston: Houghton Mifflin, 1960.

Morris, Lloyd, and Kendall Smith. *Ceiling Unlimited; The Story of American Aviation from Kitty Hawk to Supersonics.* New York: Macmillan, 1953.

Mosley, Leonard. *On Borrowed Time: How World War II Began.* New York: Random House, 1969.

Müller-Hillebrand, Burkhart. *Das Heer, 1933–1945; Entwicklung des organisatorischen Aufbaues,* 3 vols. Darmstadt: E.S. Mittler & Sohn, Gmbh., 1954.

Müller, Ingo. *Hitler's Justice: The Courts of the Third Reich,* translated by Deborah Lucas Schneider. Cambridge, Mass.: Harvard University Press, 1991.

Nicolson, Harold. *Curzon: The Last Phase, 1919–1925; A Study in Post-War Diplomacy.* New York: Harcourt, Brace and Co.

Odom, William O. *After the Trenches: The Transformation of U.S. Army Doctrine, 1918–1939.* College Station, Tex.: Texas A&M University Press, 1999.

Offner, Arnold A. *American Appeasement; United States Foreign Policy and Germany, 1933–1938.* Cambridge, Mass.: Harvard University Press, 1969.

Oliver, A. C. Jr., and Harold M. Dudley. *This New America; The Spirit of the Civilian Conservation Corps.* New York: Longmans Green and Co., 1937.

Orlovius, Heinz. *Flieg, Deutscher Adler, Flieg! Ein Fliegerbuch für unsere Jungen.* Berlin: Union Deutsche Verlags Gesellschaft, 1935.

Orlow, Dietrich. *The History of the Nazi Party, 1933–1945,* 2 vols. Pittsburgh: University of Pittsburgh Press, 1973.

Orvik, Nils. *The Decline of Neutrality, 1914–1941, with Special Reference to the United States and the Northern Neutrals,* 2d ed. London: Cass, 1971.

Pappas, George S. *Prudens Futuri; The U. S. Army War College, 1901–1967.* Carlisle Barracks, Pa.: Alumni Ass'n of the U.S. Army War College, 1967.

Perret, Geoffrey. *Days of Sadness, Years of Triumph; The American People, 1939–1945.* New York: Coward, McCann & Co., 1973.

———. *Old Soldiers Never Die: The Life of Douglas MacArthur.* New York: Random House, 1996.

Persico, Joseph E. *Roosevelt's Secret War: FDR and World War II Espionage.* New York: Random House, 2001.

Peukert, Detlev J. K. *The Weimar Republic: The Crisis of Classical Modernity*, translated by Richard Deveson. New York: Hill and Wang, 1992.

Phillips, Cabell. *The New York Times Chronicle of American Life: From the Crash to the Blitz*. New York: Macmillan. 1969.

Pogue, Forrest C. *George C. Marshall*, 4 vols. New York: Viking Press, 1963–1987.

Post, Gaines Jr., *The Civil-Military Fabric of Weimar Foreign Policy*. Princeton, N.J: Princeton University Press, 1973.

Powers, Richard Gid. *Secrecy and Power: The Life of J. Edgar Hoover*. New York: The Free Press, 1987.

Pratt, Julius W. *A History of United States Foreign Policy*, 3d ed. Englewood Cliffs, N.J.: Prentice-Hall, 1972.

Presseisen, Ernst L. *Germany and Japan: A Study in Totalitarian Diplomacy, 1933–1941*. The Hague: M. Nijhoff, 1958.

Randolph Macon Woman's College *Bulletin*, 1959.

Rauch, Basil. *Roosevelt from Munich to Pearl Harbor; A Study in the Creation of a Foreign Policy*. New York: Creative Age Press, 1950.

Regala, Roberto. *Trends in Modern Diplomatic Practice*. Milan: A. Giuffre, 1959.

Rich, Norman. *Hitler's War Aims*, 2 vols. New York: W. W. Norton, 1974.

Riedel, Peter. "Geschwader Segeln mit Geiern," in Dr. Werner V. Langsdorff, *Flieger und was Sie Erlebten, Siebenundsiebzig deutsche Luftfahrer erzählen*. Gütersloh: Verlag C. Bertelsmann, 1939.

Ritter, Gerhard. *Die deutschen Militär-Attachés und das Auswartiges Amt, Aus den verbrannten Akten des Grossen Generalstabs*. Heidelberg: C. Winter, 1959.

———. *The Sword and the Scepter; The Problem of Militarism in Germany*, reprint, 4 vols., reprint of the original English edition published by the University of Miami Press. Princeton Junction, N.J.: The Scholar's Bookshelf, 1988.

Roetter, Charles. *The Diplomatic Art, An Informal History of World Diplomacy*. Philadelphia: Macare Smith, 1963.

Rogge, Oetje John. *The Official German Report*. New York: T. Yoseloff, 1961.

Ross, Walter S. *The Last Hero; Charles A. Lindbergh*. New York: Manor Books, 1974.

Rowley, Eric E. *Hyperinflation in Germany: Perceptions of a Process*. Aldershot: Scolar Press, 1994.

Sächsische Schweiz, Osterzgebirge, mit Dresden, Meissen, Pirna und Sebnitz, Brockhaus Reisehandbuch. Leipzig: VEB F.A. Brockhaus Verlag, 1972.

Salmond, John A. *The Civilian Conservation Corps, 1933–1942; A New Deal Case Study*. Durham, N.C.: Duke University Press, 1967.

Satow, Ernest. *A Guide to Diplomatic Practice*, 2 vols. London: Longmans Green, 1922.

Sayers, Michael, and Albert E. Kahn. *Sabotage! The Secret War against America*. New York: Harper & Bros. 1942.

Schlesinger, Arthur. *The Imperial Presidency*, Boston: Houghton Mifflin. 1973.

Schröder, Hans Jürgen. *Deutschland und die Vereinigten Staaten, 1933–1939*. Wiesbaden: Franz Steiner Verlag, 1970.

Schroeder, Paul W. *The Axis Alliance and Japanese-American Relations*. Ithaca, N.Y.: Cornell University Press, 1958.

Schell, Adolf von. *Battle Leadership; Some Personal Experiences of a Junior Officer of the German Army with Observations on Battle Tactics and the Psychological Reactions of Troops in Campaign*. Fort Benning, Ga.: Benning Herald, 1933.

Schramm, Percy Ernst. *Hitler als militärischer Führer; Erkentnisse und Erfahrungen aus dem Kriegstagebuch des Oberkommandos der Wehrmacht*, 2d rev. ed. Frankfurt am Main: Athenäum Verlag, 1962.

Schwartzkoppen, Max von. *The Truth about Dreyfus, from the Schwartzkoppen Papers*, edited by Bernard Schwertfeger, London: Putnam, 1931.

Schwipps, Werner. *Kleine Geschichte der deutschen Luftfahrt.* Berlin: Handl u. Speversche Verlagsbuchhandlung, 1968.

Seabury, Paul. *The Wilhelmstrasse.* Berkeley: University of California Press, 1954.

Seth, Ronald. *Spies at Work; A History of Espionage.* New York: Philosophical Library, 1954.

Sherwood, Robert E. *Roosevelt and Hopkins; An Intimate History.* New York: Harper and Bros., 1948.

Smith, Henry Ladd. *Airways: The History of Commercial Aviation in the United States.* New York: Alfred A. Knopf, 1942.

Snell, John L. *Illusion and Necessity; The Diplomacy of Global War, 1939–1945.* Boston: Houghton Mifflin Co., 1963.

Sontag, Raymond J. *A Broken World,* in the Rise of Modern Europe series, edited by William L. Langer, New York: Harper and Row, 1971.

Spector, Ronald H. *Eagle against the Sun: The American War with Japan.* New York: The Free Press, 1985.

Stein, Lorenz Jacob von. *Die Lehre vom Heereswesen. Als Theil der Staatswissenschaft.* Mit Vorwort von E. W. Böckenförde. Neudruck der Ausg. 1872. Osnabrück: Biblio-Verlag, 1967.

Stettinius, Edward R., Jr. *Lend Lease, Weapon for Victory.* New York: Macmillan & Co., 1949.

Stimson, Henry L., and McGeorge Bundy. *On Active Service in Peace and War.* New York: Harper and Brothers, 1947.

Supf, Peter. *Das Buch der deutschen Fluggeschichte: Vorkriegszeit Kriegszeit, Nachkriegszeit.* 2 vols. Berlin-Grünewald: Verlags Anstalt Hermann Klemm, A.G., 1935.

Tantum, W. H., and E. J. Hoffschmidt. *The Rise and Fall of the German Air Force, 1939–1945.* Old Greenwich, Conn.: WE, 1969.

Taylor, Alan John Percival. *The Origins of the Second World War.* Greenwich, Conn.: Fawcett Books, 1968.

Taylor, Telford. *Munich; The Price of Peace.* Garden City, N.Y.: Doubleday & Co., 1979.

Teske, Hermann. *Wenn Gegenwart Geschichte wird . . .* Neckargemünd: Kurt Vowinckel Verlag, 1974.

Thayer, Charles W. *Diplomat.* New York: Harper, 1959.

Thomas, David. *Nazi Victory; Crete, 1941.* New York: Stein and Day, 1973.

Thorne, Christopher. *Allies of a Kind; the United States, Britain, and the War against Japan, 1941–1945.* New York: Oxford University Press, 1978.

Tobin, Harold J., and Percy W. Bidwell. *Mobilizing Civilian America.* New York: Council on Foreign Relations, 1940.

Trefousse, Hans L. *Germany and American Neutrality, 1939–1941.* New York: Octagon, 1969.

Twichell, Heath. *Allen: The Biography of an Army Officer.* New Brunswick, N.J.: Rutgers University Press, 1974.

Ulam, Adam B. *Expansion and Coexistence; The History of Soviet Foreign Policy.* New York: Frederick A. Praeger, 1968.

Underwood, Jeffrey S. *The Wings of Democracy; The Influence of Air Power on the Roosevelt Administration, 1933–1941.* College Station: Texas A&M Press, 1991.

Vagts, Alfred. *Defense and Diplomacy; The Soldier and the Conduct of Foreign Relations.* New York: King's Crown Press, 1956.

———. *The History of Militarism, Romance and Realities of a Profession.* New York: W. W. Norton & Co., 1951.

———. *The Military Attaché.* Princeton, N.J.: Princeton University Press, 1967.

Viereck, Peter. *Meta-Politics; The Roots of the Nazi Mind.* New York: Capricorn Books, 1965.

Walters, Frank P. *A History of the League of Nations,* 2 vols. London: Oxford University Press, 1952.

Wark, Wesley K. *The Ultimate Enemy; British Intelligence and Nazi Germany, 1933–1939.* Ithaca, N.Y.: Cornell University Press, 1985.

Wecter, Dixon. "The Age of the Great Depression, 1929–1941," vol. XIII, *A History of American Life*, edited by Arthur M. Schlesinger and Dixon R. Fox. Chicago: Quadrangle Books, 1971.

Weigley, Russell F. *The American Way of War; A History of United States Military Strategy and Policy*. New York: Macmillan Publishing, 1973.

———. *History of the United States Army*. New York: Macmillan, 1967.

Weinberg, Gerhard L. *The Foreign Policy of Hitler's Germany*, rev. ed. vol. 1, *Diplomatic Revolution in Europe, 1933–1936*. Atlantic Highlands, N.J.: Humanities Press International, 1994.

———. *The Foreign Policy of Hitler's Germany*, vol. 2, *Starting World War II, 1937–1939*, rev. ed. Atlantic Highlands, N.J.: Humanities Press International, 1994.

———. *A World at Arms: A Global History of World War II*. Cambridge: Cambridge University Press, 1994.

———. *World in the Balance: Behind the Scenes of World War II*. Hanover, N.H.: University Press of New England, 1981.

Wheeler-Bennett, John W. *Disarmament and Security Since Locarno; Being the Political and Technical Background of the General Disarmament Conference, 1932*, with introduction by Maj. Gen. Sir Neill Malcolm, New York: The Macmillan Company, 1932.

———. *Information on the Reduction of Armaments*. London: George Allen & Unwin, 1925.

———. *Munich, Prologue to Tragedy*. New York: Duell, Sloane, and Pearce, 1948.

———. *The Nemesis of Power; The German Army in Politics, 1918–1945*, Compass Books Edition. New York: Viking Press, 1967.

———. *The Pipe Dream of Peace*. New York: William Morrow & Co., 1935.

Wighton, Charles, and Gunter Peis. *Hitler's Spies and Saboteurs*. New York: Award Books, 1973.

Wilmot, Chester. *The Struggle for Europe*. Harper Colophon Edition. New York: Harper and Row Publishers, 1963.

Wilson, Clifton E. *Diplomatic Privileges and Immunities*. Tucson: University of Arizona Press, 1967.

Winterbotham, F. W. *The Ultra Secret*. New York: Harper and Row, 1974.

Wolfe, Henry C. *The German Octopus; Hitler Bids for World Power*. Garden City, N.Y.: Doubleday, Doran & Co., 1938.

Wolfskill, George, and John A. Hudson. *All but the People; Franklin D. Roosevelt and His Critics, 1933–1939*. New York: The Macmillan Co., 1969.

Wood, John R. and Jean Serres. *Diplomatic Ceremonial and Protocol; Principles, Procedures & Practices*. London: Macmillan, 1970.

World Committee for the Victims of German Fascism. *Brown Network; The Activities of the Nazis in Foreign Countries*. London and New York: Knight Publishers, 1935.

Wright, Gordon, *The Ordeal of Total War*, The Rise of Modern Europe Series, edited by William L. Langer, New York: Harper and Row, 1968.

Wriston, Henry Merritt. *Diplomacy in a Democracy*. New York: Harper and Brothers, 1956.

Zimmermann, Erich, and Hans-Adolf Jacobsen, comp. *Germans against Hitler, July 20, 1944*, Bonn: Berto Verlag, 1960.

Journal Articles

Adler, Selig. "War Guilt Question and American Disillusionment," *Journal of Modern History* 23 (March 1951): 1–28.

"American Opinion about the War; Evidence Gathered by the Gallup Poll Since 1939," *Harper's Magazine* 182 (April 1941): 549–552.

Baldwin, Hanson W. "Our New Long Shadow," *Foreign Affairs* 17 (April 1939): 465–476.

Beard, Charles A. "Giddy Minds and Foreign Quarrels," *Harper's Magazine* 179 (September 1939): 337–351.

Boetticher, Friedrich von. "Feldherrentum und Generalstab," *Wehrkunde* 13 (September 1964): 453–459.

———. "The Struggle against Overwhelming Odds," *Review of Military Literature* 15 (December 1935): 5–26.

Bowers, Ray L. "After Thirty Years: Conversations on the Air War," *Aerospace Historian* 21 (Summer 1974): 65–69.

Burdick, Charles B. "Foreign Military Records of World War I in the National Archives," *Prologue: The Journal of the National Archives* 7 (Winter 1975): 212–220.

Butow, R. J. C. "The Hull-Nomura Conversations: A Fundamental Misconception," *American Historical Review* 56 (July 1960): 882–886.

Callahan, Raymond. "The Illusion of Security; Singapore, 1919–1942," *Journal of Contemporary History* 9 (April 1974): 69–92.

Cole, Wayne S. "American Entry into World War II," *Mississippi Valley Historical Review* 43 (1957): 555–619.

Craig, Gordon A. "Military Diplomats in the Prussian Army and German Service: The Attachés, 1816–1914," *Political Science Quarterly* 64 (March 1949): 65–94.

———. Reichswehr and National Socialism: The Policy of Wilhelm Groener, 1928–1932," *Political Science Quarterly,* 63 (June 1948): 194–229.

De Conde, Alexander. "The South and Isolationism," *Journal of Southern History* 24 (August 1958): 332–46.

Dick, Ronald. "Sunset on Adlertag," *Air & Space* 5 (August–September 1990): 52–63.

Doob, Leonard W. "Goebbels's Principles of Propaganda," *The Public Opinion Quarterly* 14 (Fall 1950): 419–442.

Echevarria, Antulio, II, "An Infamous Legacy: Schlieffen's Military Theories Revisited," *Army History, The Professional Bulletin of Army History* (Summer–Fall 2001): 1–4.

Ferrell, Robert H. "The Merchants of Death, Then and Now," *Journal of International Affairs* 26 (1972): 27–39.

Graml, Helmut. "Die Wehrmacht im Dritten Reich," *Vierteljahrshefte für Zeitgeschichte* 45 (July 1997): 365–384.

Greene, Fred. "The Military View of American National Policy, 1904–1940," *American Historical Review* 66 (January 1961): 348–375.

Herwig, Holger. "Prelude to Weltblitzkrieg; German Naval Policy toward the United States, 1939–1941," *Journal of Modern History* 43 (December 1971): 649–670.

Jolemore, Kenneth A. "The Mentor: More Than a Teacher, More Than a Coach," *Military Review* 46 (July 1986): 4–17.

Jonas, Manfred. "Prophet without Honor: Hans Heinrich Dieckhoff's Reporting from Washington," *Mid-America, An Historical Review* 47 (July 1965): 222–233.

Kent, George O. "Problems and Pitfalls of a Papen Biography," *Central European History* 20 (June 1987): 191–197.

Kimball, Warren F. "Dieckhoff and America: A German's View of German-American Relations, 1937–1941," *The Historian* 27 (February 1965): 218–243.

Kirk, Grayson. "Wings over the Pacific," *Foreign Affairs* 20 (January 1942): 293–302.

Kittredge, Capt. Tracy B. USNR. "A Military Danger: The Revelation of Secret Strategic Plans," *U.S. Naval Institute Proceedings* 81 (July 1955): 731–737.

Knox, Magregor. "1 October 1942: Adolf Hitler, Wehrmacht Officer Policy, and Social Revolution," *The Historical Journal,* 43 (September 2000): 801–825.

McFarland, Keith D. "Woodring vs. Johnson, F.D.R. and the Great War Department Feud," *Army* 26 (March 1960): 26–47.

Morton, Louis. "National Policy and Military Strategy," *The Virginia Quarterly Review* 36 (Winter 1960): 26–47.

"News from Clubs and Members," *Soaring* 28 (July 1937): 12

Phelps, Reginald H. "Aus den Groener Dokumenten: I Groener, Ebert, Hindenburg," *Deutsche Rundschau* 76 (Juli 1950): 530–547.

———. "Aus den Groener Dokumenten: II Die Aussenpolitik der O.H.L. bis zum Friedensvertrag," *Deutsche Rundschau* 76 (August 1950): 616–625.

Poole, DeWitt C. "New Light on Nazi Foreign Policy," *Foreign Affairs* 25 (October 1946): 136–149.

Rabemau, Fregattenkapitän Georg von. "The German Military Attaché," translated by Dermot Bradley, *An Cosantoir, The Irish Defense Journal* 29 (June 1969): 200–206.

Reilly, Brig. Gen. Harry J. "Background for Lightning War," *Infantry Journal* 47 (January–February 1940): 4–11.

Remak, Joachim. "Friends of the New Germany: The Bund and German-American Relations," *Journal of Modern History* 29 (March 1957): 38–41.

———. "Hitlers Amerikapolitik," *Aussenpolitik* 6 (November 1955): 711–729.

Showalter, Dennis. "From Deterrence to Doomsday Machine: The German Way of War, 1890–1914," *Journal of Military History* 64 (July 2000): 679–710.

———. "Mass Multiplied by Impulsion; The Influence of Railroads on Prussian Planning for the Seven Weeks War," *Military Affairs* 38 (April 1974): 62–67.

Sofair, André N., MD, and Lauris C. Kaldjian, MD. "Eugenic Sterilization and a Qualified Nazi Analogy: The United States and Germany, 1930–1945," *Annals of Internal Medicine* 132 (15 February 2000): 312–319.

Soutor, Kevin. "To Stem the Red Tide: The German Report Series and Its Effect on American Defense Doctrine, 1948–1954," *Journal of Modern History* 57 (October 1993): 653–688.

Thompson, Capt. Paul W. "Engineers in the Blitzkrieg," *Infantry Journal* 47 (September–October 1940): 424–432.

Trefousse, Hans L. "Failure of German Intelligence in the United States, 1935–1945," *Mississippi Valley Historical Review* 42 (June 1955): 84–100.

"Two Weeks of Soaring," *Soaring* 29 (August 1937): 2-3.

Ulanoff, Stanley M. "The Attache: Diplomat in Uniform," *Soldiers* 29 (January 1974): 34–36.

Watt, D. C. "German Diplomats and the Nazi Leaders," *Journal of Central European Affairs* 15 (July 1955): 148–160.

"We Are Going Ahead," *Soaring* 2 (August 1938): 2–5.

Weinberg, Gerhard. "Hitler's Image of the United States," *American Historical Review* 69 (July 1964): 1006–1021.

Wesson, Maj. Gen. Charles M. "Fundamentals of Preparedness, Some Facts and Figures of the New Ordnance Program," *Army Ordnance* 19 (May–June 1939): 329–336.

Woodring, Harry H. "Supply Preparedness," *Army Ordnance* 17 (March-April 1947): 263–265.

Yoshpe, Harry B. "Economic Mobilization Planning between the Two World Wars (Part I)," *Military Affairs* 15 (Winter 1951): 199–204.

———. "Economic Mobilization Planning between the Two World Wars (Part II)," *Military Affairs* 16 (Summer 1952): 71–83.

Theses and Dissertations

Gottsacker, Sister Mary Hugh. German-American Relations, 1938–1941, and the Influence of Hans Thomsen, Ph.D. Dissertation, Georgetown University, 1968.

Heidner, Samuel J. The Thirty-Fifth Division in the Meuse-Argonne Offensive, M.A. Thesis, Georgetown University, April 10, 1929.

Killigrew, John. The Impact of the Great Depression on the Army, 1929–1936, Ph. D. Dissertation, University of Indiana, 1960.

Kimball, Warren F. Dieckhoff and America: A German's View of German-American Relations, 1937–1941, M.A. Thesis, Georgetown University, 1965.

Index

ABOUT THE AUTHOR

Alfred M. Beck received his doctorate in European diplomatic history at Georgetown University in 1977. His career as a federal government historian has included supervisory positions at the Army Corp of Engineers' Office of History and the U.S. Army Center of Military History. From 1985 to 1994, he served as the chief editor and publisher at the Center for Air Force History, where he managed the production of more than thirty official Air Force histories. He coauthored *The Corps of Engineers: The War Against Germany* (1985), in the official U.S. Army in World War II series; and was general editor of *With Courage: The U.S. Army Air Forces in World War II* (1995). Dr. Beck also contributed to the U.S. Navy's multivolume *Dictionary of American Naval Fighting Ships* and the *Simon and Schuster Encyclopedia of World War II* (1978). After retiring from federal service, he has continued research and publishing activities. He was editor of *The Federalist*, the newsletter of the Society for History in the Federal Government, and he was production editor of the *International Journal of Korean Studies* from 1998 to 2003. Dr. Beck lives in Falls Church, Virginia.